SUMMARY JUDGMENT

"The court shall grant summary judgment if . . .
there is no genuine dispute as to any material fact
and the movant is entitled to judgment as a matter of law."

FED. R. CIV. P. 56(a)

SUMMARY

JUDGMENT

★ ★ ★ ★ ★

25 Years of
Condemning Treachery,
Tyranny, and Injustice

WILLIAM PERRY PENDLEY

Mountain States Legal Foundation
Lakewood, Colorado

ISBNs: 978-0-69254-349-8 (paperback); 978-0-692-55772-3 (ePub); 978-0-692-55773-0 (Kindle)

Library of Congress Control Number: 2015916208
Printed in the United States of America
First Printing: 2015
19 18 17 16 15   5 4 3 2 1

Cover design by Kelli Escalante of Lauren Graphics, Inc.
Page design and typesetting by Mayfly Design and set in the Adobe Garamond Pro and ITC Galliard typefaces

To order, visit www.mountainstateslegal.org or call 303-292-2021.

CONTENTS

*To those who stepped forward to battle for
constitutional liberties and the rule of law as clients
of Mountain States Legal Foundation;*

*To the Directors and Board of Litigation members
and MSLF attorneys and staff who represented or
served those clients' interests; and*

*To those who, through their generosity of spirit
and commitment to the vision of the Founding
Fathers, made MSLF's representation
and advocacy on behalf of its clients possible;*

This book is dedicated.

PREFACE

Mountain States Legal Foundation (MSLF) is a nonprofit, public-interest legal foundation (PILF) created in 1977, thanks to the leadership of Joe Coors who became its first chairman. James G. (Jim) Watt was its first president and launched it into a spectacularly successful opening as it responded to the anti-western agenda of the Carter administration, which was driven by those Ronald Reagan called "environmental extremists."

It was Reagan, however, who gave birth to the movement of which MSLF is a part. Of course, since 1968 National Right to Work Legal Defense Foundation litigated to protect employees' legal rights against forced unionism abuses, but Governor Reagan's response to the attacks on his legislative reform efforts by leftist legal groups gave rise to the first freedom-based PILF focused on a range of free enterprise, economic, and property rights issues. Reagan saw a need for a liberty-based legal defense group with that broader focus; thus, in 1973, with his full support, Pacific Legal Foundation (PLF) opened its doors in Sacramento. By the time Reagan ended his weekly radio addresses, which he began when he left the governor's mansion, liberty-based PILFs similar to PLF had spread across the country. In 1979, in his last radio address before he began his successful campaign for president of the United States, one entitled "Miscellaneous and Goodbye," Reagan began, "The first item is, in my opinion, very serious for all of us and another indication of how far we are straying from the very basics of our system. The Mountain States Legal Foundation has filed a suit with the federal government claiming that the constitutional rights of several states are being violated...."

MSLF is dedicated to individual liberty, the right to own and use property, limited and ethical government, and the free enterprise system and represents *pro bono* those who are not able to hire an attorney to fight for constitutional liberties and the rule of law. Over the years, MSLF has represented individuals, private businesses, corporate entities, trade associations, and local governments. In doing so, MSLF seeks to win for its clients, set nationally significant legal precedents that will benefit others, and educate the American people of the threats to their liberty. MSLF seeks victory—primarily in cases in which the facts are established and MSLF seeks a precedential ruling on the law—before the highest judicial tribunal possible, optimally the Supreme Court of the United States, but also a federal court of appeals, or a state's highest court.

Incorporated in Colorado and headquartered in Denver, MSLF sits amidst the vast land holdings of the federal government. One-third of the nation is owned and managed by the federal government and most of that is in the eleven Mountain and Pacific states and Alaska. The federal government owns nearly a third of Colorado, Montana, New Mexico, and Washington; it owns roughly half of Arizona, California, Oregon, and Wyoming; and owns almost two-thirds or even more of Alaska, Idaho, Nevada, and Utah. By comparison, the three non-western states with the most federal land are New Hampshire (14 percent), Florida (13 percent), and Michigan (10 percent). Even worse, in many western states, federal ownership exceeds 90 percent of the land in scores of vast rural counties. Two agencies of particular importance in the lives of westerners are the Bureau of Land Management (BLM), which controls nearly 250 million acres, and the U.S. Forest Service (USFS), which manages more than 190 million acres. The acreage controlled by the BLM and the USFS exceeds that of Alaska; it also exceeds the acreage of the next three largest states (Texas, California, and Montana) and Colorado combined. These lands are managed in accordance with "multiple-use" principles, that is, these lands are to host a variety of activities, including energy and mineral development, logging, grazing, and recreation, to name but a few. Unfortunately, these activities are opposed by environmental groups and they are all too willing to go to court to end them. That is where MSLF was meant to enter the picture and it did early and often, with great effect.

Not surprisingly, multiple use federal lands, national forests, for example, and national parks are to be found across the country and with them come the inevitable conflicts with private citizens and landowners. Thus, MSLF found itself in litigation in Arkansas, Michigan, and Minnesota, for instance.

Likewise, environmental laws, enacted with the best of intentions, have been used by these same groups to challenge the economic use of public and private lands alike. The Endangered Species Act (ESA), Clean Water

Act, Clean Air Act, and National Environmental Policy Act (NEPA) all were capable of being misused and abused, and soon. At first, the ESA and NEPA involved primarily federal and nearby private lands, but in time, the ESA, for example, was being applied with disastrous results from coast to coast and border to border. Once again, it was to respond to attacks such as these for which MSLF was created; MSLF did so forcefully.

Most MSLF litigation regarding federal land issues and environmental laws involve the rule of law—that is, ensuring that laws are implemented consistent with the intent of Congress, that agencies remain bound by the laws that govern them, and that courts rule consistent with binding legal precedents. Occasionally, however, litigation regarding federal statutes may also implicate constitutional liberties, such as the right to "just compensation" for the "tak[ing]" of "private property" for "public use."

Despite its location in "fly over country," MSLF has earned a national reputation as a staunch defender of the Constitution's provisions. MSLF won precedent-setting rulings from the Supreme Court regarding the Constitution's equal protection guarantee. As Justice Scalia put it in one landmark victory, "In the eyes of government we are just one race here. It is American." MSLF also battled for the Second Amendment, first on behalf of a rancher who killed a grizzly bear in self-defense and more recently on behalf of those seeking to exercise their rights on federal property, on vast federal recreation land, or while they travel state to state. Furthermore, MSLF has been at the forefront of challenging attempts by federal land managers, contrary to the Establishment Clause, to close public land regarded by some as sacred and on which solitude is required.

Although MSLF's legal services are free of charge, MSLF requires of its clients a priceless contribution, that is, their willingness to commit to months and even years of litigation. It is much to ask because those who oppose their efforts think nothing of attacking them during the course of legal proceedings, in the courtroom, and in the media. They must be resilient, steadfast, and brave. Over the years, MSLF has been blessed with clients who are all of that and more, as will become evident in many of the articles set forth here. It has been a pleasure and an honor to represent them. Just know that there are many other clients whose stories are not told here; MSLF is equally indebted to them.

WILLIAM PERRY PENDLEY
DENVER, COLORADO

INTRODUCTION

In March of 1989, I returned to the Rocky Mountain West from Washington, D.C. to become president of MSLF in Denver.

I was born and raised some 100 miles north in Cheyenne at the far western edge of the Great Plains, the son of a railroad man from Decatur, Arkansas in the Ozark Mountains and a coal miner's daughter from Harlan County, Kentucky—"bloody Harlan County" as my mother, who had become a Licensed Practical Nurse, put it. Both had left the South, traveled to Cheyenne—my father after a stint in Pocatello, Idaho when he got laid off from the Union Pacific Railroad (UPRR) in Cheyenne, and met as my dad was relaxing on the porch of the boarding house where he lived and my mom was walking to the public library. I grew up in "the big white house with the blue roof," as we described it to people trying to find us, on five acres east of town on a dirt road with few neighbors. My dad, with his father, built the house, which had a full-sized concrete basement where we lived until the main floor and sizeable but unfinished attic was completed. My older sister Jeri (Geraldine Mae) married Hugo Jensen and left to live with her husband and then their four children (Dawn, Kurt, Erik, and Nels) in Cheyenne, so my brother Barry and I grew up just the two of us, playing on the shortgrass prairie and up and down the vast windbreak my father had planted with shrubs, oak, and blue spruce, which was where the winter snows piled up, except for the Blizzard of 1949 when it broke through and drifted up to the attic window. I could hear the whistles from trains as they passed south of us and, from the south-facing attic window, I could see the snow-covered Rocky Mountains west of Denver—the big city for me—so I imagined far-away places, dreams my mother applauded.

Encouraged by an elderly lawyer who had befriended my mother and me—Marshall S. Reynolds, born in 1881 in Wyoming County, Pennsylvania: "If you are interested in government, you should go to Washington."—I declined swimming scholarships in the West and took the train to the Nation's Capital and the George Washington University (GWU). I returned to Cheyenne for three summers of railroading—as a sheet metal workers apprentice to my father, as a ditch-digging member of the B&B (Bridge and Building) crew, and as a uniform-wearing brakeman for the UPRR passenger line from Cheyenne or Denver to Green River, Wyoming—but after that I was gone from home. At GWU, I earned a scholarship, worked odd-jobs (cafeteria dishwasher, cleanup man, and baker's assistant; laundry service man; residence hall assistant; and test grader), and volunteered for and was hired on by Senator Clifford P. Hansen (R-WY). (I did not tell Senator Hansen, but I remember sitting at our kitchen table writing postcards with my Sheet Metal Workers, Local 103 treasurer father asking Governor Hansen to veto the Right to Work law—my politics had evolved.) I received a B.A. and then an M.A. in Public Affairs (political science and economics), but just as I was putting the finishing touches on my master's thesis after passing the foreign language test, a week before I left town, I met Elisabeth Young Jones (Lis) of Scranton, Pennsylvania, a recent graduate of Mary Washington College who taught the third grade in suburban Montgomery County, Maryland.

Back in Wyoming at its College of Law in Laramie, I joined with my fifteen male classmates for the study of what Mr. Reynolds warned me was "a jealous mistress." Advised by my local draft board, however, that it would ask me to report for a physical examination and, if qualified, for induction the following month, I secured a promise of readmission and resumption of my scholarship from Dean E. George Rudolph and signed up for the U.S. Marine Corps Officer Candidate School (OCS) for March of 1969. I returned to my parent's home in Cheyenne, did substitute teaching as the Hong Kong flu pandemic of 1968 laid full-time teachers low, volunteered with the Laramie County Republican Party for the Richard M. Nixon campaign, and spent two months touring Europe and the Soviet Union. Lis advised me to take the trip; she had done her "Europe 101" tour the previous summer; however, mine was in the midst of a brutal Russian winter. After a month visiting my parents, my brother at Washington University in St. Louis, and Lis in Washington, I entered OCS. After I graduated from The Basic School in Quantico, Virginia ("Every Marine an infantryman."), Lis and I were married.

I selected Marine Corps Aviation, trained in Pensacola, Florida, Brunswick, Georgia, and Sacramento, California, and was assigned a squadron at Marine Corps Air Station Cherry Point, N.C. With two weeks of law school, I was the perfect choice for squadron legal officer, which collateral duties I performed as I awaited aircraft availability for qualifying flights. I had chosen EA-6A aircraft, with an electronic countermeasure mission, but training slots were few so I transitioned to the RF-4B, with its photo-reconnaissance mission, so I could fly more often and qualify more quickly for overseas duty. I requested reassignment to the Far East and duty in Iwakuni, Japan, and Cubi Point, the Philippines, from whence my squadron flew missions over North Vietnam. Lis had taught elementary school in Florida and North Carolina, written for the *California Journal* when we were in Sacramento, and worked for Representative Margaret Heckler (R-10th MA), while I was overseas; however, just before she joined me for the two-month visit the Marine Corps allowed spouses, which would end my time in the service, she sent a telegram. She had applied and been accepted to Wyoming's law school, she reported—"I will be joining you there STOP Whee STOP" it read.

My five years away brought a vast change to the law school. Seventy-five of us filled the school's largest classroom—over 1,000 had applied; ten were women; five were veterans. In 1976, when we graduated the market for two lawyers married to one another who wanted to work within 50 miles of each other was scarce so we returned to Washington, Lis as an attorney at the Federal Power Commission, later the Federal Energy Regulatory Commission, and I as a legislative assistant to my former boss Senator Hansen to work on mining and energy issues. When Hansen declined to run again in 1978, I went to work as a "minority [Republican] counsel" for the House Interior and Insular Affairs Committee, today the House Resources Committee, first for Representative Philip Ruppe (R-11th MI), then Representative Don Young (R-AK), and finally Jim Santini (D-NV), who became a great friend and later a Republican.

When Governor Ronald Reagan was elected president and nominated Jim Watt to be secretary of the U.S. Department of the Interior, I went to work for Watt, was Deputy Assistant Secretary for Energy and Minerals and first Acting Director of the newly created Minerals and Management Service, and ramrodded adoption of the Exclusive Economic Zone (EEZ) proclamation and reformation of the Vietnam Veterans Memorial, which necessitated addition of a heroic sculpture, inspiring inscription, and the American Flag. I served for a time with Secretary of the Navy John F. Lehman, Jr., and then entered the private practice of law with a Marine Corps friend, Stephen W. Comiskey, my first such opportunity. I enjoyed it greatly, especially when I thought that any victories I might win would benefit others. In 1989, while worrying a case for a client with a man I had hired as a political appointee in 1981 but who was now one of the senior people left in the Reagan administration, J. Steven Griles, Steve stopped me. "I've been asked to be president of Mountain States Legal Foundation, but I'm not the right man for the job. You are. I want to tell Dave True you will take the job."

A short time earlier I had been speaking with my eight going on twenty-eight year old son Perry about being a westerner. "You may be a westerner, Dad, but I was born in Washington, D.C. and I have lived in Arlington, Virginia all of my life." I had gone to Washington like thousands of others temporarily ("Not more than five years," I had sworn to my friend, Brent Kunz with whom I had started law school in 1968), but had stayed on. The news that was covered in the bottom half of the back page of my hometown paper, the *Wyoming State Tribune*, filled the *Washington Post*, and I thought I was in the midst of all that important goings-on. By the time I spoke with Steve Griles, I realized that I was a bystander and would have been just as involved at the kitchen table back home in Cheyenne. I told Steve, "Yes," and later took a call from Casper, Wyoming independent oil-man H.A. "Dave" True. I flew out to Arizona, met with Dave and his wife and partner Jean in Nogales, and then flew into Denver to meet with Dave, MSLF Directors, and a Board of Litigation member. A few weeks later, my brother Barry flew out to Washington and helped me drive cross country to Denver. Later that summer, Lis and Perry and Luke joined me.

Barry said it was the perfect job for me: "You'll get to practice law, serve the public interest, write and publish articles, travel the country, and give talks about the battles you're fighting." He was right, of course. It is all of that, but much more because of the people for whom those battles are being fought. As I wrote in my dedication to *War on the West*:

"Their endeavors have enriched the West and the nation they love. Their embrace of the cause of freedom has encouraged others to step forward, to speak up, and to be heard. Their endurance under fire has emboldened their friends and their neighbors.

I have been on their farms and fields, on their ranches and ranges, in their mines and mills, in their forests and factories, in their cities and counties, in their homes and hotels, in their conference centers and courthouses. I know they wanted to learn something from me, but I was always the one who learned from them. I learned about their world and what makes it work and why they love it and have given their lives to it.

Even more important, I learned something about humanity, about faith, family, friends, and the fundamental principles that have governed through the ages. I feel blessed to have known them all and honored that they call me friend."

In January of 1990, my first full year with MSLF, I began to write a monthly column, which I called *Summary Judgment*. (In the law, summary judgment may be granted when no genuine issues of material facts are in dispute and it is mandated as a matter of law.) I found the issues with which I was dealing fascinating and worthy of greater circulation, the clients I was serving deserving of more attention than they were earning in the courtroom or in the rare media coverage of their litigation, and the broader public policy questions involved missing a western perspective. Each month I sought to remedy these deficiencies. There was never a shortage of subjects about which to write; as we used to say in the Marine Corps, "It is a target-rich environment." The challenge was to reduce convoluted facts and complicated legal principles (Surprise!) to an understandable mix with an exciting beginning, informative middle, and hard-hitting ending. Based on what I have heard from across the country, most of the time, I was successful. I am appreciative of the many suggestions I received.

In the pages that follow, I have set forth a selection of my favorite columns from each year over the last 25 years. Some columns were not selected because they covered issues that, in retrospect, were of but local interest, or dealt with litigation that did not proceed as anticipated and hence lost precedential value, or involved legal proceedings that were addressed more fully in a subsequent column. Other columns fell by the wayside because they were interesting only as historical novelties, but that was the rarity. All too often and unfortunately, the columns take on a depressing sameness: covetous bureaucrats, activist judges, spineless politicians; only the facts and the applicable law change. Fortunately, another unchanging feature is the endless parade of brave men and women who courageously step up to stand at the front lines of the never ending battle for freedom. If one truth emerges from all of these essays over the years, it is that expressed by Ronald Reagan in 1961:

"Freedom is never more than one generation away from extinction. We didn't pass it on to our children in the bloodstream. It must be fought for, protected, and handed on for them to do the same, or one day we will spend our sunset years telling our children and our children's children what it was once like in the United States where men were free."

CHAPTER ONE

An Environmental President

———

President Reagan called radical environmentalists—those, in his words, who would not "be happy until the White House looks like a bird's nest"—"environmental extremists" or "modern-day Luddites," because they elevated the needs of nature over the needs of mankind. "People are ecology too," said Reagan, "and most of us are looking for answers that will preserve nature to the greatest extent possible consistent with the need to have places where we can work and live." Thus, his policies ensured development of oil and gas, coal, and strategic and critical minerals, and he set aside the most wilderness areas in history, expanded wildlife refuges, and restored national parks as pleasuring grounds for the American people. As he restored and revitalized the economy, he also reined in the arrogant federal bureaucracy, quelled the Sagebrush Rebellion with a good neighbor policy, and embraced "fundamental federalism principles" that recognized dual sovereignty.

Not surprisingly, therefore, his Vice President, George H.W. Bush, was elected to Reagan's third term in an electoral vote landslide. President Bush, however, wanted to differentiate himself from Reagan. He sought a "kinder, and gentler nation" and to be an "environmental president." It was predictable that the first to feel the impact of his efforts to distinguish himself from Reagan was the American West. MSLF responded in federal court with lawsuits on behalf of those affected adversely by the federal government's policies and with friend of the court briefs on behalf of litigants locked in heated personal and public policy battles. Meanwhile, in a long-running dispute, MSLF prevailed before the Supreme Court of the United States when the Court ruled 5-4 that environmental groups could not challenge the Reagan administration's land withdrawal review program because the program itself was not "final agency action" and because the groups lacked standing—they failed to allege they used the public lands that were the subject of any final agency action that did result from the program.

BUSH ASSAILS WESTERN WATER RIGHTS

For nearly 100 years, Colorado viewed the two forks of the South Platte River as the source of Denver's water for the 21st century and, since 1982, Denver and 40 cities, counties, and districts planned construction of the Two Forks project, using only local, not state or federal funds.

The Metropolitan Water Providers—the governmental coalition that will build the project—accommodated local environmental groups' concerns by authorizing $90 million in mitigation measures, including increased and improved recreational fisheries and access to other fishing areas above the dam site now inaccessible. National groups, however, want the project stopped and wrote President Bush's Environmental Protection Agency (EPA) administrator, William K. Reilly. Thereupon, Reilly removed the nearly complete approval process from the regional administrator in Denver so he could veto it.

Over the past eight months, that EPA veto process has ground on. With each procedural step taken by the EPA, yet another nail is driven into the coffin that holds the mortally-wounded Two Forks water project. One might reasonably ask, after all this, exactly what it is that the EPA has against the project. Amazingly enough, no one seems to know. Several weeks ago, the city council of Aurora wrote to Reilly asking the basis for the pending veto. Reilly has not responded. In October of 1989, however, Reilly's representative, the regional administrator from Atlanta, who conducted fact-finding for Reilly, announced that he would recommend a veto and declared, as the basis, "Denver, you can do better."

The EPA is arguing alternatively that Denver does not need the water; or that, if it needs the water, it should do a better job conserving water; or that, there are better places to build a water storage facility. The EPA does not say where those places are, implying that Coloradoans should spend another $47 million—the amount expended so far planning Two Forks—selecting a site so the EPA can decree it too is wrong.

The ostensible authority for the EPA to make the rules with regard to when and where westerners get to store the spring runoff for use during the dry summers is the Clean Water Act provision regarding "the discharge of dredged or fill material into the navigable waters...." Ironically, this section, which was adopted to protect the quality of municipal water supplies from dumping potentially contaminating dredged materials, is being used to prevent construction of a project that would guarantee much needed municipal water supplies, while dramatically increasing quality fisheries in Colorado.

How necessary is the Denver water project? If northern Colorado had suffered a drought during the 1980s as drastic as the one suffered from 1953 through 1955, the Denver suburb of Westminster would have been able to supply only 74 percent of its customers' water needs. In addition, projected Denver growth, especially following completion of Denver's new international airport, could bring water shortage—without Two Forks—during the mid-1990s under the best water supply conditions. Denver and the Colorado foothills do not just need the water for growth; they need the water now.

The larger question is who is now in charge of western water? Ever since gold was panned in California, westerners have decided, under the prior appropriations doctrine, how their water is to be used. With Reilly's veto, for the first time in history, non-westerners will tell the West how to use its water. The future of Denver, and in fact the future of all of the West, will not be decided by those of us in the West, but by bureaucrats two-thirds of a continent away.

The day Reilly vetoes Denver's water project will be a significant day in the history of the West as surely as was the day the golden spike was driven at Promontory Summit, Utah. Only this time the spike will be driven through the heart of the West. Sadly, it will happen thanks to the Bush administration.

JANUARY 1990

Epilogue: On November 23, 1990, Reilly officially killed the project.

ENDANGERED SPECIES TAG WIDELY ABUSED

Two recent battles out west demonstrate the degree to which the Endangered Species Act (ESA) is being misused by shoddy science and litigious environmental groups.

The University of Arizona, the Smithsonian Institute, the Vatican, the University of Chicago and other astrophysical institutes, propose a $240 million state-of-the-art observatory atop Mount Graham near Safford in economically hard-pressed southeastern Arizona. Mount Graham is no wilderness peak; its vantage point has been used as a holographic site since the U.S. Army used it to rein in the Apache Chief Cochise. The University of Arizona dropped its proposal from 19 to 13 to 10 and finally to 7 telescopes but that was still too many for the observatory's opponents who asserted species on Mount Graham were endangered, not only by the observatory, but also by all other uses of the mountain, including privately owned cabins, some of which have been there for decades.

Although the bipartisan Arizona congressional delegation—including the hero of the environmental community, Congressman Morris K. Udall—secured passage of legislation that found the requirements of the ESA to have been met and ordered immediate construction of the first three telescopes, an environmental group sued arguing that construction will lead to extinction of the red squirrel. Unfortunately, much of this situation is the work of the Bush administration's Fish and Wildlife Service (FWS), which concluded that the red squirrel is endangered by mankind. Its "Biological Opinion" is filled with nonsense: the red squirrel, on seeing an intruder, *i.e.*, man: will fixate, neglect to collect cones, and starve to death in winter; or will forget to watch for the goshawk, be picked off, and eaten.

As a result, the University of Arizona and its scientific colleagues await a green light from federal court to erect a telescope that testifies to American creativity, ingenuity, and technological know-how. By comparison, scientists in the Soviet Union have been unable to construct similar telescopes. America can beat Red Ivan, but not the red squirrel.

Meanwhile, in the desert of the American southwest—comprising portions of California, Nevada, Utah, and Arizona—live as many as three million desert tortoises; 100,000 also live in captivity. Despite its abundance, the FWS concluded it is "endangered" and entitled to ESA protection. One reason for its allegedly fragile state is predation by the common raven, whose population has increased, in the California desert alone, by 1,000 percent over a 20-year period. Ravens—notoriously adaptable scavengers—have developed a taste for young tortoises that, says the FWS, will lead to the extirpation—to pull up as if by the roots—of the tortoise population! As a result, the FWS and the California Department of Fish and Game initiated a "raven control" program to kill some 1,500 of them. The FWS concluded that, while severe restrictions could be placed on mankind's activities in the desert of the southwest, such restrictions—without an aggressive raven control program—would be "fruitless!"

The American Humane Society filed a lawsuit charging that the program is inhumane to the raven. The FWS agreed to abandon its program if the Humane Society would permit the killing of 56 ravens. Instead, the Humane Society demanded, and got, an agreement from the FWS that it would only kill ravens that it could identify as "habitually preying on tortoises!"

Despite its previous admission that restriction on the activities of mankind would be "fruitless" in aiding the tortoise, less than two months after abandoning the raven control program, the FWS used its emergency authority to name the desert tortoise as "endangered." That action brought the building boom in Las Vegas to a virtual standstill and rendered highly uncertain all economic activities of mankind on the desert of the Southwest, including cattle and sheep grazing and mining exploration and development.

No doubt much greater ESA mischief, undertaken by the Bush administration and environmental groups, lies ahead for the country, landowners, and the American economy.

APRIL 1990

PROMISES MADE BUT BROKEN:
BECAUSE CONGRESS SAYS IT
DOESN'T MAKE IT SO

In the natural give and take that accompanies adoption of federal legislation, Congress seeks to accomplish that for which its proponents often credit it: the art of the possible. Since no one in a democracy can have everything he or she wants, compromises—in congressional parlance, accommodations—are made from which all emerge, if not pleased, then at least uninjured.

Unfortunately, the test of the statutory pudding is neither in the tasting of the words and phrases that make up the federal code, nor even in a sampling of the legislative history that attend those words and phrases, but in a testing of that statute in the federal courts. Once that legislation is before a federal judge, however, all bets are off, when environmental activists seek to improve on the deal to which they agreed in Congress.

When the U.S. Congress enacted the Surface Mining Control and Reclamation Act of 1977, it recognized that while it could prohibit coal mining by surface mining methods in areas where such mining had been permitted previously, that would constitute an unconstitutional "taking" of private property and would require "just compensation." Therefore, Congress protected those property rights with a "valid existing rights" (VER) provision. In fact, when some Members of Congress sought to delete the provision, the bill's primary sponsor, Congressman Morris K. Udall (D-2nd AZ), warned that the per se prohibitions of the statute could not be implemented without "paying compensation under the Fifth Amendment to the Constitution."

In economically hard-pressed southern Ohio lies the Wayne National Forest, a forest comprised almost entirely of lands purchased by the U.S. Forest Service under the Weeks Forestry Act of 1911. Over the decades, when Ohio landowners sold their property to the federal government for inclusion in the national forest, many retained their rights to mine the rich coal beds beneath the surface. Over time, Thomas J. Belville and his Belville Mining Company, Inc. acquired the rights to mine the coal underlying a small portion of the lands within the forest—its coal properties underlie only three percent of the total surface area managed by the Forest Service and only 0.6 percent of the gross area covered by the national forest.

In 1981, Belville applied for a VER determination by the U.S. Department of the Interior regarding a small portion of its property. In 1984, President Reagan's Interior Department determined that Belville had "valid existing rights" to mine that portion of its coal properties in the Wayne National Forest. Subsequently, Belville, working with the U.S. Forest Service and the State of Ohio, began a surface coal mining operation in the forest. The reclamation that followed Belville's mining—in which Belville contoured the land to the exact specifications of the Forest Service—received numerous awards.

Unfortunately Belville's subsequent applications have wandered a more tortuous course. Although Belville's applications for VER determinations were granted by the Reagan administration on December 23, 1988, the Bush administration, on August 24, 1989, under pressure from environmentalists, suspended its previous grant of VER rights. On December 21, 1989, the Bush administration formally rejected more of Belville's applications, and has yet to make a decision regarding the remaining applications. As a result, Belville has been forced to file a lawsuit in federal court to compel the Bush administration to obey an important portion of the Surface Mining Control and Reclamation Act, a constitutional protection that was crucial to the adoption of that legislation.

Americans should not be forced to go to court to defend rights that Congress granted or protected in the adoption of federal legislation. This is particularly the case when the granting or protecting of rights was an essential component of the compromise that made possible the enactment of the legislation. Yet that is what is happening. Having won some small victory in Congress, property owners are being forced to go to court to fight those battles all over again.

MAY 1990

EARTH FIRST AND THE FOREST SERVICE: WHOSE FREE SPEECH?

Earth First is an environmental terrorist organization that not only advocates sabotage, violence, and terrorism but also provides its followers handbooks and newsletters on how to perfect their craft, including "spiking" trees, which nearly decapitated a man in northern California. Earth First has published instructions on burying a device armed with a shotgun shell as a land mine aimed at the trail biker, which may indiscriminately injure the horseback rider or hiker. Earth First leaders and followers have been indicted for sabotaging nuclear power transmission lines and a ski resort chairlift, and most recently, arrested for possessing and transporting explosive devices. Even Robert F. Kennedy, Jr. decries them, "Earth First tactics must be condemned as must the tactics of anyone who favors force over democratic principles."

Earth First's objective: to frighten all users off of the public land and keep them from their lawful use of that land. Earth First style violence has been directed against loggers, cattlemen, woolgrowers, oil and gas prospectors, miners, off-road-vehicle enthusiasts, ski resort owners, and others. The one use of public lands of the West of which Earth First apparently approves is Earth First gatherings on lands managed by the federal government. Recently, Earth First requested permission from the U.S. Forest Service for 500 of its followers to "rendezvous" in the Beaverhead National Forest in southwestern Montana to "celebrate and strategize."

The Bush administration's Forest Service decided to issue the permit. The Forest Service's lawyers reached that decision notwithstanding the history of violence by Earth First and its followers, notwithstanding Earth First's advocacy of sabotage, violence, and terrorism against users of the public lands, and notwithstanding the opposition of those users of the public land who live in the small communities surrounding the Beaverhead National Forest and who make use of the Beaverhead National Forest for work and pleasure and who believe Earth First has forfeited its right to meet upon public land and has no right to gather there to strategize about ways to frighten westerners from the land.

The Forest Service's lawyers are right about one thing, the legal issue involved is prior restraint on speech—whether spoken or symbolic. There are limits, however, as to what the Constitution allows in the name of free speech. Even the judge in the federal case on which the Forest Service's lawyers relied—one involving the infamous Rainbow Family—noted that, "Where the public health or welfare is threatened, the government need not wait until after the damage has occurred in order to act, even if there happen to be criminal penalties associated with the behavior causing the threat."

It is difficult to imagine a more impermissible type of "speech" than that proposed by Earth First, that is, to gather, 500 strong, in a remote region of Montana: not only to advocate the use of violence, sabotage, and terrorism against other users of the public land; not only to be instructed on how to commit those illegal acts; but—if past is prologue—to engage in those acts in and around the Beaverhead National Forest. When Earth First last gathered—in the State of Washington—$4 million of damage was done to timber equipment located on and near the national forest where they met. This time, Earth First is meeting in a forest surrounded by 6,000 grazing cattle, tens of thousands of trees slated for a future timber sale, two operating mines, and hundreds of miles of trails used by off-road-vehicle enthusiasts, horseback riders, summer campers, and hikers.

Earth First's permit application certainly involves "free speech," but the true free speech advocates in the matter are not Earth First, but the ranchers, miners, loggers, and off-road-vehicle enthusiasts who seek to exercise their rights to symbolic speech by tending their cattle, working their claims, providing Americans wood products, and recreating on mountain trails. There is no doubt whose "free speech" is more deserving of protection.

JUNE 1990

JUDICIAL RESTRAINT WIN:
ENVIRONMENTAL GROUP
DENIED STANDING

Recently the Supreme Court of the United States resolved a lawsuit affecting 180 million acres of public land—an area the size of Texas, Vermont, and New Hampshire combined—holding that an environmental organization that had tied up the vast area for nearly five years had no right to file its lawsuit. For Mountain States Legal Foundation it is one of the most significant victories in years; a spokesman for the environmental group called it a "disaster."

For decades westerners complained that the Bureau of Land Management (BLM) used "classifications" and "withdrawals" to place vast areas of public land off limits to congressionally-mandated "multiple use" by all Americans. In 1976, Congress required the BLM to review decades-old land closures to determine which were outdated and needed to be revoked. In 1977, the BLM began that review and by 1981 had processed 180,000,000 acres of land improperly placed off-limits and removed obsolete categorizations. One such tract was in central Wyoming.

The BLM originally proposed that some 6,000 acres of federal land—lying in scattered parcels within a 2,000,000 acre tract of federal land in central Wyoming—be opened for mineral exploration. At the urging of the Wyoming Fish and Game Commission, the BLM reduced the acres opened from 6,000 to 4,500. After the BLM removed the outdated classifications and withdrawals—but not before some 7,000 mining claims, 1,000 oil and gas leases, and hundreds of other multiple use applications had been filed with the BLM on portions of the 180,000,000 acres—the National Wildlife Federation (NWF) filed a lawsuit in Washington, D.C., to stop further action.

NWF attorneys went into court armed with an affidavit from a woman from Casper, Wyoming, who asserted that she used lands "in the vicinity of" the South Pass-Green Mountain area and that she was adversely affected by the decision of the BLM to open 4,500 acres out of the 2,000,000 acre area to mineral exploration. NWF attorneys argued that the BLM should have done an environmental study on all 180,000,000 nationwide acres of land before taking any action.

Constitutional principles of "standing" necessitate that a lawsuit involve an actual "case and controversy," that the citizen bringing the lawsuit be capable of showing that she has suffered injuries different and distinct from the rest of the populace, and that the relief sought be capable of making her whole. Therefore, the Casper woman's standing was challenged—a challenged that finally reached the Supreme Court.

During oral arguments, Justice Scalia was relentless in his questioning of the NWF attorney. Justice Scalia carried that persistence into his written opinion for the 5-4 Court where, on behalf of the Court, he dismissed all bases for "standing" asserted by the NWF. He concluded that the affidavit filed by the NWF was inadequate. "[The law] is assuredly not satisfied by averments which state only that one of [the NWF's] members uses unspecified portions of an immense tract of territory, on some portion of which mining activity has occurred or probably will occur by virtue of the governmental action." Justice Scalia also concluded that federal courts are not the proper forum for testing the wisdom of a national undertaking such as the BLM's Withdrawal Review Program. "[The NWF] cannot seek wholesale improvement of this program by court decree, rather than in the offices of the Department or the halls of Congress, where programmatic improvements are normally made.... Until confided to us.... more sweeping actions are for the other Branches."

The Supreme Court, by dismissing the lawsuit filed by the NWF, not only returned millions of acres of public land to multiple use management, but also strengthened the principle of "standing" and reaffirmed the Separation of Powers doctrine. Once again, the management of the public lands is a matter for Congress and the Executive Branch—not for activist judges responding to the narrow constituencies of so-called environmental organizations.

JULY 1990

GOVERNMENT LAWYERS
AND THE SEARCH FOR JUSTICE

In western Colorado, the Roaring Fork River has rushed past the property of Dennis and Nile Gerbaz through a well-recognized channel for more than half a century. In 1985, after a neighbor completed work on a levee pursuant to a U.S. Army Corps of Engineers' permit, the Roaring Fork River washed away two acres of the Gerbaz property and a levee. When the Gerbaz brothers sought a permit to rebuild the levee, however, the Corps said, "No." After learning the law permits property owners to protect their lands, the Gerbaz brothers restored the levee to return the Roaring Fork River to its historic channel. The Bush administration's Environmental Protection Agency (EPA) sued the Gerbaz brothers for $45 million each.

This incredible display of arrogance by the federal government has been the subject of television news broadcasts, newspaper articles, and calls by public officials for abandonment of the government's litigation. In fact, Colorado's two U.S. Senators, who could not be further apart on the political spectrum, joined in challenging the EPA's legal action against the Gerbaz brothers. In the face of this onslaught, who could resist these demands for justice? The answer is federal lawyers.

The fractured decision-making process of the federal government causes more problems than just the glacial pace at which agencies move; everyone is involved, so no one is responsible. Added to this deficiency is the natural human tendency—evolved to an art form in the federal government—to deny, defer, or decline responsibility for making decisions. Moreover, in the post-Watergate era, for a government official to respond, "We must let the legal process run its course," is to avoid the allegation that the official improperly resolved a controversial issue.

Furthermore, because of all this and unlike the private sector, a federal lawyer is not a "hired gun" who responds to the requests of an autonomous client but instead is the decision-maker. Yet another difference from the private sector is the lack of concern regarding the cost of litigation. The federal government, the deepest of deep pockets, is unmoved by the number of attorneys involved, the number of hours required, or the funds expended in pursuing or defending a legal action.

The unquestionable ability of the federal government and its attorneys to pursue litigation zealously, which is the duty of an attorney representing a client, reveals yet another deficiency. Too often forgotten by government counsel is that the party on the other side of a legal controversy is a citizen, entitled to equitable treatment by his government. Simply because the federal government can target, prosecute, and outlast almost any adversary, does not mean that it should.

The Canons of Ethics provide: "[a] government lawyer ... has the responsibility to seek justice ... and he should not use ... the economic power of the government to ... bring about unjust settlements or results." Justice Robert Jackson wrote, "The United States Attorney is the representative not of an ordinary party to a controversy, but of a sovereignty whose obligation to govern impartially is as compelling as its obligation to govern at all; and whose interest, therefore, ... is not that it shall win a case, but that justice shall be done.... It is as much his duty to refrain from improper methods calculated to produce a wrongful [result] as it is to use every legitimate means to bring about a just one."

A willingness by the federal government to resolve controversial issues—that is, to settle or even to abandon litigation—is essential; however, that willingness requires greater convictions than most federal officials have shown of late, especially on environmental issues. Until government officials develop that kind of toughness and courage, men like the Gerbaz brothers will be forced to fight, in court, for one of the critical constitutional guarantees, the right to own and use property.

AUGUST 1990

WHY JOHNNY CAN'T THINK—
ABOUT ENVIRONMENTAL ISSUES

"What animal is it," my 7-year old son Luke wanted to know, "that kills other animals, pollutes the land and the water, cuts down trees and is the most dangerous animal in the world?" I pretended to guess at the answer. Finally, my son gasped in mock exasperation, "Dad, it's man!"

Luke learned all this in a book entitled *Dangerous Animals*, which he read in his first grade class. There at the end of a beautifully illustrated book filled with lions, tigers, snakes, black widow spiders, and other creatures, was man—the most dangerous creature of them all.

Earlier in the year, the third grade teacher of my son Perry, as part of Earth Day festivities, asked each child to bring his or her favorite stuffed animal to class. Once this fuzzy menagerie was assembled, Perry's teacher told the students to think of their stuffed animals—animals that they had loved since before they could remember—as endangered species; the very endangered species, she said, that are now threatened by the thoughtless acts of mankind.

Like my two sons, most Americans are now being told that environmental issues present easy decisions. They are being told that environmental issues come down to making simple choices between the despoiling evil acts of man and the survival of warm and cuddly animals; between the rapacious beast that is mankind and a gentle, nurturing, living, planet Earth. The American people are being told that environmental issues are easy. They are being asked if they are for nature, if they love animals, or if they want to save the planet. How mankind fits into this picture is ignored.

Earlier this year, I demanded the chance to speak to my son Perry's class during Earth Day discussions. We talked about the talcum powder that their mothers use on their baby brothers and sisters and I showed them a football sized piece of talc from a mine in Montana. We discussed the cinder blocks that formed the walls of their school and I showed them cinders from a mine in Nevada. We discussed the passive solar panels (windows) in their building and I showed them soda ash—out of which glass is made—from a mine in Wyoming. We talked of wood products like houses, books, and packaging and I told them there were more trees in America today than when I was their age and every year a 100-foot tree is cut down for each of us. In the end, one of my son's classmates said it best as to what he learned, "A lot of stuff comes from stuff you don't think comes from stuff."

A high school English textbook, distributed by one of the nation's major education publishing houses, contains the following question: "The coyote is: A. A benign animal with no documented record of killing cattle or sheep. Or: B. A not-so benign creature known to kill domestic animals and capable of devastating sheep herds." In 49 states in the country, the answer is A. In Utah, the answer is B because the wool growers there called the publishing house and told them that they had lost $6 million dollars' worth of sheep to coyotes the previous year. As a result of this response from Utah, the publisher printed a special text for the Beehive State.

Unfortunately the success of the wool growers of Utah is an isolated one. Yet it is a success from which all of those committed to the wise use of America's natural resources can learn at least two important lessons. First, it shows that there is much misinformation being communicated to the nation's children. Second, it shows that something can be done about it.

If we want mankind to be a part of the environmental equation then we had better start doing something about it right now and we can start where Luke is, in the first grade.

SEPTEMBER 1990

WHEN CAN A REPORTER LIE?

Imagine you are active in a matter of public policy that brings you to the attention of your fellow citizens; that is, you become what is known in the law as a "public figure." Perhaps you lead a stockgrowers, oil and gas, timber, mining, or Off Highway Vehicle (OHV) association. Perhaps you are simply in business—many businessmen and businesswomen have been held by the courts to be public figures—or you are outspoken and have been quoted in the media.

Imagine too, that you are approached by a reporter who wants to do a story about your activities. You decline, concerned that you will be misquoted. "Never fear," replies the reporter, "I'll record the interview, and provide you with copies of the tape. You can be sure that you will be quoted accurately." You agree.

Subsequently the reporter's articles appear in the local paper. To your horror you discover that the reporter did not simply misquote you. On reviewing the tapes, it becomes clear the reporter made up many of the "quotes" attributed to you. Worst of all many of those "quotes" make you look (pick one): stupid/mean-spirited/fiendish/ immoral/unscrupulous/dissolute.

You call the reporter and say that you never said the "quotes" attributed to you. The reporter declines to retract a word; in fact, the reporter advises you that Associated Press (AP) saw the story and has decided to run the article in newspapers across the country. Soon everyone in America seems to know what the reporter says you said.

Of course you decide to sue for the damage done to your reputation. Unfortunately your lawyer tells you that because you live in Alaska, Arizona, California, Hawaii, Idaho, Montana, Nevada, Oregon, or Washington, your lawsuit will be dismissed. That is because, as incredible as it sounds, the U.S. Court of Appeals for the Ninth Circuit held that a reporter cannot be sued for using fraudulent quotations. A three-judge panel of that court, sitting in San Francisco, held 2 to 1 that a reporter can make up "quotations" and attribute them to a public figure if they either are "rational interpretations of ambiguous remarks," or "do not alter the substantive content of unambiguous remarks."

Thus, as to an ambiguous statement by a public figure, no longer does a reporter need to ask, "What do you mean by that?" The reporter can intuit what was meant, write it down, and put quotation marks around it. As to an unambiguous statement by a public figure, the reporter can substitute his or her choice of words for the words used by the public figure. While "bastard" may mean the same as "his mom and dad never got married" it is neither what the public figure might have chosen to say nor does it carry with it the same implication. The panel went further, however; it also held that if the public figure made statements that constituted a "self-appraisal," then the reporter is free to attribute to the public figure any "quote" consistent with that "self-appraisal."

The panel said all this in *Masson v. New Yorker Magazine, Inc.*, in which Dr. Jeffrey Masson sought damages for allegedly fraudulent quotations attributed to him in a series of articles published in *The New Yorker*, and subsequently published in book form. The reporter, *The New Yorker*, and the publishing house were named as defendants. A California federal district court granted the defendants' motion to dismiss the case and the panel upheld the ruling.

Business leaders, politicians, and private citizens have learned to be precise in the use of their language when discussing controversial issues, given the emotional baggage some words carry. Unless the Supreme Court reverses this ruling, such caution and precision is useless, since the media will be able to use whatever words it believes are "rational interpretations of ambiguous remarks" or as long as the quotations "do not alter the substantive content of unambiguous remarks."

NOVEMBER 1990

Epilogue: On June 20, 1991, the Supreme Court unanimously reversed the Ninth Circuit. *Masson v. New Yorker Magazine, Inc.*, 501 U.S. 496 (1991). MSLF's *amicus curiae* brief was one of two in support of the ruling and was specifically discussed at oral argument.

KILLING BIRDS TO SAVE THEM

According to the *Los Angeles Times*, at the request of attorneys in the Bush administration's Justice Department, the U.S. Fish and Wildlife Service (FWS) ordered the killing of hundreds of birds in Alaska. The birds, including many from national wildlife refuges, were killed, soaked in oil, and thrown into Prince William Sound in an attempt to justify damage allegations the federal government sought to make in federal court regarding the Valdez oil spill.

These bird killings come at an interesting time. The federal government is taking steps to put up to 60,000 men and women out of work in the Pacific Northwest to "save" the northern spotted owl. The City of Las Vegas is virtually shut down to "protect" the desert tortoise because the federal government refuses to kill the common raven which, government documents show, is extirpating the tortoise. Hundreds of acres of timber in Texas have not been harvested due to the FWS's attempts to "save" the red-cockaded woodpecker. In addition, the FWS is penalizing individuals hundreds of thousands of dollars for unintentional, accidental loss of birds.

It is almost beyond comprehension that federal bureaucrats concluded that, while allegedly committed to the protection of wildlife regardless of the economic cost to the American people, it is permissible for them to kill hundreds of birds. Yet what is even more revealing about the way the FWS is being run is that these bureaucrats believed that there was no need to obtain the permission of the man in charge of the agency, Director John F. Turner. To kill hundreds of birds, at the same time the agency is taxing some companies $500,000 for the accidental loss of as few as 25 birds, without Director Turner's knowledge, indicates the bureaucrats Director Turner is supposed to be supervising believe that they have authority to do whatever they want to do. For a year and one half that is exactly what FWS bureaucrats have been doing.

What this sorry episode says about the Justice Department is even worse. The Justice Department has its pick of the best and the brightest of our nation's top law schools; nonetheless, it was these very lawyers—no doubt sitting within earshot of the nation's top law enforcement officer, U.S. Attorney General Richard Thornburgh—who decided that hundreds of birds needed to be killed to improve their likelihood of victory in court.

Thus the federal government's alleged goal of protecting wildlife had to be sacrificed so these lawyers could improve their odds of putting another notch on their jurisprudential guns. In the process not only wildlife fell by the wayside; it is entirely possible that federal law was violated as well as the government attorneys' ethical responsibilities.

The actions of the federal government in ordering these bird kills demonstrate a frightening, almost Orwellian myopia. It is further evidence of the troubling specter of an environmental passion that does not seek balance or the solving of environmental problems. While we may expect that of environmental extremists, we must neither expect it nor permit it from government officials.

It is imperative that the federal government fully investigate the circumstances behind this episode and, if necessary, bring actions against those responsible. Yet regardless of the outcome of the investigation some fundamental changes need to be made in Washington. First, Director Turner must get control of his agency or turn it over to someone who has the management skills to do the job. Second, Attorney General Thornburgh must ensure that federal attorneys seek justice and not just victory in the courtroom. Third, Congress must engage in aggressive oversight of the federal agencies to which it appropriates hundreds of billions of tax dollars annually.

If these important actions are not taken, the American people risk losing much more than the several hundred birds that our government blasted out of the sky to improve its odds of winning in federal court in Alaska.

DECEMBER 1990

CHAPTER TWO

Nonsense Runs Through It

★ ★ ★ ★ ★

———

Who are "environmentalists," what do they believe, and how many of them are there anyway? Moreover, what is the factual basis for their beliefs and how confident are we that what they say is true? After all, it was Will Rogers who warned, "It isn't what we don't know that gives us trouble; it's what we know that ain't so." With politicians, the media, and Hollywood celebrities falling all over themselves to do whatever it is that environmental groups and their leaders demand, perhaps these are questions that we ought to answer. These are certainly answers we ought to have in light of the high stakes involved in doing whatever it is that they are demanding, that is the cost to the "human environment," where people live, work, and play, not to mention the impact on the environment itself.

Take, for example, one 1991 decision by the U.S. Forest Service in the Upper Yaak River Drainage of the Kootenai National Forest in northwestern Montana. To achieve a one percent (1%) increase in grizzly bear habitat, the Forest Service lowered permitted timber harvests by forty-three percent (43%), decreased income to timber-producing communities by forty-five percent (45%), and left 3,829 acres of timber destroyed by the mountain pine beetle to rot instead of harvesting it for jobs, revenue, and fire prevention. As a result, 76,580,000 board feet of timber—enough for 6,962 homes—will provide the tinder for the next catastrophic fire to sweep through the region. Of course, this is but one decision in part of one forest by one federal agency; imagine the devastating impact of region-wide decisions such as reintroducing wolves into Idaho, Montana, and Wyoming, or putting the northern spotted owl on the Endangered Species Act (ESA) list and thus ending old-growth timber harvesting in Oregon, Washington, and northern California. That is why, in addition to filing lawsuits and friend of the court briefs, MSLF began listing endangered communities, a program later adopted by the National Association of Counties.

THE GUY BEHIND THE TREE

U.S. Senator Russell B. Long (D-LA), the former powerful chairman of the Senate Finance Committee, used to say tax policy was simple. "Don't tax me. Don't tax thee. Let's tax the guy behind the tree." What will always be true for tax policy is true increasingly for our environmental policy. Although polls indicate a heightened concern by the American people about environmental issues, most of them look to others to achieve the goals that result from that elevated consciousness.

For example, although the Earth Day issue of *USA Today* reported, "83% fear for environment," 65% of those surveyed opposed restrictions on their ability to use automobiles. A survey of 1,143 Americans last summer by Associated Press found that 61% oppose timber harvesting in "old" forests; nevertheless a "strong majority" reported they do not engage in "environmentally-ethical shopping" but instead make purchases "mainly on the basis of price and quality."

Notwithstanding the media hoopla over the environment, most Americans have not bought into the extreme rhetoric of the environmental elite and their friends in the media. Another survey by a New York City marketing and opinion research firm found that a measly 22% of the American people could be classified as environmentalists, a group equally divided between "leaders and activists" and "affluent environmental spenders—people willing to pay . . . but with little time to get involved themselves." It is not surprising that these are affluent, well-educated, well-employed and live in the Northeast and the far West. The largest single group, however, consisting of 28% of Americans, oppose environmental regulation. Another group of 24% is not involved in environmental issues or activities. These last two groups—the research firm called them "not environmentalists"—represent a majority of the American people. The remaining 26% is a "middling swing group whose attitudes and behavior can cut both ways—both pro- and anti-environment" and they represent "a portrait of Middle America." Combining this "swing group" with the "not environmentalists" 52% yields a startlingly large 78% of the American public.

Environmentalists assert that, despite their smaller numbers, they will prevail simply because they are affluent and politically sophisticated. They will triumph, however, only so long as the costs of environmental regulation do not become part of the public debate. The defeat in the last election of "Big Green" by the voters of California demonstrates that there is a difference between Earth Day and Election Day. Although 70 to 80 percent of California voters favored "Big Green's" adoption when it was first placed on the ballot, it was rejected because, using the groupings from the survey, the 28% that oppose environmental regulations persuaded, not only the 24% uninvolved in environmental issues or activities, but also another 6% of the "middling swing group" (26%) that "Big Green" was too costly.

As more Americans discover the true costs of excessive environmental policies, the wisdom of those policies will be questioned more rigorously. "Wetlands" policy, for example, once seen as the savior of swamps, bogs, and migratory bird habitat, may soon be viewed as why a Hungarian émigré will spend three years in prison for cleaning a Pennsylvania dump site he owns; why municipal water projects from San Diego to South Carolina have been scuttled by the Environmental Protection Agency (EPA); and why two Colorado farmers have been fined $45 million each by the EPA for protecting their lands from floodwaters.

Unfortunately for wise public policy, even these horror stories are too far removed to have any real meaning for most voters. While all decry such thoughtless abuses of power in the name of "environmentalism," the impact upon the individual citizen is not yet readily apparent. For far too many Americans the victims of such perversions are merely guys behind the tree, the ones who, through no fault of their own, are being required to bear the burdens of environmental policies. What we all need to realize is that soon it could be us behind that tree.

JANUARY 1991

THE MORAL EQUIVALENT OF SURRENDER

Once again Americans are on foreign shores fighting, in President George H.W. Bush's words, "to preserve and extend the blessings of liberty." While we fight to stop a madman armed with the world's fourth greatest military machine, we do so, in large part, because Saddam Hussein is a most strategically-placed madman. As President Bush asserted recently, "We cannot allow control of the world's oil resources to fall into [Saddam Hussein's] hands."

Even if America did not get half of its oil from other countries, American men and women might be fighting in the Persian Gulf; however, the fact is we do. The question is why? The answer is simple; our energy policy is a disaster. America's reliance on foreign oil has climbed from one third to one half of its total oil consumption in just five years demonstrating a lack of not wealth, but will. Consider, for example the energy beneath our oceans.

The Outer Continental Shelf (OCS)—the natural extension of the land mass of the United States into the ocean—is enormous, over one billion acres, with equally impressive energy resources. Federal government experts assert that the OCS contains enough oil to supplant all the oil that America purchases from Persian Gulf countries for the next 25 years.

Since 1954, the United States has been exploring for and producing oil and gas from the OCS. During the past 37 years the federal government has permitted the drilling of some 37,500 wells in the OCS, yielding billions of barrels of oil, trillions of cubic feet of natural gas, and hundreds of thousands of jobs—in every state in the Union. In addition, more than $90 billion has been paid into the federal treasury in the form of bonus bids and royalties, much of which has been used by the federal government to protect and enhance wildlife and recreational lands.

Today the OCS produces 12 percent of the nation's oil and 25 percent of its natural gas, the result of the leasing of 41 million acres—a mere four percent of the OCS. While this production is impressive, it pales in comparison to what might have been produced if America leased the amount of land leased by our allies. By comparison, the provinces of Canada have leased 900 million acres. Tiny Great Britain has leased some 66 million acres.

Yet that is much too much for Congress, which declared a "moratorium" on oil and gas exploration and development in most of the OCS, despite the impressive safety record of OCS exploration and development. Through 1986, 7.5 billion barrels of oil have been produced from the OCS and less than .005% has been spilled. By contrast, some 1,400,000 barrels of oil have entered our oceans due to natural seeps, which is nothing compared to the sight of some 460,000,000 gallons of oil flowing—on Saddam Hussein's orders—into the Persian Gulf.

Congress displays a dangerous elitism when it appears less concerned about sending the young men and women of this nation to war than about risking the eternal wrath of "environmentalists" by producing oil far offshore California or in an infinitesimal portion of the North Slope of Alaska. In the six months since Saddam Hussein invaded Kuwait that has not changed. In a disturbing similarity to the Vietnam War, nothing is asked of us at home. Therefore, our leaders, while voting for war, may cast what they regard as "cheap environmental votes," those opposing the development of domestic energy. With Americans in harm's way, however, those votes are no longer "cheap."

The long-term lessons of the war in the Persian Gulf have yet to be written, but one should be evident even now. If we care about the security of our nation and if we care about the quality of the human environment, we must develop our own energy resources and we must start now. Our brave men and women in the Persian Gulf deserve no less.

FEBRUARY 1991

BUT IT DOESN'T HAVE TO BE

It was with great surprise that I learned last summer that the George Washington National Forest had not only entered into negotiations with Earth First, a terrorist organization, but also had placed an Earth First representative on an official panel to develop its forest plan. I objected to Forest Supervisor George W. Kelley.

I brought his attention to the fact that, in the State of Washington, Earth First claimed, in writing, its responsibility for "spiking" trees that were part of a timber sale in a national forest in an attempt to prevent the sale from being consummated. I informed him of the sworn testimony of a law enforcement official in Oakland, California: "[Earth First is] a violent terrorist group involved in the manufacture and placing of explosive devices." I referred him to remarks by Robert F. Kennedy, Jr., a Natural Resources Defense Council (NRDC) attorney: "Earth First activists attack at night, destroy property and machinery, endanger human life and then flee[;] Earth First tactics must be condemned as must the tactics of anyone who favors force over democratic principles."

I argued that Earth First had no place on a Forest Service working group since Earth First, as a terrorist organization, denies the legitimacy of the negotiating process, reserving always the ability to achieve—through acts of sabotage, violence, and terrorism—any goal it was denied during the negotiating process. A group whose "court of last resort" is not before a black robed judge with a gavel, but via a darkly clad terrorist with a tree "spike," does not belong at a government negotiating table on national forest plans. Supervisor Kelley refused, however, to remove the Earth First representative from the Forest Service panel, asserting that Earth First represents "deep ecology interests."

I filed an appeal with the Chief of the U.S. Forest Service. Quoting from the counterterrorism policy of the U.S. Department of State, I urged Chief F. Dale Robertson to remove the Earth First representative from the panel. A month later, I met with Chief Robertson. He advised me that, in his forthcoming written response, he would refuse my request. He noted that the U.S. Forest Service had not had any trouble with Earth First in Virginia and that it did not want any trouble with it in the future. I responded, "The State Department has not had any trouble with the Islamic Jihad in

New York City, but that does not mean that it has any right to negotiate with that terrorist group there." Chief Robertson was not persuaded.

"Chief," I tried one last time, "you are standing within ear shot of stockgrowers who have had their lives threatened by these environmental terrorists," referring to the meeting of cattlemen we were attending. "Friends of mine in timber have received similar threats. You just cannot negotiate with groups that think terrorism can be used to achieve political objectives." Chief Robertson was unmoved. I then concluded, "Chief, send me your letter as soon as possible. I want you to explain to the American people why the U.S. Forest Service is negotiating with a terrorist group."

Nearly six weeks later I received Chief Robertson's letter. It was not, however, the one Chief Robertson promised me. Although Chief Robertson did not remove the Earth First representative from the working group, he did the next best thing. He disbanded the entire panel. Negotiations with Earth First had come to an end!

The decision of the Forest Service is a major victory for the freedoms guaranteed by our Constitution and a decisive defeat for those who use violence, sabotage, and terrorism to achieve political objectives. It is also a defeat for those apologists in government who capitulate—out of fear or intimidation—to terrorists.

The decision of the Forest Service is also a lesson to all of us that we can fight back and that we can win. It is a lesson we all need to remember.

MARCH 1991

DEALING WITH GOLIATH:
CAN DAVID USE A SLINGSHOT?

The Saint Croix River flows through eastern Minnesota and northwestern Wisconsin where it merges with the Mississippi River near Prescott, Wisconsin. Some 30 miles northeast of Saint Paul, Minnesota, in Polk County, Wisconsin, lays the riverfront property of Francis (Jake) and Elizabeth Bradac. Since the early 1970s the National Park Service (NPS) has been acquiring property along the river to include in the Lower Saint Croix National Scenic Riverway Project. One property the NPS condemned was that of the Bradacs.

The Bradacs disagreed with the determination of the NPS as to the value of their property. As a result, the matter proceeded to court. Despite that, two years before trial, the NPS had asserted that the property was worth $41,000, just one month prior to trial the NPS reduced its appraisal by more than half, to $19,000. Less than two weeks prior to trial, the Bradacs offered to settle for $100,000. The NPS counter-offered $90,000; however, by this time the Bradacs had an appraisal indicating their property was worth $155,000. They rejected the counter-offer.

At the one-day trial, the jury returned a verdict for the Bradacs of $170,000. Although the NPS paid that judgment, the family's attorney and expert witness fees amounted to $60,000, thus reducing their recovery to $110,000—$45,000 less than their expert said their place was worth.

As Jake and Elizabeth Bradac learned, "negotiating" with the federal government and its agents in the NPS and the Department of Justice is never easy. That is one reason Congress adopted the Equal Access to Justice Act (EAJA), providing that, when private citizens prevail over the federal government and the position taken by the government is not "substantially justified," citizens are entitled to the payment of attorneys' fees and expenses. Congress concluded that citizens should be made whole for battling unjustified positions taken by the government. For the Davids of the country, the EAJA is a slingshot to use against the Goliath that is the vast power of the federal government and the officials acting in its name. It is little more than a slingshot.

Following their victory, the Bradacs requested that their attorneys' fees and expenses be paid fully by the federal government. After all, the jury returned a verdict that represented a 900% increase over the government's last "appraisal" of the value of their property. Incredibly, the trial court ruled against the Bradacs. Their appeal to the U.S. Court of Appeals for the Seventh Circuit was denied by a two to one ruling. The majority of the panel held that the position taken by the NPS was "substantially justified" because the appraiser used by the NPS was an "experienced, qualified and competent appraiser." The majority rejected the Bradacs' claim that the NPS had engaged in bad faith during negotiations. The dissent, however, asserted that the use by the NPS of an "experienced, qualified, and competent appraiser" did not answer the question of whether or not the government's position was "substantially justified." In addition, referring to the Bradacs' "lengthy statement of alleged facts" that the government had engaged in truly bad faith negotiations, the dissent concluded that the issue of bad faith had not been addressed properly by the district court.

The Bradacs petitioned the Supreme Court of the United States to hear their appeal in light of the substantial conflict between and among the Courts of Appeals as to when, in condemnation cases, the government's actions are "substantially justified."

When landowners prevail over the U.S. Government—not in regaining their land but in receiving fair value for that land—the payment received should not be diminished by the fees incurred by the landowners in their efforts to prevail over the often oppressive tactics of government officials. If the government is able to do to others what it did to Jake and Elizabeth Bradac, even the slingshot will have been taken out of the hands of the American people.

APRIL 1991

EVEN FROM HERE YOU CAN'T SEE THE FOREST SERVICE'S REASONING

If ever an artist popularized the American West, it was Albert Bierstadt who, in 1859, ventured into the frontier, which he painted as a mythical, dream-like, and beautiful land. In the summer of 1863, he journeyed 35 miles west of Denver to gaze upon a 14,264 foot peak. To the east, over the foothills, stretched the Great Plains; to the west, towered the Rocky Mountains, angular and rock strewn, dotted with alpine lakes and covered—below timberline—with a lush carpet of pine and shimmering aspen. He painted what he saw and called it, "A Storm in the Rockies," and named the peak Mount Rosalie, after his future wife. While his painting became famous, the name lasted only thirty two years. In 1895, the Colorado General Assembly switched to Mount Evans, after Colorado's second territorial governor.

Others wanted to see the view that inspired Bierstadt. Even before 1920, roads began making their way toward Mount Evans. In 1922, construction of a highway to the summit was begun. In 1930, Colorado Highway 5, or the Mount Evans Highway, was completed. It is the highest road for motorized travel in North America, the third highest in the world.

Beginning at 10,650 foot Echo Lake, the highway climbs slowly, switching back and forth in a 14-mile trip to the summit that passes through an ecological exhibit where flora and fauna flourish, including a rare and beautiful grove of ancient bristlecone pine. At 11,500 feet, the highway goes beyond timberline and into tundra whose abundant arctic and alpine wild flowers are world famous. While wildlife abounds—bighorn sheep, elk, deer, fox, badger and an occasional black bear and cougar—the most frequently-sighted wildlife are Rocky Mountain goats, which stand incautiously in the roadway or watch visitors from rocky perches overhead.

Each year more than 150,000 visitors to Colorado drive to the top of Mount Evans. In the late 1930s, three Colorado civic leaders decided those visitors needed a structure from which to better enjoy Mount Evans—the 15th highest peak in the lower 48. In 1940, construction began on what famed Colorado architect Edwin A. Francis, inspired by "the moon, stars and heavens," thought his best work. In 1941, the "Crest House" was completed. Built of native boulders and stone, the building was later deemed eligible for historic landmark status.

Over the years Crest House served millions of tourists, its employees assisted hundreds of lost, stranded, injured or ailing visitors to a summit where the atmospheric pressure is 60 percent that of sea-level, and it functioned as a vital communications center for the Alpine Rescue Team, during which Crest House employees provided first aid to trauma victims in "the golden hour"—the first 60 minutes following traumatic injury.

All that came to an end on September 1, 1979, when a propane fire destroyed the Crest House. The U.S. Forest Service, which by then owned the Crest House, received more than $500,000 in damages and insurance to use to rebuild the structure.

Incredibly, after years of study, the Forest Service decided not to rebuild the Crest House, ignoring the pleas of Clear Creek County, nearby Idaho Springs, the Alpine Rescue Team, and some thousands of visitors. The Forest Service also appears to have violated federal law requiring agencies to use proceeds from the loss of facilities to replace them. Most incredible of all was the Forest Service response to those who thought the Crest House met a safety need: "there is no requirement or obligation for the Forest Service to ensure the presence of people on a relatively continuous basis at the summit of Mt. Evans for safety related purposes." What a far cry from the day in 1941 when the local Forest Ranger wrote: "The Summit House meets a very outstanding public need, and the Forest Service is anxious to cooperate with you in any particulars that may serve to meet this need more fully."

MAY 1991

Epilogue: In *Mount Evans Company v. Madigan*, 14 F.3d 1444 (10th Cir. 1994), a three-judge panel upheld the Forest Service's refusal to rebuild the Crest House.

WOLVES AND WALT DISNEY

Recently, my son Luke and I went to see the Walt Disney Company's adaptation of Jack London's novel, *White Fang*, the tale of a young man's adventures during the Alaskan gold rush and his friendship with a wolf. As we sat through the credits, I was struck by the disclaimer: "Jack London's *White Fang* is a work of fiction. There has never been a documented case of a healthy wolf or pack of wolves attacking a human in North America."

Something about it stuck in my craw. Part of the problem was a statement bemoaning "persecution" of the wolf and calling for the introduction of the wolf into "wilderness areas." I wondered how likely was it—during the 500 years since Europeans arrived in North America—a wolf had not attacked a human being? Serendipitously, soon I discovered The Common Man Institute, which for years has collected objective information about the wolf. Its findings: while uncommon, attacks by healthy wolves upon humans have occurred in North America.

In addition to attacks that began in the 1830s, such as one in Colorado, attacks have been reported more recently in Algonquin Provincial Park in Ontario, Canada—where a 16 year old girl, while camping with a youth group, was bitten by a wolf—and also in Minnesota where two young children were attacked—one fatally—by wolves kept as pets. After reviewing this information I concluded that the *White Fang* disclaimer was wrong. While what Hollywood puts on the big screen is not usually of interest to me, the disclaimer was, for two reasons. First, most children do not realize that wolves are not just big, furry dogs with long teeth. Second, it is just this type of misinformation that permits officials in Washington, D.C. to conclude they can tell people in Idaho, Montana, and Wyoming that the wolf poses no threat to them or to their livestock.

I took my concern to Michael Eisner, chief executive officer of the Walt Disney Company, asking that the disclaimer be revised, or abandoned, before the film was released in video format. I next heard, not from the Walt Disney Company, but from a representative of Defenders of Wildlife (DOW) who advised me that DOW had recommended the language to the Walt Disney Company and that DOW stood by its "disclaimer." It asserted that all previous alleged attacks by wolves upon humans in North American had not been "scientifically" documented; were the result of attacks by "tame" wolves; were not really "attacks" since DOW "did not characterize" instances where people had been bitten by wolves as "attacks;" or were not "serious" attacks.

In asserting the absence of "scientific" documentation, DOW ignored some available information, and, in a bit of weird science, presumed that attacking wolves are not healthy unless their health has been documented "scientifically." DOW's science became even weirder when it presumed attacking wolves as tame unless it has been documented they were never in captivity. The conditions and qualifications set forth in the DOW letter would yield the following revision to the original *White Fang* disclaimer: "There has never been a [scientifically] documented case of a [wild—that is a wolf that was never, at any time, owned by a human] healthy wolf or pack of wolves attacking [in a serious manner, which does not include biting] a human in North America."

Needless to say I wrote back to Michael Eisner to bring this nonsense to his attention and to request that his company abandon DOW's propaganda. Regardless of how the company responds, I believe that it, and other studios, should be less concerned with the image of the wolf—and the political objectives of groups such as Defenders of Wildlife—and more concerned with factual accuracy. It would be unfortunate if the entertainment industry decided to take sides in the growing battle over natural resources, a battle that involves the economic future of millions of Americans.

AUGUST 1991

Epilogue: Maybe Disney learned its lesson; it rejected the Obama administration's plea to make *Frozen's* characters climate change advocates. "Disney cool on State Department pitch to use 'Frozen' to teach climate change," Colby Itkowitz, *Washington Post*, January 25, 2015. Said one Disney official, "[H]ere at Disney it's in our culture to tell stories that project optimism and have happy endings."

WEIRD OR POLITICAL SCIENCE

Years ago efforts were undertaken in western Colorado to kill the squawfish—after all, it is a trash fish; those efforts did not wipe out the squawfish but they made it a lot less abundant. In the last year, however, the U.S. Fish and Wildlife Service (FWS) has been determining if the squawfish is "threatened" or "endangered" under the Endangered Species Act (ESA). Such a designation will: jeopardize completion of a water project agreed to in a treaty between the United States and the Ute Indians; threaten an important coal-fired power plant on the Navajo Indian Reservation in New Mexico; and force the U.S. Bureau of Reclamation to change the manner in which it operates the Flaming Gorge Reservoir, which provides key power to western Colorado.

Meanwhile, along the Columbia River in Washington and Oregon, anglers are being paid three dollars for every squawfish—over eleven inches in size—that they pull in because, says the FWS, the squawfish is injuring the salmon. Say what? How is it that the squawfish merits key ESA protection—with its resultant economic hardship in Colorado and New Mexico—while the squawfish is being killed in Washington and Oregon? "No problem," says the FWS, "it's a totally different subspecies."

What smells in this puzzling conundrum is not three day old fish but, as Burl Ives' Big Daddy character in *Cat on a Hot Tin Roof* would say, "the powerful odor of mendacity." What is also evident is "weird or political science," "agenda science" or "pseudoscience," and its use to justify one public policy action after another. Weird science is increasingly in evidence in the national debate over big environmental issues: global warming, acid rain, wetlands, and, particularly, endangered species. All of which reminds me of a sign I saw while speaking at a timber rally in Forks, Washington—a town that is being ravaged by the northern spotted owl controversy. Outside the rally stood a boy holding a sign that read: "It's not the owls. It's the loons."

Lest anyone think these daily, dire, doomsday predictions by environmentalists and their so-called experts are the result of honest scientific inquiry and mistake, listen to what they tell each other regarding how they should discuss environmental issues. Liberal reporter Jonathan Schell, author of *Our Fragile Earth*, calls upon scientists, in making these "scientific predictions," to "disavow the certainty and precision that they normally insist on." Stanford professor Stephen Schneider, proponent of frightening stories of the ozone, also asserts, "[W]e have to offer up scary scenarios, make simplified, dramatic statements, and make little mention of any doubts we may have. Each of us has to decide what the right balance is between being effective and being honest."

Unfortunately, the nonsense that passes for environmental science and that is altering public policy in this country could not survive but for the silence of other scientists. After all, there are two kinds of "scientists" in this country. On the one hand are the scientists who are on top of their work, seek peer approval, publish in scholarly journals, and rarely, if ever, speak to the press. On the other hand are the scientists whose means and methods are questionable, do not seek peer approval, and publish in *People* magazine. Unfortunately too often it is the latter—as a result of the silence of the former—who play the lead role in making public policy.

In her book, *Trashing the Planet*, former Governor Dixy Lee Ray probes: "Who speaks for science?" Thus far in the debate over environmental issues, it has not been true scientists who have spoken for science, but environmental groups. More than public policy will suffer if real scientists continue to sit on the sidelines and leave the playing field to environmental groups whose "sky is falling" rhetoric fattens their wallets and facilitates their calls for more governmental regulation. Scientists could soon find themselves as highly regarded as politicians and us lawyers.

OCTOBER 1991

"ENVIRONMENTAL JOURNALISTS" — REPORTERS OR ADVOCATES?

Like millions of Americans I enjoy getting out-of-doors to bike or hike or fish or just to enjoy the beautiful country, its idyllic communities and their people; however, too few realize that those communities need more than our visits to survive. This was brought home to me recently when I interviewed a lawyer for a job. She is from Connecticut but a few years ago her family fell in love with the West; her father left his corporate job back East and hung out his shingle in a tiny town in New Mexico. Sadly, her family does not live there anymore. All of them are back in Connecticut. As the lawyer advised me, "There were two seasons outside of the tourist season, that is, the mud season and the dead season; there just was not enough activity to support one more family."

What most Americans fail to realize is the majority of the land in the West is owned by the federal government. In many rural counties 60, 70, 80, and even 90 percent of the land is federally owned; thus, if their communities are not allowed economic activity on the federal lands that surround them, they will die. They survive, not because of the visits of tourists, but because of the ranches nearby, or the timber mill down the road, or because an energy company is exploring for natural gas over the hill. As a result, wilderness designation and wilderness-like use of public lands are devastating to those communities.

Yet, it is not just because these communities are America's rural, small town, Norman-Rockwell-type roots that we should care about their survival. They are also the source of natural resources. Sixty percent of our nation's wool comes from the West and its federal lands. Much of America's strategic and critical minerals is from ore located on public lands in the West. Clean-burning natural gas is found in abundance in the West, particularly in the Overthrust Belt, which stretches through the forests of Wyoming and Montana. If we do not get these resources here, where will we get them? Our need for wood products—as well as other natural resources—is growing, not diminishing, even with recycling and conservation. If we do not cut trees in America, do we get them from Russia? As citizens of the "global village," we must realize that Russia has an abysmal environmental record.

A couple of weeks ago, I communicated these thoughts to a convention of the Society of Environmental Journalists due to the fact that, generally, their reporting on environmental issues left much to be desired. I concluded my remarks asking what they mean when they call themselves "environmental journalists?" Are their writings the reportage of journalists or the opinions of environmentalists? If journalists, I urged that they ask tough questions:

- What about the communities?
- What about the availability of natural resources?
- What about the global picture?
- What about the cost in taxes, jobs, imports, unemployment, and "takings" compensation to owners of private property?
- What about weird science and its role in environmental enforcement?
- Finally, what about these "environmentalists?" What is it that they really want?

We are all "environmentalists," but, as Meg Greenfield of the *Washington Post* writes, the word is not big enough for all of the meanings attributed to it. We all want clean air, clean water, and safe lands but most of us also want jobs. Seventy-one percent of the American people do not have discretionary income. Who are these environmentalists who say that we must do with less—that we have to tighten our belts? Is it really environmental protection that they seek, or is it something else, such as more governmental control?

I do not know if they heard me, but one thing is certain: we cannot expect better reporting from them unless we make an effort to get them the facts. If we do, then we have every right to demand that they demonstrate the professionalism that justifies their claim to and use of First Amendment protection.

NOVEMBER 1991

NONSENSE RUNS THROUGH IT

Robert Redford has completed filming Norman Maclean's *A River Runs Through It*, a story regarded by many as the greatest tribute to fly fishing ever written. Maclean's autobiographical tale begins, "In our family, there was no clear line between religion and fly fishing."

The *Chicago Tribune* recently described the care with which Mr. Redford approached the film, insisting on a precise recreation of Montana life of more than a generation ago. In addition, in order to flesh out the characters, the cast and crew combed through the memorabilia of Maclean's family and friends—searching for intimate and revealing details.

In the midst of such thoroughness was an incongruity made more incredible because it concerns the essence of Maclean's story—fly fishing. In deference to the Montana Humane Society, fish were not permitted to be caught. Instead, the "fish" tugging on the actors' lines were plastic bottles half-filled with water. The fish that were used were supervised by the Montana Humane Society to ensure that they were not traumatized; actors were instructed not to hold the fish by the gills but delicately around the body; and each night the fish were returned to a monitored tank to recover from their day's labors.

We all know that movie-making is done with smoke and mirrors, and that any relationship between the reel life portrayed by tinsel town and real life is often purely coincidental. For millions of Americans, however, particularly for young Americans—the nation's most avid movie-goers and also television-watchers—much of the information that they receive regarding the "real" world comes from the "reel" world of Hollywood.

What a world it is. From the glass bubble-like isolation of the studios and sound stages of Los Angeles a few hundred executives, producers, and writers create video versions of their vision of the world, or the world as they would have it. What America sees at the theaters and at home during prime time is affected not simply by the fact that we are looking through the lenses of one of the most liberal elements of our society, but also by the fact that these elitists use their medium in an attempt to reshape attitudes and thus change the world.

For example, what *Time* magazine refers to as the "almost complete absence of religious content on prime time" and the political correctness of Hollywood-style environmentalism found fertile ground in *The Simpsons*. The popular cartoon series not only conducted an assault on timber harvesting in America—depicting the bribery of a Congressman who shouts "Timber!"—but ridiculed religious faith by scripting this "prayer" for Bart Simpson: "Dear God, we paid for all this stuff ourselves, so thanks for nothing."

As *The Simpsons* timber episode illustrates, Hollywood's approach to environmental issues reflects its bias and its effort to influence public opinion. While Ted Turner's *Captain Planet* is the worst of the cartoon genre—with its mysticism, factual inaccuracies, and demonic portrayal of most American entrepreneurs—many other animated features also pass out environmental misinformation.

During prime time, either the hero embraces the latest trendy environmental cause, or the arch villain is discovered to be a "wealthy developer" bent on environmental destruction. Meanwhile, at the movies, an environmental subtext is often added to the most innocuous of films. For example, the only subject given serious treatment in *Naked Gun 2 1/2* was the film's characterization of the nation's energy producers as plotting criminals, a portrayal for which the film credits several environmental groups.

It is Mr. Redford's call as to how much power he wishes to give environmental groups over how he makes his films—even to the extent of not fishing in a film about fly fishing. It is our call, however, as to how much of this nonsense we endure in what we pay to see, particularly when one considers the likely consequences. As communications professor George Gerbner noted, "If you can write a nation's stories, you needn't worry about who makes its laws."

DECEMBER 1991

CHAPTER THREE

Bush Goes Green
and Loses

★ ★ ★ ★ ★

———

President Reagan's famous first Secretary of the Interior Jim Watt once opined, "You can't outrun an environmentalist to the left." He was referring to a vital lesson he learned watching, first hand, the unhappy fate of President Nixon's Secretary of the Interior Walter J. Hickel, who tried to do just that without any success whatsoever.

So it was with President George H.W. Bush's attempt to be "an environmental president." Just how far to the left are the politics of the environmentalists became clear with the release of Al Gore's book, *Earth in the Balance*. No thinking person and certainly no one who believes in the Constitution and its guarantees could embrace the "wrenching transformation of society" envisioned and in fact demanded by Gore. There was nothing that the Bush administration could do that would satisfy such zealotry; however, in the process of attempting to do so, the Bush administration alienated many millions of people who had been targeted by these environmental extremists, especially in the West and in rural America.

Two of the people targeted were Colorado brothers, Dennis and Nile Gerbaz of Carbondale, Colorado who sought to restore their land when it was flooded by the Roaring Fork River. Environmental groups were livid that the brothers had engaged in such "self-help" and demanded action by the Environmental Protection Agency (EPA) and got that action when the EPA came after the brothers for violating the Clean Water Act to the tune of forty-five (45) million dollars each. Instantly, the brothers became "poster boys" for government overkill and heavy handedness. Incredibly enough, one high-ranking Bush administration official countered: "It does not have to make sense; it's the law."

Meanwhile, besieged citizens, small communities, as well as property owners fought back in federal court and in the all-important court of public opinion. They experienced some precedent setting victories and national recognition, but all that came too late to result in a change in direction in the Bush administration.

FOSTERING FOREIGN DEPENDENCE

1991 was historic. America fought and won a war; the Soviet Union survived a coup attempt and then disintegrated; and, for the first time in as many as six years, a handful of Americans spent New Year's Eve, not chained to a wall in Lebanon, but free in the company of loved ones.

1991 was historic for a lesser known but disturbing reason: exploration for domestic sources of energy hit a 49-year low. Not since Japan bombed Pearl Harbor has America done less to provide itself with the fuel that propels our modern society.

There are a number of reasons for this incredible milestone, including the state of the economy and low oil prices; however, the most important reason was what the *New York Times*, in its article on the subject, called "environmental laws." Most Americans know the phrase "environmental laws" is a euphemism for the patchwork-quilt of federal statutes that permits no growth advocates to slow, if not stop, the search for traditional sources of energy in America.

What is not widely known is that environmental groups also oppose new energy sources. This comes as a surprise to Americans who thought they heard environmental group leaders call for the development of "alternative energy sources." This schizophrenia becomes almost surreal in the case of efforts by environmental groups to deny American workers the ability to supply the resources necessary to power electric automobiles.

The vision of fleets of electric automobiles is no Jules Verne fantasy. As a result of the Clean Air Act amendments and tough new air quality regulations adopted by a number of states, primarily California, alternatively-fueled vehicles—most likely electric—may be only years, if not months away. Such a development is good news not just for smog-clogged big cities like Los Angeles, but for the people of tiny towns like Winona, Missouri. Not only will electric cars mean fewer exhaust-emitting vehicles on the streets and freeways of our big cities, but they will also mean American jobs. After all, the development of electric automobiles requires powerful batteries, and batteries demand an abundance of lead.

Fortunately, America is the Saudi Arabia of lead. Only Australia possesses richer lead deposits. Ninety percent of America's lead lies beneath the rolling woodlands of southeastern Missouri—a hard scrabble region where jobs are few and far between.

There, some 65 air miles southwest of St. Louis, lies the Viburnum Trend, a world class deposit of lead, 25 to 100 feet thick, 50 to 1000 feet wide, stretching over 40 miles, with enough lead to power millions of electric cars. Mined from deep, underground caverns whose only surface impact is a handful of buildings that permits the entry of the miners and the extraction of the ore, the lead means more than just cleaner air for our big cities; it means American jobs.

This is all irrelevant to several environmental groups that are committed to putting an end to lead mining in southeastern Missouri. For them the outstanding environmental record of mining in southeastern Missouri is irrelevant. For them the need for high paying jobs and the boost to the region's economy that mining provides is irrelevant. For them the possibility that America could meet some of its energy needs from domestic sources, and thereby improve our balance of trade, is irrelevant. As one of them stated in a public meeting, "Maybe we should just let foreign countries sell us the lead America needs."

How very fitting that, in a year in which we went to war to protect the availability of oil from foreign sources, America seems to be starting down the path of foreign dependence regarding an energy source of the future. Australia, however, is not the Middle East. Australia is a stable, friendly nation that will probably never ask us to send our sons and daughters to war. Like its neighbor nations in the Pacific Rim, our dollars will suffice.

JANUARY 1992

NO MORE "CHEAP"
ENVIRONMENTAL VOTES

On Monday, March 2, 1992, the Supreme Court of the United States heard oral arguments in what may become the most important property rights decision in history. The case is *Lucas v. South Carolina Coastal Council*. The issue is whether government must pay landowners when government yields to the demands of environmental groups and restricts the use of private property.

In 1986, Mr. Lucas purchased two beach front lots in South Carolina. He intended to build a home for his family on one and a home for resale on the other. In 1988, however, the South Carolina Legislature enacted a law permitting setback lines to be drawn along the South Carolina coast, seaward of which no structures could be built. The line drawn by the South Carolina Coastal Council was behind Mr. Lucas' lots, preventing him from any use of his property.

Mr. Lucas sued, charging an unconstitutional "taking." The trial court found a "taking" and awarded Mr. Lucas $1.2 million, but the South Carolina Supreme Court reversed. On November 18, 1991, the Supreme Court agreed to hear the case.

Lucas provides the Court with the opportunity to establish coherent standards as to what constitutes a Fifth Amendment "taking." This is an opportunity that the Court must seize, not only because of what happened to Mr. Lucas, but also given government action being undertaken in the name of "environmental protection."

For example, under President Bush's "no net loss of wetlands" policy, bureaucrats regulate millions of acres of privately-owned land, not because the use of these lands by their owners will cause harm to their neighbors, but because federal officials believe these private lands serve a higher "public use" by remaining "wet."

Similarly, federal officials have announced their intention to designate some 3,000 more plants and animals under the Endangered Species Act. The Endangered Species Act has been interpreted to prohibit the use of private lands upon which endangered species reside, not because the prohibited uses of these private lands will interfere with the lands of others, but because bureaucrats believe that these private lands must serve the "public use" of species habitat.

While such governmental actions may be the manner in which bureaucrats seek to appease environmental groups, these actions are impermissible under the Constitution. After all, the Court has declared, "[a] strong public desire to improve the public condition is not enough to warrant achieving the desire by a shorter cut than the constitutional way of paying for the change."

Years ago, when I served as an attorney to the U.S. Senate and the U.S. House of Representatives, I was called upon to discuss various legislative proposals with Senators and Representatives. All too often they told me they were going to vote as the environmental groups demanded because, "It's a cheap environmental vote." What they meant was that while they did not agree with the environmental groups on the issue, the legislation was not thought to cost any jobs in their state or district so they were free to comply with the dictates of environmental groups.

Too much of the nation's environmental legislation and regulation has been put on the books, not because it is costless or even wise, but because it is "cheap;" that is, the cost is imposed on someone else. Off-budget environmental policy is not only unfair, inequitable, and an incalculable drain on the economy, it is contrary to the Constitution. The Fifth Amendment provides "nor shall private property be taken for public use" without paying for it.

If the American people want more wetlands and more endangered species habitat, apparently concluding that there is an important public good that merits telling property owners how they can use their land, then the American people—and not the property owner—must bear the financial burdens that accompany the benefits. We may soon have that opportunity since, after *Lucas*, implementing the agenda of environmental groups may no longer be "cheap."

MARCH 1992

KATHLEEN MARQUARDT: HEROIC ACTIVIST

In Washington, D.C., a storm was about to descend upon the home of Kathleen Marquardt from an unlikely and tranquil source: along the quiet, sunny, tree-lined street, children were coming home from school. Among them were Kathleen Marquardt's daughters, Shane and Montana. Montana was eager to arrive home to tell her mother the amazing lessons she had learned in school. "Mommy," Montana cried out as she threw open the door, "We're murderers."

For three days representatives of People for the Ethical Treatment of Animals (PETA) held forth in Montana's classroom. Using photographs, games, and stories, they told Montana and her classmates that they were no better than rats and chickens and pigs and dogs. They told them that it is not just human life that is sacred, but all life. Furthermore, they told them that anyone who hunted or fished, who wore clothing made from the fur or skin of animals, who ate fish or fowl or other creatures, who condoned animal research—even to discover the cures for cancer, AIDS, or sudden infant death syndrome (SIDS)—was a murderer.

For Kathleen Marquardt, who grew up in western Montana hunting and fishing, wearing leather and fur, eating beef, chicken and lamb, and believing that mankind was both created in the image of God and blessed with dominion over the Earth and all of its creatures, such teachings were an abomination. She could not believe there were people who thought such things, let alone believed they had the right to teach them in her children's classroom.

Kathleen Marquardt immersed herself in a study of PETA and its ilk. She read their books and studied their literature. The more she learned, the more upset she became, and the even more committed. Someone had to do something! She learned something else—little was being done to combat the evil Kathleen Marquardt saw spreading across the country.

She realized that if anything were going to be done, she would have to do it. She knew what she was up against. She had read of the terrorist response of some animal rights advocates to their opponents: the break-ins, the destruction of facilities, the trashing of reputations and careers. None of it dissuaded Kathleen Marquardt.

What would have terrified her, had she known it, was that to do what she knew had to be done, she would be required to stand in front of hundreds, even thousands, of strangers and speak. For the quiet, almost hermit-like recluse who wanted nothing more than to sit in the quiet of her home listening to classical music and being the fabric designer she had trained to be, the rough and tumble public policy arena was a foreign and horrifying place. As great as was her fear of public appearances and confrontation, however, her fear of what would happen if she did nothing was much greater.

Today, less than three years after she began, Kathleen Marquardt has turned her third child—the organization that she bore so painfully, Putting People First—into a national grassroots group, some 40,000 strong, and growing. She has testified before state legislatures, appeared on national television, spearheaded opposition to legislation, and spoken to thousands all across the country. Much more lies ahead. "We're just getting started," she says.

Many of us remember the line of anger and frustration from Paddy Chayefsky's movie *Network*: "I'm as mad as hell and I'm not going to take it anymore." Less well known are the sentences that preceded that cry of disaffection: "I'm a human being, damn it. My life has value."

Kathleen Marquardt understands the value of human life. She understands that human beings are innately more valuable than other living things. Like millions of Americans, Kathleen Marquardt cried out, "I'm mad as hell and I'm not going to take it anymore." She did not just say it, however; she did something about it. If only there were more like her.

APRIL 1992

IT'S BAD POLITICS AND BAD PUBLIC POLICY
FOR PRESIDENT BUSH TO GO GREEN

According to White House experts, President Bush must move left on environmental issues to win reelection. Unfortunately for George Bush, his political advisors, and the nation, a leftward move is not just disastrous public policy; it is also abysmal politics. Bush's advisors are correct that opinion polls reveal a majority of Americans are "environmentalists," but the *Washington Post's* Meg Greenfield says the word means too many different things to have political significance. Furthermore, a Roper Organization poll finds that only 22% of Americans are "hard-core environmentalists."

Where are these "environmentalists" and to what degree, if any, do they impact elections? The answer: Maine, Massachusetts, Minnesota, New Jersey, Oregon, Vermont, Washington, Wisconsin, and, to a degree, California. It should come as no surprise, therefore, that Governor Dukakis carried a majority of those states, winning in Massachusetts, Minnesota, Oregon, Washington, and Wisconsin. He almost carried Vermont. Frankly, it is surprising Dukakis did not do better; he had massive support from environmental organizations and was the beneficiary of eight years of trashing of the Reagan-Bush administration by the environmental lobby and its allies in the media.

Still, nervous White House types note that Dukakis "almost" carried California, losing by a "scant" 300,000 votes. They overlook that, except for the Reagan anomaly as a popular former Governor, elections for president in California have always been close. Nixon carried California by 100,000 votes in 1960 and by 200,000 votes in 1968. Ford won by 100,000 votes in 1976. Thus Bush's 300,000 vote margin demonstrates, not weakness, but strength.

In California, there are only three major counties that vote Democratic: San Francisco and Alameda, each yields a 100,000 vote Democratic margin, and Los Angeles, which yields a 200,000 Democratic vote margin. In order to win, Republicans must offset this 400,000 vote margin, primarily with the votes from southern California. Orange County yields Republican margins of 300,000; San Diego 150,000; San Bernardino and Riverside Counties 75,000 each; Ventura County 40,000 to 50,000, and

Kern County 30,000. Thus, the Republican margin statewide is some 680,000—nearly 300,000 more than that of the Democrats.

With these margins, why did Ford almost lose California in 1976? The answer: because many conservative voters in Riverside and San Bernardino County—whose families came from the South—saw Carter as the more conservative candidate. Similarly, Bush's vulnerability in California is not because he cannot win over the environmental voters—and no matter how hard he tries, he cannot—but because his leftward movement endangers the margins critical to Republican victory. In addition, the swing voters in Los Angeles County, where Bush might eat into the Democratic margin, are not those persuaded by elitist environmental rhetoric but are Hispanics and Asians—people almost totally missing from the environmental organizations and people for whom jobs, opportunity, education, and family values are of major importance.

As President Bush moves to the left on environmental issues for the sake of California, what happens in the rest of the country? The experience of Gerald Ford is instructive. In 1976, President Ford failed to carry Ohio by 11,000 votes, a key loss since Ohio, plus any other state (Hawaii, Mississippi, or Wisconsin), would have won him the presidency. Ford did not lose Ohio because Cleveland yielded bigger margins for Carter than for Humphrey or McGovern, but because Carter did better in the Republican areas of southern Ohio. As in California's Riverside and San Bernardino Counties, Carter was seen as the more conservative of the two candidates.

As important as is the impact of Bush's leftward tilt upon voters in these traditionally conservative regions is its impact on the activists—like members of the American Farm Bureau Federation—who are key to any Republican victory. The White House team may have gotten a partial answer earlier this year at the American Farm Bureau Federation Convention where President Bush became the first president in history not to receive a standing ovation. We can only wonder if President Bush got the message.

MAY 1992

PROPERTY RIGHTS VICTORY

When, on June 29, 1992, the Supreme Court of the United States decided the landmark property rights case of *Lucas v. South Carolina Coastal Council*, it reached back 70 years to an opinion written by Justice Oliver Wendell Holmes: *Pennsylvania Coal Company v. Mahon.*

For the 131 years prior to *Pennsylvania Coal*, the Fifth Amendment, and its provision that "private property" not be put to "public use without just compensation," had been applied only to "direct appropriation" or to the "practical ouster of [the owner's] possession." Justice Holmes concluded the Fifth Amendment was not limited to a physical taking: "if regulation goes too far it will be recognized as a taking." "Limits" were necessary, declared Justice Holmes prophetically, because of "the natural tendency of human nature . . . to extend the qualification more and more until at last private property disappears." To those who asserted that the challenged Pennsylvania statute served the public good, Justice Holmes gave this warning: "We are in danger of forgetting that a strong public desire to improve the public condition is not enough to warrant achieving the desire by a shorter cut than the constitutional way of paying for the change."

Over the decades that followed the ruling, it began to appear as if there were no limits to how far regulations might go without causing a taking. Finally, in 1987, the Court declared that a statute, much like the one challenged in *Pennsylvania Coal*, was not a "taking." By 1992, *Newsweek* and *Time* may have been right when, in discussing the upcoming *Lucas* case, they referred to the "takings" clause as "a quaint anachronism" and "a radical notion."

On the last day of its term, the Court decided *Lucas*. In his opinion for the majority, Justice Scalia first paid homage to Justice Holmes. Then, in language strongly reminiscent of *Pennsylvania Coal*, Justice Scalia wrote: "when the owner of real property has been called upon to sacrifice all economically beneficial uses in the name of the common good . . . he has suffered a taking." Thus, the Court reversed the decision of the South Carolina Supreme Court that David H. Lucas, prevented from building on two beach front lots, had not suffered a "taking." The case returned to South Carolina for reconsideration consistent with the Court's ruling.

As a result of the Court's holding in *Lucas*, the opinion of Justice Holmes is as alive and vital today, as it was when it was first written, perhaps even more so. The Court will no longer be satisfied with the pronouncements of state legislatures or regulatory bodies as to why their regulations do not constitute a taking. For the Court, such self-serving rationales are irrelevant. What the Court will consider, noted Justice Scalia, is the view of the property owner—what were his or her expectations when the property was purchased.

Environmental organizations and state regulatory agencies, attempting to diminish the significance of the *Lucas* decision—called "damage control" in Washington, D.C.—point to Court language requiring that "all economically beneficial or productive use of land" be lost in order to be considered a taking. What "all economically beneficial or productive use" means is uncertain, because that was not at issue in *Lucas*; however, a recent decision by the Court of Claims may provide a clue.

A company purchased hundreds of acres of Wyoming ranch land in order to mine the rich, low sulfur coal beneath the surface. Prevented by federal law from mining the coal, it sued, charging a "taking." The Court of Claims agreed and awarded the company nearly $200 million. The federal government, urging the Supreme Court to review the decision, asserted that the company had not lost "all" use of its property; after all it still could manage the surface as a livestock ranch. In a fitting tribute to Justice Holmes, the Supreme Court declined to hear the case.

JULY 1992

CONGRESS AND MEDIA IGNORE RIP-OFF

Where are they now? Where are the committee chairmen, the self-appointed congressional watch dogs, the headline-grabbing decriers of waste, fraud, and abuse, the media pontificators, the self-righteous experts on what ails the country, the intimidators of cowering bureaucrats, the defamers of accused wrongdoers?

Where are they now that the Inspector General (IG) of the U.S. Department of the Interior (DOI) has exposed the biggest rip-off since Teapot Dome? The answer: nowhere, because now the shoe is on the other foot and it hurts. Now the accusations of rip-off, self-enrichment, and cover up are directed at their friends in the environmental community.

In early June, the IG released the results of an investigation into how the National Park Service (NPS), the U.S. Fish and Wildlife Service (FWS), and the Bureau of Land Management (BLM) use "nonprofit" organizations to acquire private lands, take them off the tax rolls, and bring them into federal ownership. DOI's acquisition of privately-owned lands is no mom and pop operation. During fiscal year 1991, the NPS, the FWS, and the BLM spent more than $219 million to buy private land. Over the last six fiscal years (1986 to 1991), these agencies spend a whopping $992 million dollars—nearly a billion dollars—to increase federal land ownership.

As stunning as is the DOI's land acquisition budget, which has increased 140 percent since 1986, is the underhanded, wasteful, and maybe even illegal manner in which that money has been spent. According to the IG, the FWS paid $5.2 million more than the approved fair market value of $44 million in 64 transactions. In addition, the FWS paid "interest" and "overhead costs" of nonprofits even though payment of these "costs" has never been authorized by the DOI's top lawyer and even though the FWS did not verify that the nonprofits incurred these "costs."

Several land acquisitions are worth mentioning. In 1987, the FWS paid the National Audubon Society $1 million for 777 acres in California valued at $700,000, a 30 percent windfall. In 1988 and 1989, the FWS paid The Nature Conservancy (TNC) $4.5 million for 5,398 acres in Oklahoma valued at $3.5 million, a 28 percent gift.

Furthermore, the IG reported that these three agencies gave nonprofits a $1.9 million windfall on seven transactions, even though they had extremely limited financial involvement and almost no risk. Specifically, after TNC paid $100 for an option to buy 5,529 acres in Oregon, the BLM gave TNC $1.4 million with which the TNC paid the owner $1.26 million, a $140,000 windfall to TNC. In yet another simultaneous transaction in Oregon, the BLM paid the Trust for Public Land (TPL) $1 million, out of which the TPL paid the owner $720,000, a 38 percent profit.

According to the IG, none of these three agencies followed established appraisal and property valuation standards to ensure that property values are timely, independent, and adequately supported by market data. The appraisals used by the three agencies were an average of 400 days old. In one case, the appraisal was more than four years old. Typically, in fact, the appraisals are provided by the nonprofits themselves. In perhaps the most outrageous example, the NPS paid $4.77 million for 4,200 acres in South Carolina using a year and one half old appraisal; between that appraisal and the purchase by the NPS, Hurricane Hugo devastated the area.

Despite the shocking revelations in the IG's report, the Assistant Secretary for Fish, Wildlife, and Parks has thumbed his nose at the IG, refusing to comply with the IG's recommendations. The IG stops short of calling his colleague a liar, but publicly bemoans the "arrogance" of the FWS and the NPS.

What will happen next is uncertain; however, one thing is clear. If it were the private sector the IG had skewered, there would be massive media coverage, congressional hearings, cries of outrage from Capitol Hill, and maybe even calls for the appointment of a Special Prosecutor.

AUGUST 1992

GORE(ING) THE ECONOMY

Perhaps the nicest thing one can say about U.S. Senator Al Gore (D-TN) after reading his book *Earth in the Balance: Ecology and The Human Spirit*, is the mid-life crisis through which he admits he is passing is world class. Unfortunately, with a self-centeredness that is astonishing even for the wealthy, elitist politician that he is, Gore concludes that everyone feels his sense of ennui and despair.

Gore believes not only that we are all unhappy, rootless, and emotionally empty, but also that we are that way because we are estranged from the planet. Although Gore testifies, on the last page of his book, to a belief in God and a personal relationship with Jesus Christ, he spends the other 367 pages professing that the rest of us can be saved, physically and emotionally, only by a spiritual relationship with the Earth. Yet for all the "connection" Gore wants us to have with the planet, it is asking too much for mankind to benefit from the Earth's resources. For example, Gore questions using the yew tree to save women from ovarian cancer: "Are those of us alive today entitled to cut down all of those trees to extend the lives of a few of us[.]" Gore's vision is grim: we are "bulldozing the Garden of Eden," the results of which will be: "destruction ... on a biblical scale," "as unthinkable as the consequences of unrestrained nuclear war," and even an "environmental holocaust without precedent."

Gore's book jacket states that his book "is required reading for all who perceive the urgent need to bring the earth back into balance." Gore's publicist got that right. Gore's book is for the true believer—one who has bought into Gore's Chicken Little rhetoric and the weird science that supports it. Devoid of footnotes, Gore concludes with a narrative labeled "Notes," which reveals that Gore's book was "based on:" "conversations," "discussions," "congressional investigations," "hearings" and "investigative stories" by the media. Gore fails to note some of his academic sources have broken ranks.

Gore boldly, and erroneously, maintains that there is no genuine scientific dispute regarding his bleak observations and apocalyptic predictions. (Nearly half of all climatologists surveyed disagree with Gore.) Instead, Gore heaps abuse upon those who do not see things his way, comparing them to drug addicts (or "enablers" of addicts), child abusers and dysfunctional parents. Such people are "cynical," "unethical," and capable of "racism" or the "atrocities of Hitler and Stalin."

Gore advocates adoption of a "Global Marshall Plan" under which the free market system, having demonstrated its superiority over communism, "must undergo a profound transformation." Thus, having won a stunning victory over totalitarianism, we must now surrender meekly to green tyranny. Gore would require U.S. citizens to fund massive programs here and abroad through a host of new taxes, would restrict all development to "environmentally appropriate technologies," and finally would enter into international treaties and agreements to be enforced by a new United Nations "Stewardship Council." (Gore's aggressive advocacy of tax and spend policies is not surprising. The National Taxpayers Union labels him one of the U.S. Senate's biggest spenders.)

While Gore has little faith in technology ("we are not that clever, and we never have been"), he has great faith in the ability of government—not just national government, but international government—to determine what technologies are "appropriate," to decide what economic progress is "sustainable" (and thereby permissible), and to order our lives and our economy. Nothing can stand in the way of Gore's new programs, neither the cost, nor "individual rights" toward which Gore asserts we have already "tilted" too far. In words of song, if you think the estimated $115 billion a year environmental regulations cost this country is too much, if Gore has his way, "You ain't seen nothing yet."

In time, Al Gore may recover from his mid-life crisis, but if he and Clinton get elected in November, the odds are that the American people never will recover.

SEPTEMBER 1992

CHAPTER FOUR

Clinton's War on the West

———

In 1982, Colorado Governor Richard Lamm, a Democrat, declared that the Carter administration was a "western nightmare.... At no time did he have a western strategy. Out of uninterest or contempt, or both, Carter went to the Rocky Mountain West only four times in his term." Westerners would later wish that President Clinton had never visited the West, but that was in the future. People expected better of Clinton; after all, his unofficial slogan was, "The economy, stupid," a phrase hung at campaign headquarters to help stay on message. The campaign's official slogan was "Putting People First." Meanwhile, most Americans wanted an end to environmental extremism. In a *USA Weekend* national showdown, which reached 33.5 million readers between an Earth Day founder and me, my call to "Ease up on environmental rules," won 62 percent to 38 percent.

Unfortunately, as westerners were to learn, Clinton did not mean the western economy nor did he mean the hardworking people of the rural west, whether loggers in timber-producing communities in the Pacific Northwest, or the miners, ranchers, and oil and gas workers in communities across the West that depend on such economic pursuits. Like Jimmy Carter before him, Bill Clinton owed too big a debt to environmental extremists. Within days he would do just as they demanded; moreover, over time, those demands would escalate and so would Clinton's "War on the West."

Meanwhile, MSLF was busy fighting policies put in place or rulings made by the Bush administration. MSLF represented timber-producing communities in northern Idaho and northwestern Montana that feared catastrophic fires due to disastrous timber-harvesting decisions. MSLF represented a Montana sheep rancher who killed a grizzly bear in self-defense but was being persecuted for violating the Endangered Species Act. In addition, MSLF represented a mom and pop outfit from Colorado, which despite its low bid to install the guardrail on a federal highway, was denied the contract because of the family's race; a federal race-based quota mandated that decision.

PRESIDENT CLINTON: PUT PEOPLE FIRST

If President Clinton is committed to "Putting People First," which his campaign slogan claimed was his goal, he must repudiate the extreme, anti-human environmental policies of Vice President Al Gore and organized environmental groups.

According to Election Day exit polls, 43 percent of voters saw the economy and jobs as vitally important, while only 6 percent were concerned about the "environment." If Clinton has a mandate, it is to strengthen the economy, not to be a slave to the sky-is-falling, mankind-is-a-cancer-on-the-planet rhetoric of environmental groups. It will take courage for Clinton to dismiss the demands for power by these groups, especially given that the media reports their hysterical pronouncements as gospel, but if Clinton wants to be a growth and jobs president that is what he must do. Here are five ways to start.

Stop never-ending environmental litigation. Environmental groups litigate interminably in their effort to stop economic activity. These elitist groups—overflowing with tax-free dollars, armed with complicated federal statutes and complex regulations, and aided by judges intent on making, not interpreting, law—can delay or kill economic activity anywhere in the United States. These lawsuits cost millions, escalate federal outlays, and doom American jobs.

Reform the Endangered Species Act to consider its impact upon *Homo sapiens*. This statute, which protects "endangered" or "threatened" species "whatever the cost," compels that the federal government spend tens of millions of dollars annually. Yet those expenditures pale in comparison to the cost to the economy in lost jobs and abandoned economic activity. The Act's impact, which extends to obscure subspecies and to small pockets of creatures in abundance elsewhere, will get worse as more species are listed. Since environmental groups want the current list of 600-plus species to be increased to more than 4,000, soon every community will have a federally-protected animal or plant threatening economic activity.

Establish intelligent timber management so our forests will provide not only solace, oxygen, and ground cover, but also jobs and a home-grown natural resource. Forests left unharvested because of the endless administrative appeals and lawsuits of environmental groups are victimized by insect infestation and fuel build up. In time, nature will clear these sickly forests, with devastating results, as millions of acres go up in flames. Diseased and healthy trees will be destroyed, along with wildlife habitat and a source of jobs and economic and social well-being for mankind. The environmentalists croon that wild fires are nature's way. So was the Black Death (Bubonic Plague) until mankind found a way to prevent it.

Preserve true "wetlands" by implementing federal policy that excludes potholes, ditches, and dry lake beds. In 1989, covetous federal bureaucrats, unable to change the science of "wetlands," simply changed the legal definition of "wetlands." With the stroke of a pen, "wetlands" doubled. Millions of dollars have been spent by federal lawyers and power hungry bureaucrats battling over land that is not wet and is not covered by the Clean Water Act. Economic activity has been delayed, millions have been added to the cost of projects, and Americans will soon be paying billions to compensate citizens for the unconstitutional "taking" of private land.

Disavow a Carter-like "War on the West." While millions of westerners earn their living in pursuits that draw the inflammatory ire of environmental groups, those activities boost the economy of the nation and the West. Tourism is not a sufficient answer. There are not enough summer tourists or enough Hollywood stars and rich Americans for all of us to turn our homes into bed and breakfast operations, pouring cappuccino and fluffing duvets.

The battle over environmental policy is not over the quality of the human environment but over whether environmental elitists and their allies in the federal bureaucracy have the power they seek over the lives of all Americans. One measure of the success of the Clinton presidency will be how quickly he learns that vital lesson. Another measure will be whether he heeds it.

FEBRUARY 1993

CLINTON DECLARES WAR ON THE WEST

President Clinton, who said he wanted to grow jobs and the economy, decided that he did not mean in the West. Therefore, for westerners, Clinton's campaign sign, "It's The Economy, Stupid," becomes "Stupidly, you thought we meant your economy."

On February 17, 1993, the Clinton administration announced plans to impose a royalty on mining, increase grazing fees, adopt broad environmental taxes, reduce timber sales, and put a surcharge on agricultural use of western water. All this follows Clinton's plans to tax energy use, which hits westerners twice: first as producers and then again as consumers. The significance of this remarkable set of policies was not lost on the *Washington Post*, which labeled the plan "a direct assault on the traditional economic foundation of the West" and "a virtual wish-list of the environmental movement."

Clinton's selection to lead this onslaught is Secretary of the Interior Bruce Babbitt, aided by a Who's Who of the environmental movement. Westerners are beginning to realize what Babbitt meant when, as president of the League of Conservation Voters, he cried, "We must identify our enemies and drive them into oblivion."

As Jimmy Carter discovered in 1977 when his anti-western crusade produced the Sagebrush Rebellion, Clinton's policies are not without risks. Clinton, however, appears willing to take those risks. The *New Republic* quotes Babbitt as telling Clinton that the bad news about his environmental policies is that Clinton will lose the Rockies in 1996. The good news is that he is sure to lock up California. Of course, that is nearly four years away. Meanwhile, Clinton will try to convince the nation that his anti-western policies are necessary: "to reduce the deficit," "to move toward the market," "to eliminate subsidies," and "to take on special interests."

Clinton's newest crusade has nothing to do with deficits, the market, or subsidies; however, it has everything to do with "special interests." Clinton is heeding the demands of environmental groups to kill mining, grazing, timber harvesting, energy development, and other like uses of federal lands. If adopted, these policies will wreck the West. Gutting the mining law—the changes endorsed by Clinton will be undertaken with a meat axe, not a scalpel—will: eliminate nearly 30,000 jobs; cause the loss of more than $700 million dollars in federal, state, and local revenues; and cost the West $3.8 billion in annual economic activity.

A hike in grazing fees will cost more than 82,000 jobs on ranches (not to mention those lost in nearby communities) and deny the rural West over $4 billion in annual revenues. Ironically, driving ranchers off the land will require at least $16 million a year in federal expenditures for water (for wildlife) and road maintenance.

Elimination of so-called "below cost timber sales" ("below cost" only because of voodoo accounting and the inclusion of costs not carried by the private sector) will cost more than 22,000 jobs with an annual payroll of $822 million. The Clinton proposal will also deprive rural counties of over $20 million in timber receipts and will doom millions of acres of decaying forests to cataclysmic fires.

While the West has its urban areas, most western counties are rural in character and cannot survive economically without the wise utilization of federal lands. It is not just rural communities that will be hurt, however; western states are built upon natural resources activities. Even the most urban among them rely on such activities for vital tax revenues.

The rebellion in the West will hardly be partisan. The ink was not yet dry on Clinton's directives when U.S. Senator Ben Nighthorse Campbell (D-CO) threw down the gauntlet, asserting Clinton's plans are an attack "on my neighbors and my friends."

Now that President Clinton has declared War on the West, only two questions remain: will he win that war; and, will he be reelected in 1996? If past is prologue, the answer to both is "No."

APRIL 1993

CLINTON'S READING ASSIGNMENT

On June 3, President Clinton withdrew the nomination of Lani Guinier to be Assistant Attorney General for the Civil Rights Division of the U.S. Department of Justice. The position is not without substance. With hundreds of lawyers and an arsenal of civil rights legislation, the division has the power to bring individuals, corporations, school districts, universities, and state governments to their knees, if it but has the will.

There is no question but that Ms. Guinier, a law professor at the University of Pennsylvania, has the will. What brought down wrath upon her, however, was her desire to go beyond what has long been the essence of civil rights: "a color-blind Constitution." For Ms. Guinier, it was not enough that members of a minority group be assured the ability to vote; they had to win. It was not enough that members of the U.S. Senate and U.S. House of Representatives be duly elected—they had to be "representative" of America. Thus, Ms. Guinier challenged, and sought to alter, the very underpinnings of the democratic system.

As the nation's top civil rights "cop," with the power, not just to wear down even the strongest adversary, but also to threaten thousands of others with litigation, Ms. Guinier would have been in a unique position to achieve the fundamental change of which she wrote so often. In the end, it was those writings that doomed her, not just with the American people and Senators who were asked to confirm her, but also with President Clinton. As Clinton admitted, "At the time of the nomination, I had not read her writings. Had I read them before I nominated her, I would not have done so."

If that is what it takes for Clinton to withdraw a nomination and abandon a long-time ally, I suggest that he take a hard look at the writings and pronouncements of all the leaders of the environmental movement. Unfortunately, it is probably too late for a review of Vice President Al Gore ("Are those of us alive today entitled to cut down all of those [yew] trees to extend the lives of a few of us [who suffer from cancer]?") or of Secretary of the Interior Bruce Babbitt ("We must identify our enemies and drive them into oblivion.")

It is not too late, however, to reconsider Clinton's nominee as Assistant Secretary for Fish, Wildlife, and Parks—former Wilderness Society leader, George Frampton. His full embrace of environmental radicalism is well-known, given such statements as: "[Alaska is] a curiosity ... we ought to make the whole state an historical park so people can go there and see how folks thought in the 19th Century. ..." Frampton's views are not unusual; in fact, elitists who lead environmental groups demonstrate an appalling anti-people bias that puts them at odds with the most basic dreams and aspirations of the American people.

Paul Ehrlich: "We've already had too much economic growth in the United States. Economic growth in rich countries like ours is the disease, not the cure."

Stewart Brand: "We have wished ... for a disaster or for social change to come and bomb us into the Stone Age, where we might live like indians in our valley, with our localism, our appropriate technology, our gardens, our homemade religion—guilt free."

While President Clinton campaigned to "put people first," environmental leaders have made it clear that people come last, that jobs, growth, property rights, and individual liberty carry almost no weight with them. Given the Guinier precedent, Clinton must do some serious soul searching about the environmental movement with which he has allied himself.

When Bill Clinton abandoned Ms. Guinier, he concluded, "I cannot fight a battle ... if I do not believe." If Clinton continues to stand by the radical environmentalists, then we can only conclude, unlike his policy disputes with Ms. Guinier, he embraces the anti-human orientation of the nation's environmental leaders.

JUNE 1993

FEDERAL LAWYERS ABDICATE
THEIR RESPONSIBILITY

When Earth First proposed to meet, 500 strong, in late June and early July, atop Mount Graham in the Coronado National Forest in southeastern Arizona, the U.S. Forest Service was concerned. After all, Earth First has a well-deserved reputation for what it euphemistically calls "monkeywrenching," the admittedly illegal sabotage or vandalizing of federal and private property to terrorize men and women into not engaging in legal pursuits.

Although Earth First leaders have been convicted of federal crimes for their operations, the threat they pose remains. A recent call, by a Montana Earth First publication, for the fiery destruction of logging equipment, drew this response from the U.S. Forest Supervisor: "I would not take these things as idle threats. There are some members of that organization who would carry out those acts."

Forest Service professionals in the Coronado National Forest had other causes for concern. First, the 1992 gathering of Earth First, in the San Juan National Forest in Colorado, resulted in a fire that cost more than $8,000 to extinguish. Although billed by the Forest Service, Earth First refuses to pay. The Forest Service's 1992 experience is important, what with temperatures in southeastern Arizona soaring into the 100s, with Mount Graham in a severe fire hazard condition, and with wildfires plaguing the area.

Second, the Coronado National Forest is a true multiple use forest with recreation, cabin sites, a *Bible* camp, cattle grazing, and two world-class, multi-million dollar telescopes. Those telescopes merit special mention given the warning of Earth First founder, Dave Foreman: "There are people who are prepared to make them put the scopes up there several times . . . a telescope doesn't see the stars very well if its mirror is broken."

Third, the Coronado National Forest is home to the Mount Graham red squirrel, an "endangered" species. It is the red squirrel that made the University of Arizona's world-class observatory so controversial and so extraordinarily expensive.

The U.S. Fish and Wildlife Service (FWS) asserts that the red squirrel is "extremely vulnerable to extinction," and that even "recreational use of [Mount Graham] would adversely affect [it, especially since] [r]ecreationalists are an uncontrolled impact." While many biological experts dispute these and other FWS findings regarding the red squirrel, it is the FWS's viewpoint that the Forest Service must consider in making land use decisions, such as letting 500 Earth First members camp out there for a week.

No wonder the Forest Service was eager to have Earth First apply for the permit required of any group of 25 or more that proposes to meet in a national forest. Regulations requiring a permit have been in place for years; the latest version was adopted in 1988.

In fact, the Forest Service applied these regulations to Earth First conclaves in Madison County, Montana (1990) and Archuleta County, Colorado (1992). When the Forest Service asked Earth First to submit the required application, however, Earth First refused. Incredibly, when the Forest Service sought help from federal government lawyers, the attorneys sided with Earth First!

Although no court had ever found the 1988 regulations to be unconstitutional, and although the Forest Service had applied the regulations for five years, federal lawyers insisted that forcing Earth First to obtain a permit and to demonstrate its financial responsibility infringed upon First Amendment guarantees. Denied the regulatory authority to fulfill its statutory duty to protect the forest and its resources, as well as the rights of others, the Forest Service did the only thing it could: it mobilized as many law enforcement officers as possible atop Mount Graham.

How ironic that the Clinton administration—with its alleged commitment to making users pay and to ensuring the protection of the environment—would so blithely turn its head, plead impotence in the face of a band of anarchists, and abandon professionals whose duty it is to protect the forest. No wonder cynicism regarding the federal government is at an all-time high.

JULY 1993

HUGGING TREES NOT PEOPLE

The little girl was weeping hysterically yet striving mightily to maintain her dignity. It was not working. Overwhelmed with emotion, she dissolved into tears. With her tiny hand clasped in the man's grip, her head fell against his chest, her left arm hanging limply at her side, his left arm around her slender shoulders. The photograph was on the front page of nearly every newspaper in the country. The city was Des Moines, Iowa. The girl was Christina Hein, whose family had lost everything in the floodwaters of the Midwest. The man was President Clinton waging, in the words of Laurence McQuillan of *Reuters*, "an unusual high-profile campaign of concern" with "pledges of aid and empathy."

Taking calls later on WHO radio in Des Moines, President Clinton said, "I talked to people who had lost everything, their farms and businesses. It was a very moving thing." Clinton might have been discussing, not the Midwest and its flood waters, but the Pacific Northwest and the logging ban caused by the lawsuits filed by environmental groups.

The comparisons between Molalla (Oregon) and Montrose (Iowa), between Crescent City (California) and Dallas City (Illinois), between Aberdeen (Washington) and Alexandria (Missouri) are striking. The menace creeps noiselessly into cities and communities, forcing the evacuations of homes and even entire towns. Houses sit vacant; businesses are boarded up. Everywhere there is despair. Gathering together in town halls and community centers, seeking comfort from one another, people ask: "Will it ever be the same?" "What will we do?" "How will we ever recover from the loss of everything we worked for our all of our lives?"

There the similarities end and the contrasts begin. For in the timber-producing communities of the Pacific Northwest the disaster that has befallen them is not a freak, once-in-a-thousand years, act of nature, but a conscious decision by mankind, specifically President Clinton. It was after all, on July 1, 1993, that Clinton announced his "solution" to the timber crisis in Washington, Oregon, and northern California. Under the Clinton plan, timber harvesting will proceed at only 25 percent of normal and Congress will be asked to spend (who knows if Congress will do it) $1.2 billion over the next five years for "job retraining."

While Clinton admits that 15,000 to 20,000 jobs will be lost, the number is more likely 85,000 jobs, given the impact on timber-related services and local economies. Even if Congress appropriates the money and job retraining works (it rarely does), the new jobs will pay half of what these workers earned before environmental elitists decided to put them out of work.

There is more. Hundreds of millions of dollars in federal revenues from the sale of timber and the taxes generated in the woods, and in the mills, and in the villages and towns that once supplied timber to the nation will be lost. In these deficit reducing days, where we will find new revenues and new tax-paying jobs, let alone wood products (the price of which continues to skyrocket), is anybody's guess. Furthermore, the meager timber harvest goals set by Clinton are only proposals, achievement of which likely will be frustrated by more environmental lawsuits.

In early April, President Clinton led his highly publicized Timber Summit in Portland, Oregon, during which he promised to end the quagmire, end the litigation, restore balance and put people to work. The only promise he kept was his campaign commitment that environmental groups would decide timber policy.

Last month, when news of Clinton's decision came to the Pacific Northwest, hundreds of men, women and children gathered in Portland in silent protest—all hope that Clinton could hear their cries and feel their pain was gone. Many wept openly and then silently followed the coffins that bore the names of the towns they love to a pyre near the federal building. For all of these people of the Pacific Northwest, the only hugs from Clinton were for the trees.

AUGUST 1993

PROGENY OF PROGRESS

On Election Night 1992, Senator Al Gore stepped before the television cameras and announced, "We [Bill Clinton and Gore] are the children of modern America." Former Secretary of Education Bill Bennett later responded, "That's right, Mr. Vice President, you are the children of modern America and now it is time to grow up."

Clinton and Gore are of a generation that came of age during the Vietnam War and passed through the defiance, disaffection, and dissidence of the sixties. While those rites of passage have not made their generation any more homogeneous than any other generation, there are some areas in which Clinton and Gore are representative, not just of a generation, but also of a nation. They should not be so eager to admit it. When it comes to science and technology, Clinton and Gore represent, not the nation's best hopes, but its worst fears; they are not proponents of progress, but advocates of apocalypse. Rather than providing critical leadership and seeking to moderate the nation's illiteracy on matters of science, Clinton and Gore have emerged as sky-is-falling demagogues seeking political gain from fear, superstition, and dread.

Last February, ABC's Peter Jennings, accompanied by some children whose remarks had been planned carefully, visited President Clinton in the White House. One poignant moment came when Pernell of Garyville, Louisiana, spoke of his brother's death from "a very rare brain tumor" that "may have resulted from ... environmental contamination" because of nearby petrochemical plants. President Clinton, while empathizing with the tragic loss of a young brother, could have calmed the boy's and the nation's fears. Instead, Clinton fed upon them: "I think there are now all kinds of health hazards that we never knew about before ... from some of the things we've done. And we need to do a lot of environmental cleanup in that part of Louisiana where you live and throughout the country.... We'll do it for your brother, okay?"

Vice President Gore's demagoguery on matters of science and technology are well known. Fred Barns of the *New Republic* advises, Gore rants "against the scientific revolution[,] the industrial revolution[,] biotechnology, [and] the internal combustion engine." Gore's view of technology appeared in his book: "[W]e are not that clever, and we never have been."

Speak for yourself, Mr. Vice President. Contrary to the politically-correct panderings of Clinton and Gore and their environmental elitist allies, science and technology have led, in the words of former governor and author Dr. Dixy Lee Ray, "to a longer and healthier life."

As Dr. Ray wrote in *Trashing the Planet*, "The belief that the 'good old days' were simple, benign, and kind is wrong! The reality is those days were dirty, disease-ridden, and smelly.... We have been privileged to live through the most extraordinary five decades of expanding knowledge and its use for bettering life that the world has ever known. Little wonder that some people cannot cope."

Unfortunately, scientific illiteracy in America is more than a problem for "some people." It poses a grave threat to wise public policy and to the nation's ability to address and to resolve important technological and social problems. Obviously, the willingness of Clinton and Gore to echo anti-technology utopians is not helping. Neither is the media. There is hope, however. Three years after Dr. Ray's ground-breaking *Trashing the Planet*, and the appearance of her notable sequel, *Environmental Overkill: Whatever Happened To Common Sense?*, weird or political science is the subject of several new books, including, in particular, Michael Fumento's outstanding *Science Under Siege*.

As one considers the momentous interplay between science and public policy, the admonition of James Madison once again rings true: "Knowledge will forever govern ignorance; and a people who mean to be their own governors must arm themselves with the power which knowledge gives."

SEPTEMBER 1993

WHALES AS WEAPONS IN A CULTURAL WAR

Recently I saw a car with two bumper stickers. One read, "Celebrate Diversity," the other, "Save the Whales." I wonder if the car's owner knows what the federal government plans to do to the diverse peoples of Norway in the name of saving the whales?

For centuries hardy Norwegians have been taking to the high seas, not for sport, but for the stuff of their very survival. Anyone who has ever visited the Lofoten Islands, from whence the whaling vessels have been launched since time immemorial, cannot help but be stricken, not just by the raw beauty of these glacier carved, mountainous islands of rock, but also by the ruggedness of the people who have clawed out an existence in this barren land, far north of the Arctic Circle. That existence depends on the sea and its resources, including whales—primarily the minke whale.

Today the minke whale swims the world's oceans in great abundance, thanks to the careful husbandry of the Norwegians. According to the unanimous finding of the Scientific Committee of the International Whaling Committee (IWC), there are 86,700 minke whales in the northeast Atlantic, more than one million worldwide.

Of this vast population, Norway will harvest, during 1993, 296 minke whales (160 for food and 136 for ecological research). For harvesting less than one half of one percent of local whales, David Phillips, of the Earth Island Institute in diversity-loving San Francisco, called Norway, in a *Rocky Mountain News* article, an "environmental . . . pariah" that warrants "world-wide scorn." Animal rights zealots, environmental radicals, and their politically-correct allies in Hollywood instigated "a global boycott," aimed at costing Norwegians hundreds of millions of dollars in lost business.

While we expect little else from groups that depend, for their existence, upon sky-is-falling rhetoric and ever-escalating demands, what is shocking is the official U.S. response. Commerce Secretary Ron Brown, kowtowing to the dictates of animal rights groups, says that trade sanctions will be imposed on Norway. If President Clinton does not reverse that decision, on October 8, the United States will declare economic war on a nation that courageously fought the only animal rights fanatics ever to lead a nation—Adolph Hitler, Hermann Göring, and Heinrich Himmler.

The manner in which Hollywood entered this conflict is instructive. Theaters showing *Free Willy* distributed slick fliers that ask: "How far would you go for a friend?" The flier then tells how far one must go: so far as to stop Norway's whaling. Why? Because whales are "majestic, gentle, warm-blooded mammals that mate for life, travel in family groups, feel pain and are incredibly intelligent."

Once again, as with most environmental or ecological crises, this is not about science. If it were, Dr. Phillip Hammond, the highly-regarded Chairman of the IWC Scientific Committee, would not have resigned in protest over what he condemned as "the [IWC's] contempt for the recommendations of its Scientific Committee [that minke whaling could be resumed.]"

Like so many other environmental "calamities," the attack on Norway is not about safety, or survivability, or sustainability, but about ascetics and cultural values. Some Americans imagine whales as friends. Norwegians ingest whales for food. What we have here is true cultural imperialism. If we tell Norwegians they should not eat whale meat, why should Japan not force us to give up venison, or India compel us to stop eating beef?

Providentially, there is an emergent backlash in the United States. Putting People First, of Washington, D.C., is leading the charge to convince President Clinton and Congress to overturn Secretary Brown's decision, to respect good marine science, and to stand courageously beside America's long-time ally, Norway.

I plan to do my part. In addition to shopping for Norwegian cheese, I am going to buy a "Celebrate Diversity" button to wear on the t-shirt I received from a Norwegian fisherman. Under the picture of a minke whale are the words: "Big Norwegians Need Big Food."

OCTOBER 1993

MEDIA MADNESS

In 1963, I was a high school student in Cheyenne, Wyoming. When Paul Harvey spoke at the University of Wyoming in Laramie, I drove over to hear him. Although I had long admired him and wanted to hear him in person, there was another reason for my drive to Laramie. I headed a youth group and hoped he would address its awards banquet. I carried a written invitation to that effect.

I arrived early and waited back stage for Paul Harvey. When he arrived, I introduced myself, told him how much I admired him, told him the reason for meeting him, and handed him my letter. He could not have been more pleasant. He slipped the letter into his suit pocket and told me he would get back to me. I returned to my seat to hear his speech.

The next week, I chanced to see a photograph in the Laramie newspaper. It had been taken as I talked to Paul Harvey, just as he slipped my letter into his pocket. The caption read: "Paul Harvey speaks with a University of Wyoming student as he slips his notes into his pocket following his speech." Of the three facts in that one-sentence caption, all were wrong. I was a high school student, not a University of Wyoming student; he was slipping my letter, not his speech notes, into his pocket; and the photograph was taken before, not following his speech.

We have all had similar experiences. It is almost a cliché to say that, if you know anything about a subject, you will find news coverage on it replete with errors. When such lack of attention to detail is combined: with the media's well-known liberal bias, with the superficial treatment given most issues, and with the tendency to be pessimistic and to pander to people's worst fears, it is easy to become cynical. Thus, it is easy to conclude that dealing with the media is hopeless, but it is also wrong. The media is the only means by which the American people receive what information they do receive. It is our responsibility to ensure it is the best information possible. If we have any hope of doing more than preaching to the choir, we must work with the media.

I believe it is possible. I believe most journalists regard themselves as professionals, doing an important job under incredible pressure and often unrealistic time constraints. I also believe that, if we work at it, we can convince reporters, if not that we are right, at least that there is another side that should be told.

Therefore, it is vital that those of us who are knowledgeable on environmental and natural resources issues work with the media. We who are the most informed have an obligation to reach out to reporters, talk show hosts, editors, editorial boards, news anchors, and other journalists. We must appeal to their professionalism and offer them the opportunity to get the facts right, to quote from truly informed sources, and to provide the American people balanced and objective news coverage.

When, despite our best efforts, reporting does not measure up, we must follow up, with calls to the reporter and to his or her boss. In addition, both good and bad news coverage should be the subject of a trenchant, pithy letter to the editor. Since more people listen to talk radio than read the newspaper, that resource should not be overlooked. Those knowledgeable should be available as guests on radio programs. Do not hesitate to call in when a guest is right and especially when a guest is wrong. Your endorsement or factual criticism will validate or undercut a guest's point of view.

In short, become involved in reaching beyond your circle of supporters. You may not carry the day every single time, but at least you will have gone a long way to telling, in Paul Harvey's words, "the rest of the story."

NOVEMBER 1993

ALIENS AND ALLIES

In the sequel *Aliens*, Sigourney Weaver again played Ripley, returning to the planet where the fearsome monster, which killed her crew and destroyed her ship in *Alien*, was discovered. This time Ripley is accompanied by Space Marines with the mission of saving colonists unknowingly sent into the alien's lair.

As in *Alien*, the "bad guy" in *Aliens* is the corporation that seeks to return one of the aliens to Earth for weapons research. In *Aliens*, the corporation's evil deed is undertaken by an obsequious and unctuous yuppie, Carter J. Burke. When Ripley discovers his plans, he attempts to bribe her. Failing that, he appeals to her love of science: "Let's not make snap judgments, please. This is clearly, clearly an important species we're dealing with and I don't think that you or I or anybody has the right to arbitrarily exterminate them." Ripley—faced with choosing between science (the preservation of a unique species) and mankind—opts for human beings. Her decision is an easy one since Ripley has seen, first hand, the monster's destructive power. She knows the grave danger it poses, not simply to herself, her crew and the remaining colonist, but to the entire civilized world. Obviously, it depends on one's perspective.

Today, Hollywood has a new perspective on the Endangered Species Act (ESA). No longer is it an obscure federal law that applies only to Paul Bunyan logging types along the Pacific Coast, or to Marlboro men in the Mountain West, or to George ("Gabby") Hayes-looking miners in the desert. For the first time, the ESA has come to Hollywood. It came upon the hot winds that carried the recent fires across southern California, destroying hundreds of homes that were worth hundreds of millions of dollars. Unbelievably, for most of the homeowners, it did not have to happen.

Southern Californians have known for decades about the dangers of brush fires. They have also known that one of the best ways to stop brush fires is to create a fire-break, that is, to clear a strip of vegetation so that when the fire arrives there will be nothing to burn. That is what they have done, until recently, when the U.S. Fish and Wildlife Service threatened the landowners with fines and imprisonment if they protected their homes by clearing vegetation. The reason: the kangaroo rat.

Astonishingly, given all that has happened to the timber producing communities of the Pacific Northwest, the draconian nature of the ESA apparently comes as a big surprise to Hollywood. In a recent ABC *20/20* program, Hugh Downs described the plight of landowners in the fire's path and the federal law that brought it about: "Their hands were tied by a law that you may not have paid much attention to up to now. But this law might eventually threaten your home and property, too."

Added Barbara Walters, "It's the Endangered Species Act, a well-intentioned and valuable law that's supposed to see that animals and even insects aren't squeezed out by the existence of man. The question is, does this law go too far?" In the program John Stossel answered, "Yes." "The law is sort of unnatural in that it seeks to stop the clock now. And we certainly want more diversity . . . but do we want to turn life upside down to preserve all of them?"

My, oh my! At last Hollywood has proclaimed what millions of Americans already knew. Said Bruce Vincent, Libby, Montana, timber man and Executive Director of Communities for a Great Northwest: "We have effectively torched 80,000 homes in the Northwest to 'save' the spotted owl, without a hint of recognition from the media. But let 80 homes go up in smoke in southern California and the Endangered Species Act has gone too far."

Clearly, the half-life of the media's focus on the ESA will be short, but it is possible to get their attention.

DECEMBER 1993

CHAPTER FIVE

A Shift to the Right

★ ★ ★ ★ ★

———

In *It Takes A Hero: The Grassroots Battle Against Environmental Oppression* (Free Enterprise Press, 1994), I profiled heroes with whom I had been privileged to work. The Credo said it all.

"We are the true environmentalists. We are the stewards of the Earth. We're the farmers and ranchers, the hunters and trappers, the fishermen and watermen—people who've cared for the land and the waters for generations. We're the men and women who have clothed and fed the nation and the world. We're the miners and the loggers and the energy producers who have provided this nation with the building blocks of a modern civilization. We're the workers, the builders, the doers. Together, we hard-working Americans built this country, made it strong and prosperous, delivering to generation after generation not just a better and more abundant life, but also the hope for such a life. We're the landowners, the home owners, the holders of a piece of the American Dream, secure that it belongs to us and to our children and that we have the right to use that land—prudently and properly—as we wish. We know that it is this one right, to own and use property, which has provided the incentive for generation after generation to dream, to strive, to build and to prosper. We're the consumers of the products of a technological society. We know that all of our material needs are met, first and foremost, by natural resources that would remain unavailable to mankind but for the greatest resource of all: human creativity. We know that it is technology, developed by the indomitable human spirit, unfettered by the yoke of oppression, which made this nation so richly blessed. We know as well that our ability to use the out-of-doors for recreation and revitalization is sustained by those few who work and live in the nature we only visit."

"We believe in clean air, clean water, and safe lands. We believe in being good stewards, in taking care of the land and waters of the world around us. We believe that mankind and nature can live together in productive harmony.... [We] want a safe and healthy environment just as much as we want jobs and opportunity and progress. We know that the battle being fought today is not about safety or survivability or sustainability. It is about the future of America's precious freedoms and with them the American Dream."

DIXY LEE RAY: IN MEMORIAM

In 1981, Dixy Lee Ray stepped down as governor of the State of Washington. After years in the rough and tumble world of politics, Dixy Lee Ray was "wrung out" and "exhausted." She needed a rest, but she also needed to provide for herself. Dixy Lee Ray let it be known that she would accept speaking invitations.

Selecting the topic was easy. Although she was nationally-known as a public official, she had spent nearly four decades as a scientist, and more specifically, as a marine biologist. She would give speeches about science. The year 1981 was a good year to be talking about things scientific. Increasingly the media was focusing on such matters, particularly as they related to environmental issues; however, Dixy Lee Ray had a unique perspective on these issues.

Years earlier, in the late 1960s, when most Americans were first becoming aware of the environmental movement, Dixy Lee Ray had already been offended by their extremism, their attacks on all things technological, their assaults on modern civilization, and their return-to-nature advocacy.

Part of the reason was philosophical. Dixy Lee Ray was an old fashioned conservationist, a believer in good stewardship, in the wise utilization of natural resources, and in the ability of mankind to live in productive harmony with nature.

Part of the reason was professional. Dixy Lee Ray was a scientist who took great pride in her profession. She was greatly troubled by the "political science" being used to "prove" alleged environmental calamities and to justify environmental "cures."

Part of the reason was personal. The "good old days" for which the environmental movement yearned and to which it wanted America to return were when Dixy Lee Ray grew up, days that were, in Dixy Lee Ray's words, "dirty, disease-ridden, and smelly."

When she returned to the lecture circuit in early 1981, it was to discuss one of the hot topics of the day: the state of the human environment and the Earth's future. What she had to say surprised those who heard her, for it was contrary to everything they had been hearing or reading in the media. Dixy Lee Ray's audiences wanted to know more. They wanted her speech in writing. They wanted to carry it around, to read it over and over, to study it, and to quote from it. In 1987, she sat down to write a book. Two years later, it became the first scientific book ever published by Regnery-Gateway Press. It became something else, the company's biggest seller, ever!

The book was *Trashing the Planet*, which, despite not being marketed by a major publishing house, sold more than 100,000 copies and was republished in paperback. Thousands of those sales were by word of mouth, as Americans eagerly welcomed a book that challenged much modern mythology on environmental issues.

Dixy Lee Ray, the 80-year old biologist had become a trend setter. As a result of the incredible success of *Trashing the Planet*, other, much younger authors were inspired to address the topics first broached by Dixy Lee Ray. Dixy Lee Ray, however, was not yet finished. She wrote another great book: *Environmental Overkill: Whatever Happened to Common Sense?*

Dixy Lee Ray became the nation's best known conservative speaker, writer, and deep thinker about environmental issues. Her opinions were sought by the nation's most influential leaders and admired by millions. Everyone who knew her held her in the highest esteem. She was beloved. With a speaking schedule that would have challenged the stamina of someone half her age, Dixy Lee Ray pressed on from audience to audience to carry her message of truth, of hope, and of a deep belief in the future of mankind.

Today she has her rest, the rest she refused to take in her all too short time here. We who grieve her passing know the world is a richer and more well-informed place for her having come this way.

JANUARY 1994

GOVERNMENT HEALTH CARE: THANKS, BUT NO THANKS

What were the odds that the Montana town of Libby would be hit with three catastrophic health care cases in such a short period of time? In February of 1992, Sally Sauer, 26-year old daughter of an unemployed forester, discovered she needed a heart transplant. In February of 1993, 5-year old Amanda Johnson, the daughter of an uninsured logging truck driver, needed heart valve surgery. Then, six months later, Kyle Rosling, 17-year old son of an uninsured sawyer, needed heart surgery.

Libby is a tiny community of 2,800 in Lincoln County where 78 percent of the land is owned by the federal government. As a result of U.S. Forest Service's timber harvest cut backs, to "protect" the grizzly bear, Libby's unemployment has been double digits for months. Nonetheless, Libby and neighboring Troy set out to save Sally, Amanda, and Kyle. Through a variety of campaigns and the generosity and vigorous work of the industries and individuals of northwestern Montana, the "Sally's Heart," "Hour Amanda," and "Kids for Kyle," campaigns raised more than $325,000. Today Sally can be seen jogging around town; Amanda is completely cured; and Kyle is wrestling in the 152-pound class on the Libby Loggers varsity team.

What happened to Libby's Sally, Amanda, and Kyle might well be cited, by the Clinton White House, as proof that America needs federal health care. Certainly Libby's experience is no less compelling than the other anecdotal evidence heard by Hillary Rodham Clinton's secret health care panel. At least that is what ABC's *The Home Show* thought.

When ABC heard about Sally, Amanda, and Kyle, it sent a crew to Libby to film men and women citing their ordeal as proof that America needs a federal health care plan. The film crew heard plenty about Sally, Amanda, and Kyle, but the lessons these people drew from their experience surprised the worldly folks from ABC. Yes, Sally, Amanda, and Kyle had been awfully sick. Yes, getting them well had cost a lot of money. Yes, many of the people in Libby did not have their own health care plan. The good people of Libby, however, were unwilling to whine about their experience or to jump to conclusions about the state of the nation's health care and what ought to be done about it.

What the ABC crew heard was not the rhetoric of the inside-the-Washington, D.C.-beltway crowd, but questions real people ask if given the chance. "What is all of that going to cost?" "Who is going to pay for it?" "Will we get to keep our own doctors?" One point the ABC crew heard over and over was that the health care proposal the people had been hearing about was a very expensive program that the American people simply could not afford.

The ABC crew heard something else. Many of the men and women interviewed had been covered by a health care plan; that is, they were until an environmental policy gone wild took their jobs. What many of them said was that if President and Mrs. Clinton wanted to do something about their health care, the Clintons could get the environmentalists off the backs of the people and allow the harvesting of trees in the forests around Libby once again. Just let the mills reopen, they said. Then health care will take care of itself.

When people talk about a federal health care program, they forget about all the other things the federal government cannot seem to get right. The people of Libby are not that forgetful. Perhaps it is because they know firsthand how the federal government operates. Perhaps it is because they have seen what federal control means to their lives. Whatever the reason, the people of Libby, interviewed on the streets of their struggling town, have said "No" to federal health care. Having heard President Clinton's State of the Union Address and his commitment to health care in 1994, they wonder what the rest of the nation will say.

FEBRUARY 1994

POLITICAL CORRECTNESS
ON FEDERAL LANDS

In 1977, President Jimmy Carter issued an Executive Order requiring federal land managers to ensure the "minimization of conflicts" between off-road-vehicle (ORV) users and hikers. In 1980, the Wenatchee National Forest in central Washington adopted a comprehensive trail plan to comply with Carter's order. In 1986, as part of its land-use planning process, the U.S. Forest Service studied whether some high alpine trails in the North Entiat/Pyramid Mountain region should remain open to ORVs.

The North Entiat/Pyramid Mountain trails are unique in all of Washington. They are one of only two trail networks offering a back-country experience on trails above 5,000 feet in elevation. In addition, they are the only trails that allow ORV access to early fall buck deer hunting and that permit access to an 8,000 foot peak.

After the Forest Service completed its planning, it decided that, because of the importance of the trails to ORV users, and because other trails are closed to ORV users, the trails should remain open. The Forest Service reached its decision despite the receipt of nearly 3,000 comments attacking use of ORVs in the nation's forests. It did so because it found the comments were "emotional and issue-generated, very general in content, with little in the way of specifics tied to on-the-ground management." While willing to "take whatever action is needed to attempt to resolve this conflict," when and "if real conflicts do become a major problem," the agency knew it had other obligations. "In fairness to all of our users, we need to have the facts when conflicts occur and cannot base our actions on philosophical differences or emotional response to an issue."

The Forest Service decided "to monitor user conflicts" but, more than a year later, it had to report, "[s]o far, no on-the-ground conflicts between users have been documented in the area." There was a reason: "use in the area is relatively light." At some point, however, the Forest Service changed its mind. Citing the comments by those opposed to ORV use, the Forest Service closed the trails. After this new conclusion became final, the Northwest Motorcycle Association (NMA) challenged the decision in federal court.

The federal district court agreed with the Forest Service that the anti-ORV comments were primarily "general" and "emotional." "[A] majority of the public comments did not specifically state that [off-road-vehicle] use 'conflicts' with non-motorized uses and ... many of the comments focused on the philosophical aversion many people hold toward [off-road-vehicle] use. ..." Therefore, the court found "a philosophical struggle" that existed, not on specific trails, but "[i]n the minds of the individuals who commented on the issue."

Thus, the NMA argued that the comments did not provide a basis for closing the trails since they were not specific, were merely philosophical, and did not substantiate any actual "conflicts" to "minimize." Responded the court: "The court might be persuaded by the [NMA's] argument if the [Forest Service was] instructed to minimize actual conflicts; however, this is not the case."

The district court's decision, now on appeal, is a distressing precedent. For the first time, a federal court has held that the number of comments received by the government is a factor in managing federal lands. Even more stunning is the court's holding that alleged conflicts need not be actual, on-the-ground conflicts but may be merely philosophical, present just in the minds of those commenting.

The danger is two-fold. First, environmental groups will be able to control federal decision-making by swamping managers with a plethora of negative comments. Second, all that will be needed to stop a statutorily permitted use of federal lands will be the presence of a "philosophical" conflict.

Today, ORV use appears to be politically incorrect. If the decision stands, however, it will not be long before hunting, logging, horseback riding, mining, seismic work, and practically any other activity that involves humans will be forbidden on federal lands. No wonder James Madison feared the "tyranny of the majority."

MARCH 1994

Epilogue: A panel of the U.S. Court of Appeals for the Ninth Circuit upheld the district court's ruling. *Northwest Motorcycle Association v. U.S. Department of Agriculture,* 18 F.3d 1468 (9th Cir. 1994)

LOCAL HEROES FIGHT BACK

"At one time or another, I have belonged or contributed to just about every environmental group you can name," says Cheryl Johnson. "That ended in 1991." That was the year Cheryl Johnson traveled to Washington, D.C., for a gathering of grassroots property rights activists. Fresh from her very early battles over the proposed designation of the Pemigewasset River through her home town of Campton, New Hampshire, as "wild and scenic," she went looking for ideas, for support, for solutions. She found friends and herself.

"I met and talked with Oregon loggers about what was happening to them and to their families. I had read the National Wildlife Federation stories about the northern spotted owl. Having heard both sides, now I believe the loggers." Cheryl Johnson was changed forever. "When I got home, I packed up an eleven year collection of *National Wildlife* magazines and mailed them directly to Jay Hair. I included a note: 'Since I don't have a recycling facility in my town, I would appreciate it if you would take care of them for me. I suggest recycling them into something more useful, such as pay checks for Pacific Northwest loggers. If you are too busy to do it yourself, perhaps your chauffeur can drop them off.'"

Cheryl Johnson was ready for the impassioned battle over the Pemigewasset River. Earlier that year she had attended a public hearing on the fate of "the Pemi." Two things bothered her: the deceptive tactics of those presiding when they concluded the meeting by announcing "overwhelming support" for the proposal, and the push for what Cheryl Johnson called "environmental socialism," controlling the property of those living along the river in the name of environmental protection. Cheryl Johnson concluded that it was not plants and animals that were "threatened," but private property.

Although she had never been politically active, never voted, never watched the news, never stood in front of a group and spoke—she was too terrified—and was almost painfully shy, Cheryl Johnson knew she had to do something. Although the Pemi had been one of the most highly industrialized rivers in New England, although it flows through the center of town after town and is crossed by bridges, power lines, and trestles and is paralleled by roads, railroad tracks, as well as houses, condos, golf courses, and sewage treatment plants, the National Park Service argued that the Pemi should be designated because of its "unique and outstanding values." Cheryl Johnson knew a federal government land grab when she saw one.

Cheryl Johnson caught the National Park Service officials in distortion after distortion, arrogant misrepresentation after arrogant misrepresentation, half-truth after half-truth, fraudulent denial after fraudulent denial. By networking with her newfound friends from all across the country, she learned the truth about what happens to the private property along wild and scenic rivers and about the heavy hand of the National Park Service and its allies in the environmental organizations once a river is designated. Cheryl Johnson, the quiet wildlife artist, started speaking up, started leading. She helped found the New Hampshire Landowners Alliance, Inc., (NHLA), which held forums, meetings, and rallies. NHLA staged various public events including responding to a planned canoe trip by a National Park Service study committee by posting "Go Home NPS" and "NO Wild & Scenic" signs up and down the river.

In the spring of 1993, Cheryl Johnson's NHLA proudly proclaimed victory. "We won, despite being out-spent by at least a ten-to-one margin—maybe even fifteen or twenty-to-one," says Cheryl Johnson, "because we refused to compromise. We learned to use the media. We were not afraid to be controversial."

Like thousands of others throughout the country, Cheryl Johnson has gone from being a bystander, to a potential victim, to a heroic activist. Today, she and others like her are stepping to the front lines of the battle over property rights, economic freedom, and constitutional liberty. It is a battle they cannot afford to lose.

JUNE 1994

PROPERTY RIGHTS WIN

Near the close of oral arguments in *Dolan v. City of Tigard*, the Clinton administration presented its views to the Supreme Court. Although the case did not involve the federal government—it was, after all, a legal dispute between a landowner and a Portland, Oregon suburb—the Solicitor General opted to take sides. Other entities had done the same. Two stacks of briefs—a set for Florence Dolan, a widow, and a set for the City of Tigard—accompanied each one of the justices. Environmental groups and others argued for the right of the City of Tigard to restrict Mrs. Dolan's use of her land. Property rights groups argued that the Fifth Amendment's Takings Clause required Mrs. Dolan to be paid for the City's use of her land.

The Solicitor General's brief on behalf of the City of Tigard, however, was somewhat unexpected. After all, Clinton and Gore had called their campaign "Putting People First." Argued the Clinton administration, once a government—federal, state or local—decides it wants someone's land, the burden is on people like Mrs. Dolan to prove the government is going too far. Said Justice Scalia: "That's an awful burden to put on the ... small individual property owner. ..."

There is no question that the City of Tigard wants Widow Dolan's land. When she and her late husband sought to expand the use of their property, the City ruled that, in exchange for a building permit, the Dolans had to: (1) cede all of their land within the 100-year flood plain; (2) cede a 15-foot swath for a bike path; and (3) build the bike path. What was the reason for these demands? The City coveted their property because it is "the backbone of the City's open space system." While Mrs. Dolan thought that the Constitution required the City to pay for taking her property, the City argued it should be able to create its "open space system" for free.

The City of Tigard was not the only one. A number of states weighed in, not on behalf of the Widow Dolan and property owners, but in support of governments' right to demand that landowners hand over property as the cost of dealing with a unit of government. Among the states taking that position were Nevada, New Mexico, and Wyoming.

Although environmental groups and several states, whose leaders lost touch with their constituents, were selling that position, the Court was not buying. Held the Court: "We see no reason why the Takings Clause of the Fifth Amendment, as much a part of the Bill of Rights as the First Amendment or Fourth Amendment, should be relegated to the status of a poor relation. . . ." Neither was the Court persuaded by the environmental values being pursued by the City of Tigard and other governmental units. Pronounced Chief Justice Rehnquist: "The city's goals . . . are laudable, but there are outer limits to how this may be done. 'A strong public desire to improve the public condition [will not] warrant achieving the desire by a shorter cut than the constitutional way of paying for the change.'"

One has to wonder at what point politicians stop seeing things as their constituents see them and start looking at things like covetous bureaucrats. The bad news is that some politicians have not gotten the message on property rights; the good news is some have. As Governor Fife Symington proclaimed on signing the Arizona Private Property Protection Act: "[Does] environmentalism require[] its adherents to denigrate the principle of private property as it has been known in America from the very dawn of our national existence? If so, then they have embraced an environmentalism which is foreign to me. . . . The right to property is a civil right, no less than the rights to freedom of speech and worship, and the rights to due process and equal protection under the law."

AUGUST 1994

"OUR FOREST IS BURNING"

"They've ordered the turkeys," P.J. Vincent, wife of timber man Bruce Vincent, told me. "The crews ordered their Thanksgiving turkeys. They'll be fighting fires here through November."

The fires that leaders like Bruce Vincent had predicted have come to northwestern Montana. Today 150 fires of consequence are burning, from 100 acres to 5,000 each. The true extent of those fires will not be known until it is over. For now the U.S. Forest Service keeps track with infrared aerial photography. At the agency office, a large map of the Kootenai National Forest depicts the daily sweep of the devastation. It looks like a war zone.

It looks like a war zone on the streets of Libby too. More than 7,500 members of the Armed Forces have been mobilized in the Kootenai Valley, nearly doubling the population of Lincoln County. They are there to fight the fire, but they are not doing much fighting. Instead they are in a holding action, in what the Forest Service calls "containment," to keep the fire away from Troy, Eureka, and Libby. They are there to watch the forest burn down.

The people of Libby are watching too. From downtown they can see Scenery Hill burn while all about them the sky is dark with smoke. But you do not need to see to know the forest is burning—the air is thick with the stench of burned pine and gritty with the ash that floats on the winds that these powerful blazes create.

A senior firefighting "hot shot," brought out of retirement, is in charge of the crews that have flown in from around the country. Every available fire truck is in Libby. None of it is enough to stop the fires. The hot shot says he has never seen fires behave like these conflagrations. He would have if he had been in Lincoln County in 1910, when three million acres went up in flames in a matter of days. It is not just coincidence that the lifespan of lodgepole pine—80 and 90 years—is the same amount of time that has passed since the devastating fires of 1910.

For many years the trees of the Kootenai have been ready for harvesting, either by mankind, or by nature. Using appeals and litigation, environmental groups determined that it would not be mankind. Bruce Vincent and others told the people what would happen, told them that the forest would burn, maybe even as hot as 1910. It probably will not, not this time. This time a mere 650,000 acres will burn up—an area the size of Rhode Island.

In legal briefs filed in court, the federal government said the fact that the Kootenai had not burned meant that it would not burn. Environmentalist said, if it did, it would be nature's way. Today the people of Libby know Bruce Vincent was right and they are not fond of "nature's way." It has taken their jobs, their tax base, their sense of self, and now it is taking their forest and its habitat. All the while it has filled the air with carbon dioxide and the streams with ash.

The other day Secretary Babbitt came to Lincoln County for a "photo op." He was brave enough to stand on the line with the crews to face the fire, but he was not brave enough to face the people of Libby and see the fire in their eyes. All of them had one question: "If you knew this was going to happen, why did you let it?"

Next year, after the crews have eaten their turkeys and the fires are gone, next year after the November elections and a new Congress has gone to Washington, D.C., one of the turkeys they might serve up before congressional hearings is Babbitt, so he can explain why he and his environmental friends are doing this to America's forests and to people like Bruce and P.J. Vincent.

SEPTEMBER 1994

A COLOR-BLIND CONSTITUTION?

On August 23, 1963, the Reverend Dr. Martin Luther King, Jr. delivered his "I Have a Dream" speech from the Lincoln Memorial steps. While thousands stood along the Reflecting Pool and millions more watched on national television, King delivered his most unforgettable words: "I have a dream that my four little children will one day live in a nation where they will not be judged by the color of their skin but by the content of their character." More than 31 years have passed and still men and women of racial and ethnic groups are being "judged by the color of the skin" not "by the content of the character." Remarkably, much race-based decision making occurs, not due to the extreme prejudice of their fellow citizens but because of the explicit policy of the federal government.

For the first time in nearly fifteen years, this national policy of making decisions based on race may be on the verge of extinction. Appropriately, the beginning of the end may occur within a few days of the nation's celebration of the birth of Dr. King. In early January of 1995, the Supreme Court of the United States will hear oral arguments in *Adarand Constructors, Inc. v. Peña.*

Adarand is a family-owned, highway construction company in Colorado Springs, Colorado, that specializes in installing guardrail systems and highway signs. In 1989, the federal government awarded a contract for the construction of a 4.7 mile section of highway in the San Juan National Forest in southwestern Colorado. Adarand submitted a bid to perform the guardrail subcontracted portion of the project. Although Adarand submitted the lowest bid, the subcontract was awarded to another firm. The reason? Since Adarand is operated by a white male, the prime contractor "felt economically compelled to award its subcontract to [a firm owned and operated by a racial minority] because [the prime contractor] was entitled to a bonus of . . . $10,000.00 for [doing so]."

This remarkable program—whereby Americans are paid tens of thousands of dollars to make decisions based on race—is the result of a federal statute that has been in place for more than a quarter of a century. Under federal law between 5 and 100 percent of all government contracts must be awarded to members of specified racial and ethnic groups, which Congress determined to be "socially and economically disadvantaged." Adarand filed a lawsuit, challenging the program as unconstitutional.

A reading of the equal protection guarantee causes one to wonder how such a law, which uses race as the primary basis for federal decision making, could survive a constitutional challenge. Such doubts are heightened on reading that the Supreme Court has held that the Constitution's guarantee of equal protection is violated when persons of different races "are not accorded the same protection," and that the promise applies to Congress: "It would be unthinkable that the same Constitution would impose a lesser duty on the Federal Government."

Not since 1980, however, has the Supreme Court heard a lawsuit involving a federal contracting program similar to the one challenged by Adarand. In 1980, the Court upheld Congress's authority to engage in such race-based decision making, albeit on narrow grounds: the program was temporary; it was limited; and it might not be applied in inappropriate situations. So it continued.

Times have changed, however. In 1986, the Supreme Court held the use of race in decision making must be subjected to "strict scrutiny." In 1989, the Supreme Court struck down a city's race-based system for awarding contracts, holding the city had failed to show a "compelling governmental interest" or that the race-based program was "narrowly tailored."

Fifteen years after the 1980 ruling, it is anyone's guess how the Court will decide *Adarand*; however, the justices are not the only ones asking whether it is time to ensure that at least the federal government makes decisions based on character and not color.

NOVEMBER 1994

A SHIFT TO THE RIGHT

The 1994 midterm elections could be called Ronald Reagan's fourth national election victory—after 1980, 1984, and 1988—since President Clinton sought to make him the issue. If Clinton prevailed in focusing attention on Reagan's record and not on his own, then the American people voted for Reagan. Reagan, however, was not the issue. Instead it was Clinton, his record, and his vision for America. All were rejected. On Election Day 1994, the public voted for an unprecedented shift to the right.

For the first time since 1872, more than half of the Senators, Representatives, and governors from the South are Republicans. For the first time since the mid-1800s, a Speaker of the U.S. House of Representatives was voted out of office. For the first time in half a century, a party out of power picked up 52 seats in the U.S. House of Representatives. For the first time in four decades, Republicans control both sides of Capitol Hill.

In the Senate, conservative Republicans replaced liberal Democrats: Wofford (Pennsylvania), Metzenbaum (Ohio), Riegle (Michigan), DeConcini (Arizona), Sasser and Gore, whose vacated seat was up in 1994 (Tennessee). A less conservative Republican (Olympia Snowe) replaced a liberal Democrat (George Mitchell) in Maine, and a more conservative Republican (Jim Inhofe) replaced a sometimes conservative Democrat (David Boren) in Oklahoma.

That is only part of the story in the Senate. Not only did Democrat Senator Richard Shelby of Alabama switch parties after the election, but also two more liberal Republican Senators yielded their seats to very conservative successors: Rod Grams for Senator Durenberger in Minnesota and John Ashcroft for Senator Danforth in Missouri. Conservative Republican Senators once targeted as vulnerable swept to very easy victories: Gorton (Washington), Burns (Montana), and Hutchinson (Texas).

In the U.S. House of Representatives, it was more of the same. Republicans picked up two seats each in Florida, Illinois, Kansas, New Jersey, Oklahoma, Tennessee, and Texas; three seats each in Georgia and Indiana; four seats each in California, North Carolina, and Ohio; and an astonishing six seats in the State of Washington.

Washington is a particularly interesting example given the agony of timber producing communities resulting from lawsuits by radical environmentalists and the decision by Clinton to turn his back on timber workers. Senator Slade Gorton, an unabashed supporter of timber communities, was slated for defeat by environmentalists as liberal Democratic Representatives appeared in their ascendancy, for example, Congresswoman Jolene Unsoeld (D-3rd WA) of Olympia. It was Gorton who won and Unsoeld and five of her colleagues who lost, including the Speaker of the House Tom Foley (D-5thWA), whose lukewarm support of miners, loggers, and gun owners was a prime factor in bringing his three decade career to an end.

The best example of Clinton's impact was Wyoming. Two-term Democratic Governor Mike Sullivan had an excellent chance of winning Republican Malcolm Wallop's Senate seat, given his state-wide popularity and personal charm. In the end, it was not close. Sullivan lost by 20 percent, mostly because of the "War on the West" declared by Sullivan's friends, Clinton and Babbitt. While Clinton's environmental and gun control policies dominated the debate in the West and the South—southerners discovered that federal "wetlands" and Endangered Species Act policies apply to them—that was not all. The overriding issue was the federal government itself, and the view of the American people that it has gotten too big, too powerful, too intrusive, too arrogant, and totally out of control.

In 1980, Ronald Reagan campaigned saying he would get the federal government off of the backs of the American people. Although Reagan tethered world communism, he did not put the federal government on a short enough leash. If there is a conclusion to be drawn from the 1994 elections, it is less government that the people want. No time is better than the present. As Reagan used to say, "If not us, who? If not now, when?"

DECEMBER 1994

CHAPTER SIX

Victory before the Supreme Court

On September 26, 1994, I was driving to Lusk, Wyoming to deliver a dinner speech to seventy-five ranchers. On U.S. Highway 85 in the middle of nowhere my telephone rang. It was Todd Welch, MSLF Senior Attorney. The Supreme Court of the United States, he excitedly related, granted our petition in *Adarand Constructors, Inc. v. Peña*, a challenge to the federal government's policy of awarding highway construction contracts based on race. I was lucky to keep my car on the road; it is every lawyer's dream to argue a case at the Supreme Court, but only one percent of petitions are granted.

It was not MSLF's first appearance before the Court on this issue. In *Wygant v. Jackson Bd. of Educ.*, 476 U.S. 267 (1986), MSLF represented a teacher and won a 5-4 ruling that her school district had violated the Equal Protection Clause when it made employment decisions based upon her race. MSLF continued to seek an end to race-based decision making by all governmental entities.

A most hectic schedule of drafting and filing briefs "on the merits," holding "moot courts" with colleagues, and preparing alone for hours followed for when, on January 17, 1995, I stood before the Court and began:

"Mr. Chief Justice and may it please the court. Adarand is a small, family-owned corporation that does business in Colorado Springs, Colorado.... In 1989, Adarand submitted a bid to do the guardrail work on the subcontract as a subcontractor along 4.7 miles of highway in the San Juan National Forest in extreme Southwestern Colorado. Although it submitted the lowest bid and although it has an excellent reputation for doing quality work on a timely basis, its bid was rejected by operation of the statute questioned here, a statute which presumes that all members of certain enumerated racial and ethnic groups are socially and economically disadvantaged. Adarand challenged the constitutionality of the statute both on its face and as applied to him in the loss of this $20,000 contract."

ENDANGERED SPECIES IN
WOLVES' CLOTHING

"Don't you have coyotes in Wyoming?" an eastern reporter asked me regarding western ranchers' opposition to Secretary Bruce Babbitt's $6 million (now $13 million) plan to put wolves in Idaho, Montana, and Wyoming. I said we do. "Then what's the difference between a coyote and a wolf?"

"About 100 pounds," I replied, "and the Endangered Species Act. Since wolves are legally protected under the Act, their presence on federal and private land has serious consequences."

Within mere days my remarks were rendered prophetic: an environmental group filed a lawsuit in Idaho to remove what few protections exist for ranchers under Babbitt's wolf plan. It will not be the last such lawsuit. In fact, the placement of wolves in the tri-state area is just the beginning of what will no doubt be a lengthy battle in which environmental groups will demand that plans for federal lands be revised to reflect the return of the wolf. (Just ask the people of northwestern Montana what has happened to their ability to recreate—not to mention harvest timber—on federal lands as a result of the presence in their backyard of the protected grizzly bear.)

The region affected by the wolf is huge. Under the Babbitt plan, wolves were released into what bureaucrats euphemistically call the "Yellowstone and central Idaho areas." Remarkably, those terms are defined to mean all of Wyoming, all or portions of 42 of Idaho's 44 counties, and all or portions of 40 of Montana's 56 counties. Ranchers anticipate that the federal government will order the removal of M-44's (cyanide charges used to kill coyotes) as well as traps and snares from all land in the wolf's new territory, exposing livestock to ever-escalating predation from coyotes.

Babbitt's plan has nothing to do with "saving the wolf," since tens of thousands of them now roam Canada and Alaska. It has nothing to do with increasing the ability of tourists to see wolves, since these reclusive beasts—according to federal officials—will avoid most human contact. (These bureaucrats swore in court that wolves prefer to take down a 1,000 pound elk rather than dine on a newborn calf.) It is not about restoring nature's "delicate balance," even if the federal officials who allowed brucellosis to become an epidemic in Yellowstone's elk and buffalo herds were capable of assuring such symmetry.

The objective behind "restoring" the wolf is the one that has driven practically every other Endangered Species Act designation—to prevent human and economic activity. That was the goal behind the listing of the northern spotted owl in the Pacific Northwest, behind the listing of the golden cheek warbler in Texas, and behind the listing of the gnatcatcher and the Delhi Sands flower-loving fruit fly in California. With each listing, millions of acres of public and private land were to be placed off limits to humans.

That may be one reason the Supreme Court of the United States agreed to hear *Sweet Home Chapter of Communities for a Great Oregon v. Babbitt*, in which timber communities seek to prevent Babbitt from ignoring the plain language of federal statute written to protect private property. A favorable ruling, however, will not protect those who depend on the use of federal lands in Idaho, Montana, and Wyoming from an increasingly restrictive federal view of what will be permitted in the wolf's vast new habitat. The needs of westerners are irrelevant to Babbitt and his minions. They have concluded that whatever economic injury westerners suffer is of little significance compared to the "existence value" the rest of the nation will receive knowing that wolves are somewhere out west.

I told the reporter that if Babbitt really wants to recover the wolf, he should put them in Rock Creek Park in Washington, D.C., since the loss of a couple of French poodles a night might change the inside-the-beltway mentality. "We can't do that," she quickly cried out. "People live there."

FEBRUARY 1995

AN END TO SOCIAL ENGINEERING?

On February 24, 1995, the *Washington Post* headlined: "Clinton Orders Affirmative Action Review." The *Post* reported that Clinton had ordered "an 'intense, urgent review' of all aspects of the government's affirmative action programs, aimed at protecting those that can be shown to work and jettisoning or altering the rest."

Clinton's actions are hardly surprising given the building momentum for ending race-based decision making by the federal government. Today there is an irresistible force in opposition to affirmative action bound for a head-on collision with the immovable object that is, in Justice Stevens' words, "racial politics."

The momentum began to build on September 26, 1994, when the Supreme Court agreed to decide *Adarand Constructors, Inc. v. Peña*, a case I argued before the Court on January 17, 1995. At risk in that case is a 15-year old decision in which the Court upheld the authority of Congress to award contracts based on race. Observers believe the Court may declare the federal program at issue in the suit, which awards contracts based solely on race, unconstitutional.

Six weeks and a day after the Court agreed to hear *Adarand*, the American people issued their ruling. According to David Frum, author of *Dead Right*, on November 8, more than 60 percent of white males voted Republican in large part due to anger over congressional policies that threaten jobs, personal freedom, and private property. Affirmative action is part of that mix.

Meanwhile, the California Civil Rights Initiative—it will compel race-neutral decision making by the nation's largest state—is all but guaranteed a place on the ballot in 1996. In Congress, House Majority Leader Dick Armey (R-26th TX) has recently become one more voice against affirmative action. Both in California and before Congress, the future of affirmative action appears bleak.

The death knell that may now be ringing tolls not just for affirmative action, but also for the once powerful philosophy that underlies it: what Professor Steven Yates calls the "Philosophy of Social Engineering." In his 1994 book, *Civil Wrongs: What Went Wrong with Affirmative Action*, Professor Yates sets out the tenets of that philosophy: there is a social elite that should determine national policies; those policies must be imposed by the federal government; American society is systemically flawed; and, it is lawful to burden individual members of society if it serves group goals.

While anger over federal race-based decision making is, in part, the result of a perception of unfairness and inequity as well as the reality of lost jobs and denied opportunities, something more is at work here. That something is the American peoples' view of the role of the federal government in their lives. More and more Americans are discovering the flawed philosophy upon which big government programs are based and they find it repugnant.

That very same thing is happening on environmental issues. While much opposition to environmental policy gone wild emanates from regulatory overkill, lost jobs, and imperiled property rights, millions of Americans are responding to the philosophy of social engineering that underlies radical environmental policies.

Today's environmental policies fit neatly in Professor Yates' construct: only environmental elitists are competent to make the rules by which all of us are to live; the rules must be imposed from Washington, D.C., in order to change dramatically a flawed society (recall, for example, Vice President Al Gore's call for "a wrenching transformation of society"); and this must be accomplished regardless of the impact on people who get caught in the agonizing metamorphosis (people like loggers, ranchers, and others).

Today, more and more people see liberal social policies—regardless of their euphemistic labels—for what they are, that is, a way to gain power and control. Those threatened by environmental policies must help others understand that the philosophical bedrocks of affirmative action are the intellectual keystones for environmental policy—notions starkly at odds with the views of most Americans.

MARCH 1995

AN END TO AFFIRMATIVE ACTION?

In southwestern Colorado, near the tiny town of Stoner, 27 miles northeast of Cortez, lies the West Dolores River. Deep in the San Juan National Forest, betwixt rolling hillsides and abutted by pine and aspen, the West Dolores takes melted snow from the foot of Mount Wilson and sends it off to the Gulf of California. Standing near the guardrail for the West Dolores Road that parallels the river amid this idyllic scene it is hard to imagine this is the origin for a Supreme Court case that is sending shock waves across America.

On August 10, 1989, the Central Federal Lands Highway Division (an agency within the U.S. Department of Transportation) issued a solicitation for bids for construction of 4.7 miles of highway along the West Dolores River. After the contract was awarded to Mountain Gravel & Construction Company, Adarand Constructors, Inc., submitted a bid to build the guardrail portion of the contract. Although Adarand submitted the lowest bid, its bid was rejected. Instead, Mountain Gravel awarded the guardrail subcontract to a "disadvantaged business enterprise" under a federal program that mandated that a percent of contracts be awarded to "socially and economically disadvantaged" businesses. Mountain Gravel was then paid a "bounty" of $10,000.

For Randy Pech who, with his wife Valery, owns and operates Adarand, the loss of the West Dolores Project was the last straw. On August 10, 1990, Adarand sued the federal government, asserting that a federal program that makes decisions on the basis of race violates the equal protection guarantee of the Constitution. That argument was rejected by a Colorado federal district court and the U.S. Court of Appeals for the Tenth Circuit because Supreme Court rulings, in 1980 and 1990, authorized Congress to make awards based on race.

Against overwhelming odds—only one percent of all cases that seek review by the Supreme Court are accepted—the Court, on September 26, 1994, agreed to hear the case, setting in motion a briefing schedule that ended days before Christmas. On January 17, 1995, I stood before the Court arguing that the standard the Court applies to state and local governments regarding racial issues also applies to Congress, and that, under that standard, the law that denied Adarand the guardrail subcontract is unconstitutional.

The key issue is that, while the law targets "socially and economically disadvantaged" individuals, it defines that phrase to include, by regulation, all "Black Americans, Hispanic Americans, Native Americans [and] Asian Pacific Americans." The economic status of minority businessmen is irrelevant; only their race matters. It is this drawing of lines solely on the basis of race and for no other reason that the Supreme Court has held violates the Constitution.

The Clinton administration, in its brief and during its oral argument, asserted that the federal statute is constitutional because Congress is seeking to "remediate" historical discrimination. What justification, however, is there for a program that entitles a Hong Kong banker, a Japanese businessman, or the son of landed gentry in Spain to the same preferences as the descendants of slaves? Further, what justification is there for such a program 40 years after *Brown v. Board of Education* and 30 years after the Civil Rights Act of 1964? Finally, what justification exists for a race-based program when the problems that Congress says it is remediating may be addressed by what Justice O'Connor calls "race-neutral alternatives?"

Another important question is whether a race-based program makes sense in light of what Justice Stevens calls its stigmatizing effect, both on those who are benefitted (because people think they are incompetent) and on those who are burdened (because people think they are to blame)? The end result, argues Justice Stevens, is racial antipathy and feelings of anger and hostility.

Thus, perhaps the greatest benefit of a decision in favor of Adarand would be that, over time, it would restore to race relations in this country the tranquility found along the West Dolores River in southwestern Colorado.

APRIL 1995

COURT RULES—BUT IT'S UP TO US!

On July 19th, President Clinton announced the results of what began on February 23rd as an "intense, urgent review" of affirmative action. It was all for naught. The *Washington Post* characterized Clinton as "moving back to the liberal side of the divide" with a "full-throated endorsement of government [racial] preference programs. . . ."

Clinton began the review after oral arguments before the Supreme Court in the landmark affirmative action case *Adarand Constructors, Inc. v. Peña*. The review's results followed Justice O'Connor's June 12th *Adarand* opinion. The Supreme Court ruled the Constitution requires the Court to apply the same standard when considering race-based decision making, regardless of the unit of government, whether federal, state, or local. That standard, held the Court, is one of "strict scrutiny," which requires the government to demonstrate a "compelling governmental interest" in using race and "narrow tailoring" in serving that interest.

The Court's decision in *Adarand* overturned its 1990 ruling in *Metro Broadcasting v. Federal Communication Commission*, where the Court upheld the ability of Congress to use race to award television broadcast licenses. The Court also reversed its 1980 decision in *Fullilove v. Klutznick*, where it first held Congress could use race as a factor in awarding government contracts. Both rulings, which applied a much more lenient standard to race-based decision making by Congress, were the basis for earlier rulings by a Colorado federal district court and the U.S. Court of Appeals for the Tenth Circuit against Adarand. The Court vacated the rulings and then remanded the case for a decision consistent with its new holding.

Justice O'Connor, writing for the Court, declared: "Despite lingering uncertainty in the details, however, the Court's cases . . . established three general propositions with respect to governmental racial classifications. First, skepticism: '[a]ny preference based on racial or ethnic criteria must necessarily receive a most searching examination'. . . . Second, consistency: 'the standard of review under the Equal Protection Clause is not dependent on the race of those burdened or benefited by a particular classification'. . . . And third, congruence: '[e]qual protection analysis in the Fifth Amendment area is the same as that under the Fourteenth Amendment'. . . ." Closed Justice O'Connor: "Taken together, these three propositions lead to the conclusion that any person, of whatever race, has the right to demand that any governmental actor subject to the Constitution justify any racial classification subjecting that person to unequal treatment under the strictest judicial standard."

The Supreme Court's decision—as to what the guarantee of equal protection means—now shifts the burden of ensuring federal adherence to the Constitution to Congress and President Clinton. Sadly, Clinton—presented with a unique opportunity to move toward a new day in race relations in America—took a giant step backward.

Despite Adarand's extraordinary victory, its operator, Randy Pech, finds himself back where he began nearly five years ago. In fact, just days before the Supreme Court's decision, Pech lost yet another contract as a result of his race—something that happens with regularity. Pech must now return to federal court in Colorado and battle the world's largest law firm: the federal government. There is no doubt—after Clinton's announcement—that federal lawyers will fight tooth and nail against Randy Pech and Adarand. Thus, the question before Congress, in light of its duty to the Constitution, is whether it should stand on the sidelines and leave it to people like Randy Pech to demonstrate that various race-based programs are unconstitutional, or whether Congress should stop funding programs of dubious constitutionality.

Despite the national rejoicing over the end to federal race-based decision making that the Supreme Court's *Adarand* decision foreshadowed, there is serious question as to whether Congress has the courage to do the right thing. Perhaps during the August recess the American people will remind their representatives of what took place last November 8—and why!

AUGUST 1995

CLINTON LEADS THE "WAR ON THE WEST"

For anyone who thought that, a few months before the 1996 election, President Clinton would push Secretary of the Interior Bruce Babbitt aside, install a recently-defeated western Democratic governor—Wyoming's Mike Sullivan has been mentioned—and seek to make peace with westerners, the wait is over. It ain't going to happen!

On August 25, with Old Faithful geyser in the background, President Clinton announced a mining claim moratorium on 4,500 acres of federally-owned land north of Yellowstone National Park. After months of pressure by environmental organizations, aided by support from the *New York Times*, Clinton decided that his success in 1996 depends more on keeping environmental extremists placated than on joining with westerners to balance environmental protection with jobs. Given the chance to come West and make peace, Clinton chose to escalate a war that until now was seen as the work of the environmental activists he appointed but not the President himself.

The target of Clinton's big announcement is the New World Mining District, far beyond the northeast boundary of Yellowstone National Park, which is the site of two underground gold-copper-silver-bearing deposits. Those deposits will support a ten-to-twelve year mine with year-round employment of some 175 people with an average annual wage of $35,000 (compared to the area's current average of $16,000), plus benefits. The annual payroll will exceed $7 million with an additional $7 million to be spent on goods and services in the local economy. Eighty secondary jobs will also be created. Annual tax revenues will exceed $2.33 million.

Clinton's announcement puts all that in jeopardy. As one environmental activist enthused, "It doesn't kill the project. But it tightens the noose." Clinton's announcement also provides *carte blanche* to Secretaries Babbitt and Glickman to erect every barrier they can during the course of environmental studies and permitting and patenting procedures conducted by federal officials.

Ironically, the New World Mine is in an area that has seen mining activity since the first white man came west. As early as 1875, ore was smelted there. By 1952, gold production in the area helped make Park County, Montana, the third highest gold producing area in the state. In

1978, when Congress created the Absaroka-Beartooth Wilderness Area to the north and east, it excluded the mining area because of the U.S. Geological Survey's expectation of future mineral development.

The fact that the New World Mine would be located on lands managed by the U.S. Forest Service, in accordance with multiple use principles, the fact that the mine is neither part of nor visible from any place in Yellowstone National Park, the fact that world-class ore bodies such as those at the New World Mine are extremely rare, and the fact that the mine will provide much needed jobs and tax revenue are irrelevant to environmental extremists and their ally, President Clinton. For them, all of the nearly 20 million acres of land around Yellowstone—as much as 25 percent of which is privately owned—should be managed as part of a vast park.

That was the essence of the "Yellowstone Vision Document" published by the National Park Service in August of 1990. The response to that document was immediate—thousands of westerners in Idaho, Montana, and Wyoming vigorously opposed the proposal. Before the dust was settled, all three governors—including two Democrats—signed a letter to President Clinton decrying the Vision Document. The two federal officials responsible for the fiasco were moved out of the region.

Now, five years after the "Vision Document" first saw the light of day, President Clinton is responding to those environmental extremists who want to put an end to all economic activity in what they refer to as the "Greater Yellowstone Ecosystem." Clinton's full embrace of the "War on the West" that Secretary Babbitt started two and one half years ago is the result of a mathematical calculation. Clinton decided that there just are not enough westerners or western electoral votes to matter. We shall see.

SEPTEMBER 1995

U.S. OR U.N.

I guess we should have seen it coming when Vice President Al Gore, speaking of the death of members of the U.S. Armed Forces in a "friendly fire" tragedy in the Mideast, honored "their service to the United Nations." Perhaps some of us thought that it was just a slip, like when the Vice President defined "*E Pluribus Unum*" as meaning "from one many." It was not a mistake, however. Gore's remarks on whose interests were being served by our men in uniform was yet another demonstration of Gore's world view— the world view that sent the then U.S. Senator to Rio de Janeiro in 1992 to embrace international agreements regarding atmospheric emissions and endangered species. Not surprisingly, the Rio de Janeiro pacts have serious ramifications for all Americans.

Until recently, the impact on ordinary citizens of such international deal making was rather vague or at least far removed. As these agreements go from the discussion stage to the international standards and enforcement stage, however, the ramifications for the nation's economy, for individual rights, and for constitutional liberty become more obvious. For example, as of January 1, 1996, Freon will no longer be available due to international acquiescence to the sky-is-falling types who say the product is destroying the Earth's ozone.

The most shocking indication, however, of the Clinton administration's willingness to place international decision making above that of domestic entities, to place the opinions of foreigners above those of American citizens, and to submit, not to the will of the people, but to the demands of international tribunals took place recently in the American West.

In an audacious attempt to kill a proposed Montana mine—even before the Environmental Impact Statement (EIS) has been completed—Babbitt's Department of the Interior asked the World Heritage Centre of the United Nations Educational, Scientific and Cultural Organization (UNESCO) to come to the United States to place Yellowstone National Park on an international "Endangered Heritage List." According to one UNESCO document—translated from French—the request was "made by the United States" and entails a "study not only [of] the mining project but also all the problems affecting Yellowstone (apparently very numerous)." As if it were not enough that federal government officials asked foreigners to help kill local economic activity, Americans are paying for the bullets. Writes the UNESCO official, "Due to the lack of available funds at the World Heritage Fund, the United States will assume the costs of the mission."

The concerns of the U.N. body go far beyond the proposed new mine, as is clear from the minutes of a meeting conducted in Paris, France, following the U.S. request and a communication from fourteen environmental groups. For example, German and Canadian delegates argued that threats to Yellowstone include "deforestation" as well as "tourism impact and wildlife policies."

What Babbitt and his subordinates seek to do is evident. The letter sent to UNESCO by Babbitt's man reads: "Considering the national and international significance of Yellowstone and in compliance with the World Heritage Convention and Public Law 96-515, the United States must assume full responsibility for assuring the integrity of World Heritage values is not compromised by . . . actions taken either internal or external to World Heritage Site boundaries." Translation: put Yellowstone on UNESCO's list and the Clinton administration will have another weapon in its "War on the West."

It is remarkable that, at a time when elected officials are returning power to the people and reviving federalism by restoring the proper balance between the federal government and the states, and at a time when the Supreme Court is breathing new life into the Tenth Amendment, the Clinton administration invites foreigners to the West to decide our future. If we are not careful, the decisions on this and other similar issues will not be made in Helena, Boise, and Cheyenne, but in Washington, Bonn, and Paris.

OCTOBER 1995

WHEN THE TRUTH HURTS

Recently, after speaking to a college audience, one student stood up. "I don't have a question," she said, "I have a comment. Your speech is filled with troubling stories of people who have been hurt by environmental policies. That's not fair! We shouldn't be talking about the impact of these laws on a handful of people but about what these laws are trying to do."

The student's comments and others like them that I have heard over the past several months are the manifestation of the criticism to which environmental extremists are subjected when the public learns of the human cost of so-called environmental laws. That comment and the irritation felt by environmental groups when forced to deal with stories of human tragedies due to environmental policy also explain the assault by environmental groups, not only upon the messenger of these tales, but also upon the victims themselves.

Several months ago, Bruce Babbitt's Department of the Interior released a thick document that sought to discount the scores of factual situations in which humans were injured by environmental policies. As evidence of the level of credibility Babbitt's agency accorded the document, it did not state it was a federal publication. In another instance earlier this summer, I appeared on an American Bar Association panel opposite Assistant Attorney General Lois Schiffer, the third ranking official at the U.S. Department of Justice. Remarkably, given the hundreds of issues she could have addressed, she launched into a diatribe arguing that none of the stories being reported about environmental victims was factual. More recently, Discovery Network ("Environment Beware: Counter Revolution!") used former CBS anchor Walter Cronkite to attack the truthfulness of environmental victims and those who deliver their message.

The reason for the assault is apparent. As long as these environmental extremists can keep the debate general, nonspecific, and aspirational, the policies that they embrace enjoy broad public support. Consider, for example, the positive response in public opinion surveys to such questions as "Do you believe we need to protect the quality of our nation's drinking water?" and "Would you be willing to spend a little extra money to protect the environment?"

Once the debate progresses from the general to the specific, however, once the goals are translated into precise legislative and regulatory language with actual consequences to people, once the human impact of the application of these very same environmental policies becomes clear, public support all but vanishes. "The devil," it is said, "is in the details." No wonder environmentalists are bedeviled by the human impact of their policies.

Much of the American public supports the vague goals of the Endangered Species Act (ESA), but very few support an ESA: that declares that a Montana rancher cannot use deadly force to protect himself from a grizzly bear attack; that allows for an "endangered" fly to stop economic activity in California; or that permits a flyspeck sized "endangered" snail to put half the farmers in a rural Idaho county out of business.

Much of the American public supports the general goals of the Clean Water Act, but few support a Clean Water Act: that allows hundred-million-dollar fines to be levied against Colorado ranchers for protecting their lands from government-induced flood waters; that permits the Environmental Protection Agency to declare dry lands in New Mexico to be "waters of the United States;" or that denies property owners the right to challenge such arbitrary and property-taking decisions in federal court.

There is scarcely a federal statute that, shorn of its impact on people and other unintended consequences, would not merit broad public support. Once those impacts and consequences become clear, however, once the national debate moves from the aspirational to the actual, from the general to the specific, from the theoretical to the applied, public support evaporates. That is why support for federal "environmental" laws is eroding. That is also why environmental extremists fear the truth!

NOVEMBER 1995

CHAPTER SEVEN

Clinton Escalates His War on the West

★ ★ ★ ★ ★

———

I n *War on the West: Government Tyranny on America's Great Frontier* (Regnery, 1995), I wrote:
          "Today, the American West is a battleground. The men and women whose families settled the West, who have lived on the land for generations, find themselves besieged by environmental elitists sitting in their glass towers in New York City and San Francisco, their ivory towers in prestigious colleges and universities, and their marble towers along the corridors of power in Washington, D.C. These 'strangers' to the West and to westerners seek to turn everything from the 100th meridian to the Cascade Mountains into a vast park. The battle now raging in the West is often couched as a fight between environmentalists (the 'good guys') and anti-environmentalists (the 'bad guys'), as powerful environmental organizations rant about ending the abuses of the past in mining, grazing, forestry, and the use of western water. However, the battle is not about the quality of the human environment or about safety or survivability or sustainability.

The War on the West is about whether westerners will have an economy, or property rights, or the ability to engage in economic pursuits that sustained their forefathers and that the nation still requires. The War on the West is more. It is about laws and culture and whether the freedoms guaranteed by the Constitution will survive. Today, the War on the West is important for millions of westerners and for those who care about the traditions and culture of the West. It is also important to anyone who loves freedom and fears tyranny. For the War on the West is only the first skirmish in what will soon become a national campaign by environmental extremists [that began] with the election of Bill Clinton and Al Gore."

In Washington, D.C., my publisher and friend Al Regnery read those words, put down my manuscript, and looked up, "You ain't seen nothing yet." The year 1996 would prove him right.

A LONG WAY TO GO

Following the congressional elections of 1994, many thought that the restoration of a proper balance between people and the planet, between economic growth and environmental goals, between property rights and prohibitory laws and regulations was weeks away. The Class of 1994, which had campaigned against the abuse of federal "wetlands" policy and the Endangered Species Act as well as the federal government's covetous approach to private property, went to Washington, D.C., committed to change. This month, as the 1996 election presidential election campaign begins in New Hampshire, it is clear we have a ways to go.

Just how far was demonstrated recently by a decision of the Denver-based United States Court of Appeals for the Tenth Circuit, a decision that addressed the most fundamental guarantee of our Constitution: the right to fair treatment or the Due Process Clause.

Laguna Gatuna, Inc. (Laguna) is a New Mexico corporation located in Hobbs. Its only business is that of disposing of waters produced from oil and gas operations on lands it owns in southeastern New Mexico. In April of 1992, the Environmental Protection Agency (EPA) served Laguna with a cease and desist order, stating that further disposal of produced waters would subject Laguna to penalties under the Clean Water Act (CWA). The EPA claimed that Laguna's dry desert lands are "waters of the United States," as defined by the CWA, because migratory birds might land on the rain water that infrequently collects on Laguna's property. Laguna's land, however, is isolated hydrologically since no streams empty into it; no streams drain out of it; and, there are no surface or groundwater connections between it and any other water body. Faced with fines of $25,000 a day and $125,000 for a "knowing" violation, plus jail time, Laguna ceased all of its operations and went out of business. Believing that the EPA's decision was in error, Laguna sued, asking a New Mexico federal judge to determine whether its lands were indeed "waters of the United States" as defined by the CWA. Laguna never got that far.

The federal government moved to dismiss, asserting that the federal district court had no jurisdiction to hear the case because Laguna was seeking "pre-enforcement review." The EPA even implied the cease and desist order that it issued Laguna was not truly final and might be withdrawn. Remarkably, the district court agreed and dismissed the case.

On appeal, Laguna argued that its inability to appear in court to challenge a bureaucrat's decision that Laguna's land met the federal definition of "waters of the United States" was a violation of the Due Process Clause. Concluded the Tenth Circuit, "Laguna's policy argument that it should not be necessary to violate an EPA order and risk civil and criminal penalties to obtain judicial review is well taken. Nevertheless…we reject Laguna's conclusion [since it would] undermine the EPA's regulatory authority." Last month, a request that the Supreme Court of the United States review the decision was denied.

There is no more fundamental guarantee for Americans than the one contained in the Fifth Amendment to the Constitution that says simply, "No person shall…be deprived of life, liberty, or property, without due process of law." It is this provision that acts as one of the few restraints on the ability of the federal government to do as it wishes. In decision after decision, the Supreme Court has held that this provision requires, at the very least, "that individuals must receive notice and an opportunity to be heard before the Government deprives them of property." In the Court's words, "the right to be heard before being condemned to suffer grievous loss of any kind, even though it may not involve the stigma and hardships of a criminal conviction, is a principle basic to our society."

Unfortunately, when it comes to environmental policy in America today, even "basic principles" seem to take a back seat.

FEBRUARY 1996

GIVING THE DEVIL ITS DUE

Never let it be said that Secretary Bruce Babbitt's minions are not creative when closing the nation's federal lands to public access. Yet for pure, unadulterated chutzpa, it is hard to beat the decision of the National Park Service (NPS) to close Devils Tower as a religious site, off limits to recreational visitors.

This is the NPS to which Congress assigned two missions on its creation eighty years ago: "to conserve the scenery and the natural and historic objects and the wildlife therein and to provide for the enjoyment of the same in such manner and by such means as will leave them unimpaired for the enjoyment of future generations." Over the years, the NPS has done all in its power to ignore, if not erase the directive of public "enjoyment." Twenty years ago the NPS rewrote—without congressional authorization—its mission regarding the first national park (Yellowstone): "To perpetuate the natural ecosystems . . . for their inspirational, educational, cultural, and scientific values for this and future generations." Gone was the word "enjoyment."

In 1991, the NPS adopted the so-called "Vail Agenda." The NPS decided that "it should not be the goal of the [NPS] to provide visitors with mere entertainment and recreation . . . [r]ather, the objective should be . . . use and enjoyment on the *park's* terms . . . [that is] entertainment, education, and recreation *with meaning*." (Emphasis in original.) Apparently one of the meanings the NPS wishes to convey is that Devils Tower, located in extreme northeastern Wyoming, is a religious site of enormous importance to American Indians.

While people of faith throughout the country find it difficult, if not impossible, under current interpretations of the First Amendment, to erect crèches and menorahs on courthouse lawns, the NPS has decided that the nation's first national monument should be set aside for religious purposes. Under a February of 1995 decision document, the NPS placed Devils Tower off limits to climbing during the month of June. The reason: "respect for the reverence many American Indians hold for Devils Tower as a sacred site. . . ."

Ironically, the activity the NPS is banning from Devils Tower predated the establishment of the national monument in 1906: rock climbing.

Climbing at Devils Tower began in 1893 when two local ranchers constructed a stake ladder on the Tower, a ladder that was last used in 1927 and thereafter listed on the National Register of Historic Places. Even more ironic is the fact that Devils Tower was never a sacred site for American Indians!

According to a 1934 document in the NPS archives there was no physical evidence that Devils Tower was significant to American Indians and their culture. Moreover, unlike nearby sacred Indian sites, there were no sightings of American Indians at Devils Tower into the mid-to-late 1800s. On the other hand, there is substantial evidence that American Indians considered Devils Tower an evil place, hence its name: "Bad God Tower."

The decision by the NPS to close Devils Tower for religious purposes puts the NPS in direct conflict with a Supreme Court ruling. Justice O'Connor, writing for the Court in 1988, declared, "No disrespect for [American Indian religious] practices is implied when one notes that such beliefs could easily require *de facto* beneficial ownership of some rather spacious tracts of public property. Even without anticipating future cases, the diminution of the Government's property rights, and the concomitant subsidy of the Indian religion, would ... be far from trivial[.] Whatever rights the Indians may have to the use of the area, however, those rights do not divest the Government of its right to use what is, after all, its land."

If the Constitution is so clear, the NPS must have an ulterior motive. The small band of climbers who sued the NPS knows what it is: to close more federal land to public access.

MARCH 1996

WHEN THE KING IS WRONG

Last week before the U.S. Court of Appeals for the District of Columbia Circuit, a federal attorney made an astonishing admission in a case involving the ability of the people of northwestern Montana and northern Idaho to challenge a decision of the U.S. Forest Service regarding timber harvesting in the Kootenai National Forest.

The people of Lincoln County, Montana, and Boundary County, Idaho, assert that when the Forest Service placed the needs of the grizzly bear—as represented by the U.S. Fish and Wildlife Service—above the people's need, the people have the right to ask a federal court to determine whether the decision is legal. In particular, they believe they have the right to challenge the Forest Service's decision that the devastating forest fires that will sweep through the diseased, dying, and dead timber of the Kootenai National Forest are preferable to the harvesting of that timber by mankind. Fearing a catastrophic fire like the one that destroyed three million acres—an area the size of Connecticut—in the region in 1910, they think the Forest Service's decision is bad for the environment and bad for the people who live in it.

The federal government responded to their lawsuit, not by attempting to demonstrate that the Forest Service's decision was correct, but by asserting that the people had no right to sue the government. When the federal district court judge agreed, the lawsuit was dismissed. On appeal, the question was simple: can local communities, faced with economic despair and environmental devastation due to a decision by the Forest Service, sue the federal government?

Last week, a member of the three-judge panel hearing the appeal asked whether it was the government's position that there were no circumstances under which the people of northwestern Montana and northern Idaho could sue the government. "That's right," he answered. Even in the face of the devastating fires the people of the region feared would result from the Forest Service's decision? "Yes," then too, responded the government attorney.

The position taken by the federal government in the Montana case is not an unusual one. In two other cases that went before federal courts of appeals last week, the government made the same claim: citizens have no right to sue their government. One was a challenge to the constitutionality of the Clinton 1993 fuel tax increase. The other was a lawsuit by a Texas landowner whose property was destroyed by negligence on the part of the U.S. Forest Service.

The basis for the federal government's claim in all three cases is "sovereign immunity," that is, the immunity of the sovereign, the king, from lawsuits by his subjects, unless, of course, the king consents to be sued. Although there are instances in which sovereign immunity applies, federal lawyers invoke this defense regularly. Said one federal judge, "The claim of sovereign immunity is one which the government raises frequently and often inadvisedly. It appears to be a boilerplate element of many of the government's motions to dismiss. . . ."

The claim of sovereign immunity has been used by federal lawyers even in cases challenging the actions of federal officials as being in excess of their legal authority, causing the U.S. Court of Appeals for the Second Circuit to declare, "law officers of the government ought not to take the time of busy judges or of opposing parties by advancing an argument so plainly foreclosed by Supreme Court decisions."

There is more. Government attorneys have an ethical duty to recognize that those who sue the federal government are not just parties against whom they may litigate zealously, but indeed are citizens who have every right to expect justice at the hands of their government. For the men and women of northwestern Montana and northern Idaho who fear the approaching fire season, that means at the very least the right to be heard in a court of law.

APRIL 1996

THE NOSE OF THE CAMEL

On the banks of Crooked Lake, near Watersmeet, in Gogebic county, in the Upper Peninsula of Michigan, sits the tiny cabin of Ben and Kathy Thrall. In 1966, the U.S. Forest Service acquired property abutting the southern portion of Crooked Lake. Although the federal government's acquisition of the land aroused concerns, its commitment to recreation eased the minds of local residents. In the 1980s, when the Forest Service recommended that federal land around Crooked Lake be designated as a wilderness area, local citizens worried. Once again the Forest Service assured them that federal action would not affect property rights, noting "valid existing rights" language in the 1964 Wilderness Act. In 1987, Congress created the Sylvania Wilderness around Crooked Lake.

In 1992, the Forest Service changed its mind, deciding that the Thralls could no longer use Crooked Lake as Michigan law said they could. Under Michigan law, an owner of lakefront property—a "riparian"—owns the surface of the lake in common with all other riparian owners and shares an equal right to a reasonable use of the entire surface of the lake. Despite the clear provision of Michigan law that no owner may interfere with another owner's reasonable use of the surface of the lake, the Forest Service adopted a regulation restricting the Thralls' use of Crooked Lake. In fact, before the Thralls could use Crooked Lake, they had to get permission. Therefore, they sued.

Remarkably, the Forest Service argued in federal court that "valid existing rights" applied only to mining claims. Though the district court rejected that argument, it ruled for the Forest Service: "It is within the power of Congress under the Property Clause to set aside federal land as wilderness and to protect, preserve and, if necessary, restore the wilderness quality of that land by regulating private as well as federal property on lakes within a wilderness area."

A panel of the U.S. Court of Appeals for the Sixth Circuit agreed, ruling that under the Property Clause the federal government may regulate private property by standing in the shoes of local government albeit with a different objective. Declared the panel: "The federal government's limits on the Thralls' [use of their land] are similar to those of [local] townships in [various Michigan Supreme Court decisions], except that the 'general public' in [the Thrall] case is the nation at large instead of the local community, and the power now comes from a highly particularized source, the Property Clause, rather than from the state's inherent powers."

In light of: 1) the court's disregard for the fact that only federal land can be made part of a wilderness and only by Congress; 2) the court's evisceration of the "valid existing rights" provision of the wilderness acts: and 3) the court's holding that the federal government can redefine state property rights and stands in the shoes of local government to regulate private property; the Thralls asked the judges of the Sixth Circuit to rehear the case.

In a surprising move, the Sixth Circuit agreed, vacating the three-judge panel's earlier decision. A federal attorney called the decision "unprecedented," noting that it is the first time that a circuit court has vacated a panel's unanimous ruling. The decision is also a setback for the federal government, which saw the *Thrall* case as a chance "to expand federal authority over split estates."

It is not just the Thralls who are at risk. Under the court's holding, the presence of federal land near private property gives federal bureaucrats the power to regulate that property under the Property Clause, not to serve local citizens, but "the nation at large." Just as important, federal bureaucrats can ignore state law in deciding what is a protected property right.

If the federal government wins regarding Crooked Lake, no property owner anywhere near federal land anywhere in the country will be safe and state property law will become irrelevant.

JUNE 1996

GOLDILOCKS AND THE CONSTITUTION

No one would ever mistake Attorney General Janet Reno for Goldilocks of nursery story fame, but in two recent filings Reno's attorneys have taken what can only be characterized as a Goldilocks' approach to the ability of citizens to sue for the loss of constitutional rights. It would appear that, for Reno's attorneys, no argument is too absurd to use to attempt to frustrate the ability of federal courts to perform their most important function: determining the meaning of the Constitution.

The government's filings come in two momentous cases that have drawn the attention of the national media, one involving the ability of the government to set aside federal land for religious worship purposes, the other involving the ability of federal officials to award government contracts on the basis of race. While these cases have earned national headlines, the outrageous filings by federal lawyers have gone unnoticed.

In *Bear Lodge Multiple Use Association v. Babbitt*, climbing guide Andy Petefish seeks to overturn the National Park Service ban on commercial climbing on Devils Tower in northeastern Wyoming during the month of June, a ban imposed to set aside the nation's first national monument for religious worship by American Indian religious practitioners. Since Petefish, like thousands of fishing guides, ski instructors, and others associated with the tourism industry, earns most of his annual income during a few months, the June ban was devastating. That is his own fault, argued Reno's attorneys. Therefore, since he has chosen his particular "lifestyle," subsisting throughout the year on what he is able to make in the summer, his income is too meager to allow him to challenge the government's violation of his First Amendment rights.

While stunning, that is not the most egregious of the arguments put forth by Reno's attorneys. In documents filed with the Wyoming federal district court, the U.S. Attorney indicated that the government would present evidence that a lifting of the ban on climbing would result in "cultural genocide." That argument drew a stinging rebuke from the judge, as did the government's assertion that the decision by noncommercial climbers not to climb due to threats by the Park Service to close Devils Tower permanently may be characterized as "voluntary."

In the second case, *Adarand Constructors, Inc. v. Peña*, Randy Pech challenges the ability of federal officials to use his race to deny him government contracts on which he is low bidder. *Adarand* is the case in which the Supreme Court of the United States issued its landmark ruling on race-based decision making a year ago. Now back in federal district court in Colorado, Pech asserts that awarding contracts on the basis of race violates the Constitution's equal protection guarantee.

In *Adarand*, federal lawyers argue that since Pech receives contracts that enable his small, family-owned company to be successful, the fact that he is denied other contracts because of his race is irrelevant. The clear implication is that Pech makes too much money to argue that his civil rights have been violated.

Taken together, these two cases paint a remarkable picture of just who, according to Reno's lawyers, may ask a federal court to determine whether constitutional rights have been violated. In their view, such a person's annual income must not be "too little" (Petefish) or "too much" (Pech), but must be "just right." Goldilocks would be proud.

While the Wyoming and Colorado federal district courts hearing these two cases will likely reject this Goldilocks' approach to constitutional law, it is unlikely that the courts will criticize the government for making the arguments. One of the reasons government lawyers raise such arguments is to signal potential litigants that the federal government will do all in its power to overwhelm its adversaries, dramatically increasing the cost, in time and money, of fighting the government, not to mention the frustration level. The other reason is that, like Goldilocks' thievery from the Three Bears, it can get away with it.

JULY 1996

HUMAN BEINGS—THE MISSING LINK

I saw it again this summer: in a national park gift shop, perhaps a book-store, or maybe a souvenir stand. Emblazoned on a t-shirt, like the hun-dreds of other times I have seen it on posters, plaques, and fundraising appeals: "'The Earth does not belong to man; man belongs to the Earth.' Chief Seattle."

The first time I heard it was 1981, when U.S. Senator Dale Bumpers (D-AR) began his questioning of one of President Reagan's appointees by reading Chief Seattle's response to the offer of President Pierce to buy his tribe's land. Some 115 years before the modern environmental movement, Chief Seattle, sounding like a prophetic visionary, warned of the dangers of pollution, the loss of habitat, the extinction of wild creatures, and the value of wilderness areas. Most striking, however, was the Chief's view of the relationship between his people and the land: to them all nature was divine. Chief Seattle saw the defining difference between the red man and the white, as being that, for the latter, "The earth is not his brother."

Thus Chief Seattle was more than an environmental Cassandra, he was the first advocate of a belief system that would find expression in the view-point of New Age mystics and radical environmentalists that mankind is a despoiler of the planet.

Bumpers' Chief Seattle, however, is a myth, "his words" written in 1970 by screenwriter Ted Perry. That is what Paula Wissel reported on National Public Radio in 1991, quoting one authority with the Seattle Museum of History and Industry who said Perry "couldn't find an 1850s Indian Chief who spoke in 1970s environmentalese," so he made one up. NPR was not the first or the last to write of the hoax. The Seattle Museum did so in papers published in 1983 and 1984, including, "The Myth of Chief Seattle's Environmental Manifesto." Marjorie Mazel Hecht wrote similarly, "Chief Seattle Myth Bites the Dust," in the fall 1991 issue of *21st Century Science & Technology*. Nonetheless, the myth lives on.

There are two problems when history is written, not by scholars and historians, but by screenwriters and hysterics. First, how can we keep from repeating the mistakes of the past if, for example, what we know of the death of President Kennedy and the life of Chief Seattle comes from Oliver Stone and Ted Perry? Second, when those with an agenda put today's words in the mouths of historical figures, what those men and women sought to tell us is lost. Thus it is with Chief Seattle.

Chief Seattle's speech was not an antecedent of modern day environmentalism or New Age mysticism. In fact, the most analogous work to Chief Seattle's speech is not Al Gore's *Earth in the Balance: Ecology and the Human Spirit*, but Rabbi Harold Kushner's *When Bad Things Happen to Good People*. Chief Seattle strives to come to terms with what happened to his people: "Your God loves your people and hates mine; he folds his strong arms lovingly around the white man and leads him as a father leads his infant son, but he has forsaken his red children."

There is another lesson Chief Seattle teaches us. It is not, as radical environmentalists wish, that the Earth is sacred in and of itself. Something more is required: the human touch. For Chief Seattle "[e]very part of this country is sacred," not because the Earth is a holy, living thing, but because '[e]very hillside, every valley, every plain and grove, has been hallowed by some fond memory or some sad experience of my tribe." Thus it is the "past events connected with the fate of my people" that gives special meaning to the land, not the land itself.

How far removed Chief Seattle's sentiments are from the statements of radical environmentalists, such as that by one National Park Service employee who denounces human happiness and productivity, calls mankind a cancer on the planet, and hopes for "the right virus to come along."

AUGUST 1996

A NICE PLACE TO VISIT, BUT YOU WOULD NOT WANT TO MINE THERE

In August, President Clinton completed another vacation in Jackson, Wyoming. Clinton's decision to come to Wyoming for a second year and what he did while he was here demonstrate his views about the West: "It's a nice place to visit, but I wouldn't want people to work there."

In a much ballyhooed photo opportunity in Yellowstone National Park, Clinton signed an agreement that, if consummated, will kill the New World Mine and its development of a gold, copper, silver deposit in southern Montana. That signing culminated a year-long effort by Clinton and by officials in his administration to kill the mine, and a nearly ten-year war by environmental groups and Hollywood celebrities against development of the $650 million ore body. Clinton's involvement began during his first vacation in Wyoming when he announced a mining claim moratorium on 4,500 acres of federal land near the deposit.

Discussions between the mining company and the Clinton administration had been ongoing since Clinton sought to stop the mine and after the United Nations declared Yellowstone National Park "endangered" as a result of timber harvesting, tourism, wildlife management, and mining in the 26-million acre Greater Yellowstone Area. The rush to consummate an agreement on Monday, August 12, however, was prompted by the Republican National Convention in San Diego, by Clinton's western presence, and by the impending release of a federal study on the New World Mine.

According to insiders, the environmental impact statement (EIS) being prepared by the U.S. Forest Service along with the State of Montana would have concluded that the mine could have been operated safely without damaging the environment. That would have been good news for working men and women in the region since the proposed mine would have employed 175 people year-round at an average annual salary of $35,000 (compared to the area's current annual average of $16,000), plus benefits. An additional eighty secondary jobs would have been created with the expenditure of $7 million annually on goods and services in the local economy. Annual tax revenues would have exceeded $2.33 million.

No doubt aware that the EIS document would calm fears generated by the $1 million public relations war waged by environmentalists against the mine, environmental officials and Clinton administration negotiators moved quickly to render the EIS finding irrelevant. Thus, as a result of the Clinton announcement, an informed public debate based on facts, not fear, that considers scientific evidence, not scary epistles from the likes of Robert Redford and the *New York Times*, will never take place.

The irony is that the area that Clinton declared off limits to mining has been a mining site ever since the white man first came west. As early as 1875, ore was being smelted there. By 1952, gold production in the area helped to make Park County, Montana, the third highest gold producing area in the state. In 1978, when Congress created the Absaroka-Beartooth Wilderness Area, it excluded the mining area as a result of the U.S. Geological Survey's prediction of future mineral development.

There is much that could be said regarding Clinton's killing of the New World Mine. For example, why the pell-mell rush to judgment before all the facts were in? Why were the governors of Wyoming and Montana not consulted prior to the unilateral federal action killing jobs in their states? If a century old mining district is not a good site for a mine, what is? If one of the richest ore bodies in the West is not worth developing, what economic activity in the West will Clinton ever deem worthy?

The bottom line is that Clinton, as his two vacations here make clear, views the West in the same manner as environmental extremists do: as a vast park through which they might drive, drinking their Perrier and munching their organic chips, staying occasionally in rural bed-and-breakfast establishments with those westerners who remain fluffing duvets and pouring cappuccinos.

SEPTEMBER 1996

"TAKE NO PRISONERS"

For the second consecutive month, President Clinton came West, sat in a beautiful place, surrounded himself with environmental leaders, and did an ugly thing. On August 12, in Yellowstone National Park, Clinton announced a plan to prevent the mining of a $650 million ore body in Montana. A month later, on September 18, in Grand Canyon National Park, Clinton decreed a land lockup twice the size of Yellowstone to kill development of a $1 trillion coal deposit—America's largest.

In both instances, Clinton not only disregarded the will of westerners, but refused to advise the states' elected officials of what he was about to do. Clinton's actions are not only disdainful of the West, they are also detrimental to the nation: Americans will be denied hundreds of billions of dollars of new wealth that would have pulsed through the nation's economy, generating jobs, opportunity, and tax revenues. The greatest impact will be upon the West, where hundreds of high paying jobs will be lost to local economies struggling to hang on.

What Clinton did with his Utah decision (announced from more than 100 miles away in Arizona) was not, as U.S. Senator Orrin Hatch (R-UT) said, to "declare[] war on the West." He did that in early 1993. What he did was to declare that he would take no prisoners. While Bob Dole and Jack Kemp openly court the vote of African Americans—who voted overwhelmingly for Clinton in 1992—Clinton punishes westerners. The media is virtually silent about such cynical mean-spiritedness.

It is not just mean. For a politician who campaigned that "it's the economy," it's stupid. Mining of the coal deposit would have meant 1,000 jobs in Utah, $1 million in annual revenues for Utah's Kane County, and $10 million a year in state and federal taxes, not to mention $2 billion or more in royalties to Utah's public school system. Clinton's asinine remark, "We can't have mines everywhere," demonstrates his ignorance of the rarity of a coal deposit like the one at the Kaiparowits Plateau.

Nor does Clinton favor jobs in tourism over those in mining. While at the Grand Canyon he planned to kill the $250 million a year industry in which 1,200 westerners allow 800,000 tourists annually to see the Grand Canyon, in the only way possible for many of them, by overflight along carefully regulated corridors. As if that were not enough, the Clinton administration plans to release the endangered condor in southern Utah to fly over an area the size of Ohio, further threatening economic activity.

Clinton's Utah land lock up may also be illegal. The Antiquities Act of 1906, under whose authority Clinton took his unilateral action, limits the power of the president to "historic landmarks, historic and prehistoric structures, and other objects of historic or scientific interest." A reading of what was said at Clinton's photo opportunity on the edge of the Grand Canyon reveals frequent mention of things "beautiful," but next to nothing about things of "historic or scientific interest." In addition, despite the requirement of the Antiquities Act that presidential action "be confined to the smallest area" possible, Clinton's decree was exceedingly broad. For example, swept up in Clinton's expansive ban are lands granted to the State of Utah for the education of its children, another potential violation of law.

Clinton's promise to protect "valid existing rights" within the new monument will last as long as, in Congresswoman Susan Molinari's words, "a Big Mac aboard Air Force One." Clinton's Justice Department has argued before an entire U.S. Court of Appeals that the phrase, "valid existing rights," in the words of one judge who heard it, is "meaningless."

Clinton's actions in Utah mean one thing: he is beholden to the most radical element of his party, extremists who demand the sacrifice of people upon the altar of environmental purity. In his War on the West, Clinton is willing to make that sacrifice.

OCTOBER 1996

THE ELECTION
ENVIRONMENTALISTS COULD NOT BUY

If the oft-repeated litany of President Clinton and Vice President Al Gore is any indication, "the environment" was to have been a winning issue for Democrats during the 1996 election. Since December of 1995, Clinton had been proclaiming his support for "Medicare, Medicaid, education, and the environment," as if the phrase were a mantra, the mere intoning of which guaranteed his reelection. Al Gore's robot-like recitation of that incantation in his debate with Jack Kemp showed he was programmed similarly.

Leaving nothing to chance, government unions (labor bosses now preside over a membership that works predominantly for governments) and affluent environmental groups waged a vicious and well-financed nationwide campaign, estimated at between $35 and $100 million, against Republican candidates, allegedly because they opposed "the environment." One would be forgiven for being perplexed, however, over where "the environment" was a deciding factor in the election or defeat of any particular candidate, from president on down. In other words, why so little bang for the tens of millions of bucks expended nationally by union and environmental leaders?

Perhaps the nation's premier battle over "the environment" was that pitting Colorado Congressman Wayne Allard (R-4th) against Denver lawyer Tom Strickland for the seat of retiring U.S. Senator Hank Brown (R-CO). Allard, a veterinarian and a conservative three-term congressman, was an overwhelming underdog to Strickland, the wealthy, handsome, and articulate candidate of the nation's powerful environmental organizations. If ever there were a state that fits Interior Secretary Babbitt's definition of the "New West" it is Colorado. It voted for Clinton in 1992 and was predicted to do so again. Nonetheless, on Election Day both Bob Dole and Wayne Allard won. Clinton's impassioned advocacy of "the environment" did not win him as many votes as his "War on the West" lost him (especially after his 1.7 million acre Escalante Escapade). Dole, saying he would end the "War on the West," carried Colorado.

Allard stunned Strickland and the prognosticators who thought the sophisticated, media-savvy, environmental lawyer Strickland, who campaigned as if Allard's middle name were Gingrich, would overwhelm folksy

Wayne Allard, the friend of rural Colorado. Aping Clinton's litany, Strickland sought to make "the environment" the issue. It was, but not in the way Strickland envisioned. Allard successfully labeled Strickland a "lawyer lobbyist," one who had become rich representing corporate efforts to obtain relief from overly burdensome environmental laws with which all everyday Coloradoans must comply. While Allard did not say so, the subtext was clear: Strickland was another environmental extremist who believes that radical environmental policies should apply to everyone but those who can afford his services.

Elsewhere in the West, conservative defenders of western economic activity and property rights won despite the hundreds of thousands and even millions of dollars spent against them. Arizona's J.D. Hayworth (R-6th), Idaho's Helen Chenoweth (R-1st), Montana's Rick Hill (R-AL), Nevada's John Ensign (R-1st), and Washington's George Nethercutt (R-5th) emerged victorious. Some conservatives were defeated, but those races had much more to do with individual factors and the states that the Dole campaign wrote off. In Maine and Washington State, which Dole wrote off early, for example, conservative, property rights candidates lost when Clinton beat Dole by 21 and 15 point respectively. (Thus Republican defeats in New England had more to do with Dole's abandonment of the region than with the views of the rest of the ticket. Dole's last minute return to New Hampshire—drawing to within 10 points of Clinton—no doubt saved conservative U.S. Senator Bob Smith.)

There was one race, however, that was determined by Clinton's views on "the environment." Utah took out its fury for Clinton's monument decree on three-term Congressman Bill Orton (D-3rd), who lost to Chris Cannon. Thus, in places where "the environment" is what is done to someone else, the issue did not matter, but where "the environment" means what happens locally, it lost votes for Clinton and his friends. Republicans take note!

DECEMBER 1996

CHAPTER EIGHT

Crimes Against Nature

———

On February 12, 1997, Abraham Lincoln's birthday, I was in Washington, D.C. at the Independent Women's Forum as it honored MSLF's clients Randy and Valery Pech for their courage in fighting racial preferences. Ward Connerly, who played a key role in ending state-sponsored discrimination with passage the previous November of Proposition 209—the California Civil Rights Initiative, received the Lincoln Leadership Award for Civic Virtue, for "leadership, courage, and integrity as an advocate of equal opportunity for all Americans." Later, Valery Pech spoke of her experiences.

"Randy and I know what it is like to be on the receiving end of abuse. During our long fight, the most insulting thing was the portrayal of Randy as an 'angry white man,' [which] was insulting because this battle was not Randy's alone. It never was and isn't now. It is our battle, both of us. When we started our company in 1976, we had more women than men owners, all family except one close friend. We were told many times that we should be certified as a 'WBE' a woman business enterprise, and so qualify for our piece of the quota pie. We refused to do that because we believe quotas are wrong! We didn't want and don't want to be judged by the sex or race of the owners or operators of our company. We did and do want to be judged on the basis of the quality and timeliness of our work, and the amount of our bid. A good highway guardrail is a good highway guardrail, regardless of the race or sex of its builder—that's what we believe. The battle we fought was Randy's and my battle for yet another reason. Men, being men, bear the injuries and insults of the business world stoically. Women are not so similarly inclined. We women have seen the pain suffered when our sons and husbands are judged, not by who they are or what they can do but instead, by their race or their gender—and we don't like it one bit. If anyone is angry, it is we mothers and wives."

GRASSROOTS NEW YEAR'S RESOLUTIONS

It will come as no surprise that property rights advocates and those seeking to make people part of the environmental equation face remarkable challenges in 1997. For those making New Year's resolutions, I offer the following to win those battles. To begin, decide to get involved, then do it. Where to start? Here is my list.

First: Save the children. One look at the Saturday morning cartoons and what passes for politically correct environmental "facts" in school demonstrates why children swallow animal "rights," dislike business, believe the nation is running out of trees and every other resource, and are convinced that pollution will doom the planet. Children can be saved from all this nonsense.

After all, children are incredible optimists. Though filled full of gloomy stories the only cure for which is a generous contribution to an environmental organization, children naturally rebel against such dreary predictions. Not surprisingly, children believe in technology. Although Vice President Al Gore opined in *Earth in the Balance* that "we are not that clever, and we never have been," children know that we are "that clever." Only environmental extremists believe technology is the problem and not the solution. It is up to us to give children the facts and to restore their hope, not just in the future, but in humankind. That begins at home and then must continue in our schools.

Second: Communicate with our communities. Too few know how important the economic activities in which we engage are to the well-being of their community. A first step in any grassroots campaign is to educate the local community, whether with lawn signs or lectures to societies and groups. The victories we have had, and there are a wealth of them, are stories of local activism. That is where it all starts.

Third: Make employees part of the solution. For too long American industry, bending over backwards to be a good corporate citizen, has given the impression that it can pay any price, bear any burden. Forgotten in such feel good rhetoric are the men and women who suddenly find their jobs sacrificed on the altar of politically correct environmentalism. These people have the right to know about all relevant public policy issues. They have the right to fight for their jobs.

Fourth: Communicate with people through the media. We all love to hate the media, often with good reason. But like it or not, it is the only game in town. If it is not reported by the media, it has not happened. The key to media exposure is knowledge and expertise combined with a desire to be heard. Become a source of information for members of the media. Talk to reporters, editors, and editorial boards. Write articles and letters to the editors. Volunteer as a guest on talk shows and call in to express your point of view.

Fifth: The world is run by those who show up. Show up! In the early years of the environmental movement, environmental activists filled meeting halls and protested outside government and corporate offices. Now they are running those government agencies from the inside and, through litigation and congressional oversight, from the outside. It is our turn "to show up." The fact that Secretary Babbitt was not appointed to the Supreme Court of the United States, even though he was clearly President Clinton's first choice, demonstrates the impact of grassroots activism and showing up.

Sixth: Help your friends. Perhaps the most important undertaking is to join and support those who share your views. There are scores of organizations out there fighting for your point of view, your rights, your liberties. All of them desperately need one thing: more members. They also need the five "p's" of any good grassroots organization: presence, participation, passion, prayers, and patronage.

The key is to start now! As one anonymous source once put it poetically: "Count that day lost whose low descending sun; views from thy hand no worthy action done."

JANUARY 1997

"ANY PERSON" MEANS "ANY PERSON!"

When farmers in Oregon were denied irrigation water to which they had a legal right as a result of the federal government's plan to "save" two types of sucker fish, the farmers sued. Asserting that the U.S. Fish and Wildlife Service (FWS) had violated the Endangered Species Act (ESA), they asked a federal judge to stop the government from taking their water. The farmers' allegations—that there was no evidence that the fish was endangered or that the FWS's plan would help the fish—are serious questions, meriting judicial review. The Clinton administration, however, opposed any such inquiry, arguing that the farmers had no right to be in court.

Remarkably, the district court and the U.S. Court of Appeals for the Ninth Circuit agreed! The Ninth Circuit held that, although the ESA provides that "any person" may sue to force the federal government to obey the ESA, the farmers were not "any person" because they were not seeking the preservation of species. The farmers were not "any person," the court ruled, because they lack "a commonality of interest" with the fish.

It was this astonishing ruling that the Supreme Court of the United States addressed in *Bennett v. Spear* and discarded in an opinion last week. That the decision was a "no brainer" was demonstrated by the unanimous opinion and by its author—Justice Scalia—who has been harshly critical of arguments propounded by environmental groups. Concluded Justice Scalia, "[T]here is no [statutory] basis for saying that [the right to sue] applies to environmentalists alone." Rejected as well were three Clinton administration arguments that the farmers could not sue.

First, Clinton's lawyers asserted that the farmers were not hurt since less water for the region did not mean less water for them; and, if injured, the farmers were injured, not by the FWS's Biological Opinion, but by the U.S. Bureau of Reclamation's response to that opinion. Second, Clinton's lawyers claimed the Biological Opinion was not "final agency action," therefore it was not reviewable by a court. Justice Scalia made quick work of both, holding that the Biological Opinion was a final decision because it had "direct and appreciable legal consequences," and that it caused the farmers' injury due to the "substantial civil and criminal penalties, including imprisonment," for violating it.

Justice Scalia also rejected Clinton's lawyers' third argument, that the farmers have no right to sue under the ESA because the ESA protects the interests of fish, not farmers. Justice Scalia, while noting that portions of the farmers' lawsuit were not permitted under the ESA, found ample authority for them in the Administrative Procedure Act. As to the interests served by the ESA's requirement for "the best scientific and commercial data available," Justice Scalia found "[t]he obvious purpose of the requirement" is "to ensure that the ESA not be implemented haphazardly, on the basis of speculation or surmise." "[W]e think it readily apparent that another objective (if not indeed the primary one) is to avoid needless economic dislocation produced by agency officials zealously but unintelligently pursuing their environmental objectives."

The Supreme Court's decision drives a stake through the heart of the Clinton administration and environmental groups' assertion that only friends of the ESA may go to court for violations of the ESA. The fact, however, that those who seek to require federal officials to obey environmental laws to prevent them from hurting people had to fight so hard for so simple a right—to be heard in court—reveals the long road ahead. In addition, the overheated response of environmental groups to the decision (the Clinton administration called it a "crushing blow") shows that environmental extremists (like those in the White House) will brook no compromise on environmental issues, not even something so fundamental as the right of all parties to be heard in court. We might remember that the next time someone asks us to find the "common ground" with environmentalists.

APRIL 1997

THE GULF THAT SEPARATES US

Recently I was interviewed by a college student who was writing a paper on the Endangered Species Act (ESA). Early in the interview she asked, "I have the impression that one principle that guides you is your belief that human beings are more important than other creatures. Is that true and why?" I told her it was true and was based on a fundamental precept of Judeo-Christian theology—that only mankind was created in the image of God and thus imbued, by God, with an everlasting soul. I told her that while mankind has important stewardship responsibilities toward creatures and the Earth, mankind's most important responsibility is to other human beings. She said my viewpoint is a rarity on her college campus.

It is also a rarity among radical environmentalists and members of the media. Bruce Vincent of Libby, Montana, tells of being interviewed by a reporter from one of the major television networks. When Bruce was asked, "What's more important, humans or grizzly bears?" he replied with a question. "If a grizzly bear came into the yard and carried away your cameraman Peter, which one would you shoot?" In answer, the reporter turned to his cameraman, "Sorry, Peter," he said. Or take the environmental extremist, quoted by *National Review*, who when asked about a jogger killed by a mountain lion stated: "It's too bad for her, but we can always get more human beings; we can't replace the mountain lion."

The belief system that drives many environmental extremists is much more than a view that animals are deserving of protection from cruelty or wanton destruction. It is that mankind has no higher moral value than do animals and trees and plants, and maybe, given mankind's "destructive" habits, even less. As a result, mankind has no special claim to privileges or priority, not even when it means survival.

Not surprisingly given the environmental radicalism espoused by Vice President Gore and Secretary Babbitt that belief system is finding its way into governmental policy. One example was the refusal by a panel of the U.S. Department of Defense to grant conscientious objector (CO) status to a medical doctor, ruling that since he participated in killing life forms in a petri dish he was not really a CO! Today, Babbitt forges ahead with ESA protection for, of all things, an endangered fly in California—the Dehli

Sands flower-loving fruit fly—as reported this month by Ike Sugg in the *Wall Street Journal* as well as by Ted Turner's CNN.

For years, many believed that the Draconian and often nonsensical demands made by federal bureaucrats in the name of saving species could not make the politically insupportable jump from the "warm and fuzzy" species to the "cold and slimy" ones. The Clinton administration obviously believes that it can make that jump. Part of the reason the Clinton administration is committed to doing so is because the real purpose of the ESA is to place enormous power in the hands of federal bureaucrats, including the power to stop economic activity. Another reason is that, at the core, the essence of the Gore/Babbitt belief system is "who is mankind to object to the needs of other creatures?"

One of the greatest sermons of the 20th century was one called "The Weight of Glory" by C.S. Lewis delivered at Oxford in 1940. Said Lewis: "There are no ordinary people. You have never talked to a mere mortal. Nations, cultures, arts, civilizations—these are mortal, and their life is to ours as the life of a gnat. But it is immortals whom we joke with, work with, marry, snub and exploit. . . . Next to the Blessed Sacrament itself, your neighbor is the holiest object presented to your senses."

The college student interviewing me asked if I had any other basis for my belief system, "other than religion," and I said no, that was enough for me.

MAY 1997

DEVILS TOWER CLOSURE
IS NOT ABOUT RELIGION

Imagine, if out of "respect" for Moslems, all women had to be covered to enter federal buildings. Imagine, if out of "respect" for Jewish dietary laws, park concessionaires were prohibited from serving certain foods. Imagine, if out of "respect" for the religion of Americans Indians, Colorado's Aspen Mountain were closed to skiing during December.

That is the nature of the legal battle over the decision by the National Park Service (NPS) to close Devils Tower, in Wyoming's northeastern corner, to recreational climbing in June and to off-trail hiking year round! (Last year a federal court found the NPS's first closure plan unconstitutional; that court is considering the NPS's latest scheme in a lawsuit brought by Mountain States Legal Foundation on behalf of climbers.) The NPS says "respect" for the religion of some American Indians requires that non-Indians not use Devils Tower—America's first national monument—as it has been used since 1893, for climbing. American Indians, however, may climb Devils Tower as part of their religion.

This is not about "respect" for or even "accommodation" of religion. American Indians wishing to worship at Devils Tower are guaranteed free access at any time. What they have demanded, however, and what the NPS has granted, is that the NPS keep all others away from Devils Tower during June. To analogize to missions or churches within park units, that demand would be like excluding visitors from, and even barring their approach to those missions and churches.

Only in the NPS's Orwellian world could its ban on recreational climbing be called "voluntary," since if people climb despite the ban, the NPS will make the closure "mandatory." Wyoming federal district court Judge Downes ruled that, if people are "coerced" by the threat, it is unconstitutional.

Only the NPS believes that its hiring of an American Indian to proselytize on federal land is permissible. Imagine the outrage if the NPS hired Mormon missionaries, evangelical Christians, or Catholic priests to instruct on their faith. While people may espouse their beliefs in public places, they cannot do so at government expense.

What is at stake is not simply the ability of "a few rock climbers" to climb on federal land set aside for, among other purposes, climbing, but the ability of the Clinton administration to deny public access to federal land because the land is "sacred." If successful in this gambit—after all, who cares about rock climbers—then the Clinton administration can say "No" to every use of federal land, including: hiking, camping, fishing, grazing, timber harvesting, oil and gas, or mineral exploration and development, or even skiing. In fact, it has; the U.S. Forest Service refused to expand the Santa Fe (New Mexico) Ski Area due to religious objections.

The NPS plan for Devils Tower is before Wyoming's Judge Downes, whose decision is expected at any time. As important as that decision is—for visitors to Devils Tower and for other federal lands alleged to be "sacred"—it is also preordained since the U.S. Court of Appeals for the Tenth Circuit and the Supreme Court of the United States have decided this question. In 1980, the Tenth Circuit held that the "[e]xercise of First Amendment freedoms may not be asserted to deprive the public of its normal use of an area," declaring that there is "no basis in law for . . . the government to exclude the public from public areas to insure privacy during the exercise of First Amendment rights." In 1988, the Supreme Court held that American Indians "or similarly situated religious objectors" could not "seek to exclude all human activity but their own from sacred areas of the public lands."

If the NPS has trouble understanding the U.S. Constitution, maybe it can read its own policy statement: "Performance of a traditional ceremony or the conduct of a religious activity at a particular place shall not form the basis for prohibiting others from using such areas."

JUNE 1997

AIR QUALITY: EAST MEETS WEST

Within the past few days summer has come to the American West, carrying with it visions of long hot days, weekends by the pool, picnics, and family vacations. For westerners in timber country, however, summer brings a more frightening specter: forest fires! The rains of spring are gone. The thick green vegetation they engendered through the valleys and along the hillsides will soon brown in the summer heat, a heat that will cook the moisture out of the needles of the conifers that stretch like a green carpet across our western states. As summer brings both storms with lightning but little rain, and the occasional careless visitor, the dried grasses and timber (drier even than the wood stacked at a lumber yard) will, with a bolt of lightning high in the trees, or a discarded match, or unwatched fire low in the grasses, ignite and burn.

Why those fires will burn hotter and more dangerously than ever is another modern reality in the West. Today millions of acres of federal timberlands are covered with pines that are diseased, dying, or dead. Lawsuits filed by environmental groups and skewed interpretations of federal laws have prevented timber harvests and allowed fuel buildup (both of toppled dead wood that is as much as 12 feet deep and of standing dead trees) to reach an all-time high.

Over three years ago, *USA Today* environmental reporter Linda Kanamine wrote, "Federal forests from Idaho to Mexico are so crowded and stressed that fiery disasters loom—unless at least half the trees are cut down." The situation is even worse today; each year of the Clinton administration fewer trees were harvested, and more fuel built up. Deadly fires in 1994 and a worse fire season in 1996 were the result. Many fear that, someday soon, the disastrous blaze of 1910—when three million acres burned in a weekend in northwestern Montana—might reoccur. Could it be this summer? A just released study of northwestern Montana's federal timber illustrates how extreme is the danger.

The Clinton administration's response has been to call for more man-made fires. Bruce Babbitt, speaking in February of 1997 in Boise, Idaho, called, euphemistically, for the reintroduction of fire to the ecosystem. In other words, he seeks to burn what he and his allies in the radical environmental community refuse to permit to be harvested. While all knowledgeable forest experts agree that fire has a role to play, it cannot play that role now. There is simply too much fuel. Without thoughtful harvests to clear out the dangerously high fuel loads, any fire, including "planned fires," will burn too hot, too long, and too quickly out of control. (That assumes fire is susceptible to surgical-like introduction, control, and safe exit, which it is not!)

There is something else, which Babbitt admitted in his Boise speech. As he so quaintly put it, "where there's fire, there's smoke." Not really a problem, he asserted. After all, he says, scientists report air in the West is "too clean." That will come as news to EPA Administrator Carol Browner who is rushing headlong, without any scientific basis, to adopt new air quality regulations that will damage huge sectors of the economy while tripling the number of counties not in compliance with federal law. Browner asserts that America's air, including the air in the rural counties most affected by her new standards, is so dirty it threatens children's lives. One of her scientists, however, admits that these standards are not based on "strict science." What they are based on is "weird science," like Babbitt's new timber policy.

George Orwell, author of *Nineteen Eighty-Four*, once wrote, "Political language ... is designed to make lies sound truthful ... and to give an appearance of solidity to pure wind." The Clinton administration, in a discussion of air quality issues in which East meets West, has mastered that "political language."

JULY 1997

CALL FOR HUMAN SACRIFICE ANSWERED?

In May of 1994, *Denver Post* environmental writer Mark Obmascik welcomed the return of wolves to Yellowstone National Park with this: "Wolves are killers.... They don't think fawns are cute and cuddly; wolves look at Bambi and see fresh meat. Sometimes wolves look at humans the same way.... [T]hey have been known to order up an occasional course of *Homo sapiens*[, which] could serve as a rude awakening for hordes of recent western visitors who now view the back country as an adventure theme park.... People will think twice before traipsing into the back country."

Obmascik's call for human sacrifice was answered recently; however, it did not happen quite the way he envisioned, by one of Babbitt's imported wolves. Nor was the victim some windshield tourist, tastelessly attired in ill-fitting, gaudy Bermuda shorts, carrying 30 extra pounds and the latest video cam, who left his car running in the middle of the road on the way to Old Faithful Lodge so he could follow buffalo into an open field.

The call was answered instead by a cougar in Colorado and the victim was a ten-year-old Denver, Colorado, boy described as an exuberant young outdoorsman, with a "vibrant smile and boundless energy," who loved to hike and camp with his family. Hiking with his family in Rocky Mountain National Park, Mark Miedema was attacked and killed by an 88-pound mountain lion. That is the trouble with calls by Obmascik, and others like him, for the loss of human life to achieve some environmental objective. Although such suggestions are made in the abstract, the loss of human life does not happen in the abstract, or to some nameless, unknown victim far, far away. It happens to real, beautiful human beings like Mark Miedema who leave family and friends behind.

Although Miedema's death is the first mountain lion fatality in Rocky Mountain National Park, it is the second such death in Colorado in recent years. In 1991, an 18-year-old runner, Scott Lancaster, was killed near Idaho Springs. Just three days before the attack on Miedema, a four-year-old from France was attacked, but survived, in Colorado's Mesa Verde National Park. In California, a couple of years ago, 40-year-old Barbara Barsalou Schoener of Placerville was killed by a mountain lion while jogging. *National Review* reported that a California environmentalist responded, "It's too bad for the woman, but we can always get more people. We can't replace the mountain lion." Remarkably, the *Denver Post* adopted a somewhat similar tone regarding Mark Miedema's death in Rocky Mountain National Park. Its lead editorial, and only one, on the subject was entitled, "Respecting the cougar," and closed with a paean to the animal: "beautiful predator, dangerous and strong."

Despite the rhetoric from environmental extremists, we are not in danger of losing the mountain lion. Twenty years ago there were 400 mountain lions in Colorado; today there are as many as 3,000. Not only are they moving into more populated areas, but also, as the chief spokesman for the Colorado Division of Wildlife pointed out, "[W]hen they were hunted regularly, they had a good reason to fear us. Now they don't."

Now it is the people who are fearful, of cougars in Colorado and California, of wolves in Wyoming, and of grizzly bears in northwestern Montana, all due to plans by environmental activists to "recover" predators into the backyards of living human beings. Only their remarkably misplaced priorities—that wildlife and not their fellow human beings deserve their sympathy and solicitude—permit them to forge ahead when others might be given pause.

As we pray for Mark Miedema's family and friends who suffered this incredible and incalculable loss, perhaps we can say a prayer for people like Obmascik, whose love of nature has blinded them to what is truly of value in this life.

AUGUST 1997

A CITIZEN'S FIRST DUTY

Recently I debated a National Park Service (NPS) official on the agency's scheme to close Devils Tower to climbing every June out of "respect" for some American Indians who believe the Tower is sacred. She related how the NPS group met, at first disagreed, but after they "shared" with and hugged one another, conceded it was acceptable to close the Tower each year for a month. Asked how I "felt" about such warm and fuzzy consensus, I responded, "That's why we have a Constitution. So that people don't get together and give up the rights of everyone not at the meeting."

I was reminded of that debate on reading the decision of the Supreme Court of the United States in *Printz v. United States*, its last decision before adjourning in June. In *Printz*, the Court held unconstitutional the Brady Act and its requirement that state officers enforce a federal program. The opinion makes fascinating and educational reading as Justice Scalia gives a history lesson on the origins of our federal system, the views of its creators, and the manner in which it has been interpreted for 200 years. Our system is, holds Justice Scalia, one of "dual sovereignty," in which the states, while surrendering many powers, retained "a residuary and inviolable sovereignty." That "inviolable sovereignty" was breached when the Brady Act pressed, or, in the words of one jurist, "dragooned," state officers into federal service.

Although Justice Scalia based his holding on the Tenth Amendment ("The powers not delegated to the United States by the Constitution, nor prohibited by it to the States, are reserved to the States respectively, or to the people."), he noted that "numerous constitutional provisions" ensure "dual sovereignty." To those who assert that those provisions are "formalistic" impediments to the "era's perceived necessity," Justice Scalia responded, "[T]he Constitution protects us from our own best intentions...the temptation to concentrate power in one location as an expedient solution to the crisis of the day."

Over the past few years, our leaders have played fast and loose with constitutional provisions created to safeguard our liberty, seeing them as troublesome impediments to vital legislation. The adoption, in 1993, of a fuel tax increase that did not "originate," as the Constitution requires, in the House of Representatives, and the adoption, in 1990, of the Gun Free

School Zones Act, which pushed local law enforcement aside in violation of the Commerce Clause, are, along with the Brady Act, three examples.

Expect more such threats to liberty. We are told there is a crisis regarding crime, so we must give up our guns. We are told there is a health care crisis, so we must give up one-seventh of our economy to government management. We are told there is an environmental crisis, so we must give up our right to own and use private property.

We are the inheritors of the greatest political system ever devised by humankind, which recognizes, uniquely, that "all men are created equal, [and] are endowed by their Creator with certain unalienable rights, [including] life, liberty, and the pursuit of happiness." With that freedom, however, comes an obligation, as the Constitution commands, to "secure the blessings of liberty to ourselves and our posterity. . . ."

We hear a lot today about the legacy that we pass on to our children and grandchildren, our posterity: the national debt, the environment, a diverse society. The most important legacy we can leave, that we are duty bound to leave, however, is the constitutional system entrusted to us by our Founding Fathers. It would be the greatest tragedy if out of apathy, or expediency, or short-term self-interest, we allowed the destruction of the only thing that ensures that we remain a free people.

As Justice Oliver Wendell Holmes once wrote, "a strong public desire to improve the public condition is not enough to warrant achieving the desire by a shorter cut than the constitutional way. . . ."

SEPTEMBER 1997

CLINTON'S RIVERS INITIATIVE:
POLITICS RUN THROUGH IT

President Clinton announced an American Heritage Rivers Initiative under which he intends to designate ten rivers annually as "American Heritage Rivers," appoint a federal overseer (River Navigator) for each river, and provide increased federal funding to make the rivers "models of innovative economic and ecologically sustainable approaches to river restoration and protection." The plan has elicited heated opposition from the West and rural America, which fear another layer of federal bureaucracy with authority to stifle economic activity and to restrict the use of private property.

Those fears are justified, especially considering the vague language of the plan and that so much remains to be decided. Nor is there legal authority for the program. (The White House assertion that the purposes section of the National Environmental Policy Act compels action is absurd.) In addition, it is Congress that regulates navigable waters and local governments that do land-use planning.

Lost in the controversy is something more fundamental: why? Given the haste with which Clinton moved on the river plan—he scuttled the *Federal Register* process to issue an Executive Order, rushing plans to name the first ten rivers by the end of the year—there must be some urgency. There is urgency: politics, and more specifically, Democratic political fortunes in the 1998 elections. According to U.S. House of Representatives Resources Committee staff, the first three rivers most likely to be named include: the Willamette in Oregon, the Yellowstone in Montana, and the Mississippi north of St. Louis. Each has tremendous political significance, especially if it is the recipient of a massive infusion of federal funds—diverted from other approved programs—delivered with great fanfare and Clinton's empathetic tender loving care.

For example, the Willamette River in Oregon borders both the First and Fifth Congressional Districts, held by Democrats who each won with a scant 52 percent of the vote. Moreover, after Oregon elected a conservative Republican U.S. Senator, Democrats cannot afford to have Oregon's seven electoral votes go the way of the rest of the rock solid Republican Rocky Mountain States.

Montana is increasingly Republican as a result of Clinton's War on the West; it went for Dole in 1996, elected a Republican to its at-large congressional seat, and nearly defeated a three-term Democratic Senator, who won with 50 percent of the vote. The Yellowstone River is in Yellowstone County, a Republican stronghold, which must go Republican by a wide margin for Republicans to carry Montana. If the margin is held to 2,000, Democrats carry the state.

It is the Mississippi River, north of St. Louis, however, that holds the most potential for Democrats. The region is Clinton's greatest strength, with Missouri, Illinois, Minnesota, Wisconsin, Iowa, and Kentucky, giving him 69 of the 270 electoral votes he needed in 1992 and 1996. Although Clinton lost some ground there in 1996, in the off-year elections of 1998, eight congressional seats will be in play, all along the Mississippi River. Those seats (with the 1996 margin of victory) include: Democrats must hold onto Illinois' 17th (52%), Wisconsin's 3rd (52%), Iowa's 3rd (49%), while trying to defeat Republicans in Minnesota's 1st (53%), Missouri's 9th (49%), Iowa's 1st (53%) and 2nd (53%), and Illinois' 20th (50%).

In all of these districts, the green of environmental group politics and the green of millions of federal dollars will make a potent political combination. Similar political calculations are possible for the other seven rivers to be designated before the end of 1997, not to mention the other twenty to be named by the year 2000. The result could be a Democratic House in 1999 and a smaller Republican margin in the U.S. Senate. But would President Clinton and his closest aides conspire with the Democratic National Committee to use an environmental initiative to influence the 1998 elections? Anyone who listened to Senator Fred Thompson's hearings or heard Senator Bob Bennett discuss why Clinton declared the Utah Monument can answer: in a New York minute!

OCTOBER 1997

CRIMES AGAINST NATURE

Years ago, when I was just starting out as an attorney, I worked on a criminal case in Wyoming that involved an alleged sexual assault. Since Wyoming had not changed the sexual assault portion of its criminal code after becoming a state in 1890, the statute contained provisions that today sound almost quaint, including, "and other crimes against nature." Nowadays, most sexual assault laws have no such language. While the phrase is rarely heard in that context, it is not dead yet. In compliant response to the demands of environmental groups, the Clinton administration prosecutes what amounts to "crimes against nature." Increasingly, government lawyers are ascribing to "nature" and "the environment" an attitude once reserved for human beings!

The U.S. Forest Service's prosecution of famed Indy driver Bobby Unser is a case in point. It was Unser who last December was caught in a blizzard while snowmobiling in a national forest in southern Colorado. So dangerous was the blizzard that Unser and a friend nearly died, endured one night in a snow cave, and spent two days hiking through waist-deep snow to safety.

When Unser approached the Forest Service about his missing snowmobiles, it cited him for use of a motorized vehicle in a wilderness area, a violation of federal law. Unser knows the wilderness area in question and the prohibition against motorized vehicles there. He also knows that when he began his snowmobile trip, when the sun was shining and the sky was clear and blue, he was far outside the wilderness boundary. Once the blizzard sprang upon him, however, when visibility dropped to less than three feet, and the wind chill plummeted, Unser had no idea where he was.

During that time, although it is still unclear, Unser may have strayed inadvertently into the wilderness area on his snowmobile. If he breached the wilderness boundary with a motorized vehicle, he did so inadvertently, or out of necessity, or during an emergency. Thus Unser lacked what lawyers call *mens rea*, or criminal intent; he did not intend to violate the law.

The Clinton administration, however, says that does not matter. It takes the position that regardless of Unser's situation or his state of mind, operating a motorized vehicle in a wilderness area is illegal since, in legalese, the Wilderness Act of 1964 has no *mens rea* requirement. Remarkably, the Colorado federal district court that heard Unser's case agreed!

The Supreme Court of the United States has held, repeatedly, that a *mens rea* requirement is the rule, rather than the exception, and is a fundamental principle of Anglo-American criminal law. Says the Court: "[*Mens rea*] is no provincial or transient notion. It is as universal and persistent in mature systems of law as belief in freedom of the human will and a consequent ability and duty of the normal individual to choose between good and evil."

Any attempt by Congress to deviate from this "first principle" must be stated clearly. Although the Wilderness Act contained no such renunciation of *mens rea*, Clinton's lawyers argued that the Wilderness Act is a "public welfare" statute and therefore *mens rea* is not required. Incredibly, again the court agreed! In the past, "public welfare" statutes were limited to activities that affect public health, safety, or welfare, and that pose a serious risk of danger or death to human beings; for example, dangerous drugs and hand grenades! In the Unser case, however, that protection has been extended to nature.

Unfortunately, Unser is not alone. All across the country, federal officials are ascribing to nature, to plants and animals, the same protective attitude once ascribed to human beings, and bringing criminal action against human beings for what amounts to "crimes against nature."

Today, as thoughtful Americans struggle with a nation that seems desensitized to human suffering, we should not limit our attention to what comes out of Hollywood. Increasingly, Washington, D.C. is demonstrating that, in its view, people are less important than nature.

NOVEMBER 1997

UTAH MONUMENT NOT IN THE "PUBLIC INTEREST"

Under the Property Clause (Article IV, Section 3, which reads: "The Congress shall have Power to dispose of and make all needful Rules and Regulations respecting the Territory or other Property belonging to the United States."), Congress has exclusive power to manage federal lands. Therefore, President Clinton's September 17, 1996, decree setting aside 1.7 million acres of land in Utah as a national monument, relies not on constitutional authority, but on the 1906 Antiquities Act.

With that statute, Congress authorized the president to set aside "historic" or "scientific" areas, limited to the "smallest area" necessary. Said the House Report: "The bill proposes to create small reservations reserving only so much land as may be absolutely necessary for the preservation of these interesting relics of prehistoric times." Added one federal official in 1911, "The terms of the [Antiquities Act] do not specify scenery, nor remotely refer to scenery as a possible *raison d'etre* for a public reservation."

Of course, over the decades, various presidents have ignored their limited authority under and the original purpose of the Antiquities Act by setting aside hundreds of thousands, instead of hundreds, of acres. These usurpations, however, do not mean they were legal. In fact, a Wyoming federal district court declared, "[I]f a monument were to be created on a bare stretch of sage-brush prairie in regard to which there was no substantial evidence that it contained objects of historic or scientific interest, the action ... would undoubtedly be arbitrary and capricious and clearly outside the scope and purpose of the Act." Nor did Congress sit idly by in the face of these presidential usurpations of power. For example, President Franklin Roosevelt's two hundred thousand acre monument decree in Wyoming did not stand. Although he vetoed Congress's abolition of the monument, Congress prevailed by dividing the monument into various classifications, including park lands. This is how constitutional federal lands decisions are to be made.

Congressional outrage over Antiquities Act abuses, like those of FDR, culminated in 1976, in the adoption of the Federal Land Policy and Management Act, when Congress reclaimed its full authority to set aside vast areas for special purposes. Congress kept the Antiquities Act for small "historic" or "scientific" set asides, but sharply limited large land withdrawals.

There are areas worthy of wilderness protection within the Grand Staircase-Escalante National Monument; their designation is supported by the Utah congressional delegation. There is also, however, a wealth of natural resources that can contribute to the Utah economy, without harming the environment: for example, a trillion dollar coal deposit, which could provide 1,000 jobs and an annual $15 million to the local economy; $2 billion of that coal is owned by Utah school children.

Clinton's defenders believe anyone concerned about jobs and economic activity is just a mouthpiece for "special interests," unlike environmental groups that espouse only the "public interest." Setting aside Utah Senator Bob Bennett's conclusion on reading secret White House documents that Clinton locked up Utah for political, not environmental, reasons, it strains credulity to say killing 1,000 jobs, turning our backs on $1 trillion worth of clean burning coal, and requiring the nation to pay $2 billion to Utah is in the "public interest." Most Americans believe we can protect the "scientific," "historic," and scenic areas and still make use of such valuable resources, but self-serving environmental groups say "No!" (Environmental groups lost the "public interest" label when they said 6.5 million electricity users and recreationists and a $500 million tourist economy should be "damned," not the Colorado River, in their call for draining Lake Powell.)

The legality of Clinton's "special interest" decree in Utah will be tested in court, while Congress will decide what limits it should place on the ostensible authority it granted to the president. In the meantime, Clinton's defenders would do well to learn more about the Constitution and to be more careful in what they label "public interest."

DECEMBER 1997

CHAPTER NINE

Grizzly Bears and Self-Defense

———

In December of 1994, when MSLF appeared before a Wyoming federal district court to oppose the Clinton administration plan to release Canadian wolves throughout Idaho, Montana, and Wyoming, MSLF and its clients stood alone. In fact, the federal attorney urged the court to take judicial notice that only the national and state Farm Bureaus and not the three states opposed the plan. The district court allowed the release, but in December of 1997 it changed its mind; the plan was illegal. Over those years, MSLF and its clients were subjected to incredible abuse from environmental groups and their media friends.

Thus it was surprising when MSLF drew support from an unlikely source. Lanny Davis, an aide to President Clinton, served as an unabashed and omnipresent Clinton defender on nightly talk shows. After he left the White House, however, he entered the practice of law in Washington, D.C., and joined in support of MSLF's litigation by demanding that all imported wolves be removed from Wyoming! Davis, on behalf of a Wyoming ranching family, asserted that the district court's ruling in favor of MSLF was correct and should be implemented immediately. Davis pointed to unacceptable losses by the ranching family to imported wolves and demanded that the court not wait until a ruling by the U.S. Court of Appeals for the Tenth Circuit. According to the lawsuit filed by Davis and his partners, the ranching family's costs were real and substantial. Imported wolves had killed dozens of cattle, killed family pets (including three dogs), cost thousands of dollars in extra expenses, and threatened the safety of family members and others on the ranch.

Meanwhile, Davis' former colleague, Secretary Babbitt, said he does not care what federal courts say, the wolves Babbitt helped to carry into place will not be removed. In an early 1998 speech to the National Wildlife Foundation Annual Meeting, Babbitt drew a standing ovation with the statement, "[N]o wolves will be removed from Yellowstone on my watch."

A NEW YEAR'S RESOLUTION FOR LEADERS

December's Kyoto global warming conference is the latest use of weird science to achieve the radical agenda of environmental extremists. From Montreal (a ban on Freon) to Molalla, Oregon (the spotted owl logging ban); from Rio de Janeiro (a bio-diversity treaty) to Reno, Nevada (attacks on western grazing); and from Kyoto (a global warming treaty) to Kane County, Utah (Clinton's land grab), weird science is distorting public policy while adversely affecting the lives of millions of hard-working Americans.

The perversion of good science to achieve extremist policy objectives is the work of three groups: 1) radical environmentalists who are at war with western civilization and seek to remake, if not destroy, it; 2) federal bureaucrats who seek greater authority—and the personnel and budget that comes with it—over the lives of every American; and, 3) millions of Americans who are unwilling to take personal responsibility for their problems, believing that others should be held accountable while demanding that the government do something, anything, about the latest crisis, real or imagined, even if it is the wrong thing, does not work, or violates legal or constitutional principles.

These groups are aided and abetted by three liberal entities: 1) the media, which recognizes that bad news, especially news of impending doom, sells; 2) academia, which as the last vestige of the institutional left seeks validation for its published predictions of doom and calls for government-based solutions; and, 3) Hollywood, whose elite seeks to assuage its guilt by becoming an advocate for leftist causes while insinuating extremist messages into music, movies, and television broadcasts.

Since these groups do not represent a majority, they could not succeed without undeniable truths: 1) Americans are woefully ignorant regarding scientific matters and easily panicked; 2) most politicians lack the courage to proclaim that there is no role for government to play in the latest "crisis," or even more courageously, that there is no crisis; and 3) real scientists, who understand matters scientific, do not challenge the audacious avowals of the doom and gloom merchants. These factors combine to put the nation on some very dangerous public policy paths, compelling the adoption of actions that are not just unnecessary, but also even counterproductive, and, most certainly, economically devastating to millions of people.

Anyone who objects is subjected to the most hateful of abuse; for example, Al Gore says such a person is like those who sought to appease Hitler!

"We can't afford to wait," say the modern Cassandras and their fellow travelers in the media and elsewhere. As the leader of the Sierra Club, sounding like a Nike commercial, in a speech in Santa Barbara, announced, "We should 'Just do it,' and if we're wrong, apologize later." How do we apologize, if we discover the predictions of global warming were wrong after the Draconian demands of the Kyoto treaty drive the price of gasoline up $.44 a gallon or home heating oil up by 50 percent, harming the poor or elderly? Obviously people who suffer from such wrong guesses by government can never be made whole, that is, if the government were in the business of apologizing for, much less admitting, its mistakes!

Not only does the federal government rarely, if ever, apologize, it refuses to abandon the most absurd policy even after being proven wrong. This is because of the very powerful institutions that support big government and their unwillingness to relinquish the power that comes with such policies.

Obviously, since there are numerous reasons why weird science influences public policy, it will take concerted action, on several fronts, to reverse this phenomenon. One small step toward that goal would be for political leaders to have the courage to admit publicly that a crisis does not exist, or if it does, to determine what role, if any, (and there may be no role) for the government to play. The Kyoto Treaty is an excellent place to start!

JANUARY 1998

OF DOGS AND CATS IN THE ROCKIES

In December of 1994, ranchers in Idaho, Montana, and Wyoming sued Secretary of the Interior Bruce Babbitt to stop him from putting Canadian wolves in those three states. The ranchers also asked Wyoming federal district judge William F. Downes to issue an order to keep Babbitt from releasing the wolves until Downes ruled on the legality of the Babbitt plan.

During the hearing on that proposed order, Judge Downes asked Babbitt's wolf expert, "What if I let these wolves [in] and ultimately determine they should be removed? What harm am I doing to the animal by that decision...?" The response was straightforward and stunning: "My recommendation would be to kill the animals. [I]f we were to terminate the project [if] we just can't do it.... [t]he cheapest way.... would be to destroy the animals. I personally would not want them put back into Canada. The Canadians made it clear.... We will not be able to take them back to Canada and release them. [Therefore], I recommend they be destroyed."

Three years later, on December 12, 1997, Judge Downes ruled that the ranchers were right; the Babbitt plan violated the Endangered Species Act (ESA) and the wolves and their pups had to go. That decision was greeted with howls of protests from Babbitt, environmental organizations, and wolf advocacy groups throughout the country.

Where were these friends of the wolf when the federal death threat was uttered in 1994? True friends of the wolf, on hearing its fate should Babbitt lose in court, would demand that the judge issue the injunction sought by the ranchers. "Your Honor, we think we will win. But the risk is too great. We will voluntarily withhold reintroduction until the court rules on our plan." They did no such thing. Instead they forged boldly ahead, believing they would win, believing that no judge would order wolf removal once wolves were in the region, and seeking to achieve their own selfish desires—for example, Babbitt's narcissistic need for a photograph of him carrying wolves into Yellowstone National Park.

Where the Canadian wolves and their pups will go, should Judge Downes' decision be upheld on appeal is anyone's guess. (They will not be killed; Judge Downes issued a supplemental order saying that Babbitt could not "euthanize [the] wolves.") But while real wolves in Wyoming are looking for a home, a nonexistent Colorado animal is guaranteed a home.

The lynx, a small and elusive cat that has not been seen in Colorado in a quarter of a century, is the subject of a lawsuit brought by environmental groups. Like the wolf, the lynx is abundant in Canada and Alaska, but environmentalists want it to be abundant in its purported historic range, that is, in the Rocky Mountain West. The groups demand forest plans be changed to accommodate the ostensible needs of the lynx. As a result of a recent federal judge's ruling, the U.S. Forest Service says that, even if the lynx does not exist in Colorado, it will have to "protect the cat's habitat."

There is a reason why environmental groups sued over the lynx. Much like the northern spotted owl, its alleged habitat is mature stands of trees— the very trees required by loggers and timber mills. For those who know what happened to the timber industry in Oregon and Washington, the reason is clear: to kill timber harvesting and to rein in the ski industry in Colorado.

What this discussion of dogs and cats demonstrates is the idiocy that the ESA has become. With its absence of good science, with its skewed definition of what constitutes protected species, with its emphasis on political rather than biological science, the ESA bears no resemblance to its original purpose. Putting wolves in Wyoming when they already have a home while preserving a home for a nonexistent lynx are just two examples of that absurd reality.

FEBRUARY 1998

COURT SHOCKER:
HUMANS MORE IMPORTANT THAN BEARS!

Late on the night of September 9, 1989, John Shuler of Dupuyer, Montana, heard the sounds of grizzly bears in his yard. He grabbed his rifle and ran outside. When Shuler saw three bears near his sheep pen, he fired into the air causing the bears to flee. Shuler then turned to go into his house, only to be confronted by another grizzly bear. It rose on its hind feet, spread its paws, and let out a roar. Believing that he was in mortal danger; Shuler shot and fatally wounded the bear.

The news of how a rancher from northwestern Montana survived a grizzly bear attack should have been a one day story, if that! It might have made the news as far away as Great Falls, Montana, 90 miles distant, but probably not. Instead, Shuler's story is nationally known. It has been reported in too many newspapers to list, including the *Wall Street Journal*, and has been the subject of two "That's Outrageous" reports in *Readers Digest*. Everyone has heard, if not of John Shuler, then of his incredible tale.

That is because when Shuler notified the U.S. Fish and Wildlife Service (FWS) of the attack and what he did to defend himself, the FWS charged Shuler with violating the Endangered Species Act (ESA) and demanded that Shuler pay a fine of $8,000.

Following a hearing, an administrative law judge (ALJ) from the U.S. Department of the Interior ruled that Shuler's belief that his life was in danger was a reasonable one. The ALJ declared, however, that Shuler could not claim self-defense, as the ESA allows, because he had "introduced himself into the zone of imminent danger," his own yard. The ALJ fined Shuler $4,000.

Shuler appealed to an Ad Hoc Appeals Board employed by Secretary Babbitt, which not only upheld the ALJ's ruling, but found another reason for rejecting Shuler's self-defense claim: Shuler's dog, which had alerted Shuler to the bear's presence by going "on point," had "provoked the bear." The Board increased Shuler's fine to $5,000.

Finally, in October of 1996, seven years and a month after surviving the bear attack, Shuler was able to file his lawsuit against Babbitt in federal district court. Shuler charged that the holdings of the ALJ and the Board conflicted with well-settled principles of law: self-defense is well recognized, is a defense under the ESA, and gives an individual the right to use deadly force when that person believes his or her life is in danger. Shuler also argued that the law is well settled that people may carry weapons on their property and may use those weapons when their lives are in danger.

On March 17, 1998, Shuler's long legal purgatory came to an end. The U.S. District Court for the District of Montana ruled for Shuler, vacating both his conviction and fine.

It is bad enough that it took Shuler and his wife Carmen nearly nine years to get out from under a fine that would have destroyed them. What is worse is that Shuler should never have been prosecuted. Any first year law student knows what Shuler did is self-defense. Nonetheless, the federal government continued its war against Shuler. Moreover, it was a war waged, not by animal rights fanatics in the bowels of the FWS or newly-minted federal lawyers eager to make a name for themselves. Top officials in the Clinton administration pressed the case against Shuler to deny Americans the right to protect their lives from grizzly bears. To these radicals, the possibility that human life would be lost should such a standard become law was less important than increasing the protection for grizzly bears!

John Shuler's story reveals not only that environmental radicalism now pervades the federal government, but also that its lawyers seek, not justice, but victory. It is a tragic day when our government values animals over humans and winning over obeying the law.

APRIL 1998

CONGRESS ABDICATES ITS ROLE!

"Failure of political will does not justify unconstitutional remedies." So wrote Justice Anthony M. Kennedy in his concurring opinion in *Clinton v. City of New York*, in which the Supreme Court of the United States declared the Line Item Veto Act unconstitutional. Kennedy, who has provided the fifth vote for some rather controversial decisions of the Court recently, got it right this time; in fact, reporters were quick to use Kennedy's succinct summary of the case.

The media, however, missed a more thoughtful analysis in which Kennedy responded to Justice Breyer's view that the Court should demur since "the political branches are adjusting their own powers between themselves." For Kennedy that proposition is based on two faulty premises. First, the public good demands it; and second, liberty is not at risk. Kennedy calls the first "inadmissible" because "[t]he Constitution's structure requires a stability which transcends the convenience of the moment." As for the second, wrote Kennedy, "Liberty is always at stake when one or more of the branches seek to transgress the separation of powers."

Justice Kennedy quotes from *The Federalist* regarding the separation of powers doctrine: "The accumulation of all powers, legislative, executive, and judiciary, in the same hands . . . may justly be pronounced the very definition of tyranny." Thus, to prevent tyranny, the Founding Fathers did not limit constitutional safeguards to the Bill of Rights, but, in Kennedy's words, "used the principles of separation of powers and federalism to secure liberty. . . ." In the vision of the Founding Fathers, "liberty demands limits on the ability of any one branch to influence basic political decisions." Furthermore, "[s]eparation of powers helps to ensure the ability of each branch to be vigorous in asserting its proper authority." Justice Kennedy recognized that "ability" does not mean the "willingness" to be "vigorous," because with the Line Item Veto Act, "Congress surrendered its authority by its own hand." Therefore, the Court must respond since "[a]bdication of responsibility is not part of the constitutional design."

Justice Scalia, writing for the Court almost exactly one year earlier, said the same thing when the Court struck down the Brady Act. Then it was federalism that prevented Congress from tyrannically ordering local sheriffs to do its biding. Dual sovereignty is a fundamental component of the

Constitution, declared Justice Scalia, not to be brushed aside for the "crisis" of the day.

Thus in the past two years, the Supreme Court has stood in the breach twice to prevent Congress from abdicating its authority under the Constitution, and more importantly for liberty, its responsibility to serve as a check on the Executive. One can understand the Brady Act, passed by a Congress controlled by the Democrats. One can understand the Line Item Veto Act, passed by Republicans who believed it would be wielded by one of their own.

What one cannot understand is the indifferent manner in which Congress has stood by while President Clinton signed Executive Order after Executive Order, declarations for which he has absolutely no constitutional or even statutory authority. After all, the president only has the power given him by the Constitution or by an Act of Congress. That has not prevented Clinton, to almost deafening silence from Congress, from signing orders: requiring federal agencies to enforce so-called "environmental justice," implementing an American Heritage Rivers Initiative, barring certain health insurers from competing for the health insurance business of federal workers, interpreting and sharply limiting the Tenth Amendment, and barring discrimination against homosexuals in the federal government. To address but two: no law gives Clinton authority to designate "Heritage" rivers, and it is the Supreme Court, not the president, that interprets the Constitution.

As Congress adjourns for the August recess and our federal elected officials return home, it might be well to ask them one question: "Why have you stood silently by in the face of the most audacious power grab since FDR tried to pack the Supreme Court?"

AUGUST 1998

DEFINING "IS," "ALONE," AND "EQUAL FOOTING"

Outrage over President Clinton's Executive Order 13083 on "federalism" culminated in a lopsided vote by the U.S. House of Representatives that the order be withdrawn. Within days it was. Notwithstanding Clinton's withdrawal of the order, with its exhaustive listing of circumstances when the federal government must exercise dominion over sovereign states, Clinton's attack on federalism, on dual sovereignty, and on the role and rights of states continues unabated.

Consider, for example, a case in federal court in Minnesota, involving the rights of Minnesota over Rainy Lake, which lies between it and Canada. In most circumstances, Minnesota would have jurisdiction over Rainy Lake, but because Rainy Lake lies within the Voyagers National Park (VNP) it is coveted by the National Park Service (NPS), which says it, not Minnesota, has jurisdiction. That is why, in August of 1996, the NPS cited Carl Brown for carrying paying passengers on Rainy Lake and why, last spring, Mr. Brown was convicted of "conducting commercial enterprises on waters of the Voyagers National Park." Brown's appeal challenges the NPS claim of jurisdiction.

The VNP was created by Minnesota's donation of over 35,000 acres of state and other publicly owned lands to the United States. But Minnesota declined to donate its water rights, retaining ownership and jurisdiction. Although Congress, in the past, had acquired water rights when creating national park lands, it did not do so regarding the VNP.

Under the "equal footing doctrine," all states enter the Union on an "equal footing" with the Thirteen Colonies, that is with the same rights as did those that entered in 1789. One of those rights, says the Supreme Court of the United States, is "the absolute right to all navigable waters and the soil under them for their own common use." The "equal footing doctrine" is fundamental, but Clinton's lawyers reject it, just as they reject two Supreme Court decisions limiting federal control over state lands and waters. In one, the Court held the NPS could not regulate automobile traffic on state and county highways within a Colorado national park. In the other, the Court rejected an attempt to use the presence of federal lands as a basis for regulating state waters.

Dual sovereignty and the "equal footing doctrine" are not the only parts of the Constitution that Clinton's lawyers dispute in the Brown case. They say the Tenth Amendment is irrelevant. They also argue that the Property Clause (regarding federal property) gives the NPS power over Minnesota's waters. Supreme Court opinions to the contrary are ignored. One might think that because the Clinton administration favors international governance, its lawyers would defend treaties. Not in the Brown case, where those lawyers say two treaties guaranteeing "free navigation" do not apply to Rainy Lake.

Perhaps the most outrageous response of Clinton's lawyers is their willingness to ignore the clear intent of Congress. First, Congress failed to give the NPS authority over the waters within the VNP; it could have but did not. Second, Congress expressly protected Minnesota's "civil and criminal jurisdiction" within the VNP. Third, Congress made any asserted NPS jurisdiction subject to the treaty requirements of "free and open" commerce.

Unfortunately, sometimes federal lawyers have help. In an earlier case involving the VNP, a federal court of appeals held the NPS had jurisdiction over Rainy Lake, despite Minnesota's failure to cede its jurisdiction. The court concluded Minnesota's consent to and active participation in the creation of the VNP was "tantamount to a cession of jurisdiction" over its waters. Minnesota has since made it clear that it did not cede its jurisdiction over state waters.

Obviously, the battle over federalism in defense of dual sovereignty was not won with the House vote on Clinton's Executive Order or Clinton's withdrawal of that order. Instead the battle goes on in federal courtrooms where Clinton's lawyers argue that the words of the Constitution are as indistinct and imprecise as those Clinton uses during sworn testimony.

OCTOBER 1998

DOING EVERYTHING BY THE BOOK

On a snowy September night in 1989, John Shuler stepped out of his ranch house in northern Montana when he heard grizzly bears attacking his sheep. Clad only in his shorts and socks, but carrying his rifle, Shuler saw three bears near the sheep pen and frightened them off with shots over their heads. Thinking the danger was over, Shuler turned toward his house. Suddenly a grizzly bear appeared a mere 30 feet from him, stood up on its hind legs, spread its mighty forepaws, and roared a frightening roar. Shuler realized he was in mortal danger, swung his rifle in the direction of the bear, and fired. With that shot, Shuler saved his life, but he also unleashed a legal battle that is having repercussions almost a decade after he escaped death in his own yard.

Within hours of Shuler's rifle shot, the U.S. Fish and Wildlife Service (FWS) decided to bring a legal charge against him, accusing Shuler of violating the Endangered Species Act (ESA), which protects grizzly bears as "threatened." The FWS brought the charge despite the fact that the ESA contains a "self-defense" exception. According to the FWS, Shuler was at fault for a variety of ever-changing reasons: Shuler was not in real danger; Shuler was at fault for going into his yard; Shuler provoked the bear by going into his yard; Shuler's dog provoked the bear; Shuler shot the bear in the back, etc. The FWS ordered Shuler to pay an $8,000 fine.

On September 27, in Wyoming's Bridger-Teton National Forest south of Togwotee Pass, an elk hunter spotted a grizzly bear 25 yards from him. The hunter started to move away, but spooked one of the sow's three yearlings. When the cub "whined," the grizzly charged the hunter. Armed with a powerful rifle, the hunter could have killed the bear; instead, he threw his rifle at the bear and pulled out a can of pepper spray, which he emptied into the bear's face. The bear charged through the spray, in an attack the hunter called "more violent than you can imagine." "She had every intention of killing me." "I knew I was going to die."

The hunter did not die because his partner rushed to his aid by killing the 475 pound bear. Within an hour, the hunter was airlifted to Idaho to undergo emergency surgery for multiple injuries, from which he is now recovering. The most incredible aspect of this story is why the hunter threw down his rifle. "I actually had a rational thought process. I knew I didn't want to shoot [the bear] because I didn't want to go to jail and lose my hunting privileges." Instead, he wanted to do "everything by the book" because he had heard about what happened to John Shuler.

Fear of federal prosecution, fear of failing to do "everything by the book," and fear of "go[ing] to jail" nearly cost the hunter his life. Thus the events set in motion by the FWS in northern Montana in the late summer of 1989 claimed another victim in Wyoming nine years later. After all, it took John Shuler nearly nine years to clear his name and to get out from under the $8,000 fine the FWS wanted him to pay. Had he been required to pay for the free legal services he received from Mountain States Legal Foundation, he would have paid more than $225,000! He certainly could not look to the federal government to pay his legal fees. For despite losing the case, the government refuses to pay, saying its position was "substantially justified." If this is the cost of preserving the self-defense provision of the ESA, for all intents and purposes, it does not exist.

Doing "everything by the book" should not require people to allow grizzly bears to kill them, but until the federal government plays "by the book," that is what it will mean.

NOVEMBER 1998

CHAPTER TEN

U.S. Government – Like Nobody's Business

On Tuesday, April 20, 1999, I dropped my son Luke at Evergreen High School—my older son Perry and his mother were in Boulder for a physical for his Navy ROTC scholarship—and drove to MSLF's downtown office where I presided over staff and lawyer meetings, read my mail, and made some calls. As I drove to the Capitol for my talk to the Colorado General Assembly House Republican Caucus, I thought about my work over the weekend and on Monday on MSLF's second petition for *writ* of *certiorari* in the *Adarand* case—*Adarand Constructors, Inc. v. Slater* (Clinton's Secretary of Transportation). I would discuss *Adarand* in light of related Colorado issues. I would also discuss that, days before, I had filed a petition for *writ* of *certiorari* on behalf of Bobby Unser in the notorious case of him being charged by the Clinton administration with operating a snowmobile in a wilderness area. A Colorado federal district court and then a three-judge panel of the U.S. Court of Appeals for the Tenth Circuit had rejected our arguments that Bobby was neither in the area nor possessed criminal intent (*mens rea*); the panel even held it was up to Unser, not the Forest Service, to prove where he was in the forest in the middle of a blizzard. Just before leaving my car, I turned on the radio. There was a shooting at Columbine High School, but little more was known. I turned it off.

After my talk, I returned to the office, but then received a call from Luke. The school was on lock down; he had to leave. On the way to Evergreen, I listened, for the first time, to the news of the shooting. When I arrived at the school, Luke was out front alone. Shortly after we got home, Perry and his mother returned. With my sons home and safe, for the first time in weeks, I was not thinking about *Adarand* or *Unser*.

MEANWHILE OUT WEST

When Attorney General Janet Reno announced she would not seek appointment of an Independent Counsel to investigate President Clinton's alleged campaign-financing abuses, she gave a simple answer. President Clinton lacked criminal intent; that is, he had no intent, at the time of the alleged criminal activity, to commit the elements of the crime.

If Clinton did not intend to commit a violation of federal campaign financing laws, the Attorney General Reno is right to raise the legal issue of *mens rea* or criminal intent. I wish that she would alert her attorneys, both in Washington, D.C. and in Colorado, that meanwhile out west, a man is being prosecuted for a federal crime for which he lacked criminal intent.

Bobby Unser, on a beautifully clear December day, almost exactly two years ago, went for a snowmobile ride in a national forest in southern Colorado. When a dangerous blizzard swept down upon Mr. Unser and his friend, they were in deadly peril. Quickly they became disoriented and then lost as they struggled to find their way to safety. Eventually, they made it to civilization, but not before they had abandoned their snowmobiles in the deepening snow, had spent the night shivering in a hastily carved snow cave, and had hiked out of the national forest, through waist-deep snow, for eighteen hours.

Although Mr. Unser's safety was assured, his legal peril was just beginning. The Clinton administration charged him with operating a snowmobile in a federal wilderness area. Mr. Unser asserted that he had not been in the federal wilderness area, but if he were, he was there out of necessity or as a result of an emergency. That is, he had no intention of being within the federal wilderness area, an element of the crime. Federal prosecutors insisted that, given the gravity of the offense—despoiling a wilderness area—criminal intent should not be required. A federal district court agreed; Unser was convicted without proof of criminal intent.

On another front, Clinton defenders assert that Independent Counsel Ken Starr's investigation was unfair. What would they say about the fact that, meanwhile out west, Clinton's officials are conducting an investigation that reads like George Orwell's *Nineteen Eighty-Four*.

In mid-December, Secretary Babbitt's agency mailed a frightening letter to those with hunting licenses for November near Luna, New Mexico, demanding a response "within seven days" to "preclude ... Special Agents from meeting with you in person." The instructions are chilling: "Every word is important. This is not a draft. Only write your answers once. [B]efore you write, please think as to how you are going to phrase your answers." "Use only a pen while writing (no pencils). No typing allowed."

It gets worse. "[A] Mexican Gray Wolf was found dead from a gunshot wound ... during the time that you were hunting, November 1998. How would you explain this? Please write in DETAIL your ideas." "List the 5 most important causes that could have created this situation." "Would you like to change any of the information you have provided?" Then this, "Before you answer the following questions, we would like to inform you that each word of your answers will be evaluated. [T]ake your time and think before you answer. Do you know who shot the wolf? Did you shoot the wolf? Did you take part in shooting the wolf?" "Write in detail about you hunting trip ... beginning from the time you left home until you returned." "How do you feel now that you have completed this form? Should we believe your answers to the questions? If the answer to the last question was yes; give us one reason why." "What were your emotions while filing out this form? Did you feel afraid while completing this form?"

It is not merely that Clinton and his officials believe that he is above the law, but also they believe that, meanwhile out west, the American people are beneath the law and beyond the protections of the Constitution.

JANUARY 1999

IT'S UP TO CONGRESS

For 25 years, the U.S. Court of Appeals for the District of Columbia has heard lawsuits by Members of Congress challenging the actions of either their colleagues in Congress or the president and his appointees. While Members of Congress lack the "personal injury" required for "standing" (the right to sue), the appeals court found injury to "the members' rights to participate and vote on legislation in a manner defined by the Constitution." Thus, it held, in 1974, that U.S. Senator Ted Kennedy (D-MA) had standing to challenge a "pocket veto" of legislation by President Richard Nixon and, in 1984, that U.S. Representative Henson Moore (R-6th LA) had standing to challenge revenue-raising legislation that did not "originate" in the House.

It appears, however, this quarter of a century old precedent will be overturned. That reversal will come in *Chenoweth v. Clinton*, in which Representative Helen Chenoweth (R-1st ID) and four of her colleagues challenged President Clinton's authority to implement his American Heritage Rivers Initiative (AHRI), asserting that the AHRI is legislation that only Congress may enact. In the long tradition of the D.C. Circuit, Chenoweth argues that Clinton's usurpation of the role of Congress denied her the "right to participate in a constitutionally prescribed method of enacting ... legislation." Consistent with precedent, she challenges, not the implementation or the constitutionality of the law, but the manner in which the AHRI became "law," that is, in violation of the "constitutionally mandated process of enacting law."

Remarkably, when the district court ruled on standing, it decided the issue, not in accordance with the appeals court's cases on point, but on the basis of a recent ruling of the Supreme Court, *Raines v. Byrd*. That case was a challenge by Senator Bob Byrd (D-WV) and others to the constitutionality of Line Item Veto Act. The Court dismissed their challenge, holding that they had suffered no injury; "their votes were given full effect. They simply lost that vote." Added the Court, "[T]he alleged cause of [their] injury is not [the Executive's] exercise of legislative power but the actions of their own colleagues in Congress in passing the Act."

Even more remarkably, when *Chenoweth* was appealed, the three-judge panel concluded that the appeals court's earlier holdings in *Kennedy* and

Moore had been overturned by *Raines v. Byrd*. Although the Supreme Court case was decided on different grounds and the facts differed from cases where the appeals court gave standing to Members of Congress, the panel threw in the towel. If that view holds and if the appeals court's anticipated decision is not overturned, the ability of Members of Congress to sue for usurpation of their authority will end.

What recourse will there be then when a president exercises powers neither given him by the Constitution nor delegated to him by Congress? Of course, an injured private citizen or group of citizens may sue, but such litigation faces all but insurmountable challenges. The better answer is for Congress, as an institution, to object, not necessarily to what the president is doing or why he is doing it, but how it is being done. After all, in our constitutional system, there is a right way and a wrong way for doing things, even worthwhile things that deserve doing. Sadly, too few Members of Congress seem concerned about the Constitution. In discussions of the AHRI, for example, many Members of Congress agreed that Clinton lacked authority for the program, but refused to object, saying, "It sounds like a good idea."

If the federal courts opt out of the battle between Congress and the Executive, as the D.C. Circuit seems likely to do, protection of niceties such as the "constitutionally-mandated process of enacting laws," may be left up to the handful of citizen groups able to go to court and stay there. That, however, is not where the responsibility lies. It is up to Congress to defend the Constitution. Whether Congress is up to the task remains to be seen!

FEBRUARY 1999

KILLING LYNX TO SAVE THEM

In December of 1994, farm bureaus in Idaho, Montana, and Wyoming were in Wyoming federal district court to bar Secretary Babbitt from releasing Canadian wolves in their states. During the testimony of Babbitt's wolf expert, the judge asked what would happen if he permitted the reintroduction to take place and then decided it was illegal and ordered removal of the wolves. "We would have to round up the wolves and kill them," testified the expert, "because Canadians don't want them back."

Had Babbitt and his attorneys cared about the wolves, that news would have compelled them to put their plan on hold. Environmental groups, which had been passionate in their advocacy for the wolf, should have done the same. Babbitt, his lawyers, and the environmental groups said nothing; the wolves were introduced. In December of 1997, the judge declared the program illegal and ordered the wolves removed. Then, and only then, did Babbitt, his lawyers, and environmental groups worry about the wolf's fate.

A year later, in December of 1998, Colorado agricultural groups were in federal district court objecting to a similar plan by federal agencies and the Colorado Division of Wildlife. This time the plan involved the lynx, which has not been spotted in Colorado for more than 25 years. The groups objected to the lynx plan because the agencies, both federal and state, admitted they knew "almost nothing...about lynx ecology and biology in Colorado."

They did not know if there was sufficient prey to eat or if the lynx would extirpate the populations of some prey animals, such as the ptarmigan and the mink. They did not know if the lynx could survive other predators, such as the bobcat, the mountain lion, and the coyote. They did not know if the lynx could survive in southern Colorado, which they admitted was in the extreme southern part of its range. Worst of all, they had not done an environmental study to publicize the facts. One such fact: New York State's lynx program has failed; after 10 years, all 83 lynx imported by New York are gone, killed by bobcats or cars.

The groups had fears, not only for the lynx, but also for themselves. They feared that if the lynx were brought in they would be wiped out, or they would wipe out other wildlife, and people who use federal land in

Colorado would be blamed. As a result, access to federal land would be restricted to "save the lynx."

On New Year's Eve of 1998, a Colorado federal judge let the lynx plan go forward. There was no requirement for an environmental study, ruled the judge, because the federal government was not involved, even though the lynx would live on federal land and even though the federal government had been involved in the development and implementation of the plan. Despite the fact that information is required before agencies commit funds and resources, the judge said the plan was necessary so the agencies could "acquire information on . . . Canada lynx in Colorado."

Well, now Colorado has its "information." Three of the original four lynx are dead of starvation, the fourth has been recaptured, and the fate of the others is unknown. Animal rights advocates protested in Boulder, Colorado, what the *Rocky Mountain News* calls "the politics of dead lynx" drew rebukes from throughout Colorado, and the Colorado General Assembly is finalizing a statute to deny authority for such projects.

Incredibly, one Colorado wildlife spokesman admitted that the agencies had rushed the lynx into the wild to frustrate thoughtful consideration of the program. "We felt if lynx were on the ground, there would be less point for an appeal." In other words, lynx plan officials behaved just like Babbitt four years before.

The next time someone waxes emotional about the fate of animals and who cares about whether they live or die, tell them this story about dogs and cats in the West.

APRIL 1999

FIRST STEPS TO THE DARK SIDE

Throughout America people are wondering how the killers at Columbine High School in Littleton, Colorado, could do it. Days before their rampage, they had gone to the prom with their classmates, hours before they had gone bowling with some of them, and minutes before they saw one of them: "I like you man," said one killer, "Get out of here!" Then they began killing students in cold blood, because they were "jocks," because of their race, because of their faith in God, and for absolutely no reason at all. As they did so, they laughed.

Searching for some answers, religious scholars like Reverend Kenneth Williams, Ph.D. of Golden, Colorado, says the process leading to such murderous sprees involves three steps: denial of the existence of God, abandonment of religious morality, and rejection of the sanctity of human life. (If God is dead, human beings were not created in His image.)

It was Friedrich Nietzsche (1844-1900) who declared, "God is dead. God remains dead." While Nietzsche also rejected "conformist moralities," modern culture embraces a moral ambivalence and nonjudgmentalism of which Nietzsche only dreamed. Finally, it is a powerful part of our culture that asserts that it is not human life that has intrinsic value, but the environment and non-human life forms.

Nietzsche's philosophy was an important source for Hitler's fascist ideology. It was Nietzsche who said, "Without God, anything is permissible." It was Hitler who defined "anything." What is less well known, but hardly surprising, is that Hitler was a committed vegetarian. On one famous occasion Hitler told Herman Göring that eating meat was "like eating a corpse!" Hitler's compassion toward non-human species (He vigorously opposed animal research.) contrasts starkly with his pitiless genocidal murder of millions.

Compassion for animals is not a failing. To the contrary, psychologists advise that one of the warning signs of a troubled youth is cruelty to animals. What is a character flaw is when, as in Hitler's case, animals have inherent value and worth, but not human beings. Unfortunately, such a repudiation of the Judeo-Christian view of the sanctity of each human life did not die with Hitler. Today, radical animal rights and environmental advocates reject that view with as much vigor as did Hitler. Consider these statements: "There are no clear distinction between [humans] and animals." "A rat is a pig is a dog is a boy." or this book title, *A Declaration of War: Killing People to Save Animals and the Environment.*

Remarkably, one hears such things well short of the radical fringe. A Maine high school student, for example, responded to concern that the needs of mankind were being sacrificed by environmental laws to "trees, rocks, and species of insects." He defended insects thusly: "Who are we to say [that insects must die for the needs of humans]?" Here is the marriage of today's cultural moral ambivalence with Hitler's rejection of the value of human life. Note, as well, the shift of emphasis, from protecting the environment to ensure human health, safety, and well-being, to saving other life forms that have an intrinsic worth greater than humans!

While the Littleton teenage killers were devotees of Hitler, there was something else insidiously at work there, something that is all too common today. For they viewed their victims, not as human beings, but as mere members of one hated group or another: "jocks," "[Blacks]," or "Christians." Regrettably, it is not unusual to hear such demonizing language from environmental extremists, who describe loggers as "tree killers," miners as "the rape, ruin, and run boys," and ranchers as "welfare cowboys." By this language, the speaker assures the audience that people in these groups are "others," unworthy of concern, and without value.

Where does it all start? The day of the Littleton tragedy, less than 20 miles from Columbine High School, I saw a car with a bumper sticker that read, "Save an Elk. Hit a land developer."

MAY 1999

THE ECONOMY, THE ENVIRONMENT, AND EQUITY

Clinton's poverty tour brought angry responses from many westerners. They know that while Clinton is not to blame for the poverty he saw, any more than he may claim credit for the surging economy, he is the reason for the crises facing some western towns.

Libby, in northwestern Montana, is one example. Blessed with abundant and renewable timber, Libby began as and could remain a timber town. It is not, despite expenditure of millions of dollars in state-of-the-art equipment; lawsuits by environmental extremists and anti-logging policies by Clinton's officials closed the mills. Libby thought it could rely, for economic activity, on a world-class mineral deposit able to provide hundreds of high-paying jobs while complying with all environmental laws. Unfortunately, those hopes appear to have been dashed by the opposition of environmental groups and Clinton officials. But Libby never expected to make Clinton's "I feel your pain," photo-opportunity tour. After all, when Libby tried to get Interior Secretary Babbitt, who flew into the area to be photographed "fighting" a forest fire, to come talk about lost jobs, Babbitt said, "No."

The Endangered Species Act, the Clean Air Act, the Clean Water Act, the National Environmental Policy Act, and other well-meaning statutes, under the zealous enforcement of former environmental activists turned Clinton bureaucrats, are the tools used to achieve, at least in the West, Vice President Gore's *Earth in the Balance* goal: "a wrenching transformation of society." It began with Clinton's northern spotted owl policy, which put scores of timber communities in Oregon and Washington on life support, and continues to this day. It is not just the environmental laws. Federal land managers and officials in the ever-expanding Environmental Protection Agency (EPA) are engaged, in Gore's words, in "an all-out effort to use every policy and program, every law and institution, every treaty and alliance, every tactic and strategy, every plan and course of action" to stop economic activity in the rural West.

One of those laws is the Antiquities Act of 1906, which Clinton used to kill 1,000 jobs in economically hard-pressed Garfield and Kane Counties in Utah when he closed 1.7 million acres of federal lands to economic activity by designating the Grand Staircase-Escalante National Monument. Kane and Garfield Counties could have used those jobs; Clinton had killed 1,000 jobs to "save" the Mexican spotted owl. But the folks in the Kane County seat of Kanab did not expect Clinton to visit to talk about lost jobs. After all, when Clinton announced the monument, he did so in Arizona, not in Utah.

The Utah coal mine is not the only one Clinton killed. He acceded to the demands of environmental groups by killing one in southwestern Montana that would have employed hundreds in high paying jobs. When Congress responded by passing a law to compensate Montana by transferring federal coal near Ashland, the poorest part of the poorest state, Clinton and Babbitt arrogantly refused to comply. Add Ashland to the list of towns Clinton could have visited to see poverty; instead, he went to the Pine Ridge Indian Reservation in nearby South Dakota.

Clinton's visit to the reservation was steeped in irony. For despite all of Clinton's rhetoric about helping the disadvantaged, he has made it much more difficult for minority and low-income communities to attract businesses. After all, Clinton's Executive Order on "Environmental Justice" ordered federal officials to raise the regulatory bar for industries attempting to locate there. For example, environmental groups and Clinton's EPA killed a job-producing facility in rural Convent, Louisiana, another hard-pressed, African-American community.

Earlier this summer, Congressman Patrick Kennedy (D-1st RI), Chairman of the Democratic Congressional Campaign Committee, told reporters that Democrats had "written off the rural areas." After enduring the environmental policies of Clinton, Gore, and Babbitt for the past six years, Congressman Kennedy's statement did not surprise those people living in the pockets of poverty President Clinton did not get around to visiting.

AUGUST 1999

"STOP ME IF YOU CAN!"

Recently, in a front-page story, the *Washington Times* reported on President Clinton's aggressive use of Executive Orders that "push the limits of presidential power." In what one expert referred to as "a deliberate plan to usurp legislative function," Clinton has been, in the words of a congressional critic, "running roughshod over our Constitution." Although Clinton's 301 Executive Orders are not a record, his willingness to issue orders for which he has no authority in a direct challenge to the prerogatives of Congress is unprecedented. No wonder long-time aide Paul Begala laughed, "Stroke of the pen, law of the land. Kind of cool!"

Much has been written of the pitiful inability of Congress to respond to Clinton's clear abuses of power, let alone rein him in. From inflated agency appropriations through illegal recess appointments, to zero congressional oversight of fraud, waste, and abuse in a host of agencies, Congress too often appears more like a bystander than a co-equal branch in the Constitution's system of checks and balances. While the passivity of Congress in the face of Clinton's aggression does severe damage to Congress's vital role and the individual rights that role is intended to protect, there are other constitutional implications that are not so obvious.

In September of 1996, President Clinton, in clear violation of the Constitution and several federal statutes (not the least of which was the statute he cited as his authority), Clinton locked up 1.7 million acres of federal land in south central Utah. Over the next three years, the response of Congress was negligible. Attempts by westerners to limit Clinton's power went nowhere. Meanwhile, several minor legislative acts, including: one to compensate Utah for state land taken by the Clinton decree, one to remove some small towns from the new area, and one to appropriate funds for federal agencies to manage that area were adopted.

Despite the non-controversial and inconsequential nature of these acts, they were enough for Clinton's lawyers to claim, in response to a lawsuit challenging Clinton's 1996 decree, that Congress had "ratified" Clinton's unilateral act. In other words, argued Clinton's lawyers, by passing minor bills, by passing appropriations legislation, by rejecting other legislation, and simply by inaction, Congress had approved of what Clinton had done and, as a result, the lawsuit against Clinton had to be dismissed.

Wisely, the Utah federal district court refused. Concluding a strongly worded, forty-page denial of Clinton's motion, the court declared: "If the court were to find congressional ratification based on the limited record in the present case it could quite possibly be the final act in a drama...in which not one branch of government operated within its constitutional authority. It could be in effect an unintentional conspiracy of the three branches of government to do something none of them actually legally did, and thereby rob the people of their voice."

Not all courts reject such arguments. Two-thirds of a continent away, a federal appeals court facing much the same question ruled for Clinton. In a lawsuit brought by Representative Helen Chenoweth (R-1st ID) and three colleagues, challenging Clinton's ability to enact the American Heritage Rivers Initiative (AHRI) by Executive Order, first the district court and then a three-judge panel of the court of appeals ruled that the Members of Congress could not sue Clinton for usurping the constitutional powers of Congress. The appeals court relied, in part, on the failure of Congress to repeal Clinton's AHRI Executive Order. If Congress really objected to what Clinton did, said the court, it would have adopted legislation saying so!

How other federal courts will view the issue of congressional ratification remains to be seen. If more and more courts rule for Clinton on the issue, however, it will be each Member of Congress and not Clinton who will be crying out, "I'm relevant!" It will be the American public, however, who will suffer the greatest loss: the liberties guaranteed by the Constitution.

SEPTEMBER 1999

THE U.S. GOVERNMENT—
LIKE NOBODY'S BUSINESS

Stanley K. Mann claims title to a geothermal lease issued by the Bureau of Land Management (BLM) of the U.S. Department of the Interior on October 20, 1981. Over the years, Mr. Mann and others spent more than $1 million making the lease capable of producing geothermal resources—a clean, efficient, renewable energy source—in commercial quantities.

In September of 1989, Mr. Mann began teaching at Pepperdine University where he received his mail, including all mail forwarded from his prior address. Over the next several months, Mr. Mann was in frequent telephone and written communication with the BLM and the Minerals Management Service (MMS), to which Mr. Mann submitted royalty payments. Mr. Mann repeatedly advised both the BLM and the MMS of his address to ensure that he received all correspondence regarding his lease.

In April of 1991, in response to a BLM inquiry regarding the bond on his lease, Mr. Mann wrote to the company handling the bond. As a courtesy to BLM, Mr. Mann sent an unsigned copy of that letter to the BLM. Remarkably and inexplicably, especially given the difficulty Mr. Mann had getting the BLM and the MMS to use his correct address, BLM employees noticed that the return address on Mr. Mann's unsigned letter to his agent differed from the address the BLM had been using and changed Mr. Mann's address!

In November of 1993, the BLM issued an order indicating that certain geothermal leases were not in compliance with federal law and would be cancelled within 30 days unless the BLM was notified that the leases were in compliance. The BLM sent that notice, by certified mail, return receipt requested, to the address it had assigned, without authorization, to Mr. Mann. Not surprisingly, given that Mr. Mann did not reside and had never resided at that address, the BLM letter was returned "unclaimed." Two years later, when Mr. Mann visited the BLM office, he was told that the lease had been cancelled in 1994.

Mr. Mann appealed that cancellation to the Interior Board of Land Appeals, but his appeal was denied. As a result, Mr. Mann is now in the U.S. Court of Federal Claims asserting that his geothermal lease was cancelled illegally.

What took place with regard to Mr. Mann's lease is hardly exceptional in the business world. "To err is human," as Alexander Pope once said. Or, as it is more popularly stated, "These things happen." The federal government's response to Mr. Mann differs markedly, however, from what one sees in the business community. While almost every business that committed such a mistake would make it right, if not immediately, as soon as it became apparent that litigation would be throwing good money after bad, the federal government's response was to call in the lawyers. Only the federal government, the nation's largest law firm, can afford to litigate hopeless causes, attempting to drive the private citizen who has to pay for his lawyers into submission.

Ironically, to Mr. Mann's assertion that his own government has denied him the "due process of law" guaranteed by the Constitution, government lawyers responded that because the government was operating in its proprietary capacity it had no obligation to accord Mr. Mann "due process." Thus, while the federal government seeks to evade its obligation to treat its citizens in accordance with the Constitution by saying it is acting as a land owning business, it refuses to behave as any such real business would behave.

There is one final irony. Remember the letter the BLM sent to the wrong address to inform Mr. Mann that his leases were subject to revocation? That letter contained three BLM lease numbers, but not one of those numbers was for Mr. Mann's lease! Thus even had Mr. Mann received the letter he would not have been put on notice that his lease was at risk. As they say, the U.S. Government, it is like nobody's business.

OCTOBER 1999

RAILROADING PROPERTY OWNERS

In 1995, Assistant Attorney General Lois Schiffer, the highest-ranking environmental lawyer in the U.S. Department of Justice, spoke in Denver, Colorado. Remarkably, given the topics she might have addressed, she spent an hour attacking congressional proposals to expedite the time-consuming (often a decade or more) process by which landowners seek "just compensation" when the government "takes" their "private property." There was no need for legislation, she said, because her office quickly pays all takings claims.

Tell that to Maurice and Delores Glosemeyer of Marthasville, Missouri. Their "takings" claim, filed on March 4, 1993, is still pending in federal court. That is not the half of it. Ms. Schiffer and her attorneys have done everything to prevent the Glosemeyers' claim from being heard. Worse yet, the Glosemeyers are not alone.

Before the turn of the century, a railroad purchased easements across the property that the Glosemeyers came to own. By their express terms, the easements were for a railroad "right-of-way" and "for no other purpose." The property owners knew, and Missouri law ensured, that if the railroad abandoned its right-of-way, the property would revert to the landowner.

In 1983, Congress passed the "Rails to Trails Act," under which, when railroads asked the Interstate Commerce Commission (ICC) for authority to abandon a right-of-way, the ICC could mandate that the right-of-way become a trail. When property owners challenged the Act, the Supreme Court of the United States upheld its constitutionality, but held that the inability of property owners to get their land back was probably a "taking" for which "just compensation" had to be paid. In 1996, the U.S. Court of Appeals for the Federal Circuit held that when a Vermont family's property was turned into a trail after being abandoned by a railroad it was "taken." "Just compensation" had to be paid.

The Glosemeyers' situation differed slightly. Because the rail line across the Glosemeyers' property flooded on an almost annual basis and the track was "mostly obsolete because of its age" (half the bridges were installed before 1930), the railroad: found alternative means of moving its freight, abandoned the line, and began tearing out its tracks. When the railroad asked the ICC for authority to abandon the right-of-way, however, the ICC told the railroad to give it to the Missouri Department of Natural Resources (DNR) for use as a trail. That was fine with the railroad; whether the right-of-way was abandoned or given to the DNR, the railroad's responsibility was terminated.

The Glosemeyers also believed that it made little difference whether the ICC granted the abandonment or gave the trail to the DNR. After all, the railroad had abandoned its use of the right-of-way and had torn up its tracks. Furthermore, because a trail is not a "railroad purpose" under Missouri law, the Glosemeyers had to be paid. Ms. Schiffer and her lawyers disagreed, arguing that the trail was a railroad purpose because it was "saving" the right-of-way for future railroad use ("rail banking"). Not surprisingly, this absurd notion (One federal judge called it a "fig leaf.") has been rejected by Missouri courts.

Knowing that, Ms. Schiffer and her attorneys argued for six years that the case was not ready for trial or for a ruling from the judge. In hearing after hearing, federal lawyers asked for time to learn the facts. Each time their request was denied. Now, at long last, time for Clinton's lawyers may be running out. Recently the federal judge hearing the case, in response to a government lawyer's request for more depositions to learn if the railroad had pulled up its tracks, responded: "Why don't you drive out and take a look!"

Maybe, after nearly seven years, attempts by the Clinton administration to cheat railroad property owners out of "just compensation" have reached the end of the line. Maybe now, the thousands of property owners facing the same situation as the Glosemeyers will be able to receive, if not justice, then "just compensation."

NOVEMBER 1999

CHAPTER ELEVEN

Life, Liberty, and Property

———

As 2000 began, MSLF had five petitions pending before the Supreme Court of the United States. Although just one percent of all petitions are granted, MSLF's grant rate was twenty percent (20%).

United States of America v. Unser: **Facts:** Bobby Unser, caught in a blizzard, may have accidentally crossed into a federal wilderness area on a snowmobile, a motorized vehicle barred in wilderness areas. **Issue:** Whether the United States must prove Unser had criminal intent (*mens rea*)? **Outcome:** The Court denied the petition but must one day decide if "environmental crimes" are "public welfare offenses" for which *mens rea* proof is not required.

Chenoweth v. Clinton: **Facts:** President Clinton created a new federal program (the American Heritage Rivers Initiative) by Executive Order. **Issue:** Whether Members of Congress may challenge a president's unconstitutional usurpation of the powers of Congress? **Outcome:** The Court denied the petition but must one day determine its role in allowing Congress to check attempts by the Executive to usurp the powers of Congress.

United States of America v. Brown: **Facts:** Carl Brown was charged with boating on Rainy Lake—next to Voyageurs National Park—but Minnesota has jurisdiction of the lake. **Issue:** Whether the Constitution's Property Clause gives Congress authority to regulate nearby state and private property? **Outcome:** The Court denied the petition but must one day decide whether federal agencies may regulate state and private land near federal property.

Bear Lodge Multiple Use Assn. v. Babbitt: **Facts:** Acceding to demands by American Indians, the National Park Service closed Devils Tower to recreational climbing by visitors. **Issue:** Whether closing lands to serve a group's religious demands violates the Constitution's Establishment Clause? **Outcome:** The Court denied the petition regarding "standing" but must again rule if "sacred" federal lands may be closed to recreational and economic activity.

Adarand Constructors, Inc. v. Slater: **Facts:** After a victory before the Court in 1995 and a return to federal district court and a federal court of appeals, the challenge to government contracting on the basis of race was dismissed as moot. **Issue:** Whether the lawsuit is moot? **Outcome:** A unanimous Court (*per curiam*) granted the petition and reversed and remanded the case.

LIFE, LIBERTY, AND PROPERTY

Whether property rights will emerge as a major political issue in the upcoming presidential campaign remains to be seen, but it should. After all, on no other single issue is there a greater difference between the two parties and their leaders than that regarding the constitutional right to own and use property. Not only has the Clinton administration opposed every property rights proposal by Republicans in Congress and resisted every attempt by property owners in federal court to be compensated for the "taking" of their property, but also Vice President Gore has called the Constitution's "Takings Clause" the "pay the polluters provision." In fact, the disdain of the Clinton/Gore administration for "property rights," as evidenced by the statements and actions of Secretary Babbitt and others, is positively palpable.

Meanwhile, not only have Congressional Republicans, in general, been supportive of property rights, but the candidates for the Republican presidential nomination have indicated their support for property rights. For example, George W. Bush's 1994 gubernatorial campaign received a boost from an August of 1994, Austin, Texas property rights rally protesting Secretary Babbitt's use of the Endangered Species Act to commandeer private property in 33 counties around Austin on behalf of a bird. More importantly, greater than permitting a distinction between the two political parties and their candidates, a property rights debate during the 2000 presidential campaign would facilitate public recognition and understanding of the critical role that property rights plays in guaranteeing liberty in our constitutional system.

Property rights is addressed, for the first time, in two recent and remarkable books: Tom Bethell's *The Noblest Triumph: Property and Prosperity Through the Ages* (St. Martin's Press, 1998) and Richard Pipes' *Property and Freedom: The Story of How Through the Centuries Private Ownership Has Promoted Liberty and the Rule of Law* (Knopf, 1999). Professor Pipes concludes "property, in both the narrow and broad senses of the word, provides the key to the emergence of political and legal institutions that guarantee liberty." Moreover, writes the Harvard professor, "there is an intimate connection between public guarantees of ownership and individual liberty: that while property in some form is possible without liberty, the contrary is inconceivable." Mr. Bethell agrees, setting forth "four great blessings that cannot easily be realized in a society that lacks the secure, decentralized, private ownership of goods: liberty, justice, peace, and prosperity." As a result, concludes Bethell, "private property is a necessary (but not a sufficient) condition for these highly desirable social outcomes."

The scholarship of Pipes and Bethell is in sharp contrast to the demeaning, demonizing demagoguery of the Clintons, Gore, and Babbitt in attacking private property advocates. Too often such believers are characterized as rich, egoistic, and selfish owners of vast, luxurious estates. Ironically, as Pipes and Bethell point out, because property ownership is an essential guarantor of freedom from oppression, whether by wealthy citizens and corporations or big government, the most ardent advocates of property rights are small landowners. Such truths would be the largest beneficiary of a property rights debate in the upcoming election.

Remarkably, the thorough and thoughtful analysis of the role of private property rights in a free society engaged in by Pipes and Bethell and anticipated for the 2000 election has never been conducted. (Bethell: "The many blessings of a private-property system have never been properly analyzed. . . ." Pipes: "[W]e lack an explanation, based on concrete historical material, of just how property gives rise to freedom and how its absence makes possible arbitrary authority.") Yet the groundbreaking work of Pipes and Bethell verifies the wisdom of a decision made nearly 224 years ago.

The "unalienable Rights" set forth in the Declaration of Independence as having been "endowed by [the] Creator" were, originally, "Life, Liberty, and Property," not "Life, Liberty, and the Pursuit of Happiness." What Pipes and Bethell make clear is that the words were interchangeable; it is, in fact, "Property" that guarantees "the Pursuit of Happiness."

JANUARY 2000

SACRIFICING WOLVES TO SAVE THEM

An unassailable feature of the 1973 Endangered Species Act (ESA), which became clear with the 1978 decision of the Supreme Court of the United States in *Tennessee Valley Authority (TVA) v. Hill*, is that each and every one of an ESA species is sacrosanct. In *TVA v. Hill*, the Court ruled that, because Congress "viewed the value of endangered species as 'incalculable,'" each member of an ESA species must be protected from "harm" (defined to include even being annoyed) "whatever the cost." As a result, as the most casual observer knows, federal agencies, federal courts, and litigious environmental groups have used the ESA to detour, delay, and derail any activity that could "harm" a single member of an ESA species.

Recently the U.S. Court of Appeals for the Tenth Circuit in Denver, at the urging of the Clinton administration and environmental groups, issued a ruling that turns *TVA v. Hill* on its head. In *Wyoming Farm Bureau Federation v. Babbitt*, the Tenth Circuit held that individual members of an ESA species are not irreplaceable, but irrelevant. Not only does the Tenth Circuit's ruling conflict with decades of legal precedent, it contradicts biology.

The Tenth Circuit's decision comes in the lawsuit in which farm groups from three states challenged Secretary Babbitt's plan to bring Canadian wolves into all of Wyoming, 42 of 44 counties in Idaho, and 40 of 56 counties in Montana. Although Babbitt ignored the objections of rural residents, he could not ignore the fact that Canadian wolves were moving into the region. As a result, Babbitt's plan violated the congressional mandate that introduced species be "wholly separate geographically" from indigenous species.

Therefore, the Wyoming federal district court ruled, in December of 1997, that—because individual wolves from Canada and Montana were in the areas into which Babbitt was importing Canadian wolves—the imported wolves were not "wholly separate geographically" and had to be removed. The district court's holding was grounded in the controlling principle of the ESA, as announced in *TVA v. Hill*, that each and every one of an ESA species merited federal protection.

The district court relied, not just on substantive precedents of the Supreme Court, but on scientific principles of biological experts. For the term "lone wolf" is not simply a meaningful metaphor in common parlance or an idyllic image for wolf advocates; it has roots in scientific reality. The lone wolves that leave their packs in search of mates and territories ensure the biological diversity of a healthy wolf species. Thus, according to the experts, lone wolves are not expendable; they are indispensable.

The Tenth Circuit found none of this persuasive, let alone compelling. Instead the Tenth Circuit chose to "defer to [Secretary Babbitt's] interpretation" of "wholly separate geographically," taking Babbitt's word that putting imported wolves in the midst of indigenous wolves does not violate the ESA. The Tenth Circuit, however, turns the phrase upside down, reading it to mean, not that imported and indigenous populations must never inhabit the same area, but that they may commingle so long as they are not "wholly congruent geographically."

That is not the worst of it. Contrary to the Supreme Court's *TVA v. Hill* ruling and the testimony of biologists, the Tenth Circuit held that lone wolves are not protected by the ESA! The Tenth Circuit thus ventures where no court has gone before, holding that when Congress adopted the ESA, its concern was not "individual specimens" or "individual animals," but "species." Therefore, federal agencies have no duty to "protect isolated individuals" if they say they are trying to "conserve a species." "We find nothing in the [ESA] that . . . requir[es] the protection of individuals to the exclusion or detriment of overall species recovery."

Years ago, when the federal government said it had to destroy villages to save them, people laughed. Today, when federal officials say they must sacrifice wolves to save them, it is taken as gospel.

FEBRUARY 2000

WAR ON THE WEST: VOTING BY RACE

It is not as if the rural West did not have enough to worry about. Since the first days of the Clinton administration, westerners have been sent reeling by a War on the West that has done incalculable harm to rural economies, recreational pursuits, a way of life, and even life itself. New federal rules, a willingness to ignore and violate federal laws, never-say-die litigation, and unilateral presidential directives all have been used by Clinton officials to return the West to radical environmentalists' vision of "pre-settlement conditions." As a result, many rural West economies (forestry, mining, oil and gas, ranching, farming, and tourism) are dead or dying. At risk too are the people as, for example, Clinton officials challenge the right of westerners to defend themselves against grizzly bears and condemn western forests under a "let them burn" management policy.

Now comes the latest attack on rural westerners. This time the attack comes, not from Secretary Babbitt and his Department of the Interior, the doom-saying enforcers of the Endangered Species Act (the Fish and Wildlife Service and the National Marine and Fisheries Service), the anti-use partisans in the U.S. Forest Service, or even Clinton's lawyers in the Environment and Natural Resources Division of the U.S. Department of Justice. Westerners may now add one more division of the Clinton administration sent to the front in the War on the West: the Civil Rights Division of the Department of Justice.

Westerners may not recall the rancorous debate that ensued with President Clinton's nomination of Bill Lann Lee as Assistant Attorney General for the Justice Department's Civil Rights Division. When the smoke cleared on Capitol Hill, Lee's nomination had been rejected due to what a majority of Senators regarded as his racial politics and his unwillingness to adhere to the rulings of the Supreme Court of the United States in such cases as *Adarand Constructors, Inc. v. Peña*. Clinton would not be denied; he appointed Lee to the post, some say illegally and unconstitutionally, anyway. Then Lee set about to prove the Senate's misgivings about his commitment to the Constitution were justified.

In the late summer of 1999, Lee sent three of his lawyers into tiny, rural, isolated Chinook, Montana (population 1,500) to deliver an ultimatum to the Blaine County Commissioners. Either Blaine County admits to denying the civil rights of Blaine County's American Indians in violation of the Voting Rights Act and redraws the county commissioner districts to guarantee the election of an American Indian Commissioner, or the Department of Justice will sue! Blaine County, which sits in north central Montana, next to the United States border with Canada, its 7,000 citizens, and three county commissioners (one of whom had received 99 percent of the American Indian vote in the last election) were stunned.

After all, Montana law requires Blaine County to elect commissioners as it does. In addition, Blaine County votes predominantly for Democratic Party candidates in county, state, and national elections, all three commissioners and most other officers are Democrats, and the overwhelming majority of the County's Americans Indians are Democrats. No one has been denied the right to vote or the ability to run for office. In fact, running for commissioner is as easy as signing a piece of paper.

Adherence to the Constitution apparently is not enough for Clinton, Gore, Attorney General Janet Reno, and Bill Lann Lee. Despite years of Supreme Court decisions rejecting racial gerrymandering, including the Supreme Court's most recent 7-2 Hawaii decision, the Clinton administration embraces, not the Constitution, but racial politics.

There is more at risk in the Clinton administration's lawsuit against Blaine County than whether the Constitution's equal protection guarantee means what it says. There is as well the issue of Montana's sovereignty under the Constitution, particularly the Tenth Amendment. The next time people say there is no War on the West, tell them about the battle raging in Blaine County, Montana.

MARCH 2000

"THERE HE GOES AGAIN"

On June 1, Secretary of the Interior Bruce Babbitt announced that he had asked President Clinton to issue another national monument decree using the Antiquities Act of 1906 to close more than a half million acres of federal land in Arizona, Colorado, Oregon, and Washington State. If Clinton issues the proclamation, it will bring the land area designated as monuments by Clinton to 3.7 million acres, the second most in history. Although Clinton has declared or expanded 10 monuments, his most famous was the 1.7 million-acre Grand Staircase-Escalante National Monument in southern Utah, proclaimed weeks before the 1996 election.

The Utah decree served three purposes. First, Clinton killed an underground coal mine that would have employed 1,000 workers in economically hard pressed southern Utah and provided $20 million annually to communities devastated by Mexican spotted owl job losses. Second, Clinton firmed up the allegiance of radical environmental groups to ensure their support in the 1996 presidential election. Third, Clinton reportedly rewarded the Riady family for its financial support, by killing one of the few sources of low-sulfur coal that could compete with Riady's Indonesian coal.

If the purpose of the Utah Monument was to ensure Clinton's re-election in 1996, the purpose of subsequent monument decrees, including earlier ones in Arizona and California and those in Babbitt's latest proposal, is to enhance Clinton's place in history. As U.S. Senator Ben Nighthorse Campbell (R-CO) said, "One way for him to get past the Monica legacy is to create the public land legacy by locking up public property." Bereft of any accomplishments and burdened by ethical and moral lapses that yield themselves better to stand-up comedy than to historical veneration, Clinton seeks a legacy on the backs of westerners.

The Antiquities Act allows a president to set aside "historic and prehistoric structures, and other objects of historic or scientific interest" as national monuments, confining any such designation to "the smallest area." Although several presidents have used the Antiquities Act to lock up millions of acres, to which Congress acquiesced, that acquiescence ended in 1976 with adoption of the Federal Land Policy and Management Act (FLPMA). In FLPMA, Congress reasserted its constitutional authority over federal lands and severely restricted exactly how and how much federal land could be closed by a president. Although Congress left the Antiquities Act intact, read with FLPMA, the 1906 Act clearly is limited to "antiquities."

In designating the Utah Monument, Clinton said he was protecting "geological treasure" and "outstanding biological resources," neither of which is permitted by the Antiquities Act. Similarly, in Babbitt's proposals, the Act would be used to protect "critical spawning ground for salmon" in Washington State, "ironwood trees that can live more than 800 years" in Arizona, and "bats and old growth habitat" in Oregon. These may be important purposes; however, they are to be achieved using the Endangered Species Act and the Wild and Scenic Rivers Act. Use of those statutes, however, requires congressional action, which necessitates the support of westerners. For Clinton, that is the rub. Westerners oppose such land lock ups!

Not surprisingly, for a president who disputes the meaning of "is," "alone," and "false," Clinton says the Antiquities Act gives him whatever power he chooses to exercise, unless and until Congress or a court says otherwise. To date, while some western senators and representatives have objected to Clinton's unilateral actions, Congress has looked the other way and the one federal court presented the question has been unable, due to Clinton stonewalling, to issue a ruling.

That may change. The day before Babbitt's latest monument proposal, Texas Governor George W. Bush attacked Clinton, Gore, and Babbitt on the issue. "We have seen millions of acres of land declared off-limits and designated national monuments—just like that, with no real public involvement and no regard for the people affected by those decrees." Nearly four years after the designation of the Utah Monument, someone seems to be listening.

JUNE 2000

DO WHAT I SAY, NOT WHAT I DO

What is it that federal officials may do on public lands in Wyoming that high school officials may not do on school grounds in Texas? The answer: support religion! At least that is the situation following the ruling of the Supreme Court of the United States on June 19, 2000, in *Santa Fe Independent School District v. Doe.*

In *Santa Fe*, in a 6-3 ruling, the Court struck down student-led prayer at high school football games in a tiny Texas town, ruling that the prayer sends a "message to members of the audience who are nonadherants 'that they are outsiders, not full members of the political community, and an accompanying message to adherants that they are insiders, favored members of the political community.'" The Court rejected the school district's argument that the prayer is voluntary, declaring, "[w]hat to most believers may seem nothing more than a reasonable request that the nonbeliever respect their religious practices, [in this] context may appear to the nonbeliever or dissenter to be an attempt to employ the machinery of the [government] to enforce a religious orthodoxy."

Ironically, the Court issued its decision just before the National Park Service (NPS) bragged that it had achieved an eighty percent (80%) compliance rate with its demand that all visitors to Devils Tower National Monument in Wyoming "respect" American Indian religion. The NPS policy was adopted in 1995 in response to the demand by American Indian religious practitioners that, because Devils Tower is "sacred," visitors must be barred from climbing. That policy has a simple and straightforward objective: all visitors "will show respect" for American Indian religion.

Thus federal officials in Wyoming are now doing what the Supreme Court has ruled that high school officials in Texas may not do, "enforce a religious orthodoxy." In fact, the words of the Court in the *Santa Fe* case are even more applicable to the NPS actions at Devils Tower, "[T]he realities of the situation plainly reveal that [the school's] policy involved both perceived and actual endorsement of religion" because the prayer was delivered at a "school sponsored function conducted on school property [and was] broadcast over the school public address system, which remains subject to the control of school officials."

The "realities of the situation" at Devils Tower reveal an even more direct and heavy-handed effort to force the public, not only to acknowledge that Devils Tower is "sacred," but also to modify its behavior at the federal site to show its "respect" for that religion. The NPS has a major nationwide campaign, conducted through its official website, press releases, and numerous interviews, to ensure compliance. More specifically, would-be climbers who approach Devils Tower during June are advised by uniformed and armed NPS officials that the NPS opposes climbing during American Indians' June holy days.

Devils Tower is not the only federal site where the Clinton administration enforces American Indian religion by barring the use of public lands. At the Santa Fe Ski Area in New Mexico, federal officials barred the expansion of the ski area, declaring that the national forest lands are "sacred." In the Bighorn National Forest in northern Wyoming, all of Medicine Mountain and other areas have been declared off limits to economic activity because they must be managed as "sacred site[s]." In Montana, three quarters of a million acres of federal land have been declared off limits to oil and gas exploration because of assertions that large areas of the Lewis and Clark National Forest are "sacred." Finally, in Utah, visitors to the Rainbow Bridge National Arch are barred, by NPS officials, from walking beneath the Arch because it is "sacred."

Thus while federal courts, including the Supreme Court, strike down the most attenuated involvement by state officials in the religious lives of their citizens, the open and notorious involvement by federal officials in enforcing religion on federal lands continues.

JULY 2000

"SHAME ON YOU!"

Near Conner, in Montana's Bitterroot Valley, within miles of Idaho, stands a sign: "To the Fire Fighters: Thank you for all your efforts. To the U.S. Forest Service: Everything that we love is gone. . . . up in smoke. The mismanagement of our forests has turned our beautiful valley into an ASH HEAP! To Bill Clinton & Al Gore: Because of your environmental policies, the jobs are GONE, the way of life is GONE, and now the beauty is GONE. What's next? Shame on you!"

As Clinton signs one national monument edict after another, closing millions of acres to economic and recreational activity, pursuing what the *Washington Post* calls an "environmental lands legacy," that sign in the Bitterroot Valley may be Clinton's real lands legacy, that sign and the fires throughout Idaho, Montana, and the West to which it refers. Today, the West is facing the worst fire season in half a century. Before heavy snows fall in the Rocky Mountains—the only thing that will end this inferno—it could be the most destructive fire season ever!

Today, nearly 75,000 fires have destroyed 6.3 million acres, a third of that in Idaho and Montana. Montana is particularly hard hit: 200 fires are out of control on 712,000 acres, affecting all 56 counties and hundreds of communities. The number of fires will drop ominously as the fires burn together into more dangerous blazes. All national forests, affecting 20 million acres, are closed. Governor Racicot declared a state of emergency and asked for and received a national disaster area designation. More than 11,000 fire fighters, not including volunteers, are involved, including the National Guard, the U.S. Army, the U.S. Marines, and people from 27 states and 3 countries.

Unfortunately, westerners saw it coming. For example, the Forest Service and rural residents near the Kootenai National Forest in northwestern Montana, where 165 fires are now out of control, predicted catastrophic fires if fuel loads were not reduced by forest management. Environmental groups filed never-ending appeals and noisy objections, demanding a return to "nature's way." In response, the Clinton administration cut timber harvesting across the West by 75 percent; in the Kootenai, timber harvesting has been all but stopped. As a result, says Bruce Vincent, third generation logger from Libby, "We are a four-hour wind away from the fires that took out three million acres here in 1910."

Clinton, Vice President Al Gore, and Secretary of the Interior Babbitt did more than end thoughtful timber management; they sought the obliteration of 6,000 miles of national forest roads annually, the roads that serve as fire breaks and access corridors for fire fighters. (Babbitt says helicopters take him to the fires. But Montana fire fighters ride school buses!) Babbitt says his goal of pre-settlement conditions requires burning 5 million acres annually!

Recently Clinton demonstrated his commitment to "nature's way;" when viewing the fires from a helicopter, he said, "Mother Nature will burn our forests one way or another." For the first boomer president, Clinton is remarkably anti-technology, as is Gore who seeks to end timber harvesting on 40 to 65 million acres of the national forest. As Al Gore wrote in *Earth in the Balance* regarding technological solutions, such as forestry, "[W]e are not that clever, and we never have been."

Gore has been criticized for his "us against them, the people vs. the powerful" (quoting ABC's Cokie Roberts) Democratic Convention speech. But in Libby, Gore's statement, "Often powerful forces and powerful interests stand in your way and the odds seem stacked against you and your family," had special meaning, although not in the way Gore intended. In Libby, the "powerful forces and powerful interests" include Gore and the environmental groups with which Gore aligns himself. Not surprisingly, Gore's promise, "I'll stand up for you," is not being heard above the sounds of hundreds of thousands of western acres exploding into flame. Shame indeed.

SEPTEMBER 2000

AL GORE'S MIND AND HIS MINE

Over the last few months, critics of Al Gore's public pronouncements have addressed four general areas. First are Gore's flip-flops on issues: for example, abortion, gun control, and tobacco. While many politicians "evolve," Gore refuses to admit, for example, that he was once pro-life, or, most famously, that he did not become anti-tobacco at his sister's deathbed, as he told the 1996 Democratic Convention, but years later.

Second is Gore's habit of exaggerating or misrepresenting his actions. He claims to have invented the Internet, introduced the earned income tax credit, discovered Love Canal, created the Strategic Petroleum Reserve, and written Senator Humphrey's 1968 presidential acceptance speech. When caught, Gore attributes this decade-old tendency (aides first warned him about it in his 1988 presidential campaign) to "faulty memory, faulty memory." But these lies and scores like them reveal that Gore, like Clinton, has problems with the truth. Even more Clintonesque are Gore's evasions regarding criminal allegations, such as "no controlling legal authority" and "It depends on how you define fundraising."

Third is what Gore's tall tales may reveal about his psychological health. After all, Gore grew up in the lap of luxury, attended the nation's most expensive and elite educational institutions, and led a charmed professional and personal life. Nonetheless, he remains in deep need of public approval. Why else would a man with Gore's life story ask the public to believe that he and Tipper were the inspiration for Erich Segal's *Love Story*?

Fourth is Gore's radical worldview, as revealed in *Earth in the Balance*. Tony Snow of Fox News compared Gore's writings with those of the Unabomber and was unable to differentiate the two. Snow noted Gore's call for a "wrenching transformation of society" in which the "environment" is the sole governing principle. Others noted Gore's belief, not only that there is "growing evidence of an ecological holocaust," but also that the first instance of pollution occurs in the *Bible* "when Cain slays Abel and his blood falls on the ground."

Yet as fascinating as Al Gore's mind, is Al Gore's mine. Yes, Al Gore's mine, the zinc mine that has operated on his Tennessee farm for 25 years and from which he has received an annual royalty of $20,000, for a total of $500,000! Although the *Wall Street Journal* ran "Al Gore, Environmentalist and Zinc Miner," in late June, the story died, everywhere that is, but in the West. Here the story of Al Gore, zinc miner, is told wherever the radical environmental policies of Clinton and Gore have killed mines and with them thousands of high-paying jobs and millions of dollars of locally generated revenue.

In Garfield and Kane County, Utah, 1,000 high paying mining jobs and $20 million a year were lost when Clinton and Gore proclaimed the Grand Staircase-Escalante National Monument. In Park County, Montana, hundreds of mining jobs, with salaries double the local average, were lost when Clinton and Gore killed the New World Mine. In southeastern and northwestern Montana, two of Montana's poorest areas, hundreds of mining jobs have been axed due to Clinton/Gore environmental policies. Further, in Arizona, one mine employing predominantly Navajo people was driven out of business by Clinton/Gore policies while another mine was included in one of Clinton's monuments for which Gore claimed credit. Little wonder that many rural western counties are in economic distress.

The western miners who talk about Al Gore have heard about his flip-flops, exaggerations, lies, tall-tales, and radical pronouncements. They are curious, however, about only one thing regarding Al Gore, who is worth millions, who earns hundreds of thousands of dollars a year, who annually pockets $20,000 from mining on his own property, and who knows that mining can be economically beneficial and environmentally benign. Why does Al Gore begrudge them working for a living as miners? It is a good question. Perhaps it will be answered during the upcoming presidential debates.

OCTOBER 2000

WHY THE ENVIRONMENT IS IMPORTANT

During the second presidential debate, Vice President Gore demanded, as he did in *Earth in the Balance*, that the environment be the "central organizing principle for civilization". Days later Senator Lieberman (D-CN), speaking in Wisconsin, declared, "If you believe in God, I think it's hard not to be an environmentalist because, you see the environment is the work of God." Now in the campaign's final days, Gore and Lieberman are campaigning hard on the environmental issue.

Both say their environmental views are "a matter of faith." Lieberman cites Genesis and God's placement of Adam in the Garden of Eden "to work the garden but also to guard it." Gore also cites to Genesis, writing in *Earth*, "Indeed, the first instance of pollution in the *Bible* occurs when Cain slays Abel and his blood falls on the ground, rendering it fallow." Gore references, as well, the New Testament, citing "the Parable of the Unfaithful Servant," in three of the four Gospels, where the master, departing on a journey, instructs his servant "to protect the house against ['vandals or thieves']." Gore says the parable tells us to be alert to "the global vandalism now wreaking such unprecedented destruction on the earth."

Lieberman's Genesis reference in my *Bible* says Adam is "to work...and take care" of the Garden, not "guard it." "Guard," from a word meaning "to watch," is defined as "to protect from danger," while "care" is defined as "to give proper use and maintenance." In the modern context, the distinction is comparable to that between "preservation," as used regarding national parks, meaning "to guard or defend from evil," and "conservation," as used regarding federal multiple use lands, which means "the wise utilization of a natural product."

The parable of which Gore writes is neither referred to by that name in my *Bible* (instead it is either "The Day and Hour Unknown" or "Watchfulness"), nor does it address the guarding of household possessions. Instead, the master tells the servant to remain watchful for the master's return. In one Gospel, the servant is punished by the master, not for failing to protect his possessions from vandals and thieves, but for "beat[ing] his fellow servants." Although these may be quibbles, what is important here is the fact that Gore's views the chief concern as relating to the planet, not its people, as illustrated by Gore's peculiar take on the story of Cain killing Abel, which Gore describes as pollution, not murder. Elsewhere in *Earth*, Gore concludes that the story of Noah commands, "Thou shalt preserve biodiversity," pursuant to a covenant that "affirm[s] the sacredness of creation." Moreover, Gore equates the extermination of six million souls by the Nazis with the world's environmental problems: "[We are facing] an environmental holocaust without precedent."

For most people, it is not the creation that is sacred, but other human beings. Thus we are called upon to protect the environment not because the planet is "sacred" and may not be soiled, but because we wish to ensure the health and safety of the human environment for this generation and for those to come. This distinction is not lost on the nation's most needy. According to a recent survey of 69 environmental justice groups, a scant 6 percent rank the environment as their top priority, which is not surprising given that 63 percent of them say the poor and minorities pay the greatest cost in lost jobs and higher prices when "the environment" comes first.

With the environment as "the central organizing principle for civilization," Gore asks: "when giving us dominion over the Earth, did God choose an appropriate technology?" to which Gore answers, "The jury is still out." When people come first, we ask, "Am I my brother's keeper?" and are compelled to answer, "Yes!" These two questions ask us to consider what is more important: the planet or its people, and cause us to question, not God, but ourselves.

NOVEMBER 2000

CHAPTER TWELVE

Whither the War on the West

★ ★ ★ ★ ★

O n September 11, 2001, I drove to a 7:00 a.m. men's *Bible* study at my church. On the way I stopped at Walmart to buy gifts the church was sending to children in Africa. Store employees were gathered in the food service area around a television; I assumed it was a training session. Just then I saw a neighbor who, surprised I did not know, told me the news of the attack on America.

After I dropped off the gifts and sat in the circle of men, reading and discussing the *Bible* and praying, I wondered how many knew; I was not going to raise it. On my drive out of the foothills from the church, I prayed. At the office, MSLF's staff was gathered around the television. I had work to do, I thought; in a little over a month I would once again be before the Supreme Court to argue *Adarand Constructors, Inc. v. Mineta* (Bush's new Secretary of Transportation). I would read and learn about it all later and not piecemeal with bits of news from breathless reporters. At one point, my son Perry, a Navy ROTC student at the University of Pennsylvania, called: Muslim students were dancing in the halls of the dormitories. I was glad I was not watching television.

Later, MSLF attorney Stephen P. Gilmartin stuck his head in my door. The plane that hit the Pentagon was carrying a CNN reporter, did I know her? It was my friend, the remarkable Barbara Olson, wife of the Solicitor General of the United States, Theodore (Ted) Olson. I stopped work and stared out my thirtieth floor window at the foothills and rolling prairie off in the distance.

On October 31, 2001, Ted and I stood shoulder to shoulder before the justices of the Supreme Court, meeting for the first time since 1935 somewhere besides their Courtroom (The anthrax scare had forced the building's evacuation.). My wife Lis whispered that the justices looked out of sorts. I looked over at Ted; it was Ted's first appearance before the Court since his wife's murder. Then I looked back at my clients, Randy and Valery Pech, and wondered if their brave fight, which they started with me in 1989, was to be a casualty of the new war in which our country suddenly found itself.

THE LONG VIEW

In a few days, Larry Squires of Hobbs, New Mexico, will get his "day in court" as the U.S. Court of Federal Claims begins the trial in Larry's suit against the United States for unconstitutionally taking his property for "public use" without "just compensation." It has been a long time in coming.

In 1969, when Larry considered going into the business of disposing of salt water in the sinkholes on his arid property, he had concerns. After all, "I'm an environmentalist." But an expert hydrologist said "Okay." Larry's lands are 40 miles from the nearest stream; there is no ground water under his lands; and, the sinkholes are lined with 300 feet of impermeable clay. Later, Larry checked with the Environmental Protection Agency (EPA), which said, in 1987, that the Clean Water Act (CWA) did not cover his lands; he could continue with his plans. So Larry did.

In 1992, the EPA served Larry with a cease and desist order declaring his lands "waters of the United States" under the CWA. The EPA said that Larry's lands fell under the Migratory Bird Rule, adopted in 1987, because every 100 years it rains hard enough that water collects in the sinkholes; until that water evaporates, migratory birds could land there. Facing $100,000 a day fines, Larry was driven out of business.

In 1993, Larry sued the EPA, asserting that the Migratory Bird Rule violated the intent of Congress. The EPA answered that Larry could not challenge its order because it was not "final," though it was a death sentence for Larry's business. The New Mexico federal district court agreed with the EPA. Subsequently, although the U.S. Court of Appeals for the Tenth Circuit was concerned about Larry's inability to challenge the order, it did not want to undercut the EPA's enforcement authority! In 1996, the Supreme Court of the United States declined to hear Larry's appeal.

With his business destroyed, Larry sued the United States for taking his property contrary to the Constitution's Fifth Amendment. Federal attorneys raised every possible objection, each of which was rejected. Then, as Larry's trial date approached, federal lawyers said that Larry should have known, with passage of the CWA, that his arid lands are "waters of the United States." "Why, everyone knows that!" they said.

Apparently not everyone! On January 9, 2001, the Supreme Court not only ruled that it did not know that; it also ruled that Congress did not know that. As a result, the federal government's attempt, through the Migratory Bird Rule, to extend "waters of the United States" to ponds like Larry's violated the CWA! In *Solid Waste Agency of Northern Cook County v. Army Corps of Engineers*, the Court struck down the rule because it "result[s] in a significant impingement of the States' traditional and primary power over lands and water use." Larry Squires had been right all along; but that is no consolation to him. He anticipates that federal lawyers will find more reasons for not awarding him "just compensation."

There is another important and instructive observation regarding this tale, which may have become obvious in its telling. The Migratory Bird Rule was adopted in 1987, during Ronald Reagan's presidency. Larry was served with the EPA's order in 1992, during George H.W. Bush's presidency. Larry's attempt to have the merits of his case heard by a federal court was stonewalled for the eight years of Bill Clinton's presidency. Larry has no expectation that anything will change when trial starts later this month, notwithstanding George W. Bush's presence in the White House. Why should he expect otherwise?

Westerners, small business people, and property owners expect big changes at the presidential level with Bush's arrival. In the federal government, however, with millions of federal employees including thousands of lawyers, implementing hundreds of laws and tens of thousands of pages of regulations, any change at the ground level—where people live, work, and play—if it comes, will come slowly. Therefore, taking the long view, folks like Larry Squires must keep going to court.

FEBRUARY 2001

RESTORING THE RULE OF LAW, STARTING IN NEVADA

"[O]ur constitutional system is in disarray. The rule of law is severely damaged. The Department of Justice is no longer a neutral zone in the government. There is an appearance that the powerful are treated better by the law than the powerless...." declared Griffin B. Bell, President Carter's Attorney General, in the Cato Institute's "The Rule of Law in the Wake of Clinton."

John Bernt of Jarbidge, Nevada has not read "The Rule of Law" and has not heard what Mr. Bell has said on this subject. He did not need to do so. Bernt knows, first hand, what happened to the rule of law during the Clinton administration!

On January 3 and 10, 1996, Bernt staked mining claims on federal lands in Nevada. On January 19, federal officials withdrew the land upon which Bernt had staked his claims from mining availability, placing notice of that withdrawal in official documents. Because Bernt had staked his claims before the withdrawal, however, he had pre-existing rights, which Bernt told federal officials in early February and March. Meanwhile, federal officials notified Bernt that the withdrawn lands were being considered for a land exchange, but that his claims predated the withdrawal.

Then, on April 12, federal officials told Bernt that the lands had been withdrawn, not on January 19, but on November 27, 1995. If true, Bernt's claims were invalid. So, on April 17, Bernt examined official withdrawal documents, but those documents showed the January 19 date. Later, Bernt saw documents with the November 27 date; however, visible on those documents was the January 19 date, entered before the November 27 date. Later, when Bernt sought more documents, he was told they had been destroyed.

On May 24, 1996, the Bureau of Land Management (BLM) declared Bernt's claims "null and void." A month later, Bernt reexamined the "official" records and discovered that they had been altered once again, this time by placing the November 27 date above the January 19 date. When Bernt appealed the BLM's decision to the Interior Board of Land Appeals (IBLA), the BLM never filed a response, but secretly provided documents to the IBLA. On March 1, 1999, the IBLA, using those documents, ruled against Bernt.

Months later, Bernt discovered documents that the BLM had not provided to the IBLA, documents that proved Bernt's case, documents that Bernt had been told did not exist. Later, using the Freedom of Information Act, Bernt obtained other BLM documents that he had been told had been destroyed, some containing admissions that federal officials had altered documents. Bernt sued, seeking to have his claims reinstated and to hold accountable the federal officials who had altered documents fraudulently so as to invalidate his claims. He sued the agency and the officials who had altered the documents, naming them personally.

One would have thought that such serious allegations would give the U.S. Department of Justice attorneys pause. After all, Bernt had evidence federal officials had altered documents fraudulently to void his claims. But Clinton administration lawyers could not have cared less; they perfunctorily certified that the individuals were acting "within the scope of their employment" and moved to dismiss the fraud counts against them. Justice Department attorneys not only resisted Bernt's efforts to discover what had happened, but they also filed affidavits from individuals with no knowledge of the events of late 1995 and early 1996 who swore that nothing had happened!

Recently, relying on the head-in-the-sand-representations of Clinton's Justice Department, a Nevada federal district court judge dismissed Bernt's lawsuit, declaring, "This happens all the time." Sadly, after the last eight years, the judge may be right! But John Bernt does not think so. At least he hopes not; he intends to appeal.

Those desiring to restore the rule of law and the U.S. Department of Justice as, in the words of Griffin Bell, "a neutral zone in the government," can start with John Bernt in Nevada.

APRIL 2001

WESTERNERS FEAR BEARS AND
BUREAUCRATS

In July of 1992, Sarah Muller of Bozeman, Montana, was attacked by a grizzly bear while hiking in Yellowstone National Park. "Bites broke her left arm and tore open her shoulder and her legs. One crushed seven ribs that will never heal, collapsing a lung. The bear shook her like a terrier does a rat. She heard cracking sounds when the bear bit into her ribs, but the crunching of teeth in her skull, the bear's top teeth in the back of her head, the bottom ones in her eye and forehead, was even louder." Then, as Scott McMillion writes in *Mark of the Grizzly*, "She remembers flying through the air.... hoping she wouldn't die...."

Given the ferociousness of grizzly bear attacks, it is little wonder that, nearly three years earlier, on a stormy night in September of 1989, when John Shuler of Dupuyer, Montana, was attacked, he shot to kill. Although the Endangered Species Act (ESA), which lists grizzly bears as "threatened" and bars their killing, has a self-defense exception, the Fish and Wildlife Service prosecuted Shuler. After eight years, Shuler was vindicated when a federal district judge ruled that he had acted in self-defense. The Clinton administration did not appeal.

The lesson of Shuler's legal battle is that federal bureaucrats will prosecute those using deadly force to protect themselves from attacking grizzly bears. Those prosecutions and the cost of fighting back (if not *pro bono*, Shuler's legal bill would have exceeded $200,000) have rendered the ESA's self-defense provision a nullity. That is the lesson learned by Wyoming's Pat VanVleet.

In October of 1998, VanVleet was hunting near Dubois, Wyoming, when he was attacked by a grizzly bear. Armed with a powerful hunting rifle, he threw the rifle down because, in his words, "I wanted to do the right thing." No doubt Shuler was on his mind. "Everyone in grizzly bear country has heard about Shuler," he said later. In addition, federal officials had posted warnings throughout northwestern Wyoming telling hunters not to shoot grizzly bears. When VanVleet's pepper spray proved useless, he was nearly killed.

Is it any wonder that a Clinton administration plan to put grizzly bears (*Ursus arctos horribilis*) in rural central Idaho and western Montana elicited such a strong, prolonged, and negative reaction? The Clinton plan envisioned 280 grizzly bears roaming over an area nearly as large as Massachusetts, New Hampshire, and Vermont combined. Although the grizzlies were to be managed by a 15-member citizen committee, the committee's authority could be revoked if federal officials concluded it was not acting in the bear's best interest. Further, environmental groups could sue for even stricter regulations.

It should surprise no one that the people who live, work, and recreate in this area have no desire to have the type of grizzly bear encounters suffered by Sarah Muller, John Shuler, Pat VanVleet, and others. Plus, they do not want to see their ability to live their lives, to work for a living, and to enjoy the outdoors with their families restricted by some federal bureaucrat's dreamy vision of grizzly bears out "in the middle of nowhere." That is why the plan elicited such an unfavorable reaction, including hundreds of comments, a notice of intent to sue by those in rural Idaho and Montana, and a lawsuit by Idaho's Governor Dirk Kempthorne.

No wonder the *Washington Post* reported recently that Secretary Gale Norton will scuttle the Clinton plan. No doubt Norton recognizes what westerners know. The grizzly bear does not face extinction, even in the lower 48. Grizzlies thrive and are in abundance in Canada and Alaska. The grizzly bear does not belong in people's backyards and in multiple use forests upon which rural people depend. Chalk one up for President Bush for having, in this instance, fulfilled his promise that "the western mentality [will be] represented in this administration." Chalk one up as well, for the people of rural Idaho and Montana.

MAY 2001

"JUST COMPENSATION" AND THE
U.S. DEPARTMENT OF JUSTICE

Recently a federal court ordered the United States to pay Paul and Patricia Preseault of Burlington, Vermont, more than a quarter of a million dollars, plus interest—which could triple the award—and attorneys' fees. The ruling culminated the Preseaults' fifteen-year battle, which began when the federal government used the National Trails System Act Amendments of 1983 (Rails to Trails Act) to seize their property. Under that statute, an easement that was to have reverted to the Preseaults when abandoned by the railroad was withheld for public use as a trail. Thus, the Preseaults' property was opened to tens of thousands of hikers, runners, bikers, riders and rollerbladers, who—up to two hundred people an hour on weekends—pass the Preseaults' front door. After an earlier holding that the Preseaults' property had been taken without just compensation, on May 22, that compensation was held to be $234,000, as of 1986.

Shortly after passage of the Rails-to-Trails Act in 1983, the Preseaults challenged Congress's authority to vitiate the contract by which the railroad easement was to have reverted to them. In 1990, the Supreme Court of the United States held that, although the Commerce Clause gave Congress power to take the Preseaults' private property for a public use, the Fifth Amendment might require the United States to pay just compensation for that taking. The Preseaults returned to federal court, with New England Legal Foundation as their attorney, seeking just compensation. The United States responded that federal railroad legislation had redefined and destroyed state-created property rights; thus, it owed the Preseaults nothing! In 1996, the U.S. Court of Appeals for the Federal Circuit rejected that argument, ruling that the federal occupation of the Preseaults' property was "a taking.... for which the Constitution requires that just compensation be paid." Now, nearly five years later, the amount of that compensation has been determined.

Maurice and Delores Glosemeyer of Marthasville, Missouri, know about Paul and Patricia Preseault. Like the Preseaults, the Glosemeyers had a railroad right-of-way across their property that, under the easement's terms, was to revert to them when the railroad went away. Like the Preseaults, the Glosemeyers had their reversionary rights invalidated by the Rails-to-Trails

Act. Like the Preseaults, the Glosemeyers spent years in state and federal courts, challenging Congress's authority to seize their property and seeking just compensation for that seizure. In fact, for years their litigation was delayed, by court order, until resolution of the Preseaults' litigation.

Finally, in early 1997 when the Preseault decision became final, the stay on the Glosemeyers' case was lifted. In mid-1997, the Glosemeyers, seeking an expeditious ruling, filed a summary judgment motion arguing that, applying Missouri law to the undisputed facts, compelled a ruling in their favor. The United States sought more delay, asserting that it had to conduct additional fact finding. For more than two years, the United States demanded more fact-finding delays. Then, in November of 1999, during oral arguments in Washington, D.C., Justice Department attorneys repeatedly pleaded for delay, ostensibly for more fact finding, pleas the U.S. Court for Federal Claims flatly rejected. In January of 2000, the court ruled that the Glosemeyers' property rights had been taken unconstitutionally by the federal government.

One would think that, after all this time, the Glosemeyers, like the Preseaults, would be on the verge of receiving the long overdue just compensation owned them by the federal government. Within the past few days, however, Department of Justice attorneys refused to pay, not only the value of the property taken from the Glosemeyers as determined by the Glosemeyers' expert, but also interest and attorneys' fees! Instead, the Department of Justice demands that the matter of just compensation go to trial.

The dictionary defines "just" as "in accordance with or adhering to the principles of justice." It is not surprising that the Glosemeyers find that definition somewhat ironic given the refusal of the Department of Justice to pay the Glosemeyers their just compensation.

JULY 2001

THE BUSH ADMINISTRATION AND ENERGY FROM FEDERAL LANDS

In making its case for producing more domestic energy, the Bush administration declared, "The federal government owns about 31 percent of the nation's land.... Public lands provide nearly 30 percent of annual national energy production, and are estimated to contain a substantial majority of the nation's undiscovered domestic energy resources. [But portions] of federal onshore...lands are off-limits to oil and gas exploration and development[:] about 40 percent of the natural gas resources on federal lands in the Rocky Mountain region have been placed off-limits."

One area now off limits is the Rocky Mountain Division of the Lewis and Clark National Forest in north central Montana, which sits astride the Overthrust Belt, a geological formation known for decades to contain abundant natural gas. In 1986, the U.S. Forest Service sought to determine whether energy leasing could occur upon "potentially oil and gas-rich land[s]" in that area. In 1996, the Forest Service began another study on whether to authorize leasing.

Recognizing that "[t]he entire [area] has been rated as having a high potential for the presence of hydrocarbons [and that] [m]ost of the past oil and gas activity, and projected future oil and gas activity, is located [there]," the Forest Service concluded that it had an obligation to "help meet the present and future needs of the Nation . . . , [and to] contribute to the economic well-being of local communities and the strategic interest of the nation. . . ." But the Forest Service limited leasing to a one-mile strip along the boundary of the Lewis and Clark and required drilling to occur outside that boundary.

Then, inexplicably, in August of 1997, the Forest Service announced that the area would be closed to leasing. The Forest Service admitted that leasing would not harm "wildlife or other surface resources values" but barred it anyway in response to the "emotions," "feel[ings]," and "perceptions" of leasing opponents. The Forest Service admitted those opponents had "not read the environmental analysis.... [They were simply venting] heartfelt emotions. . . ."

Oil and gas operators sued. A Montana federal district court ruled that the operators had no right to sue and that it was legal for the Forest Service to "allow public sentiment to override scientific [analysis]." The U.S. Court of Appeals for the Ninth Circuit agreed, holding that the operators could not sue and, because their interest was economic, could not compel the Forest Service to obey the law. Finally, the Ninth Circuit held "psychological harms," unconnected to changes in the environment, suffered by people far from Montana, was a legal basis for closing federal lands to leasing.

There is no indication that the Bush administration is aware of what occurred in the Lewis and Clark or the decisions of the federal courts; briefings were completed before President Bush took office. That will change soon, however; Bush officials must respond to a recent petition that the Supreme Court of the United States hear the case.

The primary reason why the Bush administration may want to join in asking for Supreme Court review is the energy potential of the Lewis and Clark. But there are other reasons. The Ninth Circuit's decision bars all oil and gas operators from challenging illegal closures of federal lands to energy leasing. Environmental groups may sue to stop energy development, but energy groups may not sue to spur that development. Because of a similar decision by the Tenth Circuit, in the states that contain 93 percent of the nation's federal lands, illegal closures are beyond challenge. There is one more reason: the Ninth Circuit's decision regarding "psychological harms;" it is hard to imagine a better mechanism for stopping the Bush administration's energy plan!

The Bush administration makes the case that energy from federal lands is a vital part of the nation's future. It is one thing to say that; it is something else to take that case to the Supreme Court. How serious the Bush administration is will be clear in a month.

AUGUST 2001

IS IT PROPERTY IF CONGRESS
SAYS IT CAN'T BE SOLD?

In November of 1999, Timothy Kornwolf opened the door of his home in Stillwater, Minnesota, to Ivar Husby, who introduced himself as a Norwegian collector of Laplander artifacts interested in Indian artifacts. In reality, Husby was a Norwegian police chief working undercover for the U.S. Fish and Wildlife Service. Carrying a briefcase filled with cash and a hidden audio and video recorder, Husby intended to purchase an eagle feather headdress and a Sioux dance shield. He got what he wanted; thereafter, Kornwolf was arrested and charged in an eight count federal indictment.

Kornwolf had violated the Bald and Golden Eagle Protection Act and the Migratory Bird Treaty Act, together "the Feather Act," which prohibits the sale of golden eagle feathers. The headdress and shield, however, had been in Kornwolf's family since 1904, acquired by his mother's mother's brother, "Uncle Nick," Nicholas J. Klein, who had been in Buffalo Bill's Wild West Show, which was when he acquired the headdress and shield he gave Kornwolf.

At the U.S. District Court for Minnesota, Kornwolf's attorney argued that because the Feather Act permitted Kornwolf to possess the golden eagle feathers but prohibited him from selling them, it violated the Constitution's Fifth Amendment. The district court rejected that argument, relying on a 1979 Supreme Court of the United States decision, *Andrus v. Allard*. In *Allard*, the Supreme Court, focusing on the property rights the Feather Act allowed owners to retain, rather than on the rights the law removed, ruled that the Feather Act was constitutional: "At least where an owner possesses a full 'bundle' of property rights, the destruction of one 'strand' of the bundle is not a taking, because the aggregate must be viewed in its entirety."

In 1987, however, the Supreme Court faced the same issue. In *Hodel v. Irving*, a federal law denied tribal members the right to pass their property to their heirs. Justice O'Connor declared that although the law took but one "stick in the bundle of sticks" that constitutes property ownership, that "stick" is an essential one: "In one form or another, the right to pass on property, in particular to one's family, has been part of the Anglo-American legal system since feudal times." The Court reached the same holding ten years later in *Babbitt v. Youpee*.

The significance of *Irving* was not lost on three members of the Court. Justice Scalia, joined by Chief Justice Rehnquist, and Justice Powell, wrote, "In my view the present statute, insofar as concerns the balance between rights taken and rights left untouched, is indistinguishable from [the Feather Act, which was] at issue in *Andrus v. Allard*. Because that comparison is determinative of whether there has been a taking..., in finding a taking today our decision effectively limits *Allard* to its facts."

Remarkably, the Minnesota federal district court did not ask what was left of *Allard* after the Supreme Court's rulings in *Irving* and *Youpee*. Nor did the district court accept Justice Scalia's invitation to compare the facts of *Allard* with Kornwolf's case. Had it done so it would have found that those prosecuted in *Allard* had not presented evidence of preexisting ownership, while Kornwolf had! As a result, after the district court ruled against him, Kornwolf entered a plea of guilty to four counts of the indictment, reserving his right to withdraw that plea if the U.S. Court of Appeals for the Eighth Circuit declares the Feather Act unconstitutional.

Kornwolf hopes the Eighth Circuit will do what the district court did not do, hold that the Supreme Court has abandoned its 1979 holding that it is constitutional for the federal government to deny an owner the right to sell his property. As Kornwolf wonders whether the Eighth Circuit will free him, the rest of us might wonder what the Fish and Wildlife Service is doing sending foreign undercover agents, with suitcases full of cash, into the homes of American citizens to urge them to break the law!

SEPTEMBER 2001

THEN AND NOW: PRESIDENT BUSH'S
LAWYERS AND ELECTIONS

Last year, Governor Bush's lawyers were filing briefs regarding elections in Florida. This year, President Bush's lawyers are filing briefs regarding elections in Montana. Then, Governor Bush's attorneys argued that those elections demonstrated the will of Florida voters, with which a court could not interfere. Now, President Bush's attorneys argue that those elections demonstrate racism by Montana voters, which mandates court intervention.

In 1999, Clinton's Acting Assistant Attorney General, Bill Lann Lee, sent lawyers to rural Chinook, Montana, to deliver an ultimatum to Blaine County, population 7,009. Either admit it had violated the Voting Rights Act and agree to redraw county commissioner districts to guarantee election of an American Indian or the United States would sue! County Commissioners believed they had done nothing wrong; after all, Montana law requires Blaine County to elect commissioners as it does. Moreover, no one in Blaine County had been denied the right to register or vote or the ability to run for office. For Clinton and Lee, however, the Voting Rights Act guarantees not just the right to register and vote, regardless of race; it guarantees results. Thus, American Indians had a right to elect one of their own as commissioner.

After Governor Bush's lawyers prevailed at the Supreme Court of the United States and Bush became president, some thought Bill Lann Lee's lawsuit would be dropped. After all, Lee was "acting" because his views were so radical that a majority of U.S. Senators refused to confirm him, one was Senator Ashcroft (R-MO), Bush's Attorney General. In addition, Lee's assertions about Blaine County could be made against most western rural counties, the vast majority of which voted one-sidedly for Bush; Bush beat Gore in Blaine County 51% to 45%.

The Blaine County lawsuit was not abandoned; it is not clear whether that was due to a conscious decision by Bush or Ashcroft. For example, Ashcroft was one of the last cabinet officials sworn in, after a bruising confirmation battle. Moreover, for weeks, he was the only presidential appointee at Justice. Then came the attack on America and Bush and Ashcroft turned to fighting terrorism. Exactly a month after the attack, the very same lawyers

Bill Lann Lee had sent to Chinook, Montana, in 1999 were in Great Falls, Montana, in the midst of a two-week trial against Blaine County.

Bush's lawyers argued that Montana laws enacted between 1871 and 1919 and in 1941 and 1949 discriminated against American Indians. Blaine County answered that those laws had not been adopted for discriminatory purposes and had been repealed, at the latest, more than half a century earlier. Bush's lawyers then argued that Indians vote as a bloc to elect American Indians, but are thwarted in those efforts because non-Indians vote as a bloc to prevent American Indians from being elected to countywide office. Blaine County disproved that assertion with expert statistical evidence, but Blaine County had even better evidence: Charles Hay, an American Indian, had been elected both justice of the peace and sheriff with the overwhelming support of American Indians and non-Indians alike. Bush's lawyers said, "But Charles Hay did not run as an Indian." In part Hay agrees: "I ran as Charles Hay!" A federal judge will decide who won that argument early next year, but there is already a loser.

In 2000, Governor Bush proclaimed, "I don't like [racial] quotas. Quotas tend to pit one group of people against another. Quotas are bad for America." Today Bush's lawyers "pit one group of people against another," arguing that race is relevant in Blaine County even if folks there have shown that it is not. Plus, the future envisioned by Bush's lawyers is one in which: districts are racially gerrymandered, race is all that matters, and race is forever relevant. With Americans united as never before, that vision is not just antagonistic to the Constitution; it is an anachronism from America's shameful past, not an aspiration for America's shining future.

DECEMBER 2001

CHAPTER THIRTEEN

Clinton's Justice Department's Tenth Year

───────

As the white-gloved bugler trumpeted "Morning Colors," three U.S. Marines in dress blues raised the American flag over MSLF's new headquarters at its June 6, 2002 gala. Then, without a doubt as to its constitutionality, the one hundred Directors, Board of Litigation members, honored guests, contributors, and MSLF staff joined in the Pledge of Allegiance and, to the accompaniment of bugler Dave Barnett, the National Anthem. The flag raising, by U.S. Marine Corps Air Control Squadron 23 Corporals Alfonso Gonzales and Quinique Harris and Lance Corporal Dante Rumore, followed an opening prayer by Reverend Kenneth Williams, Ph.D., senior pastor of Rockland Community Church in Golden, Colorado. After the ceremonial cutting of the ribbon by Chairman David B. Rovig and the entire Executive Committee, the attendees gathered inside for a short program during which portions of the building were dedicated.

MSLF's Conference Room was dedicated in the name of Adarand Constructors, Inc. and its owners, Randy and Valery Pech. Two elegantly framed artistic renderings of MSLF's appearances at the Supreme Court of the United States in *Adarand*, in 1995 and 2001, gifts from the Pech Family and Adarand, adorned the walls. The Office of the President was dedicated in the name of Helen Chenoweth-Hage, who became a MSLF client in a landmark lawsuit against President Clinton, and who then launched a nationwide fundraising campaign for MSLF. Also dedicated were the flag pole in the name of Director Donald Thorson, his brother, Thomas Thorson, and his sister, Mary Gullikson and offices in the names of: John Harnish, Thomas Hauptman, the J.W. Kieckhefer Foundation, Ellice McDonald, Jr., Bob and Marilyn Prewitt, Conley P. Smith, L. Jerald Sheffels, Lew O. Ward, Carol Ann Quigg, and Wyoming Wildcatter.

I delivered opening remarks on MSLF's 1977 origins and the progress in its first quarter century. Former U.S. Representative Helen Chenoweth-Hage (R-1st ID) delivered the keynote address, reflecting on her introduction to MSLF and her years as a MSLF client. MSLF's own building is a gigantic step and one that will make it possible for MSLF to spend more of the contributions it receives on precedent-setting, nationally significant litigation. The move was made possible by a $350,000 Capital Campaign.

IS CLINTON'S JUSTICE DEPARTMENT ENTERING ITS TENTH YEAR?

On November 30, 2001, Thomas L. Sansonetti was confirmed as Assistant Attorney General for the Environment and Natural Resources Division of the Department of Justice (DOJ). Thus Sansonetti becomes President Bush's lead lawyer for federal land issues affecting the third of the nation owned by the United States and environmental issues affecting rural Americans— those in the red tide of counties from coast to coast who voted for Bush. As Sansonetti began work, eight months after his nomination, his division and others at DOJ were ending what some observers viewed, not as the Bush administration's first year, but as the Clinton administration's ninth.

This is surprising given, not only Bush-Cheney campaign rhetoric regarding failings in the Clinton-Gore years, but also bipartisan criticism that the Clinton administration abused the rule of law. Carter's Attorney General, Griffin B. Bell, for example, wrote, "[O]ur constitutional system is in disarray. The rule of law is severely damaged. The Department of Justice is no longer a neutral zone in the government." Constitutional scholar Roger Pilon, in "The Rule of Law in the Wake of Clinton," noted Clinton "ignored both constitutional limits on government power and constitutional guarantees of individual liberty ... variously launched, encouraged, or joined assaults on centuries-old common law principles while abandoning prudence in the application of statutes ... [and] politicized the institutions of justice...." The late Barbara Olson, in her best-selling, *The Final Days*, documented Clinton's greatest abuses: his refusal to obey a landmark Supreme Court civil rights ruling and his federal land decrees. The question is, if Clinton and his officials were so lawless, why are Bush lawyers defending them?

For example, Bush lawyers argued that Clinton had unfettered discretion to designate monuments and that courts may not review his decrees. Bush lawyers defended: Clinton's closure of sixty million acres of national forest, Clinton officials who conspired to kill a mining operation, and Clinton's Environmental Protection Agency administrator who destroyed court-ordered documents. Bush lawyers also defended Clinton's closure of a million acres of oil and gas lands and then, when the case was appealed to the Supreme Court, urged the Court not to hear it. That opposition was filed, even though one Bush appointee called the decision "a disaster," both for federal land law and for Bush's energy policy.

There are three reasons for these pleadings. First, the enduring bureaucratic view in the DOJ is that the United States should never confess error, never surrender, and never lose a case. Not only will DOJ lawyers do almost anything to prevail, they will seek to dismiss a case on procedural grounds, even if the citizen suing is right on the merits! Second, at his barbaric confirmation hearing, Attorney General Ashcroft was forced to promise to enforce all laws, even if of questionable constitutionality. This unprecedented promise has been aggravated by Ashcroft's overly cautious, but understandable, refusal to exercise the supervisory discretion given every Attorney General. Third, after September 11, Ashcroft's first job is preventing terrorist acts and investigating and prosecuting crimes of terrorism; all else is secondary.

As a result, in a challenge to racial preferences, *Adarand Constructors, Inc. v. Mineta*, Bush lawyers continued the procedural slight-of-hand of Clinton lawyers to prevent a Supreme Court ruling; it worked: on November 27, the Court dismissed the twelve-year old case. To force racial gerrymandering on Montana's Blaine County, Clinton lawyers sued, litigation pressed by Bush lawyers. Then, the day the Supreme Court dismissed *Adarand*, Bush lawyers sued Colorado's Alamosa County to force gerrymandering by race. Clinton must be pleased!

Some are not pleased. The Congressional Western Caucus recently met at the White House to express disappointment over Bush's failure to reverse Clinton's "War on the West." Realizing that Bush is fighting a war on western civilization, the Members remained disturbed that policy changes have not occurred, either in the field or in the courtroom. If such changes come, they may appear first in pleadings bearing the signature of Thomas L. Sansonetti.

JANUARY 2002

LYNX, WATER, CATTLE, AND THE
FISH AND WILDLIFE SERVICE

In December of 2001, the *Washington Times* reported that employees of the U.S. Fish and Wildlife Service (FWS) had planted lynx fur on rubbing posts in two national forests in Washington State to make it appear as if lynx were there in order to compel closure of those forests. Western U.S. Representatives were livid; Congressman Scott McInnis (R-3rd CO), Chairman of the House Forests and Forest Health Subcommittee, launched a congressional investigation. Months later the story is still making news, most recently when environmental groups defended the FWS employees and attacked the investigation as "a witch hunt."

Days ago, the *Washington Post* reported the results of a National Academy of Sciences (NAS) study regarding the Draconian demands imposed by the FWS on Klamath Falls, Oregon. The FWS, pursuant to the Endangered Species Act (ESA), had shut off water, to which farmers had a legal right, because delivery of the water purportedly violated the ESA. The action came during a drought, which turned productive fields into acres of withering crops. Secretary of the Interior Norton visited the embattled and embittered community, but said her hands were tied. The NAS concluded: there was "no sound scientific basis" for the FWS's actions.

Meanwhile, the U.S. Court of Appeals for the Ninth Circuit, the nation's most liberal and most frequently reversed circuit, struck down efforts by the FWS to end cattle grazing on a vast area in Arizona. The Ninth Circuit concluded that the FWS's evidence was "vague," "speculative," and "woefully insufficient." The FWS, concluded the court, "has a very low bar to meet, but it must at least attain it," otherwise compliance with the ESA would be left "within the unfettered discretion of the [FWS], leaving no method by which [private parties] or [other federal agencies] can gauge their performance."

For those who have followed the ESA and the FWS over the years, these recent reports of FWS malfeasance are nothing new. Almost ten years ago, when the FWS was accused of basing its opinions, not on biological science, but on political science, one high ranking official responded, "If you define 'politics' in the non-pejorative sense of it being the 'balancing of competing demands,' yes, our business is.... political." At the same time Clinton's

Forest Service chief and spotted owl expert told reporters there was not a "magic number" of spotted owls, that what the FWS was doing was making "moral judgments between the needs of the owl and the needs of mankind!"

The FWS's decisions may be political or moral and not scientific, but they have real life consequences. Every federal agency has a duty to consult with the FWS regarding any proposed public or private action that could affect species covered by the ESA. The so-called biological opinions that the FWS issues during that consultation, which bind all other federal agencies and private parties, can be a death sentence, as seen above, for public use of a national forest, for delivery of private water, or for the grazing of cattle.

What is new after all these years is that the public and the national media are starting to pay attention. Perhaps one of the reasons is that, after eight years of a president famous for quibbling over the definitions of "is," "alone," and "false," the idea that low-level federal employees might engage in unethical or illegal shenanigans is not so far-fetched. While the public may be changing its opinions, the message has yet to reach Washington, D.C. The U.S. Department of Justice, by defending the often indefensible, continues to make it difficult for citizens to obtain relief from improper, illegal, or unethical actions by federal employees. In addition, those up the chain of command have failed to signal change. Recently a federal administrative law judge declared, in a controversial ESA case, that FWS witnesses had to be believed because they had no reason to lie; they were simply doing their jobs!

MARCH 2002

"SACRED LAND" BATTLE MOVES ONTO PRIVATE PROPERTY

On April 17, 2002, Dale McKinnon and his attorney returned to federal district court in Phoenix, Arizona. Three years earlier, McKinnon had been sued, along with the United States and Arizona Department of Transportation, by the Hopi Tribe, which asserted that land owned by McKinnon, from which he mines aggregate used in highway construction, is sacred. Thus, because the aggregate was to be used on a federal highway project, the Tribe argued that the United States and Arizona had to consult with and get the tribe's permission before they could use McKinnon's aggregate. The Hopi's lawsuit was not McKinnon's first encounter with American Indians' demands that he be stopped from using his property because of their religious beliefs about the windswept rock pile he owns south of Holbrook in east central Arizona.

In 1990, McKinnon leased and then bought Woodruff Butte, near the wide spot in the road that is Woodruff, reached via a dirt road from Holbrook, which itself fell upon very hard times when Route 66 became Interstate 40. What does remain valuable is the aggregate on Woodruff Butte, the best in the region, due to its very high density and low porosity, which yield great concrete strength while using less oil in the paving process. Those constructing streets and highways in Arizona were eager to use McKinnon's aggregate.

Dale McKinnon, operating as Cholla Ready Mix, obtained a commercial source permit from the Arizona Department of Transportation to allow his aggregate to be used in bids to construct Arizona highways. But then the Hopi, and soon the Navajo, and the Zuni, asserted that McKinnon's rock pile was sacred. McKinnon's efforts at compromise failed; tribal leaders refused to identify any sacred locations so McKinnon could protect them. (Incredibly, younger tribal members who were particularly opposed to compromise asked McKinnon for directions to Woodruff Butte.) Then came the Hopi lawsuit, challenging use of McKinnon's aggregate. The harassment of McKinnon continued. Finally, in January of 2001, Arizona revoked McKinnon's commercial source permit and barred him from obtaining another one to ensure that the public shows respect for the beliefs of American Indians that McKinnon's land is sacred.

Although this is the first time American Indians have demanded that a landowner be barred from using his property because it is "sacred," over the last several years American Indians have demanded that "sacred" federal land be closed to the public. In northeastern Wyoming, tribes demanded that Devils Tower National Monument be closed to climbing; in north central Montana, tribes said that Lewis and Clark National Forest could not be used for oil and gas exploration; in north central Wyoming, tribes urged that the Bighorn National Forest be closed to timber harvesting; in southern Utah, tribes called for restricted public access to Rainbow Bridge within a national monument; in northern California, tribes insisted that a mining claim in the Plumas National Forest be nullified. In each case, federal officials acceded to these demands, either with outright closures or with "voluntary" closures whereby the public is "urged" by federal officials, some carrying weapons, to show respect for American Indians' religion by staying away. Challenges to these closures have yet to reach the appellate level; once there, they may be victorious given binding Supreme Court precedent that federal lands are "public lands."

What is different about Dale McKinnon's situation is that Woodruff Butte is his private property. Nonetheless, American Indians assert that he should be barred from using his land because of their view of it. When McKinnon returned to court last month, he said he would challenge Arizona's action as a violation of the prohibitions of the United States and Arizona Constitutions against, not only the establishment of religion, but also the adoption of "special legislation." What hangs in the balance is not only whether Arizona may, in Chief Justice Rehnquist's parlance, "take sides in religion," but whether it may do so as to private property.

MAY 2002

FEDS TAKE PROPERTY FOR A TRAIL; TAKE TAXPAYERS FOR A RIDE

On May 22, 2002, the U.S. Court of Federal Claims ordered the United States to pay J. Paul and Patricia Preseault of Burlington, Vermont, for the unconstitutional taking of their property, that is, without paying for it. The United States was ordered to pay: $234,000, plus interest from February 5, 1986, the date of the taking, for a total of $551,931.31; and $894,855.60 in attorneys' fees. The United States will be writing a check for $1,446,786.90!

The United States will be writing that check because, in 1983, Congress amended the National Trails System Act, by enacting the Rails-to-Trails Act, which prevents railroad easements that cross private property from reverting to the landowners after railroads abandon rail service. Thus, the owners are denied the reversionary rights to which they are entitled by: their deeds, the contract into which they or their predecessors entered with the railroad, and state law. Instead, if the easements are sought for trail use, the United States instructs the railroads that they may abandon rail service only if they transfer the easement for that purpose.

That is what happened to the Preseaults. Their land near the shore of Lake Champlain in northern Vermont was traversed by the Vermont Railway. In 1981, the railway right-of-way having been abandoned, the Preseaults sued in state court for their reversionary rights under Vermont law. In August of 1983, the court dismissed their case, ruling that the United States controlled the easement, a decision upheld by Vermont's Supreme Court. In 1985, the Preseaults petitioned the United States for a ruling that the rail line had been abandoned. Instead, in January of 1986, the United States authorized the railroad to end its rail service and approved the transfer of the easement to the City of Burlington for use as a bicycle and pedestrian path. In 1988, the Preseaults' challenge to the constitutionality of the Rails-to-Trails Act failed at the U.S. Court of Appeals for the Second Circuit. Then, in 1990, the Supreme Court of the United States ruled that, while the Act was constitutional, the Preseaults' property might have been "taken for public purpose without just compensation," a determination that required the Preseaults to file a claim against the United States.

On December 26, 1990, the Preseaults did so, arguing that Congress had taken their property and they were owed "just compensation." The United States said, "No;" it owed the Preseaults nothing! In 1992, the U.S. Court of Federal Claims agreed, as did a three-judge panel of the U.S. Court of Appeals for the Federal Circuit in 1995. Then, in November of 1996, the entire Federal Circuit reversed both decisions, ruling that the Preseaults' property had been taken and they were owed "just compensation." Four and one half years later, a trial was held on the amount of compensation; on May 22, 2001, a ruling was issued. One year later, the court ruled regarding attorneys' fees.

As large as is the check that the United States must write, it could have been worse; the $900,000 in attorneys' fees covers only the litigation that began in December of 1990, but, as the late Senator Everett McKinley Dirksen (R-IL) once said, "a million here, a million there, and pretty soon you're talking about real money." The taxpayers did not get the worst of it, however. Twenty-one years after the Preseaults went to court to regain their property and more than eleven years after they sought the "just compensation" to which the Constitution says they are entitled, they won. It took all those years for one reason: the federal government fought them every step of the way!

In 1995, a top official at Clinton's Justice Department gave a major speech against legislation then being considered by Congress to cut the time necessary for people like the Preseaults to obtain "just compensation." "There's no need to change the law," she argued, "We readily compensate anyone whose property is taken." Tell that to the Preseaults!

JUNE 2002

WRONG-HEADEDNESS, NOT HEAD CASES,
KILLS FORESTS

When the Hayman Fire, the largest wildfire in Colorado history, first began, the smoke billowed over my office in southwestern Denver. Outside, I could smell the fumes from flames fifty miles away. Worst yet, I could see the ash in the air! The night before, as my wife and I stood on our deck in the foothills west of Denver, we smelled smoke and feared that a fire was nearby. It was not; what we smelled was the beginning of the Coal Seam Fire some 110 miles west in Glenwood Springs. A few days later, when I called a sheep rancher in Bayfield, I was told he had gone to protect his flock; the Missionary Ridge Fire was out of control near his grazing allotment. Then, one of my attorneys was summoned home; the Hayman Fire was wildly out of control, moving much too fast toward Denver's southwestern suburbs.

My attorney was not the only one trying to figure out what he should load into his car if the reverse 911 system rang his phone and he heard the recorded message every westerner fears: "GET OUT!" Today the most frequent topic of conversation in the rural West is what to take and what to leave behind if and when the fires come. Storage facilities anywhere near timber country are quickly filling up as home owners realize that all that they value will not fit in their cars, fully loaded with gas and backed into their garages or up their driveways.

Westerners are doing something else. The hills are alive with the sounds of chainsaws as landowners cut away low lying branches and fell dead trees and the roar of mowers as owners cut bone dry native grasses. Those with trucks are loading them with raked up pine cones, needles, and the other slash that usually dot the landscape and hauling them off to county collection points. Those without trucks or friends from whom to borrow them are bagging up the debris and stacking the porcupine-looking bundles at their gates.

There is some great irony in what these homeowners are doing. Because, for years and years, their neighbors have refused to do what everyone knows must be done to limit the destructive force of wildfires. No, it is not their human neighbors who have failed to perform this essential task; it is their federal government neighbors, that is, land management agencies like the

National Park Service, the U.S. Forest Service, and the Bureau of Land Management.

The federal agencies, however, have had help. As one Forest Service official said amidst the national disaster that is Arizona's wildfires, "It only takes one person with a stamp to throw a wrench into the works [of thinning the forest]." So, armed with hundreds of millions of dollars in annual donations, environmental groups have bought stamps and lawyers to file appeals and lawsuits to halt the pursuit of forest health on our nation's public lands. Remarkably, the environmental groups that have prevented the type of prudent forestry practices that would enhance, if not ensure, forest health disclaim responsibility. As one environmental group leader testified recently before Congress, "Hey man, it's not us, it's the weather!"

There is nothing we can do about the head cases who light fires, like the sad soul who started the Hayman Fire, the sicko who lit more than 15 fires along U.S. 285 south of Denver, or the slack-jawed idiots who keep tossing cigarettes or torching campfires despite warning signs every half mile and acrid smoke billowing overhead. We can, however, do something about the wrong-headedness that creates as national policy a point of view that wildfires are "nature's way" and the proper prescription for western forests. That may sound dreamily sensible in an air-conditioned Starbucks in Washington, D.C., but from where I sit amidst the burning forests of Colorado, it is not just insane, it is also inhumane.

JULY 2002

BUSH: NINE FORMER PRESIDENTS WRONG; CLINTON RIGHT!

In 1872, Congress enacted the General Mining Law, allowing miners to enter onto federal land, locate valuable mineral deposits, and develop those minerals. Once claims were staked, they were inviolate against all others, except the United States, which could challenge their validity at any time. Miners had to perform annual assessment work or else the land was open to relocation by rival claimants as if no prior claim existed. If the original claimant resumed work before such relocation, however, the claim was preserved. Often called the "resumption doctrine," this is the "statutory right to resume work."

While the "right to resume work" protected claims against rival miners, did it apply to the United States? In 1930, the federal government told the Supreme Court of the United States that it did not: claims were forfeited if a miner failed to perform assessment work, even if the miner resumed work before a challenge by the federal government. The Court unanimously rejected that argument, emphasizing: "[I]t is ... clear that [a miner] maintains his claim ... by a resumption of work. ... Such resumption does not restore a lost estate; it preserves an existing estate." Thereafter, the federal government challenged claims for lack of assessment work only during a lapse in the work; but the Supreme Court later rejected that too, ruling that there was no authority for it. In 1970, the Supreme Court backtracked slightly: the federal government did have that authority, but the Supreme Court left its 1930 ruling standing: a miner maintained his claims if he resumed work before the United States challenged them.

Not surprisingly, given the frequent and consistent rulings of the Supreme Court affirming the right of a miner to "preserve[] an existing [claim]" by resuming assessment work, the federal government took the view, from 1930 on, that claims were invalid only if the federal government instituted its challenge during a lapse in assessment work. Then in 1993, in Clinton's first year, the federal government reversed 63 years of official policy and rejected the rulings of the Supreme Court: the statutory right to resume work was dead; in its place was a regulation that automatically voided claims upon a lapse in assessment work.

Meanwhile, in 1917, four oil shale claims were located on 520 acres in Uintah County, Utah. In March of 1989, the owner of the claims, Cliffs Synfuel Corporation, filed an application for title (patent) to those claims. In October of 1992, the federal government said Cliffs had complied with federal law and was entitled to a certificate ending its duty to perform assessment work. In 1996, however, the federal government declared the claims null and void because, during the 75 years the claims were held, there had been a lapse in assessment work, which the federal government had never challenged. A federal district court reinstated the claims, holding, "the Supreme Court knows how to say a statute is invalid;" because it did not declare the statutory right to resume work invalid, that provision was still alive!

The Bush administration appealed the decision to the U.S. Court of Appeals for the Tenth Circuit. On May 6, 2002, lawyers from Bush's Justice Department argued that 63 years of interpreting the mining law were irrelevant and the Supreme Court's decisions, which had bound the federal government for nine presidencies, were wrong. A three-judge panel, deferring to the federal government's expertise, agreed: the claims were null and void. Cliffs asked the entire Tenth Circuit to rehear the case and will petition the Supreme Court if the Tenth Circuit fails to rectify its error.

President Bush reportedly is seeking to restore stability and steadfastness to a Justice Department that had a reputation, during Clinton's years, for scandal and schizophrenia. Which, however, is worthy of Bush's embrace: three Supreme Court rulings and the official policy of nine presidents spanning more than six decades, or a dubious regulation adopted because of the anti-mining zealotry of William Jefferson Clinton? Sadly, Bush chose the latter.

AUGUST 2002

CHAPTER FOURTEEN

Government Lawyers and Justice

———

On May 8, 2003, I was at the U.S. Court of Appeals for the Tenth Circuit in Denver for arguments before a three-judge panel in *Wyoming Sawmills v. U.S. Forest Service*, MSLF's challenge to the decision of the Forest Service to close timber harvesting on and cancel a contract our client had regarding tens of thousands of acres of national forest viewed by American Indian religious practitioners as sacred. I had argued the case at a three-hour hearing before the Wyoming federal district court back on October 20, 1999. The district court did not issue its ruling—which it could have done the afternoon after our argument given the slavishness with which it tracked the federal government's brief—until December of 2001. We appealed immediately and briefs followed, including a brief from American Indians arguing their "minority religion" was exempt from the Constitution's Establishment Clause. Now, two years later, we were at the Tenth Circuit. At the conclusion of the argument, I was again disappointed that the Bush administration continued to defend lawless and even unconstitutional actions of Clinton officials.

In addition to *Wyoming Sawmills*, Bush officials pressed Voting Rights Act litigation fashioned by the last administration against Blaine County, Montana, and Alamosa County, Colorado, and continued the federal government's unethical attack on the valuable mining claim of a disabled veteran on fixed income in northern California. Meanwhile, the Internal Revenue Service took the outrageous position that Equal Access to Justice Act (EAJA) fees awarded to MSLF when it defeated the federal government—money MSLF's clients never saw—was income to them! Unhappily, my meetings in 2003 with senior IRS officials, asking that they carefully reexamine their position in ongoing litigation, fell on deaf ears.

On November 14, 2003, I was at Duke University School of Law in North Carolina to debate environmental policy. A top Bush administration official, who learned of my planned remarks, asked that I be more restrained in my criticism. I saw no reason to do so.

THE FEDERAL GOVERNMENT:
NEVER HAVING TO SAY YOU'RE SORRY

In the 1970 movie *Love Story*, Ali MacGraw's character declared, "Love means never having to say you're sorry." Whether that is true of love is uncertain, but it is true for the federal government. Witness the tale of John Bernt of Jarbidge, Nevada.

On January 3 and 10, 1996, Bernt staked mining claims on federal lands in Nevada. On January 19, federal officials withdrew the land upon which Bernt had staked his claims with notices on official documents. Federal officials told Bernt that they were considering the lands for an exchange, but that, because his claims predated the withdrawal, they remained valid.

On April 12, federal officials told Bernt that the lands had been withdrawn, not on January 19, but on November 27, 1995. If true, Bernt's claims were invalid. So, on April 17, Bernt examined the withdrawal documents, but they showed the January 19 date. Later, Bernt saw documents with the November 27 date; however, visible on those documents was the January 19 date, entered before the November 27 date! When Bernt sought other documents, he was told they had been "destroyed."

On May 24, the Bureau of Land Management (BLM) declared Bernt's claims "null and void." A month later, Bernt reexamined the "official" records and discovered they had been altered once again, this time by placing the November 27 date above the January 19 date. When Bernt appealed to the Interior Board of Land Appeals (IBLA), the BLM never filed a response, but secretly provided documents to the IBLA. In March of 1999, the IBLA, using BLM's *ex parte* documents, ruled against Bernt.

Months later, Bernt discovered documents that the BLM had not provided to the IBLA, documents that proved Bernt's case, documents that Bernt had been told did not exist. Then Bernt obtained documents that he had been told had been "destroyed," some with admissions that documents were altered. Bernt sued, alleging that federal officials had altered documents fraudulently to invalidate his claims.

One would have thought that such serious allegations would give federal attorneys pause. Clinton administration lawyers, however, could not have cared less; they perfunctorily certified that the individuals had done nothing wrong and moved to dismiss Bernt's lawsuit. In March of 2001, relying on the head-in-the-sand representations of Clinton's Justice Department, a Nevada federal district court dismissed Bernt's lawsuit, declaring that document backdating "happens all the time," and that, when federal employees altered the documents, they were acting "in the ordinary course of business." John Bernt appealed.

By now, however, the federal government had a problem. If it prevailed at the U.S. Court of Appeals for the Ninth Circuit, it might establish a troublesome precedent: the backdating of official documents is expected conduct by federal employees. If government lawyers were not troubled by the fraud perpetrated on Bernt, they were worried that they might not be able to fire employees who backdated documents. Federal lawyers agreed to settle Bernt's case.

John Bernt would get his claims as of their original location date, other land users would be told that John Bernt's claims were senior, the IBLA and district court decisions would be vacated, and John Bernt would be paid his expenses. Just before its signing, however, the settlement agreement nearly fell apart. John Bernt had sought an apology, an admission by his government that its employees had done him wrong, that it had forced him to litigate for more than six years for what was rightfully his, and that it was sorry. A senior Washington official said, "No," the United States would never apologize. John Bernt swallowed his pride and took the deal—without the apology—knowing he had been vindicated.

Perhaps federal officials emulate, not Ali MacGraw's character, but John Wayne's cavalry officer in *She Wore a Yellow Ribbon*: "Never apologize and never explain—it's a sign of weakness." Maybe, but a government big enough to be powerful is big enough to be penitent.

MARCH 2003

DOES THE EQUAL PROTECTION CLAUSE
APPLY TO INDIANS?

On April 21, amidst the long list of cases that the Supreme Court of the United States announced it would not decide on the merits and thus on which it "denied *certiorari*," was *AirStar Helicopter v. National Park Service*. AirStar, which flies recreational tours over portions of Grand Canyon National Park, asked the Court to decide if a 1974 decision of the Court had been overruled by a 1995 decision. Specifically, AirStar asked the Court to decide whether disparate treatment accorded American Indians violated the U.S. Constitution's equal protection guarantee.

AirStar found itself at the Supreme Court due to regulations adopted by the National Park Service (NPS), ostensibly to achieve "natural quiet" at the Grand Canyon. AirStar and its colleagues who provide recreational air tours there maintain that they have achieved "natural quiet" already and that the NPS, under the direction of Interior Secretary Babbitt who vowed to end air tours over Grand Canyon, was using junk science to do just that. Worse, the NPS admitted both that its regulations would be economically ruinous to the air tour providers and that the cost of the regulations would far exceed their benefit. Finally, the NPS decided that, because the regulations would be just as economically burdensome to the Hualapai Tribe, those American Indians would be exempt.

AirStar president Ron Williams was incensed by the decision of the NPS to exempt some American citizens from the environmental regulations because of their race or ethnicity. Williams had flown helicopters for the U.S. Army in Vietnam and, in his words, "When we got a call that Americans were down, we didn't ask their race; we went to get them out."

The NPS asserted that it could make such distinctions because of a 1974 Supreme Court decision in a case called *Morton v. Mancari*. In *Mancari*, the Bureau of Indian Affairs (BIA) had adopted a hiring preference for American Indians, which was challenged by a job seeker arguing that the Constitution's equal protection guarantee barred racial preferences. In a decision that it labeled *sui generis* ("the only one of its own kind; peculiar"), the Supreme Court sustained the BIA's hiring preference, ruling that "legislation that singles out Indians for particular and special treatment" will be upheld if, applying the rational basis test, "it can be tied rationally to the fulfillment of Congress' unique obligation toward the Indians...."

AirStar argued, first in briefs and argument before the U.S. Court of Appeals for the District of Columbia and then in its petition for *writ* of *certiorari* to the Supreme Court, that *Mancari* had been overturned by a 1995 Supreme Court decision, *Adarand Constructors, Inc. v. Peña*. Unlike the Court in *Mancari*, which applied the rational basis test under which almost every governmental decision is upheld, the Court in *Adarand* used the "strict scrutiny test," which has been described as "strict in theory, but fatal in fact" to every governmental action to which it is applied. In fact, Justice Stevens, dissenting in *Adarand*, recognized the threat that *Adarand* posed to *Mancari*. Thus informed, the Court of Appeals noted the implicit conflict but ruled it had no power to resolve the conflict; thus, it sustained the NPS's rules.

That the Supreme Court declined to hear AirStar's petition does not mean that the majority: fails to recognize the conflict, thinks that *Mancari* remains despite *Adarand*, or believes that federal distinctions based on race are constitutional. It merely means that four justices did not want to hear this case at this time, for whatever reason. The Court, however, will have another opportunity later this month to address this issue. A Montana woman will seek Supreme Court review because she was convicted of violating Montana's big game hunting regulations when, possessing a license and tag, she bagged a deer on her neighbor's private land. The reason: she and her neighbor are non-Indians whose property lies within an Indian Reservation. The basis: *Morton v. Mancari*!

MAY 2003

WARRING OVER "TRUE HISPANICS"

In Washington, D.C., the battle continues over President Bush's appointment of federal judges. Today, sixty-two judicial nominees await Senate confirmation. One of them is Miguel Estrada, who, if confirmed, would become the first Hispanic on the U.S. Court of Appeals for the District of Columbia Circuit. Mr. Estrada's biography is very impressive. Born in Tegucigalpa, Honduras, he immigrated to the United States as a teenager speaking little English. He graduated *Phi Beta Kappa* from Columbia College in New York and with honors from Harvard Law School, where he was editor of the *Harvard Law Review*. He clerked for Supreme Court Justice Kennedy, served as a federal prosecutor in New York, and, as an assistant to the Solicitor General, argued 15 cases before the Supreme Court of the United States. The ABA gave him its highest rating.

Despite being nominated by President Bush in May of 2001, Mr. Estrada has not been confirmed; nor has there been an "up or down" vote on his nomination by the Senate. It is likely that Mr. Estrada would be confirmed if a vote were taken; therefore, Democrats are filibustering because, according to some elected officials, Mr. Estrada is not "a true Hispanic." Representative Robert Menendez (D-13th NJ) says, for example, "Being Hispanic for us means much more than having a surname." Republican leaders vow to vote on Mr. Estrada and President Bush has gone to great lengths to get him confirmed, including making his nomination the subject of the President's Weekly Radio Address. As President Bush fights for Mr. Estrada's confirmation, in part by arguing that race does not equate with political philosophy, out west, President Bush's lawyers are arguing just the opposite.

In 2001, the United States Department of Justice sued Alamosa County, Colorado, alleging that it had violated the Voting Right Act (VRA), which, in the Bush administration's view, not only provides that the right to register, vote, and run for office may not be denied on the basis of race, ethnicity, or language, but also guarantees ethnic minorities the right to elect their "candidates of choice." Because, in the last few decades, only two Hispanics have been elected County Commissioner, the Justice Department says that local Hispanics have been denied that right.

Although VRA litigation is complex, requiring testimony of demographers, economists, political scientists, historians, and other experts, the Justice Department's case boils down to the following. Bush lawyers contend that Alamosa County Hispanics have well-defined political interests, which are unique to them and about which they care deeply, and that they vote as a block to elect officials to serve those interests. Bush lawyers also contend that Alamosa County Anglos have different political interests and that they vote as a block to frustrate the ability of Hispanics to elect their "candidates of choice."

There is absolutely no evidence of this racial polarization. Alamosa County is an ethnically and culturally diverse rural county whose economy relies on agriculture and a local state college begun in the 1920s. Alamosa (Spanish for Cottonwood Grove) County is divided approximately sixty to forty between Anglos and Hispanics, many of whom trace their roots to Spain. Plus, the two ethic groups are also proportionally represented in the various sectors of the local economy. Not surprisingly, political divisions break, not along ethnic and cultural lines, but along socio-economic and philosophical ones. Moreover, in 2002, Alamosa County elected Frank Mestas, a Republican, as one of its three County Commissioners, rejecting Ernie Roybal, a Democrat, and Gary Spangler, an Independent. Mestas got 56 percent of the vote; Roybal and Spangler got 33 and 11 percent respectively. Both Mestas and Roybal are Hispanics; Spangler is an Anglo.

Nonetheless, the Bush administration maintains that Mr. Mestas is not Alamosa County Hispanics' "candidate of choice," that Hispanics there have been and continue to be disenfranchised, and that Alamosa County must racially gerrymander its commissioner districts to ensure election of a "true Hispanic."

How curious. Estrada, *si*; Mestas, *no*.

JUNE 2003

GOVERNMENT LAWYERS CIRCLE
THE WAGONS AND LOSE!

Stanley K. Mann owned a geothermal lease issued by the Bureau of Land Management (BLM) of the U.S. Department of the Interior. Although Mr. Mann does business as Crowne Geothermal, Ltd., the lease was issued by the BLM in Mr. Mann's name. Over the years, Mr. Mann and others spent over $1 million making the lease capable of producing geothermal resources—a clean, efficient, renewable energy source—in commercial quantities.

In September of 1989, Mr. Mann moved to California where he received mail, including mail forwarded from his former address in Colorado. Over the next several months, Mr. Mann was in frequent telephone and written communication regarding his geothermal lease with the BLM and the Minerals Management Service (MMS), to which Mr. Mann made royalty payments. He repeatedly advised the BLM and MMS of his address to ensure he received all correspondence.

In April of 1991, in response to a BLM inquiry regarding the bond on his lease, Mr. Mann, as president of Crowne, wrote to the bonding company. Mr. Mann wrote the letter on Crowne letterhead because Crowne was paying the premium for the bond. As a courtesy to the BLM, Mr. Mann sent an unsigned copy of that letter to the BLM. Inexplicably, on receipt of the letter, BLM employees changed Mr. Mann's official address to the address on Crowne's letterhead. The BLM employees did this even though Mr. Mann, not Crowne, was the lessee.

In November of 1993, the BLM issued a notice requesting information from Mr. Mann regarding his lease and advising him that, if the information were not received within 30 days, the BLM would cancel his lease. The BLM sent that notice, by certified mail, return receipt requested, to Crowne's address. Not surprisingly, because Mr. Mann had never lived at that address, the BLM's letter was returned "unclaimed." Two years later, when Mr. Mann visited the BLM office, he was told his lease had been cancelled in 1994.

Mr. Mann sued in the U.S. Court of Federal Claims asserting that the BLM had breached his lease by failing to provide him the notice required by law. In response, federal lawyers defended the actions of the BLM and its employees but failed to provide a sworn affidavit from a single BLM employee as to why the BLM sent the notice to Crowne's address. Mr. Mann responded with sworn affidavits and official documents from the BLM's files and argued that the federal government's refusal to provide any facts and its attempt, instead, to rely on its lawyers' *post hoc* rationalizations should be rejected. The judge (a recess appointment by President Clinton that was not renewed) ruled for the government.

On June 3, 2003, Mr. Mann's case was heard by a three-judge panel of the U.S. Court of Appeals for the Federal Circuit. The judges were incredulous at the behavior of the federal government and its attorneys. Although tough questioning during oral arguments does not always foretell the result, it did in this case. In record time (twenty-four days), the judges ruled that the BLM had breached Mr. Mann's lease by failing to send notification of its pending action to his correct address; the appeals court remanded the case to determine damages.

Almost ten years after his lease was breached by the federal government, Mr. Mann was vindicated, but the documents that proved his case were in the federal government's hands the entire time, documents showing that: employees from one federal agency did not speak to their colleagues in a sister agency; some federal employees either did not or could not read the plain English of official documents; while other federal employees either did not know what the law and regulations provided or refused to do what they required.

Government lawyers have a duty, not to win at any cost for federal agencies and their employees, but to do justice. It would be refreshing if they would perform that duty.

AUGUST 2003

RULING OPENS LITIGATION FLOODGATES WHILE VOIDING RIGHTS

Jack McFarland owns property that he bought from his grandmother in Glacier National Park. Like his grandmother and the man from whom she bought it—who staked his homestead prior to Glacier National Park's creation and received his patent from President Wilson—Jack McFarland accesses his property in the only way possible: via Glacier Route 7. Jack McFarland's property is just three miles north of the Polebridge Ranger Station.

Because of the patent granted to the original homesteader and the rights guaranteed homesteaders by the Glacier National Park Act, the National Park Service (NPS) may not deny Jack McFarland year-round access to his property. Thus, in the 1970s, when the NPS put barriers on Glacier Route 7 to prevent the general public from driving north of Polebridge Ranger Station in the winter, the NPS guaranteed access to landowners. The NPS did so because it recognized that is what the law requires. As the NPS explained, in August of 1985 in its Land Protection Plan for Glacier National Park, "[t]he National Park Service recognizes private landowner rights [{to} 'reasonable and adequate use and enjoyment of his property' {are}] guaranteed in the enabling legislation for the park...."

In December of 1999, however, the NPS sent Jack McFarland an email informing him "that no one will drive park roads once they are closed to the public." Though Jack McFarland believes he has the right to use Glacier Route 7, he was willing to compromise. On January 6, 2000, he filed a special use permit application asking the NPS's permission to use a vehicle or snowmobile to travel between his home and the Polebridge Ranger Station. On January 24, 2000, the NPS summarily denied that application.

Jack McFarland sued. First, because he claims an easement in Glacier Route 7, with which the NPS interfered, he sued under the Quiet Title Act, by which Congress authorized landowners to get title to property to which the government asserts an adverse claim. Second, because the NPS arbitrarily and capriciously denied his special use permit, he sued under the Administrative Procedure Act (APA).

Recently, a Montana federal district court dismissed Jack McFarland's case. The court ruled that he had filed beyond the Quiet Title Act's twelve-year statute of limitations, which, according to the district court, began to run in 1976 when the NPS restricted the general public's ability to use Glacier Route 7 north of Polebridge Ranger Station. Though the NPS gave Jack McFarland complete access to Glacier Route 7, he should have known, reasoned the court, that the NPS believed it could deny him that right. The court also dismissed the APA claim because the Quiet Title Act is "the exclusive means" of resolving property disputes. Both rulings are legally suspect and terrible public policy.

Since 1910, the NPS acknowledged consistently that it could not deny people like Jack McFarland access to their property, putting it in writing as recently as 1985. That written statement came less than ten years after, in the court's view, Jack McFarland should have known that the NPS claimed just the opposite. Plus, when Jack McFarland requested a special use permit, he was not claiming a property right but seeking a license, which the NPS could revoke unilaterally. Under the APA, he has a right, as do all citizens, to have that request decided in a manner that is neither "arbitrary [nor] capricious." Thus, the court has deprived all who have property disputes with the government of their right, as granted by Congress in the APA, to fair and equitable treatment.

Finally, the court has opened the litigation floodgates. It has told property owners who access their property via federal lands that, any time the United States restricts the access rights of the general public to use those lands, it has acted in a manner adverse to the property owners and, to protect their rights under the Quiet Title Act, they must file suit.

OCTOBER 2003

DEMOCRACY BEATS RACE-CONSCIOUSNESS IN FEDERAL LAWSUIT

Recently, in the *Wall Street Journal*, author Dr. Shelby Steele, a fellow of the Hoover Institution, explored the "fundamental conflict between democracy and atavisms," "those tribal elements of ourselves that we inherit like a fate from our group and that we share with our grandfather's grandfather." Atavistic connections "are inherently anti-democratic because they exclude all outside the atavism." Plus, clinging zealously to one's atavistic identity "leads to three great sins: [1] asserting the inherent superiority of one's group over others, [2] excluding others as inferiors, and [3] invoking an enemy to fight in the name of one's superiority." Finally, seeking atavistic power instead of individual freedom "only allows for demagogic and totalitarian leaders," those who "appeal to resentment [and] victimization."

It would be ironic, given this analysis, if federal officials were not only to seek to encourage atavistic power but also to sue to enforce it! Unfortunately, that is exactly what high ranking officials in the Bush administration did, in the fall of 2001, when they filed a lawsuit against Alamosa County, Colorado, demanding that the county racially gerrymander its commissioner districts to guarantee election of a Hispanic commissioner. The U.S. Department of Justice filed its lawsuit because, as one of its complaining witnesses testified, "[t]o me, representative government means having somebody that looks like you, that understands what you do; and we didn't have that." Specifically, federal lawyers alleged that Alamosa County's use of a state-mandated system of electing commissioners at large from residential districts, in place since 1876, violated the Voting Rights Act by preventing Hispanics from electing their "candidates of choice." Government lawyers went even farther: not only was the Hispanic "candidate of choice" a Hispanic, the candidate was a Democrat!

Alamosa County, one of six counties in south central Colorado in the San Luis Valley, has a population of 15,000. Most of the county is rural with farming and ranching predominating; its one urban center, the City of Alamosa, is the location of most businesses, government offices, and Adams State College. Hispanics and Anglos have lived in the valley for more than a century intermarrying at higher than the national rate.

Fifty-four percent of residents are Anglo; 41 percent are Hispanic, seventy percent of whom were born in Colorado.

From 1900 to 1950, discriminatory practices caused or worsened the socioeconomic disparities between Anglos and Hispanics. Official action and social activism, however, both reduced the discriminatory climate and improved educational and socioeconomic conditions for Hispanics. Today, Hispanic residents live, work, and own businesses throughout the county and there is extensive integration and association between Hispanic and Anglo residents, socially and in business. In commissioner elections, since 1978, every Hispanic candidate who ran in the Democratic primary was nominated and, since 1984, Hispanic candidates have prevailed in the general election three out of five times. Despite all this, the federal government filed its lawsuit, engaged in a year and a half of discovery and depositions of witnesses, conducted an eight-day trial in May of 2003, and filed post-trial briefs. Through it all, federal officials maintained that only Hispanic Democrats could represent Alamosa Hispanics and that racially polarized voting by Anglos had prevented their election.

On Thanksgiving Eve, a federal district court rejected those arguments finding that "[t]he Alamosa Hispanic population... is not an insular, monolithic, minority group [but] is, instead, diverse according to all measures... [, which] create[s] a rich tapestry of experience and views..." This diversity yields a "fundamental electoral truth—that to be elected in Alamosa County, a candidate must appeal to both Anglo and Hispanic voters." In fact, "subtle or overt ethnic appeals" by Hispanic candidates "result[s] in failure at the polls." Finally, the court flatly rejected the government's contention that only a Hispanic and only a Democrat could represent Alamosa Hispanics. It is reassuring that the people of Alamosa County eschewed atavism and embraced democracy. It is troubling that the federal government did just the opposite.

DECEMBER 2003

CHAPTER FIFTEEN

Ronald Reagan, Sagebrush Rebel, Rest in Peace

I n May of 1983, President Reagan emerged from the Oval Office and instructed an aide, "I want to talk to this man, Adams, to find out why he dislikes me so much." Ansel Adams—famous for black-and-white photographs of Yosemite National Park—hated Reagan's "environmental policies." Adams was not alone; environmental groups opposed Reagan years before he took office. Adams, though, took his opposition to an obsessive degree, sending "a letter a day to newspapers and congressmen decrying President Reagan's 'disastrous' environmental policies." He warned of "catastrophe," "tragedy," "the Pearl Harbor of our American Earth," and finally declared in a magazine interview, "I hate Reagan."

Reagan decided it was "time to clear the air and straighten out the record on where my administration stands on environmental and natural resources management matters," which was how he began his weekly radio address on June 11, 1983. He closed, "We have made a commitment to protect the health of our citizens and to conserve our nation's natural beauty and resources.... Thanks to [our] efforts, our country remains 'America the Beautiful.' Indeed, it's growing healthier and more beautiful each year. I hope this helps set the record straight, because it's one we can all be proud of."

Three weeks later, in Beverly Hills, Reagan met Adams, whom Reagan called, "the great nature photographer." Afterward, Reagan wrote in his diary: "He has expressed hatred for me because of my supposed stand on the environment. I asked for the meeting. I gave him chapter [and] verse about where I really stand on the environment [and] what our record is. All in all the meeting seemed pleasant enough [and] I thought maybe I'd taken some of the acid out of his ink." Adams emerged from the meeting unassuaged and vented to reporters, assailing Reagan personally—faulting his intelligence, imagination, and "aura"—and attacking his policies and the people appointed to implement them. Nonetheless, noted the *Washington Post*, "For all his intense anger at [Reagan and his appointees], Adams said he is hard-pressed to document widespread environmental damage from their policies." Wrote Reagan in his diary after reading the article, "I'm afraid I was talking to ears that refused to hear." Like Adams, environmental extremists hated Reagan, lied about him then, and lie about him today.

PAUL BERGER, PATRIOT, PLAINTIFF, AND PHILANTHROPIST—RIP

"Thanksgiving," read the marquee of the clapboard church in the mountain community through which I drive to work, "is never over." That every day is one of thanksgiving is worth remembering as the New Year begins. Although I am thankful for many blessings, today I give thanks for a man I never met whose courage and life's work left the country and Mountain State Legal Foundation better for him having been here.

Paul Berger was born April 7, 1921, in Kellogg, Idaho, where his father Pete worked in the mines; his mother Ruth taught country school. Both died when Paul was young so he was raised by grandparents in Content, Montana, and then by an aunt in Valley County. After three years of school, he quit to work on the ranch and then, at thirteen, set out on his own with his horse Chum. He was a hired hand punching cows, breaking horses, and working up to 40,000 head of sheep. In the winters, he drove a truck; he logged 700,000 miles hauling cattle.

Paul Berger, however, wanted a ranch of his own. He saved his money buying one cow at a time and putting them wherever he could find pasture land. In the winter of 1949 and 1950, he leased a ranch and pastured his cattle there. In 1958, he bought his ranch on Lodgepole Creek north of Sand Springs. By 1993, through hard work and good fortune, Paul Berger and his wife Rosie had 700 head of cattle and several thousand sheep over 75,000 acres, mostly Bureau of Land Management land, with 7,000 deeded and improved acres. He loved the Missouri River Breaks and knew when he stepped out his front door he was in God's church.

Then, on March 24, 1993, disaster struck. Paul Berger's ranch was raided by armed employees of the U.S. Fish and Wildlife Service accompanied by an Assistant U.S. Attorney and a crew from Ted Turner's CNN. In a multi-car convoy, with an aircraft overhead, they swooped down, searching for evidence to "document the taking of wildlife in violation of Federal laws." When Garfield County's Sheriff arrived, he ordered the CNN crew off the ranch. They snuck back, however, and kept filming. Even though CNN later declared that the raid was a success, the agents found no evidence of any poisoned eagles. In the end, Paul Berger was found guilty of a sole misdemeanor count of illegal use of a pesticide used to kill grasshoppers.

Why was CNN there? Turns out, days before the raid, CNN inked an agreement with the Assistant U.S. Attorney to film a pre-raid briefing and the raid itself, an agreement that violated U.S. Department of Justice policy. One journalist labeled the deal an effort "by showboating federal law officers and slanted journalists to stage . . . a worldwide public-relations lynching of ranchers in the court of public opinion."

Paul Berger fought back. His case got to the Supreme Court of the United States where the Court held, "police violate the Fourth Amendment rights of homeowners when they allow members of the media to accompany them during the execution of a warrant in their home." After the case was remanded to lower courts to determine CNN's liability, it was settled for an undisclosed sum in May of 2001. For more than a decade, folks would stop Paul Berger to thank him for his fight to prevent violations of constitutional rights by federal bureaucrats and their handmaiden, the liberal media. On April 12, 2003, after a long illness, Paul Berger died.

Paul Berger left behind more than a loving extended family: his example of hard work, his commitment to the land, and his courage in fighting for what is right. He left a sizeable donation to Mountain States Legal Foundation that it might continue the type of fights that he waged so bravely. All who love freedom owe Paul Berger a debt of gratitude.

JANUARY 2004

MONTANANS BEAT FOREST SERVICE;
WHY DID THEY NEED TO SUE?

It must have been an open and shut case. Oral arguments occurred on December 10, 2003, in Montana federal district court; two days later, the court ruled for Stephen and Jean Roth of Darby. The court held the Roths own an easement in the Bitterroot National Forest, created in 1897, and the Selway-Bitterroot Wilderness Area, created in 1964, for Tamarack Lake dam and reservoir and four ditches that deliver water to the Roths' ranch.

The Roths' victory was welcome news to landowners across the West who are fighting with the U.S. Forest Service and other federal land agencies over whether they have the right to access their property. Despite: the specific language of titles and patents, even patents signed by presidents of the United States; the well-established protections afforded property owners by the common law; and, the express provisions of several federal statutes, federal agencies insist that landowners have no rights and must either apply for a revocable license to access their property or sue.

The Roths' facts are straight-forward. In 1988, they purchased 750 acres in Ravalli County; in 1990, they bought 50 adjacent acres; both purchases included water rights to operate their Trapper Creek Ranch, including Tamarack Lake dam and reservoir and four ditches. The Roths asserted that, under congressional acts adopted in 1866 and 1891, they held easements for these facilities, easements the Forest Service could not prevent them from using. When the Forest Service denied them access, the Roths sued the United States under the Quiet Title Act. In opposing the Roths' lawsuit, the federal government asserted that the 12-year statute of limitations for filing a Quiet Title Act suit had expired because the Forest Service had always disputed their claim. The court rejected the argument pointing to a 1998 document in which the Forest Service admitted just the opposite: the Roths had an easement.

On the merits, the Roths argued that, once their predecessors had constructed the Tamarack Lake dam and reservoir on federal lands, pursuant to the Act of 1891, the easement authorized by Congress vested automatically. The federal government countered that those rights did not vest automatically; the Secretary of the Interior needed to have approved that easement. The court rejected that argument because it was at odds with the position espoused by the Department of the Interior beginning in 1910, a position embraced twice by the Supreme Court of the United States. The court also concluded that to accept the federal government's new position would be to condemn the 1891 Act of Congress to "a sort of legal purgatory."

As to the Roths' ditches, which the Roths asserted were protected rights-of-way under both the 1866 Act and the 1891 Act, the federal government argued that the Roths had "not carried their burden of proof" without explaining what statutory requirements the Roths had failed to meet or citing anything in the record to support its position. The court flatly rejected the United States' argument, concluding that the Roths had "indeed met their burden. . . ." The court did so in part because, in 1975, a Forest Service District Ranger wrote "[a] review of old records reveals the ditches . . . were in place prior to [creation of Bitterroot National Forest]; [thus,] no special use permit will be required."

As to every claim made in its case with the Roths, the Forest Service knew better. The Forest Service knew it had acted adversely to the Roths' rights only recently; the Roths' case was not time barred. The Forest Service knew the Roths' rights to the dam and reservoir had vested automatically; the United States had taken that position for nearly 100 years. The Forest Service knew the Roths' ditch rights predated the Bitterroot; it admitted that in 1975.

How many others are there like the Roths, folks told by federal bureaucrats that they do not have an easement when the bureaucrats know better? It is not a happy thought!

FEBRUARY 2004

TEACHING BY RACE: WHAT LESSONS WILL THE CHILDREN LEARN?

In 1958, Ward Connerly, the first in his family to graduate from high school, was at American River Junior College in California. Born in the south, abandoned by his father, and raised by his maternal grandmother after his mother died, Connerly, who grew up poor, says he was "like someone walking in a fog." "Then," he wrote in *Creating Equal: My Fight against Race Preferences*, "I fell under the influence of an English teacher named Edith Freleigh."

"Edith Freleigh was one of those people you bump into in life whose influence is so subtle as to be almost imperceptible—a person who changes who you are and what you become without either one of you knowing [it]." She changed him "although this white woman certainly didn't 'look like me,' as they say about the need for color-coded role models in higher education these days." Because of her, he "gained enough confidence in [himself]" that today he is the nation's most recognized, respected, and outspoken advocate of equal opportunity for all Americans, regardless of race, sex, or ethnicity.

Unfortunately, those in charge of teacher training programs at four western universities think the Edith Freleighs of today need not apply, at least not for scholarships to teach American Indian children. Non-Indian teachers are "outsiders" who "don't easily connect with some aspects of Indian culture;" therefore, they are ineligible for the financial incentives used to induce teachers to work in schools with large American Indian populations. Perhaps these universities have not read the latest ruling of the Supreme Court of the United States on use of an absolute racial prerequisite, *Gratz v. Bollinger*. Because the University of Michigan's undergraduate admissions program made "'the factor of race …decisive' for virtually every minimally qualified underrepresented minority applicant," the Court held it violated the Constitution's Equal Protection Clause, Title VI of the Civil Rights Act of 1964, and 42 U.S.C. § 1981, which bars racial discrimination in making or enforcing contracts. As to the Constitution's Equal Protection Clause, the Supreme Court has held, especially since its landmark ruling in *Adarand Constructors, Inc. v. Peña* in 1995, that a governmental entity's use of race is unconstitutional unless it is "narrowly tailored" to serve a "compelling governmental interest." This is "strict scrutiny;" all programs subjected to it fail. Such a fate awaits these Indian-only programs for they are grounded on four race-based, illogical, and impermissible assumptions: first, all American Indian students are poor and need financial assistance; second, all non-Indian students are rich and need no financial assistance; third, only American Indians are capable and inspirational teachers for American Indian students; and fourth, absent racial preferences, American Indian students are unable to compete successfully for scholarships.

As to Title VI, which forbids recipients of federal money from discriminating "on the basis of race," the U.S. Department of Education's Office of Civil Rights has opined that racially exclusive programs are "extremely difficult to defend." That is why prestigious institutions like Princeton and MIT abandoned such programs. Ironically, given Title VI's bar on racial discrimination, the American Indian-only programs are funded by a grant, under Title VII, from the selfsame Department of Education. Thus, shortly after Montana State University, University of Utah, Humboldt State, and University of Oregon were advised that their programs are unconstitutional and illegal, some denied responsibility by pointing to Congress. Although *Adarand* held that Congress is not exempt from the Constitution's equal protection guarantee, some in Congress will reference the Supreme Court's 1974 ruling in *Mancari v. Morton*, which held that distinguishing between Indians and non-Indians is a political, not a racial, distinction. Scholars believe, however, that *Mancari's* analysis is risible and that *Adarand* overturned *Mancari*. Even the U.S. Court of Appeals for the Ninth Circuit has questioned *Mancari's* post-*Adarand* viability.

It will be years before any challenge to these scholarships reaches the Supreme Court. Meanwhile, university education students and K-12 American Indian children will be subjected to the pernicious teaching that, in America, race matters!

MARCH 2004

ESCALANTE RULING GIVES PRESIDENT
CARTE BLANCHE AUTHORITY

Every school child knows that, in 1803, the Supreme Court of the United States, in *Marbury v. Madison*, established the principle of "judicial review" under which the Court may declare acts of Congress unconstitutional and that, in 1955, in *Youngstown Sheet & Tube Co. v. Sawyer*, the Court ruled the unconstitutional actions of a president, even those undertaken in a time of war, may be enjoined. These rulings symmetrically set out one example of a fundamental principle of American government, its system of "checks and balances."

Although the ability of federal courts to review and restrain the exercise of power by the Executive Branch—seen most recently in the ruling by the U.S. Court of Appeals for the Fourth Circuit regarding the Executive's duty to produce enemy combatants as witnesses for an accused terrorist's defense—has been true for decades; presidents have sought consistently to expand the outer limits of their authority.

Thus, after the shock that President Bush chose to defend President Clinton's 1996 national monument decree in southern Utah—especially given Bush-Cheney 2000 campaign rhetoric—it came as no surprise that Bush lawyers did so zealously. In response to a lawsuit brought by the Utah Association of Counties and other westerners charging that the Grand Staircase-Escalante National Monument, which closed 1.7 million acres of federal land in Garfield and Kane Counties to all economic and much recreational activity, federal lawyers argued that the Utah federal district court lacked authority to review Clinton's actions. Clinton is, said the lawyers, "the sole and exclusive judge" of whether the monument, as the Antiquities Act of 1906 requires, is limited to the "smallest area" and contains things "historic" and "scientific."

What was a surprise was that, on April 19, 2004, the Utah district court agreed with that far-reaching argument. After all, the court had rejected an assertion by Clinton lawyers that Congress had ratified the Utah monument by failing to repeal it and by appropriating funds to manage it. Plus, during oral arguments last January, the court gave no sign that it believed its hands were tied; instead, it appeared dubious of such arguments.

Even more confusing was that the district court set forth the skullduggery that led to Clinton's "photo opportunity" at the Grand Canyon, in neighboring Arizona, where he signed the Utah monument proclamation. For example: Interior Secretary Babbitt, frustrated in his efforts to designate 5.7 million acres of Utah as wilderness, pressed for the monument; White House officials attempted to circumvent federal law; and a "driving force behind" the monument was to kill an underground, low-sulfur coal mine. The court went so far as to note that the coal mine would have: affected only 60 acres of surface; produced 11.3 billion tons of coal; and generated $20 billion in federal royalties, half of which would have gone to Utah.

Nonetheless, the court ruled, once Clinton used the language of the Antiquities Act in his proclamation, "[t]hat is essentially the end of the legal analysis. . . . Beyond such a facial review the Court is not permitted to go." This "magic words" approach to the Antiquities Act was rejected by the U.S. Court of Appeals for the District of Columbia, however, which held, in a challenge to six Clinton monuments, "review is available to ensure that [monument] Proclamations are consistent with constitutional principles and that the President has not exceeded his statutory authority."

The U.S. Court of Appeals for the Tenth Circuit, in which Utah lies, will be asked if it agrees with the District of Columbia Circuit. One district court within the Tenth Circuit has held, in a case relied upon by the federal lawyers, that a court could set aside a monument if it were "created on a bare stretch of sage-brush prairie in regard to which there was no substantial evidence that it contained objects of historic or scientific interest." That is exactly the allegation regarding much of Clinton's Utah monument.

MAY 2004

GOVERNMENT WORKERS:
WORKING HARD OR HARDLY WORKING?

Last month, the General Accounting Office (GAO) made headlines with its report that scores of high-ranking employees from eight federal agencies had degrees from bogus colleges or unaccredited schools. Worse yet, a GAO spokesman said, "It's a much larger problem than the evidence we have to date shows." That could be an understatement given that just three of the unaccredited schools the GAO examined revealed that 463 current or one-time students are federal employees. Still, some were unfazed; one wit commented, "I'm not as concerned with whether government workers have degrees as with whether they are working at all."

That remark bespeaks the conventional wisdom that government work—excluding the Armed Forces and those in law enforcement—is the epitome of "inside work; no heavy lifting." Moreover, it reflects personal experience: people who have waited on line or on hold or who have heard "that's not my area" too often wonder if anyone works in federal agencies let alone if those working know what they are doing. Often they do not: a 2003 study disclosed that the IRS gives incorrect answers or no answer at all 43 percent of the time!

An actual, rather than anecdotal, example of a federal employee's work ethic was revealed in testimony in a challenge to a small mining claim in the Plumas National Forest some 100 miles northeast of Sacramento, California. There Donald Eno, a disabled veteran, seeks to provide for himself by working sixty hour weeks on his gold and travertine discoveries. His years of hard work may pay off: estimates are his gold is worth $650,000; his travertine is valued at $20 million, or more! Because of oddities in federal land law, however, the federal government could eject him from his property if it can prove that his claim has no value or that it is more valuable for use as a sacred, scenic, or geological site. Because local U.S. Forest Service personnel oppose mining in general—in an area that has been mined for over 150 years—that is what they are trying to do.

In a recent administrative proceeding, the federal government called, as its expert witness, a Forest Service geologist who testified that Mr. Eno's gold has no economic value. His testimony was not persuasive for numerous reasons, including: errors in basic math, use of the wrong mining equipment, and incorrect economic assumptions. His most ludicrous assertion, however, was that every hour of dredging—the actual recovery of gold from the stream—required one and one-half hours of work. Part of that extra time was what the geologist said he needed to get ready to work each day; the other part was for frequent "work breaks." In fact, over the three days the geologist was at the claim, he averaged two hours a day in the stream recovering gold.

Mr. Eno faulted the geologist's lackadaisical approach to dredging for gold. Eight hours of work is eight hours of work, Mr. Eno argued. Lawyers for the federal government countered that the geologist's views are "standard in any business in America." Hardly; however, the geologist's views may be "standard" in the federal government.

At least the geologist was in the stream and dredged for gold, which is more than could be said of another Forest Service employee who testified that Mr. Eno's claim was "sacred" to local American Indians. The purported expert witness did not interview any of those Indians, nearly a quarter of whom disagreed with her conclusions; she called them "statistical outliers." Moreover, as to two key "sacred" features about which the witness testified, she admitted during cross examination that she had not visited the sites! Perhaps she was on one of the geologist's "work breaks."

Fortunately, the administrative law judge rejected the testimony of the Forest Service employees and ruled for Mr. Eno. Other Americans, however, may not be so fortunate in their encounter with federal "workers."

JUNE 2004

RONALD REAGAN, SAGEBRUSH REBEL
REST IN PEACE

"Count me in" former Governor Ronald Reagan proudly proclaimed in 1980, "as a Sagebrush Rebel." Reagan's common cause with westerners besieged by a host of federal agencies came as no surprise. Forty-four percent of California, which Reagan governed, is managed by federal agencies; thus, he saw hubris, hyperbole, and humor whenever a federal employee declared, "I'm from the federal government and I'm here to help you."

When Ronald Reagan was sworn in, he became the first president since the birth of the modern environmental movement a decade before to have seen, first hand, the impact of excessive federal environmental regulation on the ability: of state governments to perform their constitutional functions; of local governments to sustain healthy economies; and of private citizens to use their own property. Moreover, Reagan thought that the nation might have other, more important priorities, such as repealing confiscatory tax rates, restoring the nation's moribund military, and reviving America's crippled economy.

Professional environmental groups pitched a fit! After all, they had been in their ascendancy since the heady times of the first Earth Day in 1970. Their every demand for new laws, regulations, and judicial rulings to "save the planet" was fulfilled. Vast new agencies and programs grew unimpeded regardless of the political party occupying the White House. No one had ever questioned whether all of it was necessary, could be justified scientifically, or was consistent with the nation's more pressing priorities. When Reagan did, environmental groups unleashed a vicious and unrelenting barrage. Undaunted, Reagan pressed on. He signed an Executive Order requiring federal agencies to review proposed regulations to determine potential costs, benefits, net benefits, and other, less costly alternatives. He signed an Executive Order requiring federal regulations to be based upon scientific risk assessment procedures and to address "real and significant" rather than "remote and hypothetical" risks. He signed an Executive Order requiring that federal agencies determine the "just compensation" that would have to be paid for regulations that "took" private property for "public use," as the Constitution's Fifth Amendment requires.

Reagan thought federal agencies in the West should be "good neigh-bors." Therefore, Reagan returned control of western water rights to the states, where they had been from the time gold was panned in California until Jimmy Carter took office. Reagan sought to ensure that western states received the lands that they had been guaranteed when they entered the Union. Reagan responded to the desire of western governors that the peo-ple of their states be made a part of the environmental equation by being included in federal land use planning.

Facing an "energy crisis" and recognizing that "85 percent of the fuel we need ... is on federally-owned property," Reagan expanded the domes-tic search for energy. Aware of America's dependence on foreign sources for "strategic and critical minerals," Reagan signed a national minerals policy. Desirous that "Americans who cherish the dream of owning their own home" could do so, Reagan provided timber from federal lands on a sustained-yield basis. Reagan's remarkable legacy also includes the results of his appointments to the Supreme Court of the United States. In 1987, the Reagan Court abandoned decades of indifference to the plight of prop-erty owners by recognizing their constitutional rights. In 1990, the Rea-gan Court applied Article III of the Constitution to environmental groups mandating that they meet the "case" or "controversy" test to file federal liti-gation. In 1995, the Reagan Court held that Congress does not have unlim-ited power to legislate, giving the limits of the Commerce Clause new life.

As with President Reagan's courageous battle against tyranny, his fight against unwise environmental policies continues today. As in Reagan's fight for liberty, his opponents have been forced to cede some of the battlefield. For example, the horrific fires that ravaged the West in recent years ended any real debate over whether America should actively manage its national forests. Turns out, like in so much else, Reagan was right!

JULY 2004

CAVE BUG RULING ENDORSES
ELTON JOHN'S "CIRCLE OF LIFE"

In 1983, Dr. Fred Purcell and his brother purchased an interest in 216 acres in Travis County near Austin, Texas, which lie within 1,200 acres, which sit at the intersection of two major highways in a rapidly growing commercial and residential area. The Purcells' property, on which they installed water and wastewater gravity lines, force mains, lift stations, and other utilities, contains a number of caves. In 1988 and 1993, the U.S. Fish and Wildlife Service (FWS) declared six invertebrate species that live in the caves "endangered" under the Endangered Species Act (ESA). These cave bugs (arachnids and insects, some with eyes, some eyeless) range in length from 1.4 mm to 8 mm. Importantly, the cave bugs are found only in parts of Texas' Travis and Williamson Counties. Plus, there is no commercial market for them; nor do people travel to Texas to see them.

In 1989, the FWS told the Purcells that development of their property would violate the ESA because it would constitute a "take" of cave bugs. In 1990, in an effort to alleviate the FWS's concerns, the Purcells deeded six acres, containing caves and sinkholes in which the cave bugs were known to live, to a non-profit environmental organization. Then, however, in 1993, after Dr. Purcell cleared brush from his property, the FWS told him that he was under criminal investigation for "taking" endangered species. In 1998, after years of stonewalling, which drew a rebuke from a federal judge, the FWS barred the Purcells from using their property.

In 1999, the Purcells and their partners sued, contending that application of the ESA to the Texas cave bugs violated the Commerce Clause in much the same way that a federal law banning guns on school yards had been declared unconstitutional by the Supreme Court of the United States in *United States v. Lopez* in 1995. In 2001, a Texas federal district court ruled for the FWS, holding that application of the ESA to Texas cave bugs was "substantially related" to interstate commerce. In 2003, a three-judge panel of the U.S. Court of Appeals for the Fifth Circuit upheld the lower court's decision, ruling that, because "takes" of cave bugs threaten the "interdependent web" of all species, the cave bug's habitat may be regulated, under the Commerce Clause, by the ESA. In the panel's view, although the "takings" of cave bugs do not themselves affect interstate commerce, the takings of all ESA-listed species, when viewed in the aggregate, affect interstate commerce.

The Purcells and their partners asked the entire Fifth Circuit to rehear the case. On February 27, 2004, the Fifth Circuit refused to rehear the case *en banc* over the dissent of six judges (one shy of that necessary for a rehearing). The dissenting judges condemned the panel's opinion as giving new meaning to the term "*reduction ad absurdum*" and called the panel's circle of life analysis "unsubstantiated reasoning" that embraces "a remote, speculative, attenuated, indeed more than improbable connection to interstate commerce."

On May 27, 2004, the Purcells and their partners asked the Supreme Court to hear their case and to announce, whether, in interpreting the Commerce Clause consistent with the vision of the Founding Fathers in the Court's 1995 *Lopez* ruling, the Court really meant it. On August 6, the United States will respond. The Commerce Clause implications are quite serious given that half of all ESA-listed species exist only in one state and occur only on private land.

More is at stake than whether the Commerce Clause means what it says. The Tenth Amendment provides that states have exclusive authority over land-use planning, regulation, and zoning, as Justice Kennedy wrote, "by right of history and expertise." Justice Marshall called it, local government's "most essential function" because it is how "we protect [our] quality of life." Neither justice could have anticipated the federal government would lay claim to a higher calling: protecting Elton John's "Circle of Life."

AUGUST 2004

NINTH CIRCUIT BARS CHRISTIAN, BUT NOT PAGAN, WORSHIP

On May 12, 2004, an attorney for Dale McKinnon appeared before the U.S. Court of Appeals for the Ninth Circuit. He was seeking to reverse a decision by a federal district court in Arizona that upheld the constitutionality of a regulation adopted by the Arizona Department of Transportation (ADOT) barring McKinnon from using aggregate from his private property in state construction projects. In McKinnon's view, what the ADOT had done to him—injuring his ability both to stay in business and to provide for his family—was unconstitutional because the ADOT had placed his land off limits in response to demands by American Indians who say his property is "sacred" to them!

Back in 1990, McKinnon had leased and then bought Woodruff Butte, near Holbrook in east central Arizona. He bought Woodruff Butte because its aggregate is the best in the region, maybe even in all of Arizona, due to its high density and low porosity, which yield great concrete strength while using less oil in the paving process. Prime contractors, those who build Arizona's bridges, streets, and highways, were eager to use McKinnon's aggregate. Operating as Cholla Ready Mix, McKinnon obtained a commercial source permit from the ADOT so prime contractors could include his aggregate in their bids. Then, however, the Hopi, Navajo, and Zuni asserted that McKinnon's rock pile was sacred. A lawsuit followed, then years of harassment by state and federal officials. Finally, in January of 2001, the ADOT revoked McKinnon's commercial source permit and barred him from obtaining a new one. In June of 2002, McKinnon sued.

In January of 2003, however, an Arizona federal district court dismissed McKinnon's lawsuit, ruling that the regulation that the ADOT claimed barred the use of Woodruff Butte referred to "historical" and "cultural" not "religious" matters; therefore, it was constitutional. McKinnon countered that he was challenging the regulation not "facially" but "as applied" to him due to the fact that the sole reason the ADOT barred use of his land was, not because it had "historical" significance or held "cultural" artifacts but, because Indians considered it "sacred." The court rejected McKinnon's motion for reconsideration. McKinnon appealed.

Before a three-judge panel of the Ninth Circuit, McKinnon's attorney argued that the ADOT violated the Constitution's Establishment Clause because Arizona required McKinnon, and everyone else in Arizona, to adhere to the "religious orthodoxy" of American Indians, an orthodoxy that, because Woodruff Butte is "sacred," bars its use. This is hardly the neutrality the Constitution requires when governments address matters of religion. Moreover, said McKinnon's attorney, the ADOT's action would be unconstitutional even if the ADOT had closed state-owned land; closing "sacred" private property is, if possible, even more unconstitutional.

A month after McKinnon's oral arguments, the Ninth Circuit ruled in another case involving religion and land use. Ordering the removal of a Latin cross, which memorialized the veterans who died in World War I, from the National Park Service's Mohave National Preserve, the Ninth Circuit held, "[T]he Establishment Clause [means] government may not demonstrate a preference for one particular sect or creed (including a preference for Christianity over other religions)." The ADOT's preferential treatment of American Indian religion seemed doomed. Nonetheless, on September 1, the Ninth Circuit dismissed McKinnon's lawsuit as "premised on flawed analysis of the [Establishment Clause]." The Ninth Circuit did not just dismiss McKinnon's case; it issued a broad, published ruling that bars any challenge to the preferential treatment of American Indian religion: "[T]he Establishment Clause does not bar the government from protecting an historically and culturally important site simply because the site's importance derives at least in part from its sacredness to certain groups." Curiously, the historical and cultural importance of the Latin cross in the California desert was irrelevant to whether its presence violated the Establishment Clause.

Dale McKinnon has appealed. Meanwhile, however, the Ninth Circuit's two most recent rulings provide that governments may endorse paganism, but not Christianity.

OCTOBER 2004

CHAPTER SIXTEEN

America at War

———

On March 8, 2005, my wife Lis, our son Luke, and I were in Emerald Isle, North Carolina, near Marine Corps Base Camp Lejeune to help our son Perry, a Marine Corps 2nd Lieutenant, prepare and pack for deployment to Iraq. Since September 11, 2001, while Perry was at the University of Pennsylvania courtesy of a Marine Corps ROTC scholarship, we knew this day would come. We jammed too much gear into his duffle bags, tossed them into his car, took photographs, circled around in prayer, and said goodbye. We were immensely proud, but of course, apprehensive.

Two days later, I was in a Starbucks in New York City to interview a law student interested in working for MSLF. After the interview, I turned my mobile phone on and winced when I noticed I had missed the call from Perry just before his unit lifted off from Delaware. That day, along with Perry's wife Blair, a student at the University of Pennsylvania School of Veterinary Medicine, we four joined thousands of Americans all across the country with family members in the Armed Service serving overseas in harm's way.

Although I saw many American flags on vehicles in the days following 9/11—mine was one of the first up—nearly four years later, I rarely saw one. (I still have my current replacement flying; there is a box of one hundred in my garage.) Like the missing flags, the war and its human costs were invisible to most Americans. In the towns near military bases, however, the signs were everywhere: welcoming home, praying for safety, or bidding farewell. In their churches, filled with men with short-cropped hair, military bearing, and appropriate civilian attire, and young families in tow, and with young wives handling a rambunctious brood alone, the bulletins read of deployed officers and enlisted personnel and requested prayers. Little wonder: a Marine Corps general told me, "A Marine is in Iraq, just returned from Iraq, or is about to deploy to Iraq." I felt compelled to speak, write, and litigate about things military so that the nation might remember and be grateful. I was thankful I was able to do just that!

Perry returned safely and today serves in the U.S. Marine Corps as a Major and Judge Advocate. He and Blair (Dr. Pendley, D.V.M.) have three daughters and a son.

ELITE LAW SCHOOLS THUMB
THEIR NOSES AT THE U.S. MILITARY

As the nation celebrated the holidays, millions of Americans reached out to others. Across the country, gifts were purchased, packaged, and sent off to uniformed men and women serving in Iraq and Afghanistan. Likewise, visits were made, care given, and prayers raised for the hundreds of those injured in combat. As families gathered to welcome in the New Year, America remembered those who had made the ultimate sacrifice for their country. Confronted by such selflessness, millions are humbled and ask: "What can I do?" On America's elite college campuses, however, law schools and their professors arrogantly demand to know why they should do anything at all. Faced with a federal law requiring that they allow military recruiters onto their campuses, or lose federal funding, they sued, arguing that the law violates their freedoms of speech and of association. Incredibly, a panel of the U.S. Court of Appeals for the Third Circuit agreed, and found the so-called Solomon Amendment unconstitutional.

The case is *Forum for Academic & Institutional Rights, Inc. (FAIR) v. Rumsfeld*, which was filed on September 19, 2003, in New Jersey federal district court, against Secretary of Defense Donald H. Rumsfeld and five other Cabinet secretaries. FAIR is a self-described "association of 24 law schools and law faculties whose mission is to promote academic freedom and to support educational institutions in opposing discrimination" whose "first project is a legal challenge to the Solomon Amendment." FAIR, which refuses to disclose its members except *in camera* to a federal judge, contends that because law schools have anti-discrimination policies and the military bars homosexual activity, being forced to receive military representatives unconstitutionally suppresses their speech and compels them to associate with people whose "message" they abhor. After the federal district court rejected its arguments, FAIR appealed; the Third Circuit ruled on November 29, 2004.

One judge, a World War II Marine Corps Major, dissented, first discrediting the panel's reliance on two rulings by the Supreme Court of the United States where the Court held that parade organizers need not accept gay pride marchers and that the Boy Scouts may expel a homosexual scoutmaster. The dissent disclosed that the Third Circuit had rejected FAIR's arguments in an earlier case, barring the panel's ruling. Next, noting the sophistication of law school faculties and students, the dissent declared that they were capable of disassociating themselves from the military's "message" when recruiters came. Finally, speaking for most Americans, the dissent rejected "[t]he subjective idiosyncratic impressions of some law students, some professors, or some anti-war protesters" that military recruiters bring discredit to campus. Instead, "men and women in uniform are almost universally considered as heroes, sacrificing not only their lives and well-being, but living separate from all the comforts of stateside living. . . ."

If this case were about principle, elite law schools would be demanding that recruiters come to their campuses. As the abuses at Abu Ghraib prison and the recent alleged shooting of an unarmed Iraqi in Fallujah demonstrate, there is a vital need for highly qualified lawyers to serve as trial and defense counsels and as judges on military tribunals. America's credibility in the world community and the confidence of uniformed Americans in the fairness of military justice depend on skilled lawyers from the nation's best law schools. Obviously, this case is not about principle given that the ethical sensitivity on which it is based does not extend to those hired by colleges (former Weatherman Bernadine Dohrn is the director of a legal clinic at Northwestern University) or those invited to speak there (Laura Whitehorn, who spent 14 years in prison for plotting a 1983 bomb attack on the U.S. Capitol, spoke last year at Duke).

This case is not over. Until it is, however, Americans have to wonder why, as young men and women uncomplainingly face a brutal and dangerous enemy, law professors complain about having to provide "scarce interview space" and "make appointments" for military recruiters.

JANUARY 2005

REAGAN'S SECNAV:
"WHITE AMERICA ... AN ETHNIC FAIRY TALE"

In 1995, in what *Time* called "a legal earthquake," the Supreme Court of the United States all but killed racial preferences in federal government contracting in a case litigated for a decade by Mountain States Legal Foundation, *Adarand Constructors, Inc. v. Peña*. Therefore, in 1998, for the first time since it adopted racial quotas in government contracting in 1977, Congress debated the constitutionality of their use. Nonetheless, Congress left its racial preference language unchanged, leaving it to the courts to declare it unconstitutional.

The U.S. Court of Appeals for the Tenth Circuit and then for the Eighth Circuit, instead of adhering strictly to the Supreme Court's commandments in *Adarand*, reinterpreted that ruling and upheld government's use of racial preferences in contracting. Given three separate opportunities to rebuke the appellate courts for their refusal to follow *Adarand*, the Supreme Court declined, most recently in November of 2003, over a vigorous dissent by Justice Scalia and Chief Justice Rehnquist. Experts now await a split in the circuits. That split may soon come, from an unusual source. On February 11, the U.S. Court of Appeals for the Ninth Circuit heard arguments in a test of racial preferences in government contracting out of Washington State. Atypically for the Ninth Circuit, the three-judge panel has two conservative judges who may follow *Adarand*, sending the case to the Supreme Court.

If it gets there, it will be met by new scholarship that undermines the factual basis for governmental distinctions between European Americans and select groups of non-European Americans. James Webb, the most highly-decorated Marine officer of the Vietnam War and Reagan's Secretary of the Navy, argues, in his non-fiction work, *Born Fighting, How the Scots-Irish Shaped America* (Broadway Books, 2004), that preferences are based on two erroneous assumptions: "[A]nyone who was not a White Anglo-Saxon Protestant had grounds for complaint about his or her people's collective 'struggle.' And anyone who was a WASP was by default a privileged, less-than-deserving whipping post."

Thus, because the history of the Scots-Irish, for example, was "both unknown and irrelevant" to Congress when it adopted racial quotas, the

Scots-Irish, lost twice. "First, since the dominant forces in American society were by assumption the WASP hierarchy, to be white, Protestant, and of British heritage immediately lumped one in with the New England Brahmin elites...." ("In this perverted logic," notes Webb, it is as if all WASPS "had landed together on the same ship at Plymouth Rock and the smart ones had gone to Boston while the dumbest had somehow made their way to West Virginia.") "Second, [t]o be of Southern descent brought with it an immediate presumption of invidious discrimination and cruelty dating back to the slave system and the unequal, segregated society that followed it." This disregard for "the vast distinctions among white Americans" helped create "a statistical straw man of 'white America'" used to justify racial quotas, which "was nothing more than an imaginary façade. Indeed, white America is so variegated that it is an ethnic fairy tale."

Had Congress sought to give lie to the fairy tale, it could have done so. For example, writes Webb, in 1974, the University of Chicago's National Opinion Research Center (NORC) found that, "even prior to the major affirmative action programs, there was a greater variation within 'white America' than there was between white America and black America. [I]n terms of education and income, the whites at the bottom were in approximately the same situation as blacks." NORC's General Social Survey for 1980-2000 shows that, over the last thirty years, racial preferences have "exacerbated" the situation. Concludes Webb, "These members of our society can hardly be called advantaged in a way that justifies legal discrimination against them as interchangeable members of a supposedly monolithic white majority."

If the Supreme Court wants a basis for ending racial preferences, in addition to its 1995 *Adarand* ruling, it could use James Webb's scholarship on race in America.

MARCH 2005

A TALE OF TWO COUNTIES AND THE
FEDERAL VOTING RIGHTS ACT

In mid-1999, lawyers from Clinton's Justice Department arrived in tiny Chinook, the county seat of sparsely populated, rural Blaine County, Montana, to deliver an ultimatum. Either Blaine County racially gerrymander its commissioner election districts or government lawyers would sue, charging that Blaine County violated the federal Voting Rights Act (VRA). Montana, like many other western states, elects its commissioners at large, by election district. Unlike at-large election systems adopted by states with a history of violating the voting rights of minority citizens, the western at-large system has been in place since the states' territorial days. Because county government is "where the rubber hits the road," there is no room for commissioners, concluded early state lawmakers, who do not feel any obligation to other county voters wherever they reside.

American Indians comprise 43 percent of the residents and 39 percent of the voters of Blaine County; however, because 83 percent of them reside on the Fort Belknap Indian Reservation, which through tribal government and the Bureau of Indian Affairs receives services usually provided by county government, American Indians are sensibly uninterested in commissioner elections. As to other elections, American Indian voters involve themselves to the degree that they often determine the outcome of primary and general elections. For example, Blaine County voters elected Charles Hay, an American Indian, as sheriff and justice of the peace. It was the commissioner races, however, that interested federal lawyers: that no American Indian had been elected commissioner was proof of a VRA violation! That no American Indian could identify a reason to run for county commissioner or what he could do to serve his constituents if elected was irrelevant. As to Charlie Hay's election victories, federal lawyers said they proved nothing because, "He did not run for office as an Indian."

The United States sued Blaine County in November of 1999; however, discovery and other preliminary matters consumed the next 15 months. Although Bush officials were given the opportunity, in January of 2001, to abandon the lawsuit, they declined. After a week-long trial in October of 2001, a Montana federal district court ruled against Blaine County in March of 2002. Later, a panel of the U.S. Court of Appeals for the Ninth

Circuit upheld the ruling, opining, in conflict with other appellate circuits and the Supreme Court of the United States, that minorities could invalidate at-large voting without proof of, for example, racial animus or specific issues as to which racial minorities sought, but were denied, election. Last month, the Supreme Court, notwithstanding these clear conflicts, declined to hear, and thus ended, the case.

Meanwhile, federal lawyers fashioned a VRA lawsuit against yet another rural western county. Although the Clinton administration ended before the suit could be filed, Bush lawyers kindly filed it for them, suing Alamosa County, Colorado, in late 2001. This time the allegation was that at-large voting had deprived Hispanics of their ability to elect their "candidates of choice," that is, averred Bush administration lawyers, "Hispanic Democrats." Alamosa County, arguing the law the Ninth Circuit refused to apply in Blaine County's case, prevailed when a Colorado federal district court ruled the county had not violated the VRA. The Justice Department, fearing that the Tenth Circuit would rule in favor of Alamosa County and set a six-state precedent barring further VRA lawsuits, did not appeal.

So where does this tale leave other western jurisdictions, such as Wyoming's Fremont County, home to the Wind River Indian Reservation? It leaves them in what aviators call "the zone of confusion." For notwithstanding Mark Levin's scholarly views in his best-selling, *Men in Black*, not all problems are the result of opinions by Supreme Court justices. Some are the result of: those named to the Civil Rights Division; the arbitrary rulings issued by federal appellate judges, such as those on the Ninth Circuit; and finally, the cases that the Supreme Court, for whatever reason, refuses to hear.

MAY 2004

IF THE SENATE WANTS TO APOLOGIZE, THERE IS A FAMILY IN UTAH

On June 13, 2005, the U.S. Senate adopted a resolution apologizing for failing to override filibusters by Democratic Senators and to enact House-passed federal anti-lynching legislation on three occasions from 1920 to 1940. Syndicated columnist Mona Charen writes, "Not a single member of today's Senate was even in office" then; but, "that's the way we prefer our apologies in American politics. We don't apologize for our own sins." If Senators would like to apologize for things they, not others, failed to do, I have a suggestion.

In 1945, as U.S. Marines continued their assault on the islands of the Pacific and the units of the Japanese Imperial Army massed there, the U.S. government approached Jesse Fox Cannon of Toole County, Utah, to obtain permission to use 1,425 acres of mining claims he owned near the Army Dugway Proving Grounds in west-central Utah. Jesse Fox Cannon quickly agreed and entered into a contract that allowed the Army to test explosive munitions in a corner of his property on and near his Yellow Jacket mining claim.

The Army's "Project Sphinx" was to be conducted on mineshafts to simulate Japanese cave fortifications, like those the Marines had encountered on Saipan and Iwo Jima. Contrary to terms of the contract, however, the Army not only bombed all of Jesse Fox Cannon's claims, it also used non-explosive munitions: phosgene, mustard agent, and defoliants. In total, the Army utilized more than 3,000 rounds of ammunition, 12,000 pounds of conventional bombs, and 23 tons of chemical weapons in the testing project. To make matters worse, the Army continued using Jesse Fox Cannon's property, without permission, until the 1960s.

Although the contract between the federal government and Jesse Fox Cannon provided that, within 60 days from the end of its testing, the Army would restore the property to the same condition it was in prior to the bombing, the Army did no reclamation. Finally, in desperation, Jesse Fox Cannon filed a claim for $3,000, which the Army promptly denied.

To date, the federal government has not cleaned up Jesse Fox Cannon's property, which is now owned by other members of the Cannon family, that is, other than to perform a 1996 engineering study and to list the property in the Formerly Used Defense Site (FUDS) for future cleanup by the U.S. Department of Defense. The Army Corps of Engineers has testified that the Cannon property is scheduled for cleanup in 2008-2010, that is, if Congress appropriates the funds. Congress spends only $2 million annually on the 2,700 FUDS properties, whose total cleanup cost is $19 billion.

On April 7, 1998, Margaret and Allan Cannon filed a claim with the Army, which the Army summarily rejected. On December 11, 1998, Margaret and Allan Cannon sued the Army for $8 million, which the Army opposed arguing that the court had no right to hear the case. Nonetheless, the Utah federal district court ruled that the Army's weapons testing was a continuing trespass and nuisance and awarded Margaret and Allan Cannon $166,000. The federal government appealed contending that it could not be sued. The U.S. Court of Appeals for the Tenth Circuit agreed and reversed and dismissed the case.

This month, Douglas Cannon will file a claim against the United States, this time under the Resource Conservation and Recovery Act (RCRA), to force the U.S. government to do exactly what it compels others to do, on pain of civil and criminal prosecution: clean up its mess. No doubt, the federal government will deny that claim too.

All of this is well known to the U.S. Senate, its oversight and appropriation committees, and their knowledgeable staffs. For the last 60 years, they have been active participants in the refusal of the federal government to adhere to the contract it entered into and to obey the laws that it enforces. All is not lost, however; perhaps in 60 years the Senate could apologize.

JULY 2005

BETWEEN A ROCK AND A HARD PLACE

This month, briefs will be filed in the U.S. Court of Appeals for the Ninth Circuit in a case that may resolve what has been, over the last year, a constitutional anomaly. In 2004, one Ninth Circuit panel held that a Latin cross, erected on federal lands to honor those who gave their lives in World War I, violated the Establishment Clause and must be removed. Later, another Ninth Circuit panel held that Arizona's designation of private property as sacred to American Indians and off limits to use did not violate the Establishment Clause and could stand. Thus: "No" to Christianity; "Yes" to pantheism. The Ninth Circuit refused to hear the Arizona case *en banc* to resolve this conflict.

Now comes a case from a Nevada federal district court that could force another Ninth Circuit panel to decide which panel's view of the Establishment Clause is correct. The case, *Access Fund v. U.S. Department of Agriculture*, challenges the district court's ruling that the Forest Service's decision to close Cave Rock at Lake Tahoe to all climbing because it is sacred to some American Indians does not violate the Constitution's Establishment Clause. In rejecting the climbers' constitutional argument, the federal district court relied on the Ninth Circuit panel's ruling in the Arizona sacred private lands case. Held the Nevada court: "The Establishment Clause does not require government to ignore the historical value of religious sites[;] protecting culturally important Native American sites has historic value for the nation as a whole because of the unique status of Native American Societies in North American history."

The ruling of the Nevada district court, however, ignores that, for the past 30 years, the "history" and "culture" associated with religious symbols embraced by governments have not saved them from court rulings that those governments had abandoned their constitutionally required neutrality. For example, in last year's panel's ruling regarding the Latin cross, its historical and cultural importance as a symbol that 116,000 Americans left their homes and families and gave their lives in Europe must, indeed, be "ignore[d]" given what the cross represents. What is "unique," therefore, about American Indian religion that would permit its practitioners to demand to go where other religions dare not: the public square? In a word, nothing; in fact, that is exactly what the Supreme Court of the United States ruled back in 1988.

In *Lyng v. Northwest Indian Cemetery Protective Ass'n*, the Court, in a Justice O'Connor opinion, rejected the demands by three American Indian Tribes in northwestern California that portions of the national forest traditionally used by them for religious purposes be closed to logging and road building:

"Nothing in the principle for which [the Tribes] contend, however, would distinguish this case from another lawsuit in which they (or similarly situated religious objectors) might seek to exclude all human activity but their own from sacred areas of the public lands[.] Whatever rights the Indians may have to the use of the area[,] those rights do not divest the Government of its right to use what is, after all, its land."

Yet even if the *Lyng* case were not the binding legal precedent that it is, Establishment Clause jurisprudence makes clear that the Forest Service's decision at Cave Rock runs afoul of every traditional Supreme Court test, for the Forest Service's action "advances," "endorses," and "entangles" itself with American Indian religion. By agreeing with American Indians that Cave Rock is sacred and by rejecting the view of climbers that it is not, the Forest Service "conveys a message of endorsement," informing American Indian religious practitioners that they are "insiders" and the climbers that they are "outsiders." Indeed, the Forest Service is not demanding that non-Indians simply "respect" American Indian religion; it is "employ[ing] the machinery of the state to enforce religious orthodoxy" that views Cave Rock as sacred!

If the Ninth Circuit fails to get it right, the Supreme Court awaits.

AUGUST 2005

STEVEN VINCENT: A HERO IN
THE FIGHT FOR FREEDOM

In a July of 2004 *Reason* magazine article, New York City freelance writer Steven Vincent exposed the truth behind the Native American Graves Protection and Repatriation Act. "How did a well-intentioned piece of legislation come to provoke fears of Orwellian snooping?" he asked. "The answer involves the weighted history of Indian relations, a vaguely written federal law, and the zealous agencies that seek to enforce it, as well as aspects of Native American culture that strike some non-Indians as confusing and often contradictory."

Steven Vincent wrote forthrightly about issues with which I was intimately familiar: the escalating demands of American Indian religious practitioners, the eagerness of federal bureaucrats to accede to those demands, and the ruthlessness of federal law enforcement personnel and lawyers in defending the legality and constitutionality of that acquiescence. Would he write more about such things?

On a trip to New York City in the summer of 2004, I met with Steven Vincent in a small, neighborhood coffee shop in the East Village. We spoke about "sacred" Indian artifacts, about tribal cultures, and about the closure of "sacred" lands, but mostly we talked about other things because, as I was to learn, life had changed irrevocably for Steven Vincent.

It changed, as it did for millions of Americans, on September 11, 2001. That clear morning in the Lower East Side apartment he shared with his wife, Lisa Ramaci, he received a telephone call from a neighbor, summoning him to the roof of their building. There the two of them watched in horror as, a little more than two miles away, the north tower of the World Trade Center burned. They were there when the second plane hit the south tower. They were still there when both towers collapsed an hour later.

"Terrorists," thought Steven Vincent, and when he did he knew he was seeing unspeakable evil, evil made worse by its desire to be displayed for the world to see. When America responded in the weeks and months ahead, Steven Vincent cheered. He knew, however, that cheering was not enough: he had to do something. Too old to join the military, he joined with them, as a journalist, when the coalition forces liberated Iraq in March of 2003. There he fell in love with the country, its people longing to be free, and the world-wide fight for freedom. On his return, days before I met with him, he wrote and, in November of 2004, published, *In the Red Zone: A Journey into the Soul of Iraq*. It received universal acclaim and Steven Vincent appeared often in the media and blogosphere.

Shortly after *In the Red Zone* was released, we met again, this time in his apartment. I brought books to be autographed and he spread his maps and posters over the hardwood floor; we talked long into the darkness outside. I had a personal reason for wanting to know more: my son Perry, a Marine second lieutenant, had received orders to "the sandbox."

Over the weeks, we corresponded frequently and Steven Vincent graced me with his writings. When I sought to meet with him on my next visit to New York City, he demurred; he was already back in Iraq. His postings continued, culminating in a July 31, 2005, article in the *New York Times*. Hours later, Steven Vincent was abducted and murdered. On August 15, I joined his family, friends, and admirers in Middle Collegiate Church to pay our final respects.

A hero of 9/11 as surely as the passengers and firefighters who rushed forward on that day or the men and women in uniform on the days following, Steven Vincent served America with his courage, his insight, and his willingness to speak truth in defense of freedom. Like all heroes, he inspires us to do likewise, knowing that, when we do, whatever sacrifice we make is trivial compared to the one he made so willingly.

SEPTEMBER 2005

THE U.S. GOVERNMENT: ARE THE INMATES RUNNING THE ASYLUM?

Until Harriet Miers withdrew last week, President Bush's decision to name his long-time lawyer and current White House counsel to the Supreme Court of the United States seemed the last straw for many conservatives and libertarians. Bush's federalization of education, support of a budget-busting prescription drug act combined with his failure to veto Congress's profligate spending, and his signing and vigorous defense of "campaign finance reform " had frustrated his base, but it consoled itself with three words: Supreme Court appointments. Westerners scratched their heads too. They hardly expected the Bush administration: would defend Clinton's national monuments decrees, demand western counties gerrymander commissioner districts to guarantee election of racial minorities, and close federal land called sacred by American Indians.

There were mitigating factors: Vice President Gore's litigation over the 2000 election results delayed the Bush-Cheney transition; U.S. Senator Jim Jeffords' abandonment of the Republican Party prolonged Senate confirmation of Bush appointees; and, the 9/11 attack changed the nation's focus for months. Plus, gaining control of the federal bureaucracy is not easy. As Vice President Cheney told a New Mexico group in October of 2002, "These things take time." Is five years enough? Maybe not; take the case of ten miles of dirt road in a Utah park.

In 1964, Congress created the Canyonlands National Park in central Utah to ensure that Americans would always be able to enjoy geological marvels like Angel Arch, which was accessible via Salt Creek Road. For decades, visitors did as Congress intended: driving the ten miles from Peekaboo campsite to Angel Arch. Then, in 1995, bowing to pressure from environmentalists, the National Park Service (NPS) limited access to 12 vehicles a day. That failed to please environmentalists; they sued. In September of 1998, a Utah federal district court ruled for the environmentalists. Recreational groups, which had intervened to support the NPS, appealed. At the U.S. Court of Appeals for the Tenth Circuit, Clinton's NPS lawyers switched sides, arguing that the environmentalists were right. The tactic infuriated the Tenth Circuit, which remanded the case to determine if Congress intended that Salt Creek Road remain open to vehicular traffic.

Notwithstanding the rebuke, NPS bureaucrats and lawyers were unfazed. The NPS issued an order closing Salt Creek Road—it would have been reopened due to the Tenth Circuit's ruling—and then dragged its feet as the recreational groups and San Juan County battled to get the NPS back before the district court. Meanwhile, the Bush administration had arrived in Washington and promptly heard from the Utah congressional delegation about the NPS's refusal to do as Congress intended. As days turned to weeks and weeks to months, the NPS stonewalled. One federal official lamented that the NPS and its lawyers were "out of control." Nonetheless, the Utah federal district court declined to rein in the NPS.

All the while the NPS was preparing its studies to justify, *post hoc*, what it had decided to do years before. In the process, the NPS "discovered" that Salt Creek "support[ed] the most extensive riparian area in the Canyonlands," contained "the richest assemblage of birds and vertebrate wildlife in the park," and, most conveniently of all, was "critical habitat for the threatened Mexican spotted owl." With the books now conveniently cooked, the NPS at last appeared before the district court in May of 2005. In September of 2005, the district court ruled that, while the NPS had cut some corners, it was entitled to the benefit of the doubt; plus, after all, the court had an obligation to defer to the agency's expertise and, if the NPS says Salt Creek Road must be closed, then it must be true. Case closed!

Closed as well is practical public access to Angel Arch, notwithstanding the intent of Congress that people drive there when it made the area a park, which raises the issue: Why, after five years, are the inmates still running the asylum?

NOVEMBER 2005

WHEN DID IT START—
ACADEMIA'S HATRED OF THE MILITARY?

In *The Scariest Place in the World: A Marine Returns to North Korea*, James Brady tells of the men with whom he served in "the forgotten war." "Korea was just maybe the last war Americans fought in which everyone went, the rich and the poor, the Harvards and the high school dropouts, the cowboy and the rancher's son ..." Brady's fellow lieutenants were "[w]ell-bred college boys" from Harvard, Yale, Brown, Columbia, and Princeton; his company commander was blue-blood John Chafee.

Brady identifies Chafee as the hero of *The Coldest War: A Memoir of Korea* and the inspiration for the protagonist in *The Marines of Autumn: A Novel of the Korean War*, and Brady ends *The Scariest Place* with a eulogy to Chafee. No wonder. At Yale on December 7, 1941, Chafee enlisted and fought as a private on Guadalcanal; in the Marine Corps' last battle of WWII, Okinawa, Chafee was fighting as a 2nd Lieutenant. He returned to Yale, graduated, graduated from Harvard Law, passed the bar, and practiced law. In 1950, the Marine Corps called up the reserves, including Captain Chafee.

After Korea, Chafee returned to his law practice, was elected to Rhode Island's House of Representatives, became Governor, was Secretary of the Navy, and served 23 years in the U.S. Senate. It was a different time. Compare, for example, another Secretary of the Navy, James Webb, who entered law school 25 years after Chafee.

When Webb, a highly decorated combat Marine Captain medically discharged due to his wounds in Vietnam, arrived at Georgetown Law School in 1972, the "disdain that many of the advantaged in my generation felt for those who had fought in Vietnam," stunned him. It should not have; of the 1,800 students, Webb met three combat veterans. Law professors engaged daily in a condescending harangue of things military. One professor, knowing of Webb's experiences, gave him a test question about Marine platoon sergeant "Jack Webb," who smuggled jade in the bodies of dead Marines. Webb reported the professor, arguing he "lacked the judgment to teach at such a prestigious school." "If such a fact pattern had been written after World War II," says Webb, "the professor would have been drawn and quartered, probably by the students themselves." At Harvard in 1947, Chafee would have led the detail. Webb's professor got tenure!

This cultural shift and the resulting cultural schism is why the Supreme Court of the United States, on December 6, will hear arguments on the constitutionality of a federal statute that denies universities federal funds if they refuse military recruiters access granted other employers. In November of 2004, the U.S. Court of Appeals for the Third Circuit, by 2-1, held the "Solomon Amendment" unconstitutional, siding with elite law schools that wish to bar military recruiters purportedly due to Congress's "Don't ask. Don't tell." policy.

Although attorneys arguing the case will discuss freedom of speech and association, Congress's war powers, "compelled speech," Congress's ability to condition grants, and contract law, the case is about class hatred: that of law schools and their professors for the military and those who wear the uniform. It is also a case filled with irony: law schools discriminate racially to ensure "classroom diversity" but object to the military's need to assure unit cohesion; law professors, who rant from their podiums throughout the academic year, oppose the one-day-a-semester presence of military recruiters; law schools, weeks from pronouncing their seniors ready to practice law, argue that they are unable to discern whether the military is an ethical employer; and law professors, who demand the right to speak, deny law students the ability to hear the speech of military recruiters.

What the Supreme Court will do is unknown; however, the dissenting judge from the Third Circuit, a Marine who served in the Pacific, spoke for most Americans when he wrote, "men and women in uniform" are "heroes" who bring credit to the nation's campuses.

DECEMBER 2005

CHAPTER SEVENTEEN

A Color-Blind Constitution

★ ★ ★ ★ ★

I dedicated my third book—about fifteen years of MSLF litigation—
*Warriors for the West: Fighting Bureaucrats, Radical Groups, and Lib-
eral Judges on America's Frontier* (Regnery, 2006), to the man who
hired me, the late H. A. "Dave" True, Jr., the "Wyoming Wildcatter":

"In his professional career in the energy and agricultural industries,
Dave embodied the philosophy that man can develop and use our land's
resources while conserving our land's beauty and gifts. In his personal life,
his passion to see our laws applied justly and with accountability was second only to his passion for good fly fishing and his family. Without Dave,
none of the successes of [MSLF] chronicled here would have been possible."

I acknowledged that I was "grateful first to the men and women of
these pages who courageously stepped forward to fight for a cause because
they believed it was right. That did not make their decisions any easier, and
the realization that they were in for the long haul, not to settle or compromise but to win, made those decisions even more difficult and, in the end,
remarkable. Without them, there would be no stories to tell, no victories
and legal precedents to celebrate, and no lessons to learn, however painfully, from the long battles on their behalf." I wrote of the challenges facing
those who seek redress in court as "the battlefield onto which Warriors for
the West who wish to fight back must enter. The battle is not for the faint
of heart, those lacking in commitment to principle, or those in a hurry.
Occasionally, it has its rewards. Too often it results in heartbreak. But, for
those who love liberty and find truth and inspiration in the vision of the
Founding Fathers, it is the only way. Thus, over the last decade or so, the
men and women of these pages have been Warriors for the West, fighting
against incredible odds."

I concluded, "[I]t is not the destination, but the journey, so these tales
are not about victories and defeats but about men and women who, knowing that defeat was likely, undertook the fight anyway because if victory
came it would have been worth it, not just for them but for all the others
like them. They may not be heroes to everyone, but they are heroes to me."

NOT JUST DEMOCRATS,
REPUBLICAN LEADERS PANDER ON RACE

In 1993, President Clinton nominated Yale Law pal, Lani Guinier, as Assistant Attorney General for the Justice Department's Civil Rights Division. Seth Lipsky, in the *Jewish Forward*, questioned her views; others did likewise. One critic wrote, she "does not believe that the [U.S.] Constitution, with its system of representative democracy, adequately defends the rights of minorities. Therefore, she proposes adoption of schemes like cumulative voting, geared towards allowing the losing minority to win actual representation regardless of their election loss." Clinton dumped her, "Had I read [her writings] before I nominated her, I would not have done so."

Then Clinton nominated NAACP Legal Defense and Educational Fund attorney Bill Lann Lee, whose radical views prevented his confirmation. Nonetheless, Clinton named Lee to the post from whence Lee filed lawsuits against local governments for alleged violations of the 1982 amendments to Section 2 of the Voting Rights Act. In November of 1999, Lee sued Blaine County, Montana, asserting that the sparsely populated rural county had violated that law because no American Indian had been elected commissioner. A similar lawsuit two years later against sparsely populated, rural Alamosa County, Colorado, claimed Hispanics could not elect their "candidates of choice."

Alamosa County won when a Colorado federal district court ruled voting there was not racially polarized and that, "to be elected in Alamosa County, a candidate must appeal to both Anglo and Hispanic voters.... Subtle or overt ethnic appeals ...have resulted in failure at the polls." Blaine County, however, lost even though there was no evidence American Indians had been denied the ability to register, vote, or run for office. In fact, an American Indian had been elected sheriff and justice of the peace.

The U.S. Court of Appeals for the Ninth Circuit upheld that ruling holding that, to prevail in Section 2 litigation, the Justice Department need not prove that: (1) American Indians had been denied an equal opportunity to participate in elections and to elect their candidates of choice; (2) non-Indians had voted as a bloc out of racial animus and a desire to prevent election of American Indian candidates; and (3) American Indians had identified distinct political issues that could be addressed by the county commission. American Indians had run for office and lost; that was enough under Section 2, declared the Ninth Circuit.

Lawsuits like those filed by Clinton's officials and supported by Bush lawyers, and rulings like that of the Ninth Circuit are why Roger Clegg, Center for Equal Opportunity General Counsel, urges revision of the Voting Rights Act. "[T]he act should be changed back to its pre-1982 language, to require a showing of actual racial discrimination—that people are being treated differently because of race; the law should be amended to make clear that there is no requirement that districts be drawn with the racial bottom line in mind—and, indeed, that such racial gerrymandering is in fact illegal; the act should be amended to make clear that it guarantees nothing for one racial group that it does not guarantee for all racial groups."

Fortunately, the Rehnquist Court, in a series of decisions beginning in 1997, set forth what one appellate court called "an entirely new framework" for evaluating the authority of Congress to enact legislation such as its 1982 Voting Rights Act amendments. Four justices made it clear that those amendments may indeed be unconstitutional! Nonetheless, with the Voting Rights Act up for reauthorization in 2007, Republican leaders appear eager not only to keep intact the 1982 amendments that led to lawsuits against rural western counties, but also to go further. Representative James Sensenbrenner (R-5th WS), House Judiciary Committee Chairman, promised the NAACP quick action on the law "as is" and Senate Majority Leader Bill First (R-TN) is "fired up" for quick reauthorization; both have Republican National Committee Chairman Ken Mailman's support.

No wonder only 34 percent of Americans approve of the job Congress is doing!

JANUARY 2006

COURTS OF APPEALS THUMB NOSES AT
9-0 SUPREME COURT RULING

In 1994, as required by the Federal Land Policy and Management Act (FLPMA), the Bureau of Land Management (BLM), after extensive and active public participation, adopted a formal plan setting forth how it would manage 2.8 million acres of federal land in Phillips, Fergus, Petroleum, Judith Basin, Valley, and southern Chouteau Counties in northern Montana. Included within the "Judith Valley Phillips Resource Management Plan" were 20,000 acres in Phillips County known as the "40 Complex," which was to be used by the public for hiking, camping, hunting, and the recreational shooting of unregulated wildlife, including prairie dogs.

About that time, the U.S. Fish and Wildlife Service (FWS) decided to introduce black-footed ferrets, which are protected by the Endangered Species Act, into the 40 Complex. In 1999, at the urging of the FWS, the BLM, without notice or opportunity for public comment, summarily closed the 40 Complex to the "discharge or use of firearms" because, "The prairie dog colony provides prey base and habitat for the survival of the ferrets."

Recreational hunters in Montana believed the BLM's closure of the 40 Complex violated FLPMA's requirements for public participation in land management decisions; in September of 2001, they filed a lawsuit challenging the closure order. Meanwhile, the FWS convinced the Montana State Legislature to remove the 40 Complex from the hunting of unregulated wildlife. Thereupon, the BLM lifted its closure order and moved to dismiss the lawsuit, while defending the legality of its original order and its authority to reissue it should Montana restore hunting in the 40 Complex. In September of 2004, the District of Columbia federal district court granted the BLM's motion to dismiss the lawsuit as moot.

Before the U.S. Court of Appeals for the District of Columbia, the Montana hunters argued that the case was not moot because the BLM had maintained that it could reissue the closure order. Furthermore, they argued, the Supreme Court of the United States held the voluntary cessation of illegal activity does not moot a case unless the defendant proves that his illegal conduct would not recur. Nonetheless, a three-judge panel upheld the dismissal of the lawsuit because the Montana hunters had failed to prove that it was "virtually certain" that the BLM would reissue its closure order. As to the Supreme Court's ruling, the panel held that, although the test for mootness advocated by the Montana hunters applies against private individuals and entities, it does not apply against the federal government!

The Montana hunters urged the entire D.C. Circuit to rehear the case because the panel's ruling conflicted with two January 12, 2000, Supreme Court rulings. That day, the Court ruled a lawsuit filed by environmental groups was not moot even though the corporate defendant had ended its illegal activity unless the corporation proved it was "absolutely clear that [its] allegedly wrongful behavior could not reasonably be expected to recur." Next, in a case in which the federal government was the defendant, a unanimous Court used the same test; the case was not moot unless federal officials successfully shouldered the "heavy burden of persuading the court that the challenged conduct cannot reasonably be expected to start up again." Nevertheless, the D.C. Circuit declined to rehear the case.

The D.C. Circuit is not alone. The Seventh Circuit declared that the Supreme Court's ruling is not "the view we have taken toward acts of voluntary cessation by government officials. Rather, when defendants are public officials ... we place greater stock in their acts of self-correction...." Likewise, the Sixth Circuit held: "[W]e have noted that 'cessation of the allegedly illegal conduct by government officials has been treated with more solicitude by the courts than similar action by private parties.'"

Ninety-nine percent of cases seeking Supreme Court review are denied; that fate likely awaits the Montana hunters. No wonder many courts of appeals judges believe they can thumb their noses at inconvenient, but binding, Supreme Court precedent.

FEBRUARY 2006

SOUTH DAKOTA SUPREME COURT: CITIZENS ARE ON THEIR OWN

On November 8, 2005, a Wisconsin judge sentenced Chai Vang to six consecutive life sentences in prison without parole for the first degree intentional murder of six deer hunters and to 55 years in prison on three counts of attempted first-degree intentional homicide. The sentencing came nearly a year after the November of 2004, encounter between eight friends and a stranger who had occupied their deer stand on private woodland near Deer Lake in northern Wisconsin. The stranger, told to leave because he was on private land, seemed to comply but turned and opened fired. As the friends—only one carried a rifle—fled in terror, the stranger gave chase, murdering each in turn.

South Dakota Supreme Court justices may have missed news of the sentencing as they drafted their opinions regarding, among other matters, a constitutional challenge by two farming families to the State Legislature's 2003 amendment to South Dakota's hunting laws. Nonetheless, they had to be aware of the tragic case, which made horrifying national news the previous November. Moreover, the families—fearful that they might be victims of a similar assault should they seek to exclude hunters from their property—noted the Wisconsin matter in their court brief. Oral arguments occurred before the Supreme Court on August 31, 2005; ten days later, the Wisconsin murder trial began.

For decades, South Dakota allowed hunting along section lines or other roads if the rights-of-way were used for vehicular traffic; however, hunters were not allowed to fire over or onto privately owned land without the landowner's permission. In fact, since 1973, South Dakota barred hunting on private property without the owners' permission recognizing owners' right to exclude hunters. Plus, the Supreme Court of the United States held firing weapons over or onto private property to be a physical invasion and hence a "taking" "for public use" without "just compensation." That South Dakota law protected property rights was clear in 2002 when South Dakota's Supreme Court upheld the conviction of a hunter who shot game over private property from a public right-of-way road ditch. After that ruling, South Dakota's Legislature changed the hunting law to provide that lawful "hunting on highways or other public rights-of-way" includes shooting at game in flight over private land if the game took flight from or flew over the right-of-way. Hunters were advised of this new provision in a Hunting Manual and landowners were reminded of state law that criminalized interference with lawful hunting.

The families, who maintain private hunting on their property, sued, arguing the law unconstitutionally denies them the right to bar hunters from shooting over or onto their property. South Dakota's Attorney General argued the law only decriminalized hunting on private land: landowners may still exclude hunters, explicitly with civil lawsuits; implicitly, by telling them they are trespassing!

In November of 2004, a South Dakota Circuit Court rejected the "conflict and confusion" that view would cause; because the statute unconstitutionally took property, it had gone "too far." In January of 2006, South Dakota's Supreme Court reversed that decision, embracing instead the Attorney General's *post hoc* contrivance. Thus, to avoid ruling that the statute allowed hunters to trespass on private property, caused an unconstitutional taking, and must be stricken, the court held the Legislature had not done what it explicitly intended to do.

It is no longer criminal in South Dakota for hunters to shoot over and onto private property; however, while it is not unlawful, it remains a trespass and a tort. Wealthy landowners may hire guards and lawyers to sue hunters for trespassing on their land. Others may, pursuant to state law, use "sufficient" "force or violence" "to prevent[] or attempt[] to prevent ... any trespass." South Dakota politicians may have saved an unconstitutional statute and the hunting revenue they covet, but South Dakotans will pay in the lawlessness that may result. If the Wisconsin tragedy is any indication, some may pay with their lives.

MARCH 2006

AMERICAN INDIAN DENIED HIS CIVIL RIGHTS: DOES ANYONE CARE?

On June 13, 1999, Thomas Lee Morris, aged 16, was driving his family's vehicle, with his parent's permission, near their home in Ronan, Montana, on the Flathead Reservation, when he was stopped by a Ronan City Police Department officer, allegedly for speeding. The officer asked if he were a tribal member; Morris informed him that he was a member of the Minnesota Chippewa Tribe of Leech Lake Reservation, like his father.

Although Morris, his father, and mother—who is a non-Indian—have lived in Ronan for many years where his father runs an upholstery business and his mother works at several jobs, including caring for five children and four minor grandchildren, all of whom are tribal Indians, none of them is a member of the tribes of the Flathead Reservation. In fact, though all members of Morris's family, except his mother are American Indians, they do not qualify as members in the Salish or Kootenai Tribes because they have no Salish or Kootenai ancestors. Thus, they may not participate in the political life of the reservation tribes: they may not vote in elections, hold office, serve on juries, or help determine the laws, rules, or regulations that apply to them.

Nonetheless, Morris was ordered to appear in the Flathead Reservation Tribal Court to answer a charge of violating Tribal Code by speeding. Although non-Indians are not sent to Tribal Court but to Montana State courts where the Constitution, the Bill of Rights, and the Fourteenth Amendment apply, Morris does not have that right. Therefore, at Tribal Court, Morris, with the aid of *pro bono* legal counsel, moved to dismiss for lack of jurisdiction and requested a jury trial, which was denied. Thereupon, Morris filed a petition for a *writ* of *habeas corpus* in the U.S. District Court for the District of Montana; that too, was dismissed.

Remarkably, the U.S. Court of Appeals for the Ninth Circuit reversed the Montana district court's ruling and ordered that court to address the serious constitutional issues raised by Morris, that is, his claim that adoption by Congress of the Indian Civil Rights Act, which makes all American Indians, regardless of tribal membership, subject to any tribal jurisdiction, violates the Constitution's equal protection and due process guarantees.

Back in Montana, the federal district court asked the United States, which had filed a friend of the court brief earlier, to join the lawsuit now as a party, which it did; however, the United States argued, not in favor of the civil rights of Morris, but in favor of the jurisdiction over him by the Flathead Tribal Court. Then, the State of Montana jumped into the case with a friend of the court brief in favor of the Flathead Tribal Court.

Morris's attorney claimed that Congress had violated *Adarand Constructors, Inc. v. Peña*, a landmark 1995 ruling in which the Supreme Court held that the Constitution's equal protection guarantee applied to Congress. The federal district court, however, ruled that *Adarand* did not apply to American Indians because theirs was a political designation, not one based on race. In so ruling, the district court relied on a 1974 decision by the Supreme Court that legal experts believe was overruled by *Adarand*. Plus, as Morris could attest, tribal membership, unlike membership in other political entities, is based on blood quantum. The district court did have a solution for Morris; he could escape Flathead Tribal Court jurisdiction by giving up membership in his father's tribe. Instead, Morris appealed to the Ninth Circuit.

After the Ninth Circuit ruled against him, Morris, early last month, asked the Supreme Court of the United States to decide whether its *Adarand* ruling and its bar against unconstitutional acts by Congress applies to American Indians. Morris hopes the Supreme Court cares about such matters. It is obvious that no one else does—not Congress, not the U.S. Department of Justice, and not the State of Montana.

MAY 2006

OOPS, IT DID IT AGAIN:
9TH CIRCUIT OKAYS ISLAM IN CLASSROOM

On June 1, a California husband and wife filed a petition with the Supreme Court of the United States asking it to review a ruling by the U.S. Court of Appeals for the Ninth Circuit. In *Eklund v. Byron Union School District*, a Ninth Circuit panel upheld a federal district court's rejection of two families' claim that their children's school violated the Establishment Clause when it taught them how to "become Muslims." In a short unpublished opinion, the three-judge panel affirmed the lower court's ruling. Later, the entire Ninth Circuit declined to rehear the case.

In 2001, Excelsior Middle School in Byron, 40 miles east of San Francisco, advised a classroom of twelve-year olds that, "[for the next three weeks], you and your classmates will become Muslims." Thereafter, students memorized portions of the *Koran*, chose Islamic names, wore tags bearing their new Islamic names alongside the Star and Crescent Moon— the symbol of Muslims, completed the Five Pillars of Faith, and recited Muslim prayers. Ironically, the teacher's edition of the course textbook warned: "Recreating religious practices or ceremonies through role playing activities should not take place in a public school classroom."

In June of 2002, the families, represented by the Thomas More Law Center, sued saying that teaching Islam in the Excelsior public school violated the Constitution, which mandates government neutrality regarding religion. In particular, the school district's actions fail every Supreme Court test; they: lack a secular purpose; primarily advance religion; excessively entangle government with religion; endorse a particular religious belief; and coerce students to participate in religion. Nonetheless, a California federal district court judge appointed by Clinton ruled the course lacked "any devotional or religious intent" and was only educational. Notwithstanding a double standard between how the district court treated Islam and how federal courts have treated other religions in the classroom, the Ninth Circuit agreed.

It is not the first time that the Ninth Circuit has bent over backward to permit government endorsement of religions other than the Judeo-Christian faith. In May of 2003, a panel of the Ninth Circuit ruled that a Latin cross erected on federal land in the California desert to commemorate those lost in battle in World War I violated the Establishment Clause because it was a clear symbol of Christianity. Less than four months later, another panel of the Ninth Circuit ruled that an Arizona regulation that prohibited a man from using his private property because his land is sacred to three American Indian tribes did not violate the Establishment Clause because American Indians' religion is intertwined with their history and culture. Curiously, the historical and cultural importance of the Latin cross was irrelevant to whether its presence violated the Establishment Clause.

The Arizona man asked the entire Ninth Circuit to review its decision given the obvious conflict between panels in the manner that the Ninth Circuit treats various religions. The Ninth Circuit refused to rehear the case *en banc* and the Supreme Court declined review. Now comes the Excelsior school case with its ruling that teaching children how to "become Muslims" is permissible because such instruction involves a different culture and is educational. What makes the ruling particularly egregious is that, for decades, courts have barred all religion from the classroom, from the Ten Commandments, to nondenominational prayers, to moments of silence.

The Ninth Circuit has one more chance to get it right. Pending before the Ninth Circuit is a Nevada case where the U.S. Forest Service declared Cave Rock, a popular climbing spot near Lake Tahoe, off limits to climbers because the federal land has religious significance to American Indian religious practitioners. In fact, the Forest Service even declared that the "spiritual power" present at Cave Rock is a resource the Forest Service is obligated to protect. When a climbing group sued, the Nevada federal district court, relying on the Ninth Circuit's opinion in the Arizona case, upheld the closure.

JUNE 2006

HUNTING BY RACE IN MONTANA

Later this month, opening briefs will be filed with the Supreme Court of the United States in two landmark civil rights cases addressing race-based decision-making by public schools. The Court's ruling may turn on its 1995 decision in *Adarand Constructors, Inc. v. Peña*, in which the Court repudiated its 15-year abandonment of the Constitution's guarantee of equal protection. As the Court determines whether, in Justice Scalia's words, "we stand by [our] insistence that '[r]acial classifications are suspect,' ... and that [we will] '"smoke out" illegitimate uses of race'" when public schools assign students based on race, another lawsuit seeking to determine if the Court meant what it said in *Adarand* begins its long journey to the Court.

In 1995, Colorado Springs highway subcontractor Randy Pech, who, despite having submitted the lowest bids, had been denied contracts to install guardrails on federal highway projects, urged the Court to rule that the Constitution's equal protection guarantee applies to the federal government. The United States argued Congress is exempt from that provision. Justice O'Connor, writing for the Court, rejected the government's view and ruled that the Fifth Amendment guarantee is "for persons, not groups," and is a "personal right to equal protection of the laws [that may not be] infringed." In dissenting from the majority's opinion, Justice Stevens noted that the Court's *Adarand* ruling would imperil the Court's 1974 ruling in *Morton v. Mancari*, in which the Court upheld the constitutionality of an American Indian hiring preference utilized by the Bureau of Indian Affairs (BIA). Subsequently, legal scholars agreed with Justice Stevens; in fact, in 1997, the U.S. Court of Appeals for the Ninth Circuit concluded that, if *Adarand* controls, "*Mancari's* days are numbered."

If *Mancari* is doomed, Randy Roberts of Billings, Montana, is eager for its demise. That is the case because the State of Montana, and more specifically, its Department of Fish, Wildlife, and Parks, is using *Mancari* as its basis for barring owners of private property, like Roberts, from engaging in big game hunting on their own land if that land lies within the exterior boundaries of one of Montana's seven Indian Reservations. In fact, for the last 35 years, Roberts has been barred from hunting on 1,500 acres of deeded land on which he would otherwise have the right to hunt if it did not lie within the Crow Indian Reservation; in Montana's view, only American Indian tribal members may hunt there.

Roberts is not the first hunter to run afoul of Montana's race-based, big game rules. Sandra Shook of Sanders County in northwestern Montana was charged with hunting illegally, even though she had a deer hunting license and tag and her neighbor's permission to hunt on his land, because the land is within the Flathead Indian Reservation. The Montana Supreme Court rejected Ms. Shook's constitutional claims and, relying on *Mancari*, held that "laws that afford Indians special treatment are constitutional [if] [they] can be tied rationally to the fulfillment of the unique federal obligation toward Indians." Therefore, held the court, because "federal Indian law regarding the rights of Indians is binding on the state," Montana's hunting rule "is rationally tied to the fulfillment of [Montana's] unique obligation toward Indians."

Apparently lost on the Montana Supreme Court was the following: first, *Mancari* related to the authority of Congress and, as a result of the delegation by Congress, the authority of the BIA vis-à-vis American Indians—no similar authority has been given to Montana; second, although Congress has a special relationship with American Indian tribes, Montana has no such relationship; and finally, given *Adarand*, *Mancari* is likely unconstitutional. Nonetheless, the Supreme Court declined to hear Shook's appeal.

Randy Roberts is not waiting to be cited for hunting on privately owned land and a futile appeal to the Montana Supreme Court. Instead, he filed his lawsuit before the Montana federal district court. Today, his case is briefed and awaiting argument and a ruling.

AUGUST 2006

LIGHTING CANDLES OR CURSING THE DARKNESS

"When whale oil is gone," Paul Harvey reports an apocryphal American pessimist once proclaimed, "the world will be plunged into darkness." Fortunately, America's energy picture has turned, not on the pronouncements of such cranks, but on the wisdom of men like the late Warren T. Brookes and Julian Simon. It was Brookes, a reporter for the *Detroit News*, who declared, "the nature of all technological and innovative advance is to teach us how to produce more value for less waste and less cost," and, thus improve the human environment. It was Simon, victor in a famous bet over future mineral prices with an environmental Cassandra, who proclaimed human ingenuity and technological innovation as the twin and intertwined solutions to scarcity and shortages.

These thoughts come to mind with the remarkable news of a mammoth oil discovery in the Gulf of Mexico. Early last month, Chevron and its partners, including Devon Energy, released news that Chris Isidore of CNN reported "could be the biggest breakthrough in domestic oil supplies since the opening of the Alaska pipeline." Located 270 miles southwest of New Orleans and 175 miles offshore in 7,000 feet of water and drilled through 20,000 feet of rock, the Jack 2 well had a test flow rate of more than 6,000 barrels of crude oil a day. Although Chevron had announced the Jack 2 discovery in September of 2004, last month's test confirmed suspicions as to its potential and caused Chevron to conclude that the Gulf of Mexico's "lower tertiary region" may hold "3 billion to 15 billion barrels of oil." U.S. reserves are estimated at less than 30 billion barrels of oil. No wonder the news made headlines.

The tract is located on the Outer Continental Shelf (OCS), an area of one billion federally-owned acres that extends from the U.S. coastline, beyond waters owned by coastal states, and was leased by the Minerals Management Service (MMS) in July of 1996. The true origins of that lease, however, go back another fifteen years to when Reagan administration officials abandoned the old system of offering only those tracts thought by government bureaucrats to have energy potential and began "area-wide leasing." Under the new system, those who would spend hundreds of millions (now billions) of dollars would be able to choose where they took their chances. Moreover, bureaucrats, with nothing to gain and nothing to lose, had a terrible track record of finding oil and gas.

Not surprisingly, environmentalists screamed bloody murder. Nonetheless, the Reagan administration's approach to OCS oil and gas leasing was upheld by the Supreme Court of the United States. Environmental groups were not to be denied, however; soon, their congressional allies adopted a moratorium to prevent energy leasing on portions of the OCS. Then, President George H.W. Bush, to validate his claim to being a "kinder and gentler" environmental leader, withdrew a majority of the OCS. President Clinton followed suit.

Today Congress is working on a repeal of the Bush/Clinton ban. Sadly, it is not because Congress recognizes that energy prices are high, that oil supplies are low, or that what we use comes from unstable or unfriendly countries. Instead, Congress fears Cuba's plans to drill on the OCS and its impact on U.S. resources. Not surprisingly, environmental groups have launched a nationwide campaign to kill the proposal. Plus, Congress, responding to demands from environmental groups, refuses to open Alaska's Arctic National Wildlife Refuge to energy exploration. Finally, late last week, a federal judge halted leasing of a part of the National Petroleum Reserve-Alaska thought to hold two billion barrels of oil; environmental groups said more bird and caribou studies are needed.

As another summer ends and winter approaches, the imaginative, innovative, and indefatigable folks of the oil patch, who accomplished what many thought impossible, have shown that Brookes and Simon were right. Meanwhile, Congress and environmental groups are casting their lot with Paul Harvey's long ago pessimist.

OCTOBER 2006

BUSH ADMINISTRATION PROPOSES
MASSIVE LAND GRAB

Days ago, in a proposal unnoticed by the media, the U.S. Fish and Wildlife Service (FWS) announced the largest land grab since President Clinton designated massive national monuments across the West. When
Clinton decreed 1.7 million acres of federal land in Utah as the Grand
Staircase-Escalante National Monument to kill a vast underground coal
mine that would have employed 1,000 locals in the most economically
depressed region of southern Utah, generated $20 million in annual rev-
enue, and produced environmentally-compliant coal for generating electricity, there were protests across the West. When the Bush administration
published its plans, it caused barely a ripple.

There should have been a tidal wave of opposition. What Bush officials
propose would make Clinton and his Interior Secretary, Bruce Babbitt,
proud indeed. While Clinton's national monument proclamations affected
only federal land, the Bush plan affects primarily state- and privately-owned
land. Moreover, while Clinton designated a total of 5.9 million acres to
receive special federal protection as national monuments, the Bush plan
would impose a protective federal overlay upon 11.5 million acres (18,000
square miles) or an area the size of the states of Maryland and Massachusetts combined.

Formally entitled "Revised Designation of Critical Habitat for the
Contiguous United States Distinct Population Segment of the Canada
Lynx" and published in the *Federal Register* on November 9, 2005, the
plan results from a March of 2000 ruling by a federal district court in the
District of Columbia. There, after ten years of litigation, environmental
groups succeeded in efforts to require the FWS to use the Endangered Species Act (ESA) to protect the Canada lynx (*Lynx canadensis*) in the contiguous United States.

That was only the beginning. After the FWS placed the lynx on the
ESA list in July of 2003, Defenders of Wildlife urged the federal court to
order the FWS to designate critical habitat in the lower 48, notwithstanding that the lynx's natural habitat is in Canada—hence its name. In January
of 2004, the court issued that mandate with a November 1, 2006, dead-
line. After issuing its plan a year ahead of schedule—When was the last

time that happened?—in August of 2006, the FWS released its "Economic Analysis of Critical Habitat Designation for the Canada Lynx." A month later, the FWS published its "Draft Environmental Assessment: Designation of Critical Habitat for the Contiguous United States Distinct Population Segment of the Canada Lynx," then opened the matter up for public comments, which ended last month.

There is much that is worthy of comment, mostly of the negative variety. Under the plan, 8.4 million acres of private land would be included, at a cost, over twenty years, of $889 million. Although the plan includes Washington, Idaho, Montana, Minnesota, and Maine, its greatest impact is on the latter three with one million acres affected in both northwestern Montana and northeastern Minnesota and six million acres in northern Maine. Thousands of landowners will find their ability to use their private property greatly constrained, if litigious environmental groups have anything to say about it, and they will. Worst of all, the FWS admits that, because the historic range of lynx only marginally includes the lower 48, the designation of critical habitat will achieve little, if anything.

For radical environmental groups, however, designation of critical habitat for the Canada lynx will achieve one thing: it will provide them with yet another tool to bar the use of private property coveted by the groups. In one troubling action, the federal court that ruled on the lynx has retained jurisdiction, apparently to preside over the implementation of the habitat rule. That is very bad news for landowners, those who respect private property, and those who love freedom. No wonder scores of Members of Congress, in rare bi-partisan agreement, have introduced bills to reform "critical habitat" authority. Unfortunately, such reform will come too late for those facing the Bush administration's most audacious land grab.

NOVEMBER 2006

CHAPTER EIGHTEEN

Bureaucrats
Behaving Badly

In March of 2007, an MSLF attorney was in Hazleton, Pennsylvania to represent Mayor Lou Barletta in defending against a challenge to the city's recently adopted ordinance. Hazleton, which lies 80 miles northwest of Philadelphia near the intersection of Interstates 80 and 81 and was incorporated in 1857, had grown from fewer than 25,000 in 2000 to over 31,000; many of the new residents entered the country illegally. Frustrated by the federal government's failure to address the problems of small, cash-strapped towns facing illegal immigration, the city adopted an ordinance to tackle the issues. I learned of the city's troubles and, the previous summer, drove into Hazleton and met with Mayor Barletta.

MSLF's entry into such issues began three years earlier when I read of the enactment by an overwhelming majority of the voters of Arizona of Proposition 200, which barred receipt of "public benefits" by those illegally in the country and required proof of citizenship to vote. Randall Pullen, who put the initiative on the ballot, said Arizona spent more than $1 billion a year to provide services and benefits for over half a million illegal aliens, resulting in an added tax burden to each Arizona household of $700 per year. I learned that Arizona Governor Janet Napolitano and Arizona Attorney General Terry Goddard publicly opposed Proposition 200 and urged its defeat. Fearful that Proposition 200 would not be defended adequately when it came under legal attack, which was immediately, MSLF represented Mr. Pullen. On June 13, 2005, I argued before a three-judge panel of the U.S. Court of Appeals for the Ninth Circuit that those challenging Proposition 200 lacked standing; the panel agreed two months later.

Arizona's Proposition 200's case began anew in 2006 and continued into 2007, just as the Hazleton case began. MSLF argued on the Supremacy Clause issue that the Supreme Court held in 1976 that "regulation of immigration" involves "determining what aliens shall be admitted to the United States, the period they may remain, the regulation of their conduct before naturalization, and the terms and conditions of their naturalization." Plus, Congress has chosen to regulate only authorized entry, length of stay, residence status, and the deportation of immigrants; clearly, it has not "occupied the field" as to the matters addressed by Arizona or Hazleton.

AN EDUCATION CRISIS:
TOO FEW NATURAL RESOURCES SCIENTISTS

Next week, former Denver District Attorney Bill Ritter will become Colorado's 41st Governor. Although Ritter pledged to reform higher education, it remains to be seen if he will provide the assurance sought by a journalism student in Ritter's University of Denver debate with Congressman Bob Beauprez (R-7th CO). Writing in *National Review Online*, Greg A. Pollowitz reports she asked, "What is the government going to do to make sure I can get a job?" Regrettably, the candidates gave lengthy answers instead of responding simply, "Change your major."

That would have made clear that the student and not government is responsible for her employment prospects. Moreover, it would have been great advice. Today, energy and mining companies are paying top dollar for petroleum and mining engineers: graduates will receive a starting salary of $65,000 plus a sizeable signing bonus. A recent Colorado School of Mines Mining Engineering graduate received a $120,000 package from an energy company developing Canada's Athabasca oil sands. Unfortunately, there are too few such qualified graduates; as a result, not only are those jobs going begging, top executives in the oil patch and mining are calling the situation a "crisis."

Accepting the "Mining Man of the Year" Award from the Mining Foundation of the Southwest in Tucson, last month, Jack E. Thompson, Jr., formerly of Newmont Mining Corporation and Homestake Mining Company, delivered his acceptance speech on the crisis. Dr. James V. Taranik, Director of the Mackay School of Earth Sciences and Engineering at the University of Nevada in Reno, has been leading the Mining Educational Sustainability Task Force for the Society of Mining Engineers to develop an action plan to address the crisis, which is due in part to the state of post-secondary education.

When Jack Thompson, Jim Taranik, and other mining leaders entered college, there were over forty institutions of higher learning offering mining engineering degree programs, including Columbia, Harvard, and Yale; today there are but fifteen. There are many reasons why colleges have abandoned this field, despite the world's growing need for natural resources and environmentally-sensitive ways of providing them. Incredibly, the biggest reason is cost. Despite ever escalating tuition, many major universities abandoned practical science and engineering studies because they are not "cost effective." According to Dr. Taranik, the cost of turning out one more social scientist, or journalist for that matter, is only $1,500; it costs $45,000 to graduate a mining engineer. Coincidental with this cynical decision and consistent with it, colleges, which once sought to prepare students for the job market, now seek only to "increase knowledge."

Colleges are not the only ones to blame. Top mining expert, Dr. William H. Dresher, speaking recently in Arizona, declared, "In a decade of judging Arizona state science fairs, I have never seen an exhibit addressing geology, mining, or metallurgy. What is worse, it is hard to find a school that teaches science, let alone discusses engineering!" Astonishingly, this is in Arizona, the nation's largest copper producer. Dr. Mary M. Poulton, Chair of the Department of Mining and Geological Engineering at the University of Arizona, reports only one-third of U.S. high schools have a one-year course in earth science, mostly astronomy, in which only seven percent of high school students enroll.

As Michael Sanera and Jane S. Shaw reveal in *Facts Not Fear: Teaching Children About the Environment* (Regnery, 1999), schools do a marvelous job turning children into nonsense spouting Chicken Littles. Unsurprisingly, it is not just the facts about the environment that schools fail to teach; they are oblivious to fundamental facts regarding the building blocks of modern civilization, such as, "If it can't be grown, it has to be mined." No wonder, with children totally ignorant as to the need for raw materials—not to mention their source—that few youth entering high school consider a career in energy development or mining.

It is not surprising, therefore, that coeds who attend gubernatorial debates worry about their job prospects.

JANUARY 2007

RACIAL GERRYMANDERING IN "THE EQUALITY STATE"

On February 5, in a case that may reach the Supreme Court of the United States, a three- to four-week trial begins in Casper, Wyoming. The American Civil Liberties Union (ACLU), on behalf of five American Indians in rural, sparsely populated Fremont County, claims the County violated Section 2 of the federal Voting Rights Act (VRA) because of the alleged inability of an American Indian to be elected Commissioner. The ACLU demands that the five commissioners—heretofore elected at-large, pursuant to state law—be elected from single-member districts and that one district be gerrymandered racially to guarantee election of an American Indian.

Understanding the ACLU lawsuit requires some history. In 1965, with Section 2 of the VRA, Congress codified the Fifteenth Amendment's guarantee that citizens could not, "on account of race, color, or previous condition of servitude," be denied the vote; meanwhile, in Section 5, Congress required Justice Department "preclearance" of voting changes—in states and counties with a history of racially discriminatory conduct that denied citizens the right to vote—to determine if the change would have an adverse impact on voting equality. In 1966, the Supreme Court upheld the constitutionality of Section 5; however, in 1980, the Court refused to apply Section 5's reasoning to Section 2, holding that Section 2 incorporated the Fifteenth Amendment and therefore required proof of racially discriminatory intent. Hence, unless a mechanism, such as at-large voting, is adopted or maintained to deny citizens the right to vote—on the basis of race or color—it is constitutional.

Congress responded angrily and, in 1982, amended Section 2 to overturn the Court's ruling. Congress made clear that its "principle immediate target" was "the at-large system of election" and that it objected to the Supreme Court's "intent test" because intent in a Section 2 violation is "[ir]relev[ant] ... divisive [and] difficult [to prove]." Constitutional scholars believe Congress exceeded its constitutional authority by enacting legislation that prohibits facially constitutional conduct in the absence of a history of widespread, egregious, racial discrimination in voting. Moreover, Congress relieved those filing Section 2 lawsuits of the obligation to do what litigants must ordinarily do—carry the burden of proving intent.

Thus, lawyers in the Justice Department and in the ACLU were given the ammunition to file lawsuits, not just in the South, but across the country, including Wyoming, the Equality State.

The ACLU maintains that, to prevail against Fremont County, it need prove only that non-Indians vote as a bloc to prevent American Indians from electing, in the language of Section 2, the "representatives of their choice." Fremont County responds that the ACLU must prove that, again in the words of Section 2, non-Indians vote "on account of race or color" and that Indians have been denied the ability "to participate . . . and to elect representatives of their choice," which may not be American Indian candidates.

Hundreds of pages of evidence have been prepared; scores of witnesses, including several experts, will testify, including ACLU witnesses who say the United States and Fremont County committed cultural genocide against American Indians. Plus, in response to Fremont County's argument that Section 2 is unconstitutional, federal lawyers entered the case.

All this may be for naught; the case may turn upon the one fact that gives lie to the ACLU's claim: in November of 2006, an American Indian was elected Commissioner. Ms. Keja Whiteman of Arapahoe, member of the Turtle Mountain Band of the Chippewa, social worker, mental health advocate, policy consultant, and former school board member active in 4H and barrel racing, says she won because she campaigned in Dubois, Lander, Riverton, and Shoshoni, not just on the Wind River Reservation. Thus, consistent with Fremont County's argument and appellate court rulings, she did what it takes to win elections.

The ACLU responds that Commissioner Whiteman was elected because non-Indians got the word that, to defeat the ACLU's lawsuit, they should vote for her. Commissioner Whiteman says that is nonsense.

FEBRUARY 2007

JUDGING THE FEDS:
EVERY BENEFIT OF EVERY DOUBT

In May of 1945, the United States asked Jesse Fox Cannon of Toole County, Utah, to sign a "Construction, Survey & Exploration Permit" to allow the Army upon 1,425 acres of mining claims Jesse Fox Cannon owned near the Army Dugway Proving Grounds in west-central Utah. Jesse Fox Cannon agreed; after all, a war was on; plus, the Army promised that, within 60 days of finishing, it would "leave the property in as good condition as it is on the date of the government's entry." In September of 1945, Jesse Fox Cannon reentered his property and discovered that, instead of surveying and exploring the property, the Army had used it for "Project Sphinx," under which it dropped tons of high explosives and bombs, and incendiary and chemical weapons on Cannon's property.

Notwithstanding the demands by Jesse Fox Cannon and later his son, Dr. J. Floyd Cannon, that the United States fulfill its legal obligation to clean up their property, the federal government refused. In 1980, Dr. Cannon died, leaving the property to his children, who took up the crusade to have their land reclaimed and restored.

In 1993, nearly 50 years after the Army left the property, the federal government began a paper shuffling exercise purportedly to determine something the Cannon family already knew: whether the Cannon land was a "formerly used defense site" that presented safety concerns for federal and state government agencies. In 1996, the federal government concluded that the Cannon property was one of the most contaminated sites in the country and would cost $12.7 million to reclaim. Then, the federal government did nothing.

In 1998, the exasperated Cannon family sued the United States. The Utah federal district court awarded them the pittance of $161,000; however, in 2003, the U.S. Court of Appeals for the Tenth Circuit ruled that the family had filed its lawsuit too late. Nonetheless, the Tenth Circuit lamented that the United States "has yet to fulfill its contractual obligations to the Cannon family [or] to recognize and appreciate Jesse F. Cannon's contribution to National Security during World War II." Worse yet, "the only action the Government has taken associated with [its 1996 study] is to defend this lawsuit."

In November of 2005, members of the Cannon family, in one final effort to compel the United States to make good on its promise, filed a lawsuit against the United States, which later included Superfund claims. The federal government has used Superfund, which seeks "prompt cleanup of hazardous waste sites and imposition of all cleanup costs on the responsible party," to sue hundreds of corporations, governmental entities, and private parties. The Cannons figured the law ought to apply against the federal government too.

In response, the federal government reinitiated its paper shuffle of a decade earlier by letting contracts, in late 2005 and early 2006, to "prepare" for "site inspections" of the Cannon property. Next, it claimed that, if funds were available, it would conduct "inspection activities" at the Cannon property. Then, alleging that it was engaged in an "ongoing cleanup action" that deprived the court of jurisdiction, the federal government moved to dismiss the lawsuit. Weeks before oral arguments, it said it had found $700,000 to spend on the Cannon property.

Last month, the Utah federal district court dismissed the Cannons' lawsuit, deferring to the federal government's interpretation of the Superfund statute, which views its nonexistent cleanup efforts as sufficient to constitute "removal or remedial action" that deprives citizens of their access to federal court. That the federal government has done nothing for more than 60 years was irrelevant held the court. The dismissal was "without prejudice," however, and, if the United States abandons its "action" and the Cannons sue again, the judge told federal lawyers they do not want to appear before him. Those lawyers will not; they will be long gone and the Cannon representatives may be Jesse Fox Cannon's great grandchildren!

APRIL 2007

NINTH CIRCUIT PLAYS FATHER KNOWS BEST

Richard and Shauna Kidman operate RD's Drive-In and Exxon in Page, Arizona, and have for more than three decades. In 2000, much to their horror, they discovered that some of their employees, most of whom are Navajo from the nearby Navajo Nation, were sexually harassing fellow employees in the Navajo language. It was not just the female employees who objected to what was being said in the kitchen; many of the Kidmans' customers had heard that offensive language as well and had stopped patronizing the restaurant.

Neither Richard nor Shauna speaks Navajo, nor does their son Steve who helps to run the place; therefore, in order to ensure their ability to monitor employee behavior and preserve a proper working environment, the Kidmans, in accordance with information set out on the website of the Equal Employment Opportunity Commission (EEOC), adopted an English-language workplace policy. Nonetheless, in 2002, the EEOC filed a lawsuit against the Kidmans asserting that, by "discriminating" based on language, they had engaged in "racial discrimination" in violation of the federal Civil Rights Act.

The Kidmans, through legal counsel, responded that language is not a proxy for race and that the EEOC knows that well, having lost a number of legal cases on that specific issue. Moreover, the Kidmans claimed, because their employees' conduct had exposed the Kidmans to a sexual harassment lawsuit, which ironically would have been brought by the EEOC, they had the right to adopt the English-language policy. Nonetheless, as the trial preparations dragged on and with them their legal fees, the Kidmans reluctantly agreed to the EEOC's demand that they engage in settlement negotiations.

Unbeknownst to the Kidmans, but well known to lawyers who deal with the EEOC and its radical, agenda-driven lawyers (one Washington, D.C. attorney, after years of dealing with EEOC lawyers, calls them "lunatics"), the EEOC was engaged in its usual *modus operandi*: the EEOC sues a company, drives up the cost of responding with motions and trial preparations, and then demands that the company enter into a consent decree or settlement agreement.

For hour upon hour, the Kidmans found themselves on the receiving end of a strange type of shuttle diplomacy in an Arizona courthouse, as their attorney went back and forth between them and the EEOC and its "clients," the "offended" former employees. In the end, exhausted, they compromised and agreed to many of the EEOC's demands. The EEOC would draft the agreement and send it to the Kidmans; the Kidmans would sign it.

The next day, the EEOC's version of the agreement arrived. To the shock and horror of the Kidmans, it bore little resemblance to what they had agreed to the day before. There would be no agreement, they said; they wanted to go to trial. In time, they obtained the services of a *pro bono* law firm and prepared for a long siege. Incredibly, the EEOC filed a motion arguing that there had been a settlement agreement and the federal court should enforce it. Over the Kidmans' objections, the court ruled that there had been an agreement on some "material terms" and that the court would enforce that portion of the settlement.

Before the U.S. Court of Appeals for the Ninth Circuit, the Kidmans pointed out that well-established ("black letter") law provides that no settlement may be enforced unless there is "agreement on all material terms" and, in their case, there was no such agreement. One appellate judge agreed that that was the law; however, the other two judges held that it would be unfair to the Kidmans not to enforce their "agreement" with the EEOC. Moreover, held these two judges, Congress wants EEOC cases settled; thus, not to accede to the EEOC's demands in the case of the Kidmans would be contrary to congressional intent. This month, the Kidmans will ask the three-judge panel and the entire Ninth Circuit to rehear the case.

JUNE 2007

WESTERN REALITY SHOW:
BUREAUCRATS BEHAVING BADLY

In *Wilkie v. Robbins*, one of the final cases decided by the Supreme Court of the United States at the end of its term last month, one of the facts—in a case bursting with facts—on which all could agree was that a career bureaucrat was so offended by the conduct of his fellow employees that he retired. In his words, the way Bureau of Land Management (BLM) employees treated Harvey Frank Robbins was the "the volcanic point" in his decision: "It has been my experience that people given authority and not being held in check and not having solid convictions will run amuck and that [is] what I saw happening."

Why did Wyoming BLM officials "run amuck?" In Justice Ruth Bader Ginsburg's words, they "made a careless error:" after obtaining an easement to use a private road across the ranch owned by Robbins' predecessor, they failed to record it. Thus, when Robbins bought the ranch, he did not know about the easement, and, under Wyoming law, took title free of it. Thereupon, BLM officials, writes Ginsburg, "demanded from Robbins an easement—for which they did not propose to pay—to replace the one they carelessly lost." When Robbins offered to negotiate an agreement, they told him, "the Federal Government does not negotiate" and "[t]his is what you are going to do." When he refused he became, to the BLM, "the rich SOB from Alabama [who] got [the Ranch]" and, according to Ginsburg, the target of "a seven-year campaign of relentless harassment and intimidation to force [him] to give in."

After two appearances each before Wyoming federal district court and the U.S. Court of Appeals for the Tenth Circuit in Denver, Robbins, represented by Cheyenne attorney Karen Budd-Falen, was at the Supreme Court on a petition by the United States to determine whether he could sue named BLM officials for that "campaign." Specifically, did Robbins have a cause of action against them under the Supreme Court's 1971 *Bivens* decision for violating his constitutional rights to exclude them and to just compensation for the easement, and under the Racketeer Influenced and Corrupt Organizations Act (RICO) for trying to extort that easement from him? Over Ginsburg's strong dissent, the Court said no.

On the *Bivens* claim, Justice David Souter first addressed if the Court should create a remedy for what Robbins faced, since, although he could vindicate his complaints, he suffered, in his words, "death by a thousand cuts," in Souter's words, "endless battling" that "depletes the spirit along with the purse." Unable to answer that question, Souter then balanced the government's need for "zeal on the public's behalf" against a citizen's need to battle "illegitimate pressure" by "unduly zealous" bureaucrats. On that too, Souter fell short of a "workable cause of action." Congress was in a "better position" to write it, he concluded.

As to RICO, which bars obtaining property by threat or under color of official right, Souter held Congress was concerned with the "harm of public corruption, by the sale of public favors for private gain, not [with] the harm caused by overzealous efforts to obtain property on behalf of the Government." Otherwise, wrote Souter, a RICO action "could well take the starch out of regulators who are supposed to bargain and press demands vigorously on behalf of the Government and the public." If Congress meant differently, it would have said so.

Robbins' experience, although extreme, is not exceptional. Thus, it is unfortunate the Supreme Court declined to provide beleaguered property owners a remedy, but it is not alone. Congress has little interest in oversight; elected officials demur if matters are "in litigation." Moreover, bureaucrats operate largely without supervision; likewise their lawyers, who never question their clients' motives and seek, not justice, but victory. Finally, in court, agencies, their employees, and their lawyers receive the benefit of every doubt. No wonder bumper stickers in the West read, "I love my country, but fear my government."

JULY 2007

DEFENSE DEPARTMENT DENIZENS
CODDLE CALIFORNIA COLLEGE

On April 5, 2005, the University of California at Santa Cruz (UCSC) hosted a job fair for students seeking to learn about post-graduate employment opportunities. Along with representatives of 60 companies such as Broadcom, Infineon, and American Express were Army, Navy, and Marine Corps recruiters. Within moments, however, 100 student protesters infiltrated the job fair, surrounded the recruiters' tables, linked arms to deny access to those tables, and chanted anti-military rants. Meanwhile, another 200 student protesters remained outside the building, barricading the entrances and cheering in support of their compatriots. After what one reporter called "an hour of chaos and tension," during which the job fair came to a halt, UCSC officials asked the military recruiters to leave and advised protesters that they could distribute their anti-military literature.

On April 11, 2006, UCSC again hosted a job fair. Once again, recruiters from the Army and National Guard joined with other prospective employers; however, this time the U.S. Armed Forces representatives were placed in a separate room, apart from the other job fair participants, a room guarded by a dozen campus police. It was not enough; a riot broke out as protestors, which, according to one press report, included students and faculty, blocked the entrances and demanded that the recruiters be ejected from campus. Police responded as the violence escalated: one arrest was made and an automobile belonging to a recruiter was damaged. As in the previous year, the recruiters were asked to leave the campus, which they did to the regret of at least one student: "It's frustrating. I'm not a Republican. I'm not a conservative. I don't support the war. It's about finding a career."

There was one difference: the riot at UCSC made national news. Bill O'Reilly of Fox News opened his show the next evening with footage of the disturbing images from California, which included darkly clad, mask-wearing, noisy protesters marching shoulder-to-shoulder across the UCSC campus. Much of O'Reilly's discussion with his guests concerned the Solomon Amendment, which requires colleges and universities, on pain of losing federal funds, to grant military recruiters the same access allowed other prospective employers. Just one month earlier, the Supreme Court of the United States, in an 8-0 ruling, upheld the constitutionality of the law, to which various unidentified law schools and professors had objected. One of O'Reilly's guests, noting the unanimous ruling, stated that he had urged Secretary of Defense Rumsfeld to withhold the $80 million that UCSC receives annually.

Nonetheless, the Department of Defense took no action regarding the inability of its recruiters to appear at UCSC job fairs. Then, in January of 2007, the UCSC cancelled a job fair scheduled for later that month given safety concerns related to its expectation of the type of protest that took place in 2006. Finally, on April 25, 2007, UCSC "anti-war activists held a celebratory rally" after learning that Army and Marine Corps recruiters had pulled out of the April job fair, just one day after UCSC officials warned them that as many as 400 students would protest their presence on campus. While one student had the courage to speak out against the inability of military recruiters to appear on campus ("There's actually quite a few moderate and conservative students on this campus who are likely to be in the closet for fear of reprisal."), there was no comment from the Defense Department.

There will be one now. On July 25, 2007, Young America's Foundation (YAF), a nonprofit organization committed to ensuring that young Americans understand and are inspired by the ideas of individual freedom, a strong national defense, free enterprise, and traditional values and one of the nation's most active groups on America's college campuses, sued Secretary Robert M. Gates. YAF's demand is simple: declare UCSC in violation of the Solomon Amendment and withhold federal funds that it would otherwise receive until military recruiters can appear safely at its job fairs.

AUGUST 2007

NINTH CIRCUIT: FEDS MAY CLOSE LAND FOR INDIAN WORSHIP

In 2004, within four months of each other, two three-judge panels of the U.S. Court of Appeals for the Ninth Circuit decided cases involving the Constitution's Establishment Clause and its requirement of government neutrality regarding religion. In May, a panel held that a Latin cross on federal lands in honor of American servicemen killed in World War I violated the Establishment Clause and must be removed. That the memorial commemorated American "history and culture" was irrelevant to the panel; after all, the cross symbolizes Christianity. In September, another panel held that Arizona's designation of private property as sacred to American Indian religious practitioners and off-limits to use by its owner did not violate the Establishment Clause. Because American Indians' religion, said the panel, is intertwined with their history and culture, governmental action supporting their religion is constitutional.

In February, the Ninth Circuit was asked, during oral arguments in San Francisco, to decide between these conflicting interpretations of the Establishment Clause. That is, does the Establishment Clause, which has been interpreted for nearly four decades as barring Judeo-Christian religion from the "public square," notwithstanding its 4,000 year history and culture, apply to American Indian religious practitioners; or is American Indian religion uniquely exempt from the Establishment Clause. Last month, in *The Access Fund v. U.S. Department of Agriculture*, the Ninth Circuit ruled that the Establishment Clause did not bar the U.S. Forest Service from closing Cave Rock, on Nevada's Lake Tahoe, to recreational climbing because, for 1500 years, Cave Rock has been "the most religious feature within the Washoe religion" and a key part of the Washoe Tribe's "mythology," "cosmology," and culture.

The panel discussed, at length, Washoe religious beliefs, including that Cave Rock is akin to a church and is to be avoided by all but religious practitioners who "seek power or knowledge...." The panel also commented briefly on Cave Rock's archeology, discussed Cave Rock's history as a transportation corridor, and set forth the record of rock climbing at Cave Rock. The panel concluded by noting that the Washoe view rock climbing as a desecration and much worse than the traffic that roars through the two tunnels blasted through the rock itself.

The Forest Service's deference to these religious concerns is not unconstitutional, held the panel, because the Washoe history, culture, and religion are intertwined. Moreover, the climbers failed to show that the Forest Service would not protect sites of "historical, cultural, and religious importance to other groups." Finally, a religious site may be set aside for practitioners if it is also arguably historically and culturally significant. In so ruling, the panel relied on the Ninth Circuit's 2004 decision upholding the closure of a privately owned gravel pit in Arizona because the Navajo, Hopi, and Zuni regard the site as sacred.

The Ninth Circuit's ruling conflicts most directly with a 1988 ruling by the Supreme Court of the United States; in *Lyng v. Northwest Indian Cemetery Protective Ass'n*, the Court rejected demands by three American Indian Tribes in northwestern California that portions of the national forest historically and culturally used by them for religious purposes be closed. Even without *Lyng*, Establishment Clause jurisprudence makes clear that the Forest Service's Cave Rock decision runs afoul of every traditional Establishment Clause test, because the Forest Service's action "advances," "endorses," and "entangles it with" American Indian religion. By agreeing with American Indians that Cave Rock is sacred and by rejecting the view of climbers that it is not, the Forest Service, as one landmark Supreme Court ruling puts it, "conveys a message of endorsement," informing American Indian religious practitioners that they are "insiders" and the climbers that they are "outsiders." Indeed, the Forest Service is not demanding that non-Indians simply "respect" American Indian religion; it is, in the Court's words, "employ[ing] the machinery of the state to enforce [Washoe] religious orthodoxy."

Whether the Ninth Circuit is right is up to the Supreme Court!

SEPTEMBER 2007

CHAPTER NINETEEN

The Right to Keep
and Bear Arms

★ ★ ★ ★ ★

———

On March 18, 2008, I sat with lawyers admitted to practice before the Supreme Court of the United States as the justices heard *District of Columbia v. Heller*, the Second Amendment lawsuit filed against the federal enclave of Washington, D.C. As to the origins of the Second Amendment, Justice Kennedy asked, "It had nothing to do with the concern of the remote settler to defend himself and his family against hostile Indian tribes and outlaws, wolves and bears and grizzlies and things like that?" I sat upright. Justice Kennedy's question appeared to have been informed by the friend of the court brief MSLF filed and its well-known client John Shuler who killed a grizzly bear in self-defense but was prosecuted by federal lawyers who argued that he had no right to take his gun outside his home to defend himself against grizzly bears.

MSLF's defense of Shuler may have been MSLF's first entry into the battle for Second Amendment rights, but it would not be the last. After the Court ruled 5-4 for gun rights in *Heller*, MSLF filed in support of citizens in *McDonald v. Chicago*. In fact, in Justice Alioto's 5-4 ruling for citizens' gun rights, he cited MSLF's brief.

Meanwhile, on December 11, 2008, near the Denver campus of the University of Colorado (CU), I held a press conference announcing that MSLF had filed a lawsuit against CU on behalf of Students for Concealed Carry on Campus (SCCC) and three CU students with permits who sought to exercise their rights on campus. "Colorado law is quite clear," I told the reporters. "Because Colorado passed a law and set procedures for obtaining a concealed carry permit, local jurisdictions, including the Regents, may not interfere with that right. It is a sad fact, as Coloradoans have discovered, that 'bad guys' do not respect so-called gun free zones."

FEDS GIVE RADICAL COLLEGES
"GET OUT OF JAIL FREE" CARD

When radical law school professors and administrators created the Forum for Academic and Institutional Rights (FAIR) to permit them to sue then-Secretary of Defense Donald Rumsfeld anonymously to challenge the constitutionality of the Solomon Amendment, which ensures the ability of military recruiters to appear on campus, the Bush administration responded aggressively. When FAIR filed a lawsuit in New Jersey federal district court, federal lawyers vigorously defended the constitutionality of the law, which, although enacted by overwhelming margins in Congress in 1996, was not enforced until after September 11, 2001.

The district court denied FAIR's motion for an injunction; however, a three-judge panel of the U.S. Court of Appeals for the Third Circuit, by 2-1, ruled that the Solomon Amendment was unconstitutional and barred its enforcement. Federal lawyers could have returned to the district court for a ruling on the merits; instead, denied the ability to seek *en banc* review at the Third Circuit—too many judges had recused themselves— they asked the Supreme Court to hear the case despite its preliminary footing. The Solomon Amendment is too important, they reasoned, to allow the preliminary injunction to stand and perhaps to spread to other federal circuits for the years necessary to take a ruling on the merits to the Court.

Arguments took place in December of 2005 and it was at once clear that FAIR was going to take a beating notwithstanding that the nation's top law schools and professors had filed friends of the court briefs in its behalf. Sure enough, in March of 2006, the Court ruled 8-0; the Solomon Amendment is constitutional. One constitutional challenge remained; a Connecticut federal district court had ruled in favor of Yale Law School professors. Curiously, the U.S. Court of Appeals for the First Circuit did not dismiss the case summarily by relying on the Supreme Court's March ruling. Nonetheless, in September of 2007, the Second Circuit ruled the professors' claims either were "lacking in merit" or had been rejected by the Supreme Court.

Meanwhile, in July of 2007, the Young America's Foundation (YAF), a nonprofit group active on college campuses, sued Secretary of Defense Robert Gates demanding that he enforce the Solomon Amendment against the University of California at Santa Cruz (UCSC), which, for three years running, let near riots by professors and students drive military recruiters from the campus. UCSC's antics were known to the Department of Defense (DOD); not only had they made national news, the U.S. Army Recruiting Battalion Commander for UCSC's region had informed DOD of them and urged that it withhold the more than $80 million in federal funds UCSC receives annually.

Given the vigor with which federal lawyers had defended the Solomon Amendment, many assumed that DOD would acknowledge its duty to enforce it against the UCSC and its intent to do so. Instead, the first filing by federal lawyers was not an "answer," which would have allowed the case to proceed to the merits but a motion to dismiss. Federal lawyers raised a host of procedural barriers to YAF's lawsuit, the worst of which was their embrace of the UCSC's claim that the recruiters' inability to appear on campus was not the UCSC's fault! It "complied with.... the Solomon Amendment," said the UCSC, but "individuals or groups" exercising their "right.... to hold a legal and nonviolent protest" drove recruiters away.

In their motion, federal lawyers echoed these sentiments, arguing, first, that the case may not proceed in the absence of the "third parties" who had caused YAF's injuries, that is, the protesting "individuals or groups," and second, that withholding $80 million from the UCSC will not ensure the ability of recruiters to appear on campus. A ruling on the motion is likely this spring; however, one thing is sure. After years defending the Solomon Amendment, Bush administration lawyers have now handed radical campuses and their rioting students the way to escape its enforcement.

JANUARY 2008

THE WEST, WASHINGTON, D.C.,
AND WEAPONS

In 1989, John Shuler of rural Dupuyer, Montana, heard grizzly bears outside his house; fearing they would kill his sheep, he grabbed his rifle and ran into the night. The good news is he survived his encounter with four grizzly bears, as did his sheep. The bad news is his lawyers spent eight years and a quarter of a million dollars to get him acquitted of charges that he violated the Endangered Species Act by killing one of those bears. Early on in that legal battle, the federal government ruled that, although Shuler justifiably feared "death or serious bodily injury"—the test for a self-defense claim—he had no right to arm himself and enter into what the government called "the zone of imminent danger."

That conclusion conflicted directly with an 1895 opinion of the Supreme Court of the United States, in which, quoting authority, the Court ruled, "Where an attack is made with murderous intent. . . . the person attacked is under no duty to flee. He may stand his ground, and, if need be, kill his adversary." Plus, the government's view of Shuler's right to arm himself and confront danger conflicted with the ethos of the American West, which stretches from the midst of the Great Plains to the Cascades, from Canada to Mexico.

In the West, the virtues of individualism, independence, self-sufficiency, and self-governance yield, not only a strong distrust of government, but also a citizenry that forms the bedrock of America's gun culture. Their state constitutions go further than does the U.S. Constitution as to their right to "keep and bear arms"; their laws include "make my day," "castle doctrine," and "stand your ground" provisions; and their supreme courts interpret broadly the right of self-defense outside the home. Little wonder then, that the story that captivated the nation last December of a voluntary security guard who saved scores of churchgoers by shooting a heavily armed killer took place in the heart of the West—in Colorado Springs, Colorado. "[I]t was me, the gunman, and God," she humbly proclaimed.

Washington, D.C. may only be 1,500 miles from Colorado, but it is light years away in the distance that separates two cultures. In fact, Washington proves the truth of the ubiquitous western bumper sticker, "When guns are outlawed, only outlaws will have guns." For while Washington has had, since 1975, perhaps the nation's most stringent gun control laws and boasts more law enforcement officers per capita than any other city, it annually competes for and often wins designation as the nation's "Murder Capital." No wonder that, for decades, law-abiding Washingtonians complained that they may not keep weapons in their homes to provide effectively for their own self-defense.

One of those was Dick Anthony Heller, a District of Columbia special police officer permitted to carry a handgun while on duty but barred from keeping a gun in his home for self-defense. When his application to do so was denied, he sued under the Second Amendment. After his lawsuit was dismissed by the district court, the U.S. Court of Appeals reversed in March of 2007. Last November, the Supreme Court agreed to decide whether the Constitution protects, as the Court of Appeals ruled, an individual's right to keep and bear firearms unrelated to militia operations.

Scores of briefs will be filed and the March arguments watched closely. Nowhere will the Court's likely June ruling be more anxiously anticipated or closely scrutinized than in the West. Westerners believe what the Founding Fathers believed, that they have the right to keep and bear arms to defend themselves and loved ones from danger and their society from tyranny. While westerners may abide the Court discovering new rights in the shadows of the Constitution (its famous "penumbras"), westerners will not accept the Court destroying a right that has been clearly in the bright light of the Bill of Rights since 1791.

FEBRUARY 2008

FREE SCHOOL FOR ILLEGALS:
TIME FOR SUPREME COURT REVIEW?

Last year, a senior at Roswell (New Mexico) High School was ticketed for blocking a fire lane outside a middle school and for driving without a license. When the Roswell police officer who stopped her discovered that she had no proof of legal U.S. residency, he notified immigration authorities; rather than fight deportation, she agreed to be sent back to Mexico. Over the past weeks, newspapers across the country have discovered the tale and used it to lecture Americans on the "rights" (thanks to a 1982 Supreme Court of the United States ruling) of school-age children illegally in this country.

For example, in March the *Chicago Tribune* described the events in New Mexico and declared, "A 1982 Supreme Court ruling guarantees children who are in the U.S. illegally the right to a public education and says schools cannot inquire about their immigration status." The *Chicago Tribune's* depiction of the holding in *Plyler v. Doe*, 457 U.S. 202 (1982), proves Will Rogers was right when he opined, "It isn't what we don't know that gives us trouble; it's what we know that ain't so." That landmark ruling held only that, because illegal aliens are "persons" under the Equal Protection Clause, if states deny them free primary education, states must have a basis that passes "intermediate scrutiny." Specifically, the Court held that a new Texas law did not pass that test. Thus, contrary to the claim by the *Chicago Tribune*, *Plyler*: (1) does not apply to secondary and post-secondary education; (2) did not hold that public education is a right; (3) does not confer legal status on illegal alien children; (4) does not prevent an illegal alien from being arrested and deported; and (5) does not prevent a school from inquiring as to the legal status of and reporting illegal aliens. Finally, *Plyler* does not prohibit a state from denying primary education to illegal aliens; *Plyler* holds only that, if a state does, it needs a better reason than Texas set forth back in 1982.

The *Chicago Tribune* failed to note that the ruling is the epitome of "judicial activism." Five liberal justices, acting as if they were elected to Congress, ruled "illegal alien children" a "special class" and that Texas had not shown that its law "had a substantial relationship to a substantial state interest" when it voted to deny them free education. The justices admitted that free school was not a "right" but said it was a special benefit whose denial violated the Equal Protection Clause. They relied on these "facts": there are only 3 million illegal aliens in the United States; Congress might declare illegal aliens to be citizens; illegal aliens will never leave so citizens should pay to help them improve themselves; citizens are "callous" toward illegal aliens so courts must protect them from "neglect"; and the cost of paying to educate illegal aliens is not as important as the psychological toll on them of not having free education.

Chief Justice Burger, with Justices White, Rehnquist, and O'Connor, responded with a vigorous dissent: "in an effort to become an omnipotent [] problem solver[,]. . . . the court distorts our constitutional function"; "the importance of a governmental service does not elevate it to the status of a fundamental right"; "assum[ption of] a legislative role [is] one for which the court lacks both the authority and competence"; "[i]llegal aliens have no right whatever to be here, and the state may reasonably, and constitutionally, elect not to provide them with governmental services at the expense of those who are lawfully in the state"; "the constitution does not provide a cure for every social ill, nor does it vest judges with a mandate to try to remedy every social problem."

More than a quarter century later, it is not just the wisdom of the dissent that throws *Plyler* into doubt; it is the "facts" relied on by the majority that "ain't so!"

APRIL 2008

STATES' DECADE-OLD "DIALOGUE ON RACE" DOOMS QUOTAS

On March 18, Senator Barack Obama (D-IL) urged what the media labeled a "national dialogue on race." One week later, Colorado's Secretary of State approved a ballot initiative to permit Colorado voters to participate, along with three other states, in a dialogue on race that began over a decade ago. If past is indeed prologue, on Election Day, these four states will join California, Washington, and Michigan in embracing Supreme Court Justice Scalia's sentiment, "In the eyes of government, we are just one race here. It is American." Other states will join them.

What is it that foreshadows Americans' view that their governments may not distinguish between and among their fellow citizens on the basis of race? One answer is the Declaration of Independence, which the Reverend Martin Luther King, Jr., called a "promissory note" to the American people. Sadly, more than two centuries passed before that note came due for all Americans when, in 1965, Congress adopted the Civil Rights Act, which, Senator Humphrey assured his colleagues, did not allow racial quotas or preferences.

A mere 12 years later, in 1977, Congress reneged, providing for racial quotas in a public works bill. Then, in 1980, the Supreme Court of the United States upheld that law as limited in extent and duration. Thus emboldened, Congress extended racial quotas to nearly every federal agency. State and local governments joined in.

In 1990, the Court revisited what was termed, inaccurately, "affirmative action"; by 6-3, it vitiated Richmond, Virginia's race-based system of awarding contracts. Then, in 1995, in *Adarand v. Peña*, a Colorado case *Time* called "a legal earthquake," the Court declared, "Distinctions between citizens solely because of their ancestry are by their very nature odious to a free people," mandated "strict scrutiny" when Congress uses race, and doomed affirmative action. Unfortunately for the family bringing the suit, Randy and Valery Pech, who own Adarand Constructors, Inc., the Court remanded it for fact finding.

That same year, University of California Regent Ward Connerly, who had tired of California's use of racial preferences for college admission, sponsored a successful resolution ending the practice. In 1996, he placed on the ballot the California Civil Rights Initiative (CCRI), which was modeled after the Civil Rights Act of 1965. Opposed by California's media, educational, and political elite, it passed 55 percent to 45 percent. Two years later, Connerly led a similarly successful effort in the State of Washington.

Meanwhile, spurred by the Supreme Court's *Adarand* ruling, Congress, for the first time, debated the constitutionality of awarding contracts based on race. Not surprisingly, it demurred, leaving the matter to the courts. In 2001, *Adarand* returned to the Supreme Court, where it, at the Bush administration's urging, declined to rule. Thus, it left standing a U.S. Court of Appeals for the Tenth Circuit ruling that turned the Court's 1995 ruling on its head by authorizing use of racial quotas. Then, in 2003, the Court ruled the University of Michigan Law School could grant admission on the basis of race for another 25 years. Later that year, the Court, over the dissent of two justices, refused to hear an appeal by Marc Lenart of Lafayette, Colorado, who sought to overturn the Tenth Circuit's perversion of the Supreme Court's *Adarand* ruling.

The "national dialogue on race" as to government, race-based decision making was over at the Supreme Court; however, it was not finished in Michigan. Jennifer Gratz, lead plaintiff in a successful challenge to Michigan's undergraduate admission program, returned to fight for the Michigan Civil Rights Initiative (MCRI) and end the Michigan law school's race-based policy. In 2006, by a vote of 58 percent to 42 percent, the MCRI passed; Gratz had snatched victory from the jaws of defeat.

In Colorado, Randy Pech, Valery Pech Orr—co-proponents of the Colorado initiative—and Marc Lenart hope for a similar victory. If they get it, it will be without Senator Obama's help; he opposed the MCRI.

MAY 2008

EARTH TO FCC: "WHAT PART OF 'UNCONSTITUTIONAL' IS UNCLEAR?"

In 1990, the Supreme Court of the United States, in a 5-4 ruling, upheld the ability of the Federal Communications Commission (FCC) to award broadcast licenses based on race. The decision, in *Metro Broadcasting v. Federal Communications Commission*, came as a surprise; a year earlier, the Court, again by a 5-4 vote, had ruled against Richmond, Virginia's plan to use racial preferences to award city construction contracts. Writing for the Court, Justice O'Connor had rejected Richmond's claim that its program would redress societal discrimination that had prevented minorities from participating in the construction industry. In *Metro Broadcasting*, however, the FCC's claim that it sought to ensure "diversity" in programming was sufficient to persuade Justice White to abandon O'Connor, whom he had joined in *Richmond*, and join with Justice Brennan's majority opinion in *Metro Broadcasting*.

In 1995, former Justice Brennan was in the Courtroom to hear arguments in another challenge to government racial preferences, this time as to federal highway construction. If Brennan was there to exert moral suasion over his former colleagues, he failed. In *Adarand Constructors, Inc. v. Peña*, Justice O'Connor, for the 5-4 majority, wrote, "Distinctions between citizens solely because of their ancestry are by their very nature odious to a free people"; thus, "any person, of whatever race, has the right to demand that any governmental actor. . . . justify any racial classification. . . . under the strictest judicial scrutiny," to "smoke out" "what classifications are in fact motivated by illegitimate notions of racial inferiority or simple racial politics." The equal protection guarantee, ruled Justice O'Connor, is for "persons, not groups," and is a "personal right to equal protection of the laws [that may not be] infringed." In conclusion, the Court overruled *Metro Broadcasting*.

The Constitution is clear, declared the Court, the FCC may not use racial preferences! Thirteen years later, it appears the FCC did not read *Adarand*, did not understand Justice O'Connor's ruling—let alone Justice Scalia's concurrence ("In the eyes of government, we are just one race here. It is American.")—or deemed them irrelevant. In the FCC's consideration of the proposed merger of Sirius Satellite Radio Inc., and XM Satellite Radio

Holdings Inc., the FCC demanded that the companies adopt race-based set asides like the ones struck down in *Adarand*.

The FCC had help. In May of 2008, aides to members of the Congressional Black Caucus lectured a Sirius executive that their bosses wanted a 20 percent set-aside for minority owned companies, an idea that came from the head of a minority-run private equity firm. In June, in a "close[d] door" meeting, "angry" Black Caucus members repeated their demands to Sirius and XM executives. FCC Chairman Kevin J. Martin got the message and announced his support for the merger if Sirius-XM "voluntarily" agreed "to lease 4 percent of their radio spectrums, or 12 channels, for programming run by minorities and women." Nonetheless, the Black Caucus found Martin's scheme "completely unacceptable" "crumbs.... off the table." Occasionally, the Black Caucus and FCC say that they seek "minority programming," which is laughable given the diversity of programming long available on both Sirius and XM. XM's channels, for example, include "hip-hop urban," "jazz & blues," "Latin," "comedy," and "talk and entertainment," and feature artists, comedians, and performers of every hue.

Instead, the demand by the Congressional Black Caucus is reminiscent of Congress's 1977 adoption, for the first time, of racial preferences in government contracting in response to the demand by former Maryland Congressman Parren Mitchell that "minority businesses" be given "a piece of the action." Sadly, his tiny plan has expanded unabated for the last thirty-one years and, despite the *Adarand* ruling, is included today in nearly every government agency and its annual appropriation. The FCC's final order on the Sirius-XM merger is pending; however, it appears that the FCC—the agency to which *Adarand* most directly applied—will resume the "odious" activity struck down in 1995.

AUGUST 2008

NINTH CIRCUIT GETS IT RIGHT:
NO INDIAN RELIGION VETO

Arizona Snowbowl is an alpine ski area, seven miles north of Flagstaff, which occupies 777 acres on Humphrey's Peak, amid the San Francisco Peaks in the Coconino National Forest. Organized skiing has existed there since 1938; ski lifts were built in 1958 and 1962. In July of 1977, Arizona Snowbowl proposed more parking and ski slopes, new lodge facilities, and additional ski lifts, which the U.S. Forest Service authorized in December of 1980. American Indian religious practitioners sued, arguing that use of "sacred" land violated the Free Exercise Clause, which bars government action that burdens religious beliefs or practices, unless it serves a compelling governmental interest that cannot be achieved otherwise. In May of 1983, the U.S. Court of Appeals for the District of Columbia rejected that claim: "Many government actions may offend religious believers, and may cast doubt upon the veracity of religious beliefs, but unless such actions penalize faith, they do not burden religion."

The case did not reach the Supreme Court of the United States, but a challenge by American Indian religious practitioners to a Forest Service timber-harvesting and road-building plan in California did. In April of 1988, Justice O'Connor, for a 5-3 Court, wrote, "Nothing.... would distinguish this case from another lawsuit in which they (or similarly situated religious objectors) might seek to exclude all human activity but their own from sacred areas of the public lands.... Whatever rights the Indians may have to the use of the area, however, those rights do not divest the Government of its right to use what is, after all, its land."

Nonetheless, land managers, citing Clinton's 1996 "Indian Sacred Sites" Executive Order, "exclude[d] all human activity" from "sacred areas of the public lands" at Devils Tower National Monument and in the Bighorn National Forest in Wyoming, in the Lewis and Clark National Forest in Montana, at Rainbow Bridge National Monument in Utah, and in the Plumas National Forest in California. Challenges by non-Indians were dismissed. In September of 2004, the U.S. Court of Appeals for the Ninth Circuit held Arizona's bar on using gravel from "sacred" private property was constitutional because American Indian religion and culture are intertwined.

In August of 2007, the Ninth Circuit, relying on the Arizona case, upheld the Forest Service's ban on climbing at "sacred" Cave Rock at Lake Tahoe.

Meanwhile, in September of 2002, to ensure its economic viability, Arizona Snowbowl proposed to make artificial snow with reclaimed water purchased from Flagstaff. When the Forest Service approved that proposal in June of 2005, American Indian religious practitioners sued under the Religious Freedom Restoration Act (RFRA), enacted in 1993 to strengthen judicial review of government acts affecting religion. Although the Supreme Court ruled the RFRA unconstitutional as to States, it arguably remains applicable to federal actions. An Arizona federal district court rejected the claim; however, a Ninth Circuit panel held the plan tantamount to a government edict that Christian "baptisms be carried out with 'reclaimed water.'" In December of 2007, the Ninth Circuit reheard the case *en banc*.

In August of 2008, by 8-3, the Ninth Circuit, relying on the Supreme Court's 1988 ruling, reversed the panel's decision, rejected the RFRA claim, and held that "[G]iving one religious sect a veto over the use of public park land would deprive others of the right to use what is, by definition, land that belongs to everyone." Left undecided was an issue federal lawyers, for unknown reasons, did not raise: whether the RFRA applies at all to federal land.

American Indian religious practitioners vow an appeal to the Supreme Court. Unless they succeed there, they may use neither the Free Exercise Clause nor the RFRA as a sword to close "sacred" federal land to the public. Undecided is whether they may use either as a shield to defend against claims by non-Indians that managing the government's land according to the demands of "religious objectors" violates the Establishment Clause.

SEPTEMBER 2008

ENVIROS GO NUCLEAR,
BUT NOT IN A GOOD WAY

After Paul Newman died on September 26, news broke that, although he contributed to environmental causes, he was also a secret supporter of something anathema to environmentalists: nuclear power. His interest began with filming of *Fat Man and Little Boy*—a 1989 movie about the Manhattan Project, where he met the nuclear power advocate who authored the book that served as the movie's primary source—and continued with soirees on New York City's Fifth Avenue and tours of nuclear facilities from coast to coast. In fact, when Robert F. Kennedy, Jr., tried to get Newman to oppose the Indian Point Nuclear Station, Newman refused and instead toured Indian Point and praised its "[clear] commitment to safety," generation of electricity for a million New Yorkers, and zero greenhouse gases.

Newman's clandestine cause was reported by William Tucker, whose writings, for 25 years, on the environment and energy have generated articles in publications, such as the *Wall Street Journal* and *Harper's*, and three books. Tucker's fourth book is *Terrestrial Energy: How Nuclear Energy Will Lead the Green Revolution and End America's Energy Odyssey* (Bartleby Press, 2008). His timing is exquisite because a "nuclear renaissance" is underway—there are 440 active reactors worldwide in 30 countries (the USA has 104); 50 more countries have either started construction of reactors or announced they are going nuclear. In the USA, applications for 31 new reactor licenses have been or will be filed with the Nuclear Regulatory Commission. Nonetheless, the "renaissance" faces a major hurtle—opposition by environmental groups—as demonstrated by a battle now underway in federal court in Arizona.

The Monday following Paul Newman's death, three environmental groups filed a lawsuit in federal district court in Phoenix demanding that the Secretary of the Interior be compelled to withdraw more than a million acres of federal land from uranium mining. The lawsuit follows the refusal of the Secretary to comply with a June 25, 2008, resolution by the U.S. House of Representatives' Natural Resources Committee. The Secretary argues that the resolution failed to comport with congressional rules; legal experts say it is unconstitutional. Whatever the case, a federal judge could decide whether Arizona's uranium deposits, which boast high-grade ore, a minute surface footprint, no water impacts, and a nearby milling facility in Blanding, Utah, will ever be used to fuel nuclear power in America.

The resolution, which was adopted by a vote of 20-2 after Republicans walked out of the committee in protest and is under the auspices of Section 204(e) of the Federal Land Policy and Management Act (FLPMA), orders the Secretary to "immediately withdraw" 1,068,908 acres of federal land in Arizona "from all forms of location and entry under the United States mining laws. . . . for a period not to exceed three years." Resolution proponents argue that 1,100 uranium mining claims are within five miles of the Grand Canyon and past uranium mining operations had adverse environmental consequences.

Ranking Member of the House Committee Don Young (R-AK) and Ranking Member of the House Subcommittee on National Parks, Forest and Public Lands, Rob Bishop (R-1st UT), both oppose the resolution because of the resultant dependence on "foreign sources of uranium." They also argue that the resolution "short circuits the Constitution, escapes review by both bodies of Congress and the American people, [and] is political grandstanding at its best on an unconstitutional resolution which will have no force of law."

On the constitutional issue, Young and Bishop are right. In 1983, the Supreme Court of the United States ruled that a federal law authorizing a "one House legislative veto" of decisions by the Attorney General violated the Constitution's bicameralism and presentment requirements. The Court held that Congress may exercise its legislative authority only "in accord with a single, finely wrought and exhaustively considered procedure." Even so, if the Supreme Court must strike down the House resolution, the nuclear revolution will continue, if at all, without Arizona uranium!

NOVEMBER 2008

CHAPTER TWENTY

Sue and Settle— Unconstitutional Tactic

In early May of 2009, I received a newspaper clipping from long-time MSLF Board of Litigation member David William West, Esq. of Arizona. The small article mentioned a lawsuit filed by environmental groups in northwestern Pennsylvania and a planned settlement of the lawsuit by the U.S. Forest Service that would end oil and gas activity in the area where the nation's first successful oil well was drilled. "It may be worth checking out," he penned. On May 6, I looked up an attorney I had identified as being involved in the matter and placed a call to what turned out to be a retired Marine Judge Advocate. We chatted about the Marine Corps and then turned to the lawsuit. "This is far from over," he told me and invited me to Warren, Pennsylvania. On May 26, I flew into Buffalo, New York and drove to Warren. Thus began the earliest and one of the most successful challenges to the attempt by the newly installed Obama administration and its allies in environmental groups to use "sue and settle" tactics to shut down economic activity.

The battle in the Allegheny National Forest, which covers some 500,000 acres in Elk, Forest, McKean, and Warren Counties, involved private property rights, high paying jobs in one of the most depressed regions of the country, and the search for energy in one of the hottest gas prospects in the nation, Marcellus Shale. MSLF entered the suit on behalf of the world's oldest family-owned independent oil company under the continuous management of one family (Minard Run Oil Company), and the Pennsylvania Oil and Gas Association (today the Pennsylvania Independent Oil and Gas Association or PIOGA).

Together they challenged an agreement by the Forest Service to conduct National Environmental Policy Act (NEPA) review of all oil and gas operations involving private oil, gas, and mineral rights even though the agency owns only the surface. The NEPA process promised to shut down oil and gas operations for years! A lawsuit was filed in June, hearings conducted in August, and briefs filed in September. On December 15, 2009, a Pennsylvania federal district court issued a preliminary injunction barring the Forest Service from implementing the settlement agreement. Even though a long battle to finalize and sustain the initial victory remained, MSLF helped win a more Merry Christmas for the people of the region.

COLLEGE STUDENTS SEEK TO USE
CONCEALED CARRY PERMITS

One minute, Suzanne was eating lunch with her mother and father. The next, the happy hubbub of the restaurant was silenced when a pickup truck crashed through the brick, mortar, and glass. How could that happen? The driver emerged, but Suzanne noticed he was not dazed or drunk; he was angry and purposeful. Then, she saw the guns. He stepped over the debris and began to shoot patrons. She must be dreaming. Her father leaped to his feet, charged the gunman, was shot, and fell to the floor. When the gunman turned his back to shoot others, she remembered she had a gun! Where was it? She had to find her gun! Oh no, it was in her car. She crawled, then ran toward a window to escape, to get her gun, and to return to save her mother. Was it only a nightmare?

Tragically, for Suzanna Gratia Hupp and scores of others, the murder and mayhem on October 16, 1991, at Luby's Cafeteria in Killeen, Texas— 60 miles north of Austin—was real: 23 men and women were murdered in cold blood; another 20 were wounded in the deadliest killing spree in American history. (The killer turned one of his two weapons upon himself when cornered by the police.) Dr. Hupp, a chiropractor, had indeed brought her gun to Luby's that day; however, it was illegal then to carry a concealed weapon in Texas. Despite the admonition of a friend, "Better to be tried by 12 than carried by 6," she feared losing her license if she violated the law. Instead, she lost both her father and her mother; she had thought her mother would follow her through the window, but her mother had returned to comfort her dying husband and had been murdered. Dr. Hupp blames herself to this day.

As a result, Dr. Hupp became one of the nation's leading advocates for concealed carry permits; in fact, at her urging, in 1995 the Texas Legislature adopted a "shall-issue" gun law requiring all qualifying applicants to be issued a Concealed Handgun License. In 1996, she was elected to the Texas House of Representatives; then she traveled the country giving personal testimony why states should enact concealed carry laws. Most recently, she filed a friend of the court brief when the Supreme Court of the United States considered the constitutionality of Washington, D.C.'s ban on handguns for personal safety, *District of Columbia v. Heller*.

One of the states that enacted the law advocated by Dr. Hupp was Colorado, which, in 2003 created statewide standards for issuing concealed carry permits, adopted a narrow list of exclusions—locations prohibited by federal law, K-12 schools, public buildings with metal detectors, and private property—and prohibited local governments from enforcing any contradictory laws and policies. Despite the Colorado General Assembly's intent to supplant local rules as to concealed carry, the Regents of the University of Colorado (CU) refused to withdraw their 1994 policy barring concealed carry on CU's campuses throughout the state.

The massacre that killed Dr. Hupp's parents was the deadliest shooting rampage in American history, that is, it was until the Virginia Tech Massacre of April 17, 2007, when 32 were killed and 17 wounded. Subsequently, on February 14, 2008, a gunman killed 6 and wounded 18 at Northern Illinois University. Little wonder, therefore, that students on CU's campuses in Boulder, Denver, and Colorado Springs—who have a license to carry concealed weapons almost anywhere else in Colorado—wish to exercise that right in what, in their view, is one of the most dangerous settings they will encounter: "a gun-free zone."

Students for Concealed Carry on Campus (SCCC), a national advocacy group with over 30,000 members that supports the legalization of concealed carry by licensed individuals on college campuses, agrees. Last month, SCCC, two CU students and a recent CU graduate filed a lawsuit in Colorado state court seeking a ruling that CU's policy is illegal and unconstitutional!

JANUARY 2009

SUPREME COURT TO DECIDE MEANING OF OBAMA ELECTION

Northwest Austin Municipal Utility District No. 1, in the City of Austin in Travis County, Texas, but independent of both, is a political subdivision that performs various governmental functions; its five-member board is elected to staggered, four-year terms in biannual nonpartisan elections. Under Texas law, Travis County controls voter registration; however, the District runs its own elections, which, before 2004, were conducted in private residences. Eventually, the District decided to hold elections at public locations, such as the neighborhood elementary school. Later, the District contracted with Travis County to put its elections on the larger county ballot, to delegate the task of conducting the elections, and to benefit from Travis County's election apparatus, which includes minority and language-minority election officials and workers and early-voting opportunities.

Because the District is within a "covered jurisdiction" under Section 5 of the 1965 Voting Rights Act, these changes required the prior approval— the "pre-clearance"—of the Attorney General of the United States. This requirement applies to the District even though no election-related lawsuit has ever been filed against it, no person has ever questioned its voting procedures, and no one has ever filed a complaint about its elections. In fact, despite the more than 40 years since enactment of the 1965 Act and the very favorable record of Texas, Travis County, and Austin in protecting the right to vote, when Congress reauthorized the Voting Rights Act in 2006, it continued to require "pre-clearance" by the District and all other "covered jurisdictions."

In 1965, Section 5 and what the Supreme Court of the United States, in 1966, called its "uncommon exercise of congressional power" were essential given persistent, pervasive, and intransigent state action undertaken to deny African-Americans the right to vote. The Court held that, "under the compulsion of these unique circumstances, Congress responded in a permissibly decisive manner." In reaching that conclusion, the Court had before it a voluminous legislative history that demonstrated that an "insidious and pervasive evil" had been "perpetuated in certain parts of the country through the unremitting and ingenious defiance of the Constitution" and that the past remedies prescribed by Congress had been unsuccessful.

Thus, the Court held that Congress's response was harmonious with and in proportion to the historical record.

Not all enactments undertaken pursuant to Congress's powers under the Fifteenth Amendment, such as the Voting Rights Act of 1965, pass judicial scrutiny, however, given that congressional involvement in matters normally left to the states is extraordinary and extra-constitutional. Thus, beginning in 1997, the Supreme Court, consistent with its 1966 Voting Rights Act ruling, demanded that Congress set forth a historical record to justify "exceptional" and "unique" actions, such as those undertaken three decades earlier. Over the next several years, the Supreme Court struck down acts of Congress that failed to meet that test.

It was in this context that, in 2006, the District filed a federal lawsuit arguing, among other matters, that Congress's 2006 reauthorization of Section 5, lacking any record as to why the "exceptional" action adopted in 1965 was still justified in 2007, was unconstitutional. In May of 2008, a three-judge panel of the federal district court for the District of Columbia brushed the challenge aside. On January 9, 2009, the Supreme Court agreed to review it.

One week after Election Day of 2008, Abigail Thernstrom and Stephan Thernstrom, authors of *America in Black and White: One Nation Indivisible* (Simon & Schuster, 1997), and the nation's top experts on race relations, writing in the *Wall Street Journal,* called for an end to the "aggressive federal interference in state and local districting decisions enshrined in the Voting Rights Act. ..." They concluded, "[With the election of President Obama,] American voters have turned a racial corner. The law should follow in their footsteps." Sometime in June of 2009, the Supreme Court will decide if the law will or if, notwithstanding the fanfare and hoopla, Obama's election means nothing after all.

FEBRUARY 2009

COMMON SENSE ON THE ENVIRONMENT IN TIME FOR EARTH DAY

Thirty-three years ago, Keith Rattie, armed with an electrical engineering degree, went to work for an oil company because he believed that, soon, the world would not be running on fossil fuels. He knew that Chevron was seeking alternative energy sources and he wanted to be part of that transition. Today, he is Chairman, President, and CEO of Questar Corporation, which explores for, produces, and delivers natural gas. In early April, perhaps in anticipation of Earth Day (ironically Lenin's birthday), he gave advice to students at Utah Valley University because they are being told, as he was, "that by the time you're my age the world will no longer be running on fossil fuels." In short, he reported, the scientific consensus, the politicians, and the media were wrong then; they are wrong today!

In an attempt "to do something that seems impossible these days.... have an honest conversation about energy policy, [and] global warming," he told them what the "doomsters" were saying when he was their age: the world is running out of oil and natural gas, the planet is cooling off, and fossil fuels are the reason; we have to break our fossil fuel habit, and fast! The crisis is so serious, said the politicians, that solutions cannot be left to the free market system; instead, the federal government has to mandate "massive taxpayer subsidies for otherwise uneconomic forms of energy." In fact, the world did not run out of oil and gas; both are more abundant today even though, during the last three decades, humans have consumed over three times the world's known 1976 oil reserves. Oh, and global cooling? It ended abruptly in the late 1970s!

Today, Mr. Rattie told the students, you are being told, not that America is running out of fossil fuels, but that "we're running out of time!" "[T]he earth is getting hotter, humans are to blame, and we're all doomed unless we find alternatives to oil, gas and coal—fast." Despite that the threat differs significantly from the one 33 years ago, the politicians' answer is the same: the crisis is too serious for the market; the federal government must take over!

Once, admits Mr. Rattie, he believed global warming science was solid and settled; however, today he is a skeptic (what Al Gore calls a "denier") due to a dramatic breakthrough a decade ago after he examined inputs to a global circulation model. He concluded that those inputs were selected based on "little more than the opinion of the scientist—in some cases, just a guess." His conclusion, therefore, is that there is no scientific consensus.

There is, however, a political consensus, which is that Congress and President Obama must "do something," specifically, enact a tax on carbon energy, "cap and trade," which, they say, will reduce the nation's use of fossil fuel and shrink the massive federal deficit. Senate Majority Leader Harry Reid (D-NV) promises such legislation this month. What they are trying to achieve, says Mr. Rattie—an 80 percent reduction in carbon dioxide emissions by 2050—is insane; the last time each American's carbon footprint was as low as Congress and Obama want it to be in 40 years was when "Pilgrims arrived at Plymouth Rock in 1620." Concludes Mr. Rattie, "with today's energy technologies, we can't get there from here."

True, but that may not be the goal. With cap and trade: the federal government will increase dramatically in size and control vast sectors of the economy; taxes and the cost of all goods and services will skyrocket; and, Americans' quality of life will be reduced. That is not to mention the loss of liberty! One hopes the students hearing Mr. Rattie and millions of others take his message to heart. Otherwise, to paraphrase Mike + The Mechanics' 1989 hit, *The Living Years*, future generations will have good reasons to "blame[] the one before."

MAY 2009

NEPA NEEDS SUPREME COURT
INTERVENTION

On New Year's Day 1970, President Richard Nixon signed into law the National Environmental Policy Act (NEPA), the purposes of which, among other objectives, were to "encourage productive and enjoyable harmony between man and his environment [and] stimulate the health and welfare of man." NEPA's most significant single provision was its requirement that federal agencies prepare an environmental study whenever any proposal for "major Federal action[]" would "significantly affect[] the quality of the human environment," in essence, the workshop equivalent of "measure twice, cut once."

Unfortunately, in the nearly forty years since its enactment, NEPA has become the weapon of choice for groups and judges to kill activities of which they disapprove. It is not just that NEPA has killed major projects like oil refineries, nuclear power plants, and pre-Katrina improvements to New Orleans' levees; it also has delayed and thus killed salvage of fire-damaged timber, transfer of a rig from one drilling site to another, and movement of cattle to a different grazing location. Three NEPA cases now in court provide new evidence of NEPA's pernicious effects.

In 1997, natural gas was discovered on a Bureau of Land Management (BLM) lease in New Mexico. Over the next eight years, the BLM produced thousands of pages of documents, received hundreds of comments, and held scores of meetings and hearings. In January of 2005, it issued an oil and gas plan that allows a maximum surface disturbance of only 1,589 acres in Otero and Sierra Counties from well pads, roads, and pipelines— less than one-tenth of one percent of the total surface area. Because only 141 exploratory wells could be drilled with no more than 84 producing wells, the plan was the BLM's most restrictive ever. Nonetheless, neither environmental groups nor Governor Bill Richardson was satisfied; they sued. Last month, the U.S. Court of Appeals for the Tenth Circuit held that the BLM had not taken the "hard look" that NEPA requires and sent the BLM back to the drawing board.

In 2008, in the wake of the Supreme Court's ruling in *District of Columbia v. Heller*, as to the right "to keep and bear arms," and following a request from 51 Senators, the National Park Service (NPS) adopted a new rule regarding the possession of guns in parks and wildlife refuges. That rule—like those of the U.S. Forest Service (USFS) and the BLM—provides, in accordance with principles of federalism, that state law determines whether park visitors may possess guns. Anti-gun groups sued, claiming that the NPS should have conducted a NEPA study to assess the environmental impact. The NPS argued there was no environmental impact, hence no NEPA requirement. The judge ruled that, because guns will be used for "self-defense against persons and animals," the NPS's rule "will obviously have some impact on the environment, whether direct, indirect, or cumulative." The NPS was sent packing.

In the Allegheny National Forest in northwestern Pennsylvania where oil and gas activity is underway on privately owned resources beneath the federal surface, environmental groups filed a "sweetheart lawsuit" to require the USFS to do a NEPA study when an oil and gas company advises the agency that it is operating in the forest. Notwithstanding that the agency, like every other surface owner, can do nothing short of a lawsuit to deny oil, gas, or mineral owners access to their property, the USFS appears to have concluded that the mere receipt of the notice—as to which it has no discretion and can take no action—is "major federal action[]" and triggers NEPA. A recent ruling by the Supreme Court of Pennsylvania reaffirming the property rights of oil and gas operators should have ended the USFS's plans; instead, the agency says it will prevent all oil and gas activity.

What NEPA needs now is an intervention by the Supreme Court of the United States; whether it will get it remains to be seen.

JUNE 2009

FEDS SETTLE "SWEETHEART SUIT"
AND KILL SEARCH FOR ENERGY

One hundred and fifty years ago this month, the first successful commercial oil well was drilled in Titusville, Pennsylvania, thus beginning an oil and gas industry that has thrived both across the country and within forty miles of Titusville in the Allegheny National Forest (ANF). Just weeks ago, the *Wall Street Journal* reported renewed interest in the region's Marcellus Shale given massive gas discoveries in the Barnett Shale in Texas, Fayetteville Shale in Arkansas, and Haynesville Shale in Louisiana. The search in the ANF will have to wait, however, thanks to a "sweetheart lawsuit" by environmental groups and a decision by the Obama administration to admit defeat, settle that lawsuit, and impose a moratorium on energy exploration in the ANF.

In June of 2009, the Pennsylvania Oil and Gas Association (POGAM) and Minard Run Oil Company, America's oldest family-owned and operated independent oil producer, and others sued Attorney General Eric Holder, the U.S. Forest Service, and its officials, and three environmental organizations. At stake in the case are private property rights, high-paying jobs in one of the most depressed regions of the country, and the search for energy in one of the hottest gas prospects in the nation.

The ANF covers 500,000 acres in Elk, Forest, McKean, and Warren Counties in northwestern Pennsylvania. Because the lands within the ANF were once privately owned and were purchased during the 1920s and because the United States bought only the surface, most oil, gas, and mineral (OGM) rights in the ANF (93%) are privately owned. Thus, there is no basis for any federal government regulatory authority over those rights. In fact, federal law, Forest Service regulations, and federal and state court rulings say the agency has no such authority!

Although, under Pennsylvania law, owners of OGM rights may go on the surface to access their property and may occupy so much of the surface as necessary to do so, the law provides for accommodation; OGM rights must be exercised with "due regard" for surface owners' interests. That the United States owns the surface does not change the law: like other surface owners, the United States can do nothing, short of a lawsuit, to deny OGM owners access to their property. This was affirmed, as to a state agency, in a

2009 Supreme Court of Pennsylvania ruling. Therefore, the Forest Service has few options in dealing with OGM rights in the ANF, which is in accordance with the agency's longstanding practice set forth in the Forest Service Manual. This was recognized by a 1980 Pennsylvania federal district court ruling, which Congress adopted in the Energy Policy Act of 1992.

For decades, the Forest Service adhered to the law and responded to an operator's 60-day notice of its drilling plans with consultations and a "notice to proceed," which is not a decision by the Forest Service to allow OGM activity because, again, the Forest Service has no power over OGM rights. Nonetheless, in March of 2007, the Forest Service announced its decision to conduct National Environmental Policy Act (NEPA) studies on any plans to develop OGM rights in the ANF. NEPA only applies, however, to "major federal actions," which means issues as to which the agency has discretion; the Forest Service has no discretion regarding OGM rights. The Forest Service's decision is now the subject of litigation.

Meanwhile, in November of 2008, environmental groups, recognizing that the Forest Service would lose its attempt to impose NEPA on its own, sued the Forest Service asserting that a "notice to proceed" is subject to NEPA. After OGM owners intervened, federal lawyers signed a hastily executed "Settlement Agreement," and the lawsuit was dismissed.

The resultant lawsuit by POGAM and Minard Run is just beginning; however, it may well reach the Supreme Court of the United States where a favorable ruling is essential to the preservation of freedom, not to mention the search for energy in the USA!

AUGUST 2009

WYOMING MAN FIGHTS FOR HIS PROPERTY; FEDS DISSEMBLE

In 1944, Melvin M. Brandt purchased the sawmill in Fox Park, Wyoming—50 miles southwest of Laramie—from which he transported timber via a railroad owned, since 1908, by the Laramie, Hahn's Peak & Pacific Railway Company. In 1976, the United States patented 83 acres to him and his wife, pursuant to federal law, subject to a right-of-way for the railroad. Later, the Brandts' son Marvin acquired the property and, in 1991, closed the sawmill.

Meanwhile, from 1987 to 1995, the Wyoming and Colorado Railroad Company, Inc. (WYCO), which had acquired the right-of-way, operated the rail line. In 1996, WYCO filed a Notice of Intent to Abandon Rail Service with the U.S. Surface Transportation Board (STB) seeking to abandon its rail line in Albany County, Wyoming, including the portion on Mr. Brandt's property. In 1999 and 2000, WYCO removed the track and ties; in 2003, the STB approved abandonment of the rail line; and, in 2004, WYCO completed abandonment of the rail line. This was good news for Mr. Brandt who now owned, not only the reverted rail line right-of-way, but also, pursuant to the original patent, a U.S. Forest Service road that had been reserved by the agency, but then abandoned.

The good news was short lived. In April of 2005, the Forest Service announced plans to convert the abandoned rail bed into a 26-mile-long, high altitude (9,062 feet), recreational trail through the Medicine Bow National Forest. To do so, the Forest Service needed Mr. Brandt's property, so, in July of 2006, it filed a quiet title action against him and other property owners. Nonetheless, Mr. Brandt was confident; he owned the land!

In April of 2008, the Wyoming federal district court ruled against Mr. Brandt announcing that, notwithstanding a split among the federal circuits, which Mr. Brandt argued revealed that the correct holding was in his favor, the court was required to adhere to dated rulings by the U.S. Court of Appeals for the Tenth Circuit. That was perhaps understandable; what was not was the district court's ruling as to the abandoned road. Even though the Forest Service had closed the unneeded road, bulldozed a section of it, erected a fence and planted trees across it, directed Mr. Brandt to construct a gate at his end of it, and opened a new road to replace it, the district court ruled the agency's abandonment was "superficial."

Throughout all this Mr. Brandt remained confident. After all, that the rail line right-of-way could not revert to the United States was the better legal argument because the Supreme Court of the United States had rejected the view, adopted by the Tenth Circuit, that an easement could revert by implication. Therefore, argued Mr. Brandt, when the United States grants easements to railroads and later patents the underlying land to settlers, the United States gives up all its interest in the land, including any reversionary interest. As to the district court's ruling on the Forest Service road, the court was simply wrong.

Unfortunately, Mr. Brandt could not just appeal to the Tenth Circuit. Because the Forest Service's actions constitute a "taking" of Mr. Brandt's property without "just compensation" and because the time in which to file a "takings action" is running, Mr. Brandt was required to file a lawsuit at the U.S. Court of Federal Claims in Washington, D.C. When he did, however, federal lawyers argued that his case should be dismissed because the issues had been litigated before the Wyoming district court. Of course, they had not been and, even if they had been, a takings action would still lie. Meanwhile, federal lawyers defend the erroneous ruling that an easement granted a rail line as to patented land reverts to the United States. Given all this, the outcome of Mr. Brandt's case is anything but certain.

One thing is clear: federal lawyers seek victory, not justice!

SEPTEMBER 2009

NATIONAL PARK SERVICE:
A BAD NEIGHBOR IN NEW JERSEY

In September, the *New York Times* ballyhooed the public television broadcast of Ken Burns' 12-hour history, "The National Parks: America's Best Idea." It also announced that the National Parks Second Century Commission, chaired by two former U.S. Senators, had released a report on what the *New York Times* called "the state of the parks and a vision for the next century." These two events caused the *New York Times* to ponder the future of the national parks. One writer took the occasion to demand that the National Park Service (NPS) "be not only a good steward but also a good neighbor, by recognizing its boundaries and the constitutional and property rights of private citizens within and beyond park boundaries." The case of the Hulls of northern New Jersey reveals one reason for that demand.

In the 1950s, the United States proposed creation of the Tocks Island Dam Project along the Delaware River in Sandyston Township, Sussex County, New Jersey, which would have created a 37-mile-long lake between Pennsylvania and New Jersey and would have been the biggest dam project east of the Mississippi. Beginning in the 1960s, the U.S. Army Corps of Engineers, via purchase and condemnation, acquired 72,000 acres of private land, causing many landowners to complain about insufficient compensation and heavy-handed tactics. Ultimately the project failed due to local opposition and lack of federal funds. The land was never returned; instead, in 1978, it was transferred to the NPS.

One of the most persistent opponents of the project was Enos "Cy" Harker, a World War II veteran who refused to sell the land on which he lived for almost 50 years until he died—while tilling a hillside—in October of 2006 at age 93. By then, he was the only landowner along Old Mine Road who had not sold his property to the federal government. In fact, he included a deed restriction barring his property from being sold to the United States.

On September 17, 2007, brothers Matthew and Aaron Hull and Matthew's wife, Michelle, who were born and raised in the area and knew Harker well and had worked with him maintaining and farming his land, bought the property, which is surrounded on three sides by the NPS managed Delaware Water Gap National Recreation Area (NRA) and on one side by the Delaware River. Old Mine Road, which was abandoned by the Sandyston Township in 1988 and then reverted to the Hulls, crosses the NRA and bisects the Hulls' property for 300 yards; it passes within 20 feet of their house.

Because of the proximity of the Hull's property to the NRA and because there is no clear delineation as to where the NRA ends and the Hulls' property begins, hikers, mountain bikers, hunters, and park patrons continue to trespass on the property. Therefore, to protect their children, their property, and trespassers who might otherwise be injured on their property, the Hulls erected a gate shortly after they purchased their property.

Although the NPS had never claimed ownership of the road and had refused, always, to maintain it, on March 23, 2009, the NPS filed a federal lawsuit against the Hulls seeking damages and injunctive relief, alleging that the road was property of the United States. The NPS commenced the lawsuit by sending six federal marshals from Newark, New Jersey, to serve its neighbors, the Hulls, at sunrise. In fact, the marshals had been told to expect the Hulls to be "in the trees with guns"; instead, they were greeted by Mr. Hull holding the Hull's one-year-old daughter. Forthwith, the NPS commenced to "try the lawsuit" in the media, fomenting negative coverage regarding the Hulls. Furthermore, as always, the legal strategy of the NPS regarding the Hulls is to "bleed them dry." The reason, many believe, is simple—the NPS lacks the funds to condemn and pay for the property.

The National Parks: America's worst neighbor!

NOVEMBER 2009

THE "[UN]EQUAL ACCESS TO JUSTICE ACT"

John Shuler of Dupuyer, Montana, who raises sheep for a living, was nearly killed one night when he was attacked by a grizzly bear. Fortunately, he had his powerful rifle with him and was able to mortally wound the bear and save his own life. Unfortunately, the U.S. Fish and Wildlife Service (FWS) and its lawyers charged him with violating the Endangered Species Act (ESA) because grizzly bears are classified as "threatened" under that law. The FWS did so even though there is a self-defense provision in the ESA.

At first, the FWS argued that John Shuler had not been in fear of death or serious bodily injury by the grizzly bear; however, an administrative law judge (ALJ) ruled otherwise. Then, the FWS argued that John Shuler had been at fault because, knowing that grizzly bears were outside, he had left his house and entered into "the zone of imminent danger." That argument was rejected by a federal agency appeals board. At that point, the FWS argued that John Shuler was at fault because he had taken his dog Boone with him and, upon seeing the bear, Boone had gone "on point," "provoked the bear," and escalated the conflict. That argument was rejected too. Finally, the FWS argued that grizzly bears are entitled to a higher standard of self-defense than human beings because they are "incapable of sapient thought." At last, a Montana federal district court rejected all that and ruled that John Shuler, in killing a federally protected species, had acted in self-defense.

That was the good news for John and Carmen Shuler, who had faced a $5,000 fine. The bad news was that the victory had taken eight years and the public interest law firm that defended John Shuler had expended $225,000 in legal fees and expenses. Fortunately, there is the Equal Access to Justice Act (EAJA), which provides that citizens who sue the federal government and win are entitled to reimbursement of attorneys' fees and expenses.

John Shuler's attorneys were confident of an EAJA award; after all, the statutory requirements for an award (other than bars on awards to the very wealthy) are only that the private citizen win in court and that the government's position not be "substantially justified." Incredibly, the district court ruled against John Shuler's claim, holding that the United States was "justified." On appeal to the U.S. Court of Appeals for the Ninth Circuit, John Shuler's lawyers argued that, while the United States may have been justified in seeking to determine how the grizzly bear was killed, the United States was not justified in arguing that: Shuler could not go outside with his gun; his dog could not go outside with him; or that grizzly bears are due a higher standard of self-defense. The Ninth Circuit rejected those arguments.

All this is relevant given recent concerns about the size and amount of EAJA awards to environmental groups. One study noted that, in cases involving the U.S. Forest Service from 2003 to 2005, 35 of the 44 EAJA awards made were to environmental groups. Specifically, in Idaho federal district court over the past decade, one environmental group received nearly one million dollars in attorneys' fees and expenses. In some cases, the environmental groups did not win; instead, the United States settled the lawsuits. Many believe the federal government and federal courts are too willing to make EAJA awards to environmental groups. Earlier this year, for example, Attorney General Eric Holder settled a lawsuit and paid $19,222 to three environmental groups that did little more than file a complaint!

The issue of bias in EAJA awards may get more attention. A California miner who defeated attempts by the U.S. Forest Service to eject him from his valuable mining claim—in a case experts said was "unwinnable"—but was denied his claim for $207,207 for attorneys' fees and expenses, has filed an appeal in Washington, DC.

DECEMBER 2009

CHAPTER TWENTY-ONE

The Threat of Domestic Terrorism

———

The sun rose on August 20, 2010, at 6:15 in Denver; the forecast was clear and sunny with no rain. I was up early, downed a latte, put one in a travel cup for Lis, and loaded our SUV. Long-sleeves and a broad-brimmed hat were essential and sunscreen. At just shy of 10,000 feet, the temperature might not get above 70 but it would feel like a hundred. I stopped at the local supermarket for water bottles for the MSLF crew and then headed west on I-70. By the time I hit 75 miles an hour, the sun had been up for over an hour but it was still casting long shadows in our path. We raced up Floyd Hill, crossed into Clear Creek County, and then dropped into Clear Creek Canyon and roared past Idaho Springs. We continued west as the sun lit up the rocky and pine-covered peaks around us. We passed the wide spot in the road that is Dumont and its Starbucks and climbed steadily. We took the Bakerville exit ("NO SER-VICES"), which lies near the trailhead that, years before, Perry, Luke, and I used to climb Gray's and Torrey's peaks—two of Colorado's Fourteeners. We retrieved the box of orange bags and flimsy orange vests the Colorado Department of Transportation left near an old chimney and got back onto the interstate for the quick trip past the "ADOPT-A-HIGHWAY - NEXT 2 MILES - MOUNTAIN STATES LEGAL FOUNDATION" sign and on to mile marker 219 to begin. Two miles west was the Eisenhower Tunnel at 11,013 feet elevation.

Nearly twenty years before, I picked this section. It was beautiful, all downhill walking with a narrow ledge and a steep drop off on the south for which we were not responsible, and had no snakes. There was, however, heavy traffic, especially on the Fridays we did our trash pickup. There was good news in that: a million motorists pass the sign with MSLF's name on it annually. We finished in record time—four hours—and headed to Idaho Springs to wash away the dust and consume deep-dish pizza with thick braided crust we topped with honey and washed down with Arnold Palmers.

For all the bragging environmental groups do about saving the planet, why is it that I never see their names on highway signs? It seems to me, all they do is tell the rest of us how to live our lives.

AN EARLY CHRISTMAS GIFT IN
NORTHWESTERN PENNSYLVANIA

In Warren, Pennsylvania on December 15, 2009, days before Christmas, it was overcast and cold, with a 50 percent chance of snow; in fact, daytime temperatures were not expected to break 30, nighttime readings would drop to the single digits, and "lake effect snow" off Lake Erie was a possibility. Nonetheless, the mood was bright; a federal district court had just ruled against the Obama administration by ending a moratorium the U.S. Forest Service had imposed on oil and gas operations in the surrounding Allegheny National Forest (ANF).

Warren is less than 40 miles from Titusville, where 150 years ago last summer the first successful commercial oil well was drilled making it the birthplace of America's oil and gas industry. It is no surprise, therefore, that oil and gas operations have been a mainstay of the local economy ever since, especially within the 500,000-acre ANF in Elk, Forest, McKean, and Warren Counties. Because the ANF is comprised of land purchased by the Forest Service in the 1920s and because the Forest Service bought only the surface, most (93%) of the oil, gas, and mineral (OGM) rights there are privately owned.

Under Pennsylvania law, owners of OGM rights may enter upon another's surface to access their property and to remove it; however, they must exercise their rights with "due regard" for the surface owners' interests. That the United States owns the surface of the ANF does not change the law, which was recognized in 1980 by a Pennsylvania federal district court and in 2009 by the Pennsylvania Supreme Court. Finally, Forest Service policy, manuals, and regulations, as well as federal law, provide likewise. This means that any proposed use of OGM rights in the ANF does not trigger the National Environmental Policy Act (NEPA), which is the law used by environmental groups and activist judges to stop major federal actions that they oppose. Under NEPA, whatever gets studied gets studied to death!

In early 2009, development of OGM rights in the ANF ended when the Obama administration rushed to settle a sweetheart lawsuit by environmental groups. The groups alleged that NEPA applied to the use of privately owned OGM rights in the ANF and that no one could use his rights until and unless the Forest Service had complied with NEPA. Attorney

General Eric Holder agreed to: apply NEPA to OGM rights; adopt a moratorium on any use of those rights to prepare for applying NEPA; and award the groups $20,000 in attorneys' fees. The impact on Warren and the region was "devastating." Employees were laid off, projects worth $100 million were stopped, companies faced bankruptcy, and school district funds were eroded. Oil and gas was not produced and sent to the refineries, which also faced layoffs. All of this took place with the area facing what experts called "the coldest winter in history!"

On June 1, 2009, in U.S. District Court for the Western District of Pennsylvania, Minard Run Oil Company, the nation's oldest family-owned oil company, and the Pennsylvania Oil and Gas Association (POGAM) sued Holder, the Forest Service, several Forest Service employees, and the environmental groups. Just before Christmas, the court granted Minard Run's motion for a preliminary injunction. It held that the Settlement Agreement was illegal; had caused "irreparable harm," including "significant financial losses," the possibility that companies "may be forced out of business," and the loss of "enjoyment or possession of land"; yielded equities that favored Minard Run; and, was contrary to the public interest of "preventing unreasonable interference with private property rights." Thereupon, the court enjoined implementation of the Settlement Agreement including preparation of a NEPA document, enforcement of the drilling ban, and processing of all proposed use of privately owned OGM rights in any manner other than that authorized by the federal court in 1980.

Thus, in 2009, in northwestern Pennsylvania, environmental Grinches and their helpers in the Obama administration failed to steal Christmas.

JANUARY 2010

A CHANCE IN HIGHER EDUCATION TO GET IT RIGHT ON RACE

Former Supreme Court Justice Sandra Day O'Connor has been quoted as bemoaning that some of her opinions are being set aside. When it comes to her disastrous 2003 opinion in *Grutter v. Bollinger* in which she, aided by the Court's liberal bloc, authorized colleges and universities to use racial preferences to grant admission for 25 more years, reversal could not come soon enough. Like the Court's pusillanimous 1980 ruling in *Fullilove v. Klutznick*, which approved the use of race in federal government contracting and emboldened its use by state and local governments until halted by the Court in *City of Richmond v. J.A Croson Company* in 1989, and *Metro Broadcasting v. Federal Communications Commission*, which in 1990 allowed the use of race to award broadcast licenses until ended by the Court's 1995 ruling in *Adarand Constructors, Inc. v. Peña*, *Grutter* spawned much mischief. Happily, the Court has a chance to undo O'Connor's misstep in a case now at the U.S. Court of Appeals for the Fifth Circuit.

When the Fifth Circuit ruled the University of Texas Law School's use of race to grant admission unconstitutional in 1996, Texas enacted a law granting automatic admission to any of the state's public colleges or universities to Texas students in the top 10 percent of their high school class; minority enrollment soared. Nonetheless, after *Grutter*, the University of Texas reinstituted its use of race for admission. As a result, Abigail Fisher of Sugar Land and Rachel Michalewicz of Buda were denied admission; in April of 2008, they sued. In August of 2009, a Texas federal district court ruled for the University; the Texans appealed. Although the Fifth Circuit could reverse for factual reasons, *e.g.*, the district court relied improperly on student surveys and the University's unsupported judgment of the "critical mass" of minority students it needs, legal experts are focused on whether *Grutter* squares with the Supreme Court's equal protection jurisprudence. In short, it does not!

In her opinion in *Adarand*, in which the Court overturned *Metro Broadcasting*—decided five years earlier—Justice O'Connor rejected demands by the dissenting justices that, under *stare decisis et quieta non movere* (to stand by and adhere to decisions and not disturb what is settled), *Metro Broadcasting* not be overturned. Although *Metro Broadcasting* had been decided recently, wrote Justice O'Connor, in it "the Court took a surprising turn" that "undermined important principles of this Court's equal protection jurisprudence, established in a line of cases stretching back over 50 years. . . ."

Like *Metro Broadcasting, Grutter* is a constitutional aberration because it took the same "surprising turn" by "undermin[ing]" the most "important principle[]" of equal protection jurisprudence—application of "strict scrutiny." Thus, instead of viewing racial classifications ("odious to a free people") with skepticism and demanding that those who use them carry the burden of justifying their use, *Grutter* presumed that Michigan Law School's use of racial preferences to grant admission was constitutional by assuming that the Law School had a compelling interest and that it had acted in good faith.

That is not "strict scrutiny" as applied by the Court for half a century or as discussed by Justice O'Connor in *Adarand*. There she declared that the use of race by governmental entities is "inherently suspect" and "constitutionally suspect" and requires judicial scrutiny to "smoke out" its use when "motivated by illegitimate notions of racial inferiority or simple racial politics." That is because the Constitution's guarantee of equal protection is for "persons, not groups," and is a "personal right to equal protection of the laws [that may not be] infringed."

In *Adarand*, in her final rebuke to the dissenting justices, Justice O'Connor declared that, by overturning *Metro Broadcasting*, "we do not depart from the fabric of the law, we restore it." If and when *Grutter* meets the same fate as *Metro Broadcasting*, Sandra Day O'Connor may take solace that the fabric of the law has been restored.

FEBRUARY 2010

WITH HUMANS FACING FIRE DANGER,
JUDGES WORRY ABOUT ELK

In May of 2005, the U.S. Forest Service completed its evaluation of the risk of wildfire and insect loss to 44,000 acres in the Smith Creek/Shields River area of the Gallatin National Forest, north of Livingston, Montana. The Forest Service concluded that there was a high risk of wildfire in the area, which, coupled with limited access, formed unsafe conditions for the public, including residents who live on private property within the national forest and firefighters. In addition, Park County's Wildfire Protection Plan, completed in the spring of 2006, identified the Smith Creek area as a priority "wildland-urban interface area" at high risk from wildfire and thus a priority for fuels reduction projects. In response, the Forest Service developed—with comments from adjacent private homeowners and state, county, and local officials and groups—the "Smith Creek Vegetation Treatment Project" to address the dangerous fuel buildups and mitigate the risk of catastrophic wildfire and its potentially devastating impacts on human beings.

The Forest Service project would reduce fuel loads on a maximum of 1,110 acres, in 10 separate units, by thinning medium- and large-diameter green conifers, selectively harvesting insect- or disease-damaged conifers, cutting small-diameter conifers, slashing trees that encroach into meadows or aspen stands, prescribed burning in meadows and the understory of treated stands, and piling and removing or burning downed woody debris. As well, a local, quasi-governmental association was formed to provide grant monies to local residents to conduct fuels reduction projects on their lands.

In July of 2008, after unsuccessful administrative appeals of the Forest Service plan, two environmental groups and a summer resident of the area sued the Forest Service alleging that the plan violated the National Environmental Policy Act (NEPA) as well as the National Forest Management Act (NFMA); as a result of the importance of the project, a Montana federal district court set an expedited briefing schedule. Then, in August of 2008, full-time residents and local property owners, Janet and Ronald Hartman of Wilsall, Montana, intervened in the case.

In late October of 2008, the district court ruled for the Forest Service and the Hartmans on all claims except one, regarding the mapping of key elk habitat; that matter was remanded to the Forest Service. Meanwhile, the Forest Service was enjoined from beginning the project. By the following fall, the Forest Service had completed its mapping; therefore, on October 8, 2009, the district court ruled that the Forest Service could proceed with the Smith Creek Vegetation Project, portions of which would occur during the winter season, that is, between November 1 and April 30. Before the project could begin, however, the environmental groups appealed and the U.S. Court of Appeals for the Ninth Circuit barred the plan's implementation.

Last month, after legal briefing, the appeal was argued before a three-judge panel of the Ninth Circuit. The environmental groups argued that the Forest Service plan did not provide sufficient "elk hiding cover" and must be enjoined. The Hartmans responded that the plan was needed to "slow down the rate of spread" of a catastrophic fire to "buy [them] the time" to escape with their lives when such a fire begins. At that point, one judge, asserting that the court must "balance equities," asked "how severe is the danger to life," "what's the actual danger of death," and "what's the number of people who have been killed" by these fires? When the Hartmans argued that the equities favored the people, not the elk, the judge did admit that "the elk are doing very well," but, countered another judge, with more cover there "may be even more" elk.

Not surprising, given the nature of the Ninth Circuit (the most frequently reversed federal appeals court in the country) and the questions from the judges, the panel barred implementation of the Forest Service plan. Still deep in winter in southern Montana, the Hartmans and their neighbors dread yet another fire season.

MARCH 2010

ON COLLEGE CAMPUSES, NOT ONLY
OUTLAWS SHOULD HAVE GUNS

On March 9, a Denver, Colorado, television station reported a "rash of violence" on the University of Colorado's (CU's) Auraria Campus and issued a "warning" after "several people were attacked and robbed on campus or inside their dorm rooms," including "2 students [who] were stabbed with a hatchet." Two weeks later, oral arguments occurred before a three-judge panel of the Colorado Court of Appeals regarding whether students such as those who had been warned of increasing violence and threats to their personal safety had the right, if authorized by one of Colorado's sheriffs, to carry concealed weapons on campus.

In December of 2008, Students for Concealed Carry on Campus (SCCC)—a national organization with 35,000 members—and three CU students and former students, including one enrolled at CU's Auraria Campus, filed a lawsuit against CU challenging its ban on concealed carry on its campuses. They argued that Colorado's 2003 Concealed Carry Act (CCA), with four specific, narrow, and limited exceptions, applies throughout Colorado and that CU's ban violates the CCA and is otherwise unconstitutional. CU responded that it is a state entity and is exempt from the CCA's bar on "local" regulations that are in conflict with the CCA.

In April of 2009, the El Paso County district court where the case was filed—CU has a campus in Colorado Springs in El Paso County—dismissed the suit. "[I]t is apparent from the case law," held the court, "that [Colorado] courts have not treated [CU] as a 'local government,' but rather, [as] a statewide authority with its own legislative powers over distinct geographical areas." Thus, ruled the district court, CU is not constrained by the CCA because it is not a "local government." Furthermore, ruled the district court, CU's prohibition on the "right to keep and bear arms" was a reasonable exercise of the state police power.

Less than one month following oral arguments, the Court of Appeals issued its ruling. In a stunning, unanimous decision, the court reinstated the lawsuit and remanded the matter to the district court. On both issues, the court reversed the ruling of the trial court, holding that the SCCC had a valid claim as to its assertion that CU is a "local government" and barred from enacting a concealed carry policy in conflict with the CCA and its constitutional claim as to the "right to keep and bear arms." Unless CU persuades the Colorado Supreme Court to hear its appeal and reverse the ruling of the Court of Appeals, CU's ban may be stricken.

The Court of Appeals found that the Colorado legislature had intended to "'provide statewide uniform standards for issuing permits to carry concealed handguns for self-defense' and mandatory procedures for sheriffs to follow in issuing permits" to resolve the "widespread inconsistency among jurisdictions within the state," which had created "public uncertainty" as to where in the state "it is lawful to carry concealed handguns." Because "carrying of concealed handguns is a matter of statewide concern," the legislature concluded it "necessary that the state occupy the field of regulation of the bearing of concealed handguns." Therefore, the CCA allows a permittee "to carry a concealed handgun in all areas of the state" and "[a] local government does not have authority to adopt or enforce an ordinance or resolution that would conflict with [that right]." Although the CCA contains four exceptions, those exceptions do not include public universities. Declared the Court of Appeals, "Had the legislature intended to exempt universities, it knew how to do so."

The day after the ruling the Federal Bureau of Investigation, Secret Service, and the U.S. Department of Education released a report concluding that targeted violence on college campuses is up sharply over the last two decades. The report was unnecessary for students and parents who had concluded, after the Virginia Tech and Northern Illinois University tragedies, that on the nation's campuses, others besides outlaws should have guns.

MAY 2010

TIMES SQUARE ATTACK RESPONSE:
NONE DARE CALL IT THINKING

On May 1, 2010, when news of the Times Square terrorist attack first broke, New York City Mayor Michael Bloomberg said, on national television, as to who might have done it, "If I had to guess 25 cents, this would be exactly that, somebody who's homegrown, maybe a mentally deranged person or someone with a political agenda that doesn't like the health care bill or something. ..." Bloomberg was not alone. U.S. Department of Homeland Security (DHS) Secretary Janet Napolitano declared that there was no evidence that the attack was "anything other than a one-off," a British expression for "one of a kind." At least the country was spared President Obama telling Americans that they should not "jump to conclusions," as he did after the Fort Hood Massacre when the media reported that "Major Hasan. ... killed 13 and left 31 injured after he jumped on to a desk screaming 'Allahu Akbar'—God is Great—and fired on defenseless colleagues."

Where did Mayor Bloomberg and Secretary Napolitano get the idea that the terrorist was a "lone wolf"? Perhaps they were "hoping" like MSNBC reporter Contessa Brewer, "[T]here was part of me that was hoping this was not going to be anybody with ties to any kind of Islamic country. ..." Or maybe it was this from *The Nation* ["the flagship of the left"], where Robert Dreyfuss declared, "It seems far more likely to me [he] was either a lone nut job or a member of some squirrelly branch of the Tea Party, anti-government far right."

What makes Bloomberg, Napolitano, and Obama think—if one can call it thinking or anything more than wishful thinking—that Americans should fear terrorist attacks, not from those who embrace radical Islam, but from their fellow countrymen with strong views on important issues of the day? The answer, perhaps, is an "intelligence analysis report," released on April 7, 2009, by the DHS regarding "rightwing extremists" and "rightwing terrorist groups" in the United States, which Napolitano sent to all sheriffs and police departments across the country with instructions that they report back to the DHS regarding any sightings.

Entitled, "Rightwing Extremism: Current Economic and Political Climate Fueling Resurgence in Radicalization and Recruitment," the report targeted unnamed individuals and groups because of their views on such issues as illegal immigration, centralizing power in Washington, D.C. rather than in state and local governments, restricting the right to keep and bear arms, abortion, and the loss of American sovereignty. The report asserted that people espousing these views are "rightwing extremists" and are or could become members of "rightwing terrorist groups" and that both pose a threat to national security. More shocking, the report singled out military veterans returning from service in Iraq and Afghanistan due to their "combat skills and experience."

Recently, in response to Freedom of Information Act (FOIA) demands for copies of the documents upon which the DHS relied in preparing its report, the DHS provided 411 pages of documents. As the basis for the claims made in the April of 2009 report, these documents are laughable. In fact, one critic, after viewing them, called the report, "frighteningly kooky." Obviously, there is no basis in those documents for Bloomberg, Napolitano, and Obama to maintain that those who have strong political views regarding the actions of Obama, Reid, and Pelosi are "rightwing extremists" likely to engage in acts of domestic terrorism.

There is a reason why Obama and his officials as well as Reid and Pelosi keep up the drumbeat that those espousing strong views regarding the mischief afoot in Washington, D.C., are "extremists." They seek to discredit and to silence their critics. It does not appear to be working; the American people believe that much is at stake, such as the future of the country. They remember Benjamin Franklin counseled that the Founding Fathers created, "A Republic, if you can keep it." They intend to keep it.

JUNE 2010

AMERICANS WAGE NATIONWIDE FIGHT FOR GUN RIGHTS

In the wake of the June ruling by the Supreme Court of the United States, in *McDonald v. Chicago*, that the Second Amendment right "to keep and bear Arms" applies to the states via the Fourteenth Amendment's Due Process Clause, Chicago politicians declared that they would find a way around the 5-4 ruling. That is bad news for Otis McDonald, the lead plaintiff—a 76-year old, African-American Democrat and resident of Chicago's far South Side—who has watched his neighborhood deteriorate and the danger to him and his family increase since he and his wife bought their home in 1972. If it is any consolation to him, he is not alone.

All across the country, Americans, conscious not only of their right "to keep and bear Arms"—Justice Alito called it "among those fundamental rights necessary to our system of ordered liberty"—but also of the necessity that they provide for the safety of themselves and their loved ones, are holding politicians accountable and going to court, when necessary, to protect their rights. They include an Ohio woman, an Idaho student, and a rural Colorado couple. In the days and weeks ahead, their cases, and scores of others like them, may generate news but more than likely, will also guarantee the right "to keep and bear Arms."

In Illinois, Ellen Mishaga of Mentor, Ohio, sued Jonathon E. Monken, Director of the Illinois Department of State Police who is responsible for issuing Firearms Owner Identification Cards (FOIDs), in federal district court, seeking the right to possess lawfully a firearm and ammunition when she travels to Illinois. Ms. Mishaga argues that Illinois' bar on her ability to makes such purchases because she is not an Illinois resident and thus unable to obtain a FOID violates both her Second Amendment rights and her right to travel. On April 30, 2010, and again on June 14, 2010, Mr. Monken denied her application for a FOID, stating, "No Illinois driver's license number or state identification number provided."

In Nevada, Al Baker, a law student who lives in Boise, Idaho, sued Allen Biaggi, Director of the Nevada Department of Conservation and Natural Resources, and other state officials in federal district court seeking the right to possess lawfully and, if necessary for self-defense, to discharge a firearm in a state park. Mr. Baker, a NRA-certified Home Firearms

Safety & Basic Pistol Instructor who is licensed in Idaho, Utah, and Oregon to carry a concealed handgun, is also an avid outdoorsman and camps in northern Nevada. After Mr. Baker's application for a special use permit was denied, he was advised that, if he brings a firearm for personal protection into Wild Horse State Recreation Area near Elko, Nevada, he will be in violation of state law.

In Colorado, Tab and Debbie Bonidy, a rural couple that must drive 10 miles roundtrip to the Avon Post Office because mail delivery is not available at their home, notified the Postmaster General that they will "avail themselves of other legal remedies available to them" if the U.S. Postal Service does not withdraw illegal regulations that bar them from carrying a firearm or parking their vehicle, if it contains a firearm, on Postal Service property. Both are licensed to carry a handgun and regularly carry handguns for self-defense from wild animals and criminals and believe that the Postal Service's ban prevents them from exercising their rights when traveling to, from, or through Postal Service property.

Ms. Mishaga, Mr. Baker, and Mr. and Mrs. Bonidy hope that the federal district courts will adhere to the Supreme Court's binding legal precedents in *District of Columbia v. Heller* and *McDonald* and rule in their favor and that the Courts of Appeals will sustain their victories. It is unlikely any of the cases will reach the Supreme Court; however, there too victory seems assured, at least until the Sotomayors and Kagans overwhelm the Roberts and Alitos.

AUGUST 2010

SINCE WHEN ARE CHINA AND ARIZONA MORALLY EQUIVALENT?

On May 14, 2010, the U.S. Department of State announced "no major breakthroughs" in bilateral discussions with China "after only their second round of talks about human rights since 2002." Assistant Secretary for the Bureau of Democracy, Human Rights, and Labor, Michael H. Posner, who along with Ambassador to China Jon Huntsman briefed the media, said that the United States sought a "mature relationship" with China, which would yield "an open discussion" not only of "[China's] problems," but also "[the U.S.A.'s] own [problems]." At that point, a reporter asked, "Did the recently passed Arizona immigration law come up? And, if so, did they bring it up or did you bring it up?" Posner responded, "We brought it up early and often. It was mentioned in the first session, and as a troubling trend in our society and an indication that we have to deal with issues of discrimination or potential discrimination, and that these are issues very much being debated in our own society."

The day the Associated Press reported Posner's remarks, the American Civil Liberties Union (ACLU), the Mexican American Legal Defense and Educational Fund (MALDEF), the National Association for the Advancement of Colored People (NAACP), and others filed a federal lawsuit against Arizona challenging the constitutionality of the "Arizona immigration law" (S.B. 1070) in Arizona federal district court. According to their complaint, the law violates the Supremacy Clause and the First and Fourth Amendments.

Less than two months later, on July 5, while Secretary Posner was enjoying a day off (federal offices were closed) to celebrate Independence Day, the Associated Press announced that an American geologist, held and tortured by China's state security agents for two and one half years, was sentenced to eight years in prison allegedly for spying and collecting state secrets regarding the Chinese oil industry, which "endangered [China's] national security." Ambassador Huntsman was in the courtroom; after the verdict, the U.S. Embassy in Beijing announced it was "dismayed" and urged China to grant the 45-year old Xue Feng—who was born in China, earned his Ph.D. at the University of Chicago, became a U.S. citizen, and

works for a Colorado energy company—"humanitarian release and immediately deport him."

The next day, Ambassador Huntsman's colleague in the Obama administration, Attorney General Eric Holder, join with the ACLU, NAACP,
MALDEF, and others in challenging S.B. 1070, asserting, "The Constitution and the federal immigration laws do not permit the development of a
patchwork of state and local immigration policies throughout the country."

Meanwhile, public support for the right of Arizona to respond to the
crime, chaos, and cost of unrestrained illegal immigration and the refusal
of the federal government to protect the nation's southern border, grew like
Topsy. According to a Rasmussen Reports national telephone survey conducted after the Obama administration filed its lawsuit, 61 percent favor
the Arizona law for their states and 56 percent oppose the federal lawsuit.

Before the Arizona federal district court, federal lawyers argued that,
in determining whether the Arizona law violates the Supremacy Clause,
which requires preemption of state law that conflicts with federal law, the
question is not whether S.B. 1070 conflicts with the provisions of acts of
Congress, but whether it is consistent with current White House policy,
including "foreign relations [] and humanitarian concerns. . . ." Incredibly,
on July 28, the court agreed with the Obama administration's audacious
and unprecedented argument and struck down much of the Arizona law.
The next stop is the U.S. Court of Appeals for the Ninth Circuit, en route
to the Supreme Court of the United States.

Thus, while American citizens, pursuant to the Constitution and the
rule of law, seek to address issues of great personal and national concern, an
American citizen sits in a hellhole jail in China. Remarkably, Team Obama
regards these circumstances as morally equivalent. So the question arises,
what is the more embarrassing: Team Obama or Arizona?

SEPTEMBER 2010

CHAPTER TWENTY-TWO

The Commerce Clause
and Freedom

E arly on Monday, October 17, 2011, I drove out of New York City for White Plains, the county seat of Westchester County, which lies north of New York City and its five boroughs, east of the Hudson River, and west of Long Island Sound and Connecticut. Its 500 square miles is home to nearly a million residents whose median family income makes it New York's second and the nation's seventh wealthiest county. It is known for its "old money" and is home to some of America's richest families, but it is also among the most racially diverse in the state, behind only Manhattan, the Queens, and the Bronx. Since the 1990s, it voted Democratic; in 2008, Senator Obama garnered 63 percent of the vote. Being rich, racially diverse, and substantially left of center politically, however, did not protect it from being targeted by Obama officials for a precedent-setting exercise in social engineering. I drove in to see if MSLF could help.

In 2006, a nonprofit group sued Westchester County alleging that, since 2000, the County lied to the federal government to obtain over $45 million in housing and other grants because it "knew" housing in Westchester County was racially segregated as a result of discrimination. Westchester County knew no such thing; housing patterns were due to personal choice, transportation, job availability, infrastructure, land cost, and income issues. The court rejected that argument, ruled the County had lied, and set the matter for trial.

Westchester County was in a fix, facing damages and fines of over $300 million, which were increased because the United States intervened in the lawsuit. Westchester County settled for $62.5 million: $51.6 million to build 750 affordable housing units, $8.4 million to the U.S. Department of Justice, and $4.5 million to the group's attorney. Then worse madness began. A top Obama administration official turned the settlement into "an open-ended utopian integration order." Westchester County is fighting back, but the precedent set by the newly enriched nonprofit group after teaming up with the Obama administration is striking fear into the hearts of local officials all across the country.

I thought, as I drove away after my meeting, "If this can happen to a rich, powerful, and connected unit of local government, what hope is there for the rest of us?"

THE *WASHINGTON POST* ASSAILS THE WEST AND ITS LAWYERS

Phineas Taylor (P.T.) Barnum's famous adage, "I don't care what the newspapers say about me as long as they spell my name right," was put to the test regarding Mountain States Legal Foundation (MSLF) recently.

In December of 2010, the *Washington Post* ran an article headlined, "Indians question Colo. firm's motives in vote case," in which the writer not only attacked MSLF but also questioned its ethics and asserted MSLF's *pro bono* representation of rural Fremont County, Wyoming was motivated by racism. The *Post's* article quickly went "viral." An internet search reveals the article was run by newspapers and websites across the country. Nonetheless, the *Post* refused to print a Letter to the Editor MSLF submitted that included statements of fact and law the *Post* failed to report!

Indeed, the *Post* appeared disinterested in the details of the case, which began in October of 2005, when the ACLU filed a Voting Rights Act (VRA) lawsuit against Fremont County and its elected officials in Wyoming federal district court on behalf of five Eastern Shoshone and Northern Arapahoe tribal members. The ACLU demanded that the court order single-member commissioner districts, including at least one district with a majority of American Indian voters, to guarantee the perpetual election of an American Indian commissioner.

Fremont County, whose voters are 75 percent non-Hispanic Whites and 20 percent American Indians, elects its commissioners at large in partisan races pursuant to state law. Until recently, all five commissioners were Republicans given that 60 percent of voters are registered Republicans. That changed in 2006, a bad year for Republicans, when Fremont County elected an American Indian Commissioner, Keja Whiteman, well-known for her active involvement in the community, who campaigned aggressively throughout the County.

In November of 2006, Fremont County filed a motion for summary judgment arguing that Section 2 of the VRA is unconstitutional; in December of 2006, the ACLU responded. In 2007, after the filing of pretrial briefs in January, a two-week trial was held in February. In May of 2007, Fremont County and the ACLU filed post-trial briefs and the case was ready for a ruling; however, for nearly three years, none was issued. Finally, in early April of 2010, the ACLU petitioned the U.S. Court of Appeals for the Tenth Circuit to compel the district court to decide the case. Later that month, the district court issued a 102-page document holding Fremont County violated the VRA and barred it from using Wyoming's at-large system. In August of 2010, the district court nixed a County redistricting plan; it adopted the ACLU plan instead.

There is much of interest here for the thoughtful reader. Why did the court take three years to decide; and why only after a threat from a court of appeals? Why did the court not find that the election of an American Indian commissioner proved that the county's non-Indian voters are not racially biased? Why did the court rule that the century-old history of the relationship between the United States government and American Indians tainted the modern-day voters of Fremont County? Why did the court not rule as to the constitutionality of Section 2 of the VRA, which allows courts to racially gerrymander districts to ensure election of minority candidates, given that one federal court of appeals calls it "political apartheid" and Justice Thomas decried its results as "racial balkanization"?

None of this interested the *Post*; instead, it attacked MSLF—which it claimed, based on its review of "Federal tax records," is "bankrolled" by "some of the most powerful families in the West"—as "Indian fighters" motivated "by deeply conservative political philosophy" who seek a return to "the way things were in the 1950s." Westerners saw the article for what it was, an attempt to besmirch, not only MSLF's reputation, but also that of its supporters, allies, and clients. In other words, the *Post* at its worst! At least it spelled MSLF's name right.

JANUARY 2011

THE COMMERCE CLAUSE:
IT'S NOT JUST ABOUT OBAMACARE

Ever since enactment of the Patient Protection and Affordable Care Act (ObamaCare)—signed into law on March 23, 2010—and the filing of lawsuits that very day to challenge its constitutionality, the media and the American people have been focused, as at no other time in decades, on the meaning of the Commerce Clause (Art. I, § 8, cl. 3) and whether Congress may use its power "to regulate commerce.... among the several states" to impose an "individual mandate" on Americans to buy health insurance or pay a fine.

Speaker Nancy Pelosi (D-12th CA) thinks the question laughable ("Are you serious?"), but Speaker John Boehner (R-8th OH) disagrees ("ObamaCare is [an] unprecedented, unconstitutional power grab by the federal government."). The final decision rests, of course, as it has since the Supreme Court's 1803 ruling in *Marbury v. Madison*, with the federal judiciary. To date, a Virginia federal district court has ruled ObamaCare unconstitutional; a Florida federal district court appears ready to do likewise. Meanwhile, two federal district courts, one in Virginia and one in Michigan, have upheld it. The Michigan case is before the U.S. Court of Appeals for the Sixth Circuit; the two Virginia cases are en route to the U.S. Court of Appeals for the Fourth Circuit. The matter will be heard eventually by the Supreme Court of the United States, that is, unless ObamaCare is repealed in the meantime.

Before then the Supreme Court may have an opportunity to opine on a federal law that has caused property owners and especially westerners to question the scope of the Commerce Clause for decades: the Endangered Species Act (ESA). Later this month, the U.S. Court of Appeals for the Ninth Circuit will hear oral arguments on whether Congress has the authority to authorize a federal agency—the U.S. Fish and Wildlife Service (FWS)—to regulate a tiny (three-inch) fish, the delta smelt, to the detriment of the economic well-being and property rights of tens of thousands of rural residents of central California.

In March of 1993, the FWS listed the delta smelt as a "threatened species" under the ESA but made no finding on whether it or its "taking" substantially affects interstate commerce. In fact, the FWS concluded the delta smelt "is the only smelt endemic to California" and "has no commercial value." In December of 2008, the FWS issued a Biological Opinion concluding that operation of the Central Valley Project and the State Water Project jeopardizes the smelt's existence and adversely modifies its critical habitat. The FWS then issued a "reasonably prudent alternative" pursuant to which water flows in the San Joaquin Valley were restricted.

The results have been disastrous. The *Wall Street Journal* reports that "tens of billions of gallons of water" are sent into the ocean, "leaving hundreds of thousands of acres of arable land fallow or scorched." As a result, in formerly fertile farming areas, unemployment now ranges between 14 and 40 percent.

Represented by Pacific Legal Foundation, a nonprofit, public-interest legal foundation, Stewart & Jasper Orchards, Arroyo Farms, and King Pistachio Grove—water users that were affected adversely by the FWS's decision—sued alleging that the Commerce Clause does not provide Congress authority to regulate the delta smelt under the ESA. In October of 2009, the District Court for the Eastern District of California upheld the constitutionality of the ESA as to the delta smelt, a ruling that became final in December of 2009. The water users filed an appeal at the Ninth Circuit on which briefing has been completed.

Because decisions by the Ninth Circuit are frequently reviewed and reversed by the Supreme Court, the three-judge panel's ruling on the delta smelt is unlikely to end the case. To ensure that the Commerce Clause means what the Founders intended, the Supreme Court should hear the case, vacate Congress's authority to regulate intrastate species, and use that precedent to strike down the individual mandate of ObamaCare.

FEBRUARY 2011

EPA TRASHES ECONOMIC GROWTH, JOBS, AND THE RULE OF LAW

As Congress seeks to rein in the most out-of-control federal agency in Washington, the Environmental Protection Agency (EPA), folks in West Virginia wonder whether relief from the EPA's empire building, enforcement actions, and edicts will come in time.

Coal mining is crucial to West Virginia's economy; in 2009, for example, it employed more than 30,000 people directly and 105,000 people indirectly and paid $2 billion in wages. Forty percent of the state's coal is extracted by surface mining, during which the overburden created is used to re-contour the mined area to approximate original contour; but, because not all overburden can be returned to the mined area and because of the state's terrain, the only feasible disposal site for much overburden is in adjacent hollows. Those hollows, even if they carry water only as runoff during or following rainstorms, constitute, under the Clean Water Act (CWA), "navigable waters." Thus, surface mining in West Virginia often requires a CWA § 404 permit from the U.S. Army Corps of Engineers (Corps).

In Logan County in southwestern West Virginia, Mingo Logan Coal Company, a subsidiary of Arch Coal, Inc., operates the Spruce No. 1 coal mine. In March of 1997, Mingo Logan sought a permit from the Corps, pursuant to Nationwide Permit 21; however, after two years that process, which involved the EPA, ended when, in a federal lawsuit by environmental groups that did not implicate Spruce No. 1, a district court enjoined use of Nationwide Permit 21. The Corps withdrew its proffered permit.

In March of 1999, Mingo Logan applied for a § 404(a) permit. Notwithstanding the two-year process just completed, the Corps began anew; meanwhile, Spruce No. 1's project was modified. Instead of recovering nearly all of the coal, only 75 percent will be recovered: reducing the acreage impacted from 3,113 to 2,278; halving the spoil to be removed; and, cutting the acres of "navigable waters" affected from 12 to 8.11 acres, which include: 0.12 acres of wetland (an abandoned farm pond), 1.83 acres of ephemeral (storm runoff only) streams, 6.13 acres of intermittent (seasonal only) streams, and 0.034 acres of a perennial (permanently flowing) stream.

In March of 2006, the Corps released its sixteen hundred page Draft Environmental Impact Statement (EIS), the first of its kind for an individual West Virginia surface mine, in which five state and federal agencies, including the EPA, participated. In September of 2006, the Corps released a Final EIS, which included 58 pages addressing the EPA's comments on the Draft EIS. In January of 2007, the Corps issued Mingo Logan a § 404 permit for Spruce No. 1; however, it also imposed extensive mitigation conditions requiring that Mingo Logan: create wetlands, enhance thousands of feet of existing streams, plant tens of thousands of native trees and shrubs, and engage in long-term monitoring to ensure environmental mitigation.

The Corps' review of the Spruce No. 1 project's permit application lasted seven years, generated tens of thousands of pages of administrative record, and cost Mingo Logan millions of dollars. Prior to the issuance of the Corps' permit, the EPA lodged no objections, nor did it seek to exercise its statutory authority to "elevate" a challenge to the Corps' permit. There is no question but that Mingo Logan complied with the Corps' permit.

Nonetheless, on January 13, 2011, the EPA, asserting authority under § 404(c), revoked the Corps' permit. Meanwhile, on April 2, 2010, Mingo Logan, anticipating the EPA's action given a *Federal Register* notice, sued the EPA challenging its authority to void the permit. The EPA acknowledged it had never used § 404(c) to review, let alone revoke, an already-issued permit in the 38-year history of the CWA.

In February, Mingo Logan amended its complaint and last week federal lawyers filed their answer and documents regarding the EPA's decision; the battle is joined. At stake is no less than the question of the continuing vitality of the rule of law.

APRIL 2011

ARIZONA ASKS U.S. SUPREME COURT: IS FEDERALISM STILL ALIVE?

In early May, Arizona Governor Jan Brewer announced she will provide the Supreme Court of the United States with another opportunity to demonstrate that the U.S. Court of Appeals for the Ninth Circuit is the federal appeals court whose opinions it most frequently reviews, reverses, and remands. The issue presented in her petition is whether Arizona's attempt to address the impact of illegal immigrants on its citizens is unconstitutional.

Governor Brewer's announcement follows the April 11 ruling by a three-judge panel of the Ninth Circuit, voting 2-1, that S.B. 1070—Arizona's legislation undertaking to address the safety, economic, and social issues caused by the presence of illegal immigrants in the Grand Canyon State—is contrary to the Supremacy Clause because it conflicts with federal law. The Ninth Circuit thereby upheld the July 28, 2010, ruling of an Arizona federal district court barring Arizona from implementing the law pending a final court ruling on the merits.

Almost immediately upon its enactment in April of 2010, S.B. 1070 was challenged as unconstitutional by a host of "open-border groups," including the ACLU, the Mexican American Legal Defense and Educational Fund (MALDEF), and the NAACP. The "other shoe," however, dropped when Attorney General Eric Holder, proclaiming that Arizona's law could violate its citizens' civil rights, sued the state. Ironically, his lawsuit contained no such allegation.

Despite the legal challenges, or perhaps because of them, public support for the right of Arizona to respond to the crime, chaos, and cost of unrestrained illegal immigration and the refusal of the federal government to protect the nation's southern border, remains high. A Rasmussen Reports national telephone survey revealed that 61 percent of respondents favored the Arizona law for their states and 56 percent opposed the federal lawsuit.

The Obama administration did not just have its Attorney General level inflammatory charges and file a lawsuit; it launched an unprecedented attack on a sovereign state. Obama lashed out with an imaginary tale of how any Hispanic man who takes his kid "out to get ice cream, [is] gonna be harassed." Later, Assistant Secretary of State for the Bureau of Democracy, Human Rights, and Labor, Michael H. Posner, announced that, during human rights talks with China, he discussed the Arizona law "early and often," "as a troubling trend in our society and an indication that we have to deal with issues of discrimination. . . ."

Not to be outdone, weeks later, Secretary of State Hillary Clinton included a *mea culpa* on the Arizona law in a report to the "U.N. High Commissioner for Human Rights," an inclusion that drew a stinging rebuke from Governor Brewer. The United States' first ever report to the U.N. body required that American diplomats appear, in what one expert called a "barbecuing," before a panel of U.N. bureaucrats from France, Japan, and Cameroon to defend Arizona's legislation and the nation's civil rights record and to hear testimony from non-governmental organizations (NGOs).

In November of 2010, before the Ninth Circuit, federal lawyers stood by their winning argument at the Arizona federal district court that, in determining if the Arizona law violates the Supremacy Clause—which requires preemption of state laws that conflict with federal law, the question is not whether S.B. 1070 conflicts with federal law, but whether it is consistent with White House policy on "foreign relations [] and humanitarian concerns. . . ." In April of 2011, when the Ninth Circuit panel issued its ruling, one judge dissented.

Circuit Judge Carlos T. Bea charged that the majority, in ruling for the Obama administration, ignored the mandate of Congress, deferred impermissibly to federal agencies and foreign countries, and, by adopting a view rejected even by Obama's lawyers, stripped Arizona of its ability to protect its citizens. If the Supreme Court grants Governor Brewer's petition, the real issue will be, not whether S.B. 1070 is constitutional, but whether the Constitution continues to provide for dual sovereignty.

JUNE 2011

ENDANGERED SPECIES ACT:
OUT OF CONTROL AND GETTING WORSE

Folks in the Texas Panhandle and southeastern New Mexico are in an uproar, and with good reason. At the behest of environmental groups, the U.S. Fish and Wildlife Service (FWS) moves inexorably toward a decision to place the sand dune lizard on the federal Endangered Species Act (ESA) list. As similar listings have done elsewhere—the northern spotted owl in the Pacific Northwest, for example—providing the lizard ESA protection will destroy jobs and economic activity. It will destroy something else: energy production! Today Midland, Texas, produces 20 percent of the nation's crude oil; its reserves are second only to Alaska.

Folks in the Permian Basin, as it is known, fear the type of economic privation visited upon the San Joaquin Valley in California. There, the FWS ordered waters that historically irrigated fertile croplands be dumped into the ocean to "protect" a three-inch fish, the delta smelt. The result: a modern-day dustbowl and thousands of lost jobs; the unemployment rate today ranges upwards to 40 percent. The federal government is unrepentant, neither Governor Schwarzenegger nor Governor Brown stepped in, and the U.S. Court of Appeals for the Ninth Circuit rejected arguments by local citizens that Congress lacks authority under the Commerce Clause to regulate a species that exists only in California.

Meanwhile, Congress finally did take action regarding wolves in Idaho and Montana. In 1994, over protests of westerners, including ranchers, hunters, and landowners, the Clinton administration brought Canadian wolves into Yellowstone National Park in Wyoming to spread over the tri-state area. With a range of 500 miles, no longer fearful of mankind, and standing atop the food chain, wolves proliferated; in the process, they decimated Montana's elk herds and adversely affected livestock.

During the Bush administration, Idaho, Montana, and Wyoming demanded the right to regulate the species, a wish granted as to Idaho and Montana when the FWS delisted the wolf there. (When Wyoming's regulatory regime was rejected, it sued; a federal district court has ruled against the FWS.) Not surprisingly, environmental groups challenged the delisting in federal court, which, again not surprisingly, struck down the delisting. Congress had enough. It enacted (and President Obama signed) legislation ordering the delisting of wolves in Idaho and Montana. Incredibly, environmental groups sued once again, this time arguing that it is unconstitutional for Congress to restrict a law enacted by Congress.

Further south, along the I-25 corridor, from Casper, Wyoming, to Colorado Springs, Colorado, the Preble's meadow jumping mouse (PMJM) vexed local governments, businesses, and landowners since the Clinton administration acceded to demands of environmental groups and put it on the ESA list, despite a lack of science to support the listing and notwithstanding that the PMJM is indistinguishable from other rodents. The Bush administration, in response to science-based petitions from Wyoming, finally delisted the PMJM in Wyoming.

The Bush administration could delist the PMJM in Wyoming because the Department of the Interior's Solicitor opined that the ESA permitted the FWS to delist a species in a part of its range. Not surprisingly, environmental groups sued to put the PMJM back on the list and, in the process, challenged the offending Solicitor's Opinion, which they also contested in the wolf lawsuit. The Obama administration threw in the towel, withdrew the opinion, and asked the Colorado federal district court to strike the delisting and send the FWS back for rulemaking. That the request is illegal was irrelevant to federal lawyers.

Second only to the Environmental Protection Agency, the FWS is killing jobs today at an unprecedented pace across the country. There may be some hope for the Texas Panhandle and southeastern New Mexico, however; two U.S. Senators have introduced legislation to bar the listing of the lizard, and its lady-in-waiting, the prairie chicken. Because allegations that these provisions, if enacted and signed into law, are unconstitutional will follow along with federal lawsuits, the ESA cries out for massive rewrite and reform.

JULY 2011

HOLLYWOOD'S DAVID MAMET: BRAIN-DEAD LIBERAL NO MORE

David Mamet is an acclaimed playwright, screenwriter, film director, and essayist, most famous for the films *The Untouchables*, *The Verdict*, and *Wag the Dog*—the latter two received Academy Award nominations—and plays, such as *American Buffalo* and *Glengarry Glen Ross*, for which he received the Pulitzer Prize. A Chicago native, he lived in New York City, but, for several years has lived in California. Over the years, he made one other change; he became a free market conservative. His book about his journey, *The Secret Knowledge: On the Dismantling of American Culture* (Sentinel, 2011), was released in June.

Mamet's transformation from "reformed Liberal" was years in the making; however, it began in earnest when the rabbi of his Temple, the membership of which includes Liberal film people, recommended that Mamet read the works of free-market conservatives, *e.g.* Milton Friedman, Friedrich Hayek, and Thomas Sowell (and others set out in *The Secret Knowledge's* bibliography). Mamet argues that Liberals never meet Conservatives, never engage them in discussions of first principles, and never question their own views; instead, they worship the "Sunday-only religion" that is Liberalism, whose strict orthodoxy does not apply to them, and they surround themselves with other members of a herd ruled by group-think.

Mamet tackles scores of Liberal plans, programs, and policies (granted, it is a "target-rich environment"); but, he has special disdain for race-based decision-making by governments. After noting that his family fled Poland and its pogroms, just escaping Hitler's assassins, he asks: On what basis may a government undertake a plan to harm one individual to ameliorate an injury done to the long dead ancestor of another? If there were a defensible basis, he asks: when would that program end; for what facts could prove the historic wrong had been righted?

Ironically, the Supreme Court of the United States will ask Mamet's questions in its October 2011 Term. First up for review is Justice O'Connor's 2003 *Grutter* ruling allowing professional schools, specifically the University of Michigan Law School, to admit students based on race for another 25 years. In Texas, which had ensured diverse university student bodies with a race-neutral law, the University of Texas–Austin was not satisfied; it used *Grutter* to reinstitute quotas. Two young, non-minority coeds denied admission sued.

A Texas federal district court, using *Grutter*, ruled for the University, as did a U.S. Court of Appeals for the Fifth Circuit panel by a 2-1 vote; the dissent criticized *Grutter* and the University's numerology. A request for rehearing *en banc* was denied 8-7, bringing another stinging dissent. A grant of *certiorari* is certain and only *stare decisis* could save *Grutter*, not likely since nearly a decade has passed. Just five years after the Court upheld a federal racial diversity program in 1990, it overturned that ruling in *Adarand Constructors, Inc. v. Peña*.

After *Adarand*, which legal experts said doomed affirmative action, and Congress's refusal to overturn Clinton's scheme to "mend, not end" race-based decision-making, citizens took matters into their own hands. Civil rights ballot initiatives—constitutional amendments that barred any use of race—were adopted by wide margins in California (1996), Washington (1998), and Michigan (2006), over objections of politicians, business leaders, and the main-stream media. Liberals, however, were not finished; they sued. In early July, the U.S. Court of Appeals for the Sixth Circuit in Ohio ruled the Michigan plan unconstitutional because it disadvantages racial minorities. Not to be undone in pursuing liberal orthodoxy, the U.S. Court of Appeals for the Ninth Circuit in California took up a new challenge to California's Proposition 209. Both rulings will meet at the Supreme Court on the slam dunk question of whether states may vote to require adherence to the commands of the Constitution's equal protection guarantee.

If the Supreme Court hears these two sets of equal protection cases the same day, the Courtroom scene will rival a screenplay written and directed by David Mamet.

AUGUST 2011

VINDICATION FOR DR. LARRY SQUIRES
OF HOBBS, NEW MEXICO

In 1992, Larry Squires of Hobbs, New Mexico, veterinarian, rancher, entrepreneur, and self-proclaimed environmentalist, received unwelcomed news from the Environmental Protection Agency (EPA). The EPA, notwithstanding extensive factual presentations by Dr. Squires, determined that lands upon which he was conducting a business operation into which he sunk more than a $1 million were "wetlands" under the Clean Water Act (CWA), that his use of those lands was illegal, and that he was subject to a "cease and desist order." Failure to observe the EPA's order would result in fines of $125,000 a day. Dr. Squires abandoned his business, but he also went to federal court.

The EPA order was based upon a November of 1986 rule that declared that the potential use of any waters—even intermittent water bodies such as those that infrequently develop in the dry sinkholes on Dr. Squires' arid property—by migratory birds magically converts dry lands into "waters of the United States." Dr. Squires did not think his lands were "wetlands," after all, water from occasional rains quickly evaporated; moreover, there was three feet of impermeable clay under the sinkholes, there was no ground water in the area, and the nearest navigable stream was forty miles away.

Dr. Squires proposed that the EPA levy a fine certain to allow him to ask a federal court to determine: did the CWA phrase "waters of the United States" unambiguously include Dr. Squires' sinkholes; did Congress intend the phrase to include Dr. Squires' property; and was the EPA's rule reasonable? The EPA and its lawyers reacted with anger and hostility. Dr. Squires was threatened with criminal charges, resultant jail time, and "the full weight of the federal government."

Subsequently, the EPA advised the New Mexico federal district court that it could not hear Dr. Squires' case because: the EPA's order was only a "pre enforcement decision[]"; the EPA had not yet taken "final" action; the United States had not waived its sovereign immunity; and Dr. Squires' constitutional rights had not yet been violated. The district court dismissed the lawsuit. In 1995, the U.S. Court of Appeals for the Tenth Circuit upheld the district court's ruling. Although the Tenth Circuit expressed sympathy with Dr. Squires' plight, "[the] policy argument that it should not be necessary to violate an EPA order and risk civil and criminal penalties to obtain judicial review is well taken[,]" the appeals court did not find the situation "constitutionally intolerable[,]" especially given its concern with "undermin[ing] the EPA's regulatory authority." In 1996, Dr. Squires' petition for Supreme Court review was denied. (Too late for Dr. Squires, in 2001, the Supreme Court answered the questions he asked and declared the Migratory Bird Rule unconstitutional.)

In the summer of 2007, Michael and Chantrell Sackett of Priest Lake, Idaho moved dirt on their property to build a house on land with a sewer hookup, in a developed area zoned for residential construction. That November, the EPA declared the Sackett property a "wetland," barred the Sacketts from building a house, and mandated that the Sacketts restore their land to its previous state or pay civil penalties of up to $32,500 per day. Like Dr. Squires a decade before them, they were denied a hearing and their lawsuit in Idaho federal district court was dismissed; the court held that the CWA bars judicial review of "compliance orders" before any EPA "enforcement action." In 2010, the Ninth Circuit upheld the district court's decision, ruling that the bar on judicial review did not violate the Sacketts' constitutional rights. On June 28, 2011, the Supreme Court agreed to hear the Sacketts' case.

Given that the EPA recently asserted CWA jurisdiction over isolated, intrastate, non-navigable waters and wetlands, including vernal pools, prairie potholes, natural ponds, and playa lakes, the Supreme Court must step in. In Hobbs, New Mexico, Dr. Squires is smiling at the prospect that, all these years later, his position will be vindicated.

OCTOBER 2011

CENSUS BUREAU RUSHES
UNCONSTITUTIONAL BALLOT DEMAND

In mid-October, the Obama administration, through the U.S. Census Bureau, put three states and 248 counties in 25 states on notice that the election materials they provide must be printed, not only in English, but also in 68 additional languages. The mandate is not new—its announcement is required upon completion of the decennial census; however, what is new is the speed with which it was issued after the 2010 Census. The Bush administration published its *Federal Register* notice on the 2000 Census in 2002.

Cynics may suggest the notice has something to do with the 2012 elections, but the focus should be on the remarkable requirement that, in a country where English language fluency is necessary for citizenship, ballots must be in a variety of foreign languages and the insult that demand gives to the Constitution, as well as its public policy failings, including, that it: imposes a costly unfunded federal mandate in the middle of a recession; Balkanizes the body politic; and contributes to voting fraud. Little wonder that, with the Census Bureau's announcement, many are asking, "Why are we doing this?"

In 1975, Congress amended the Voting Rights Act of 1965 to require that ballots be prepared in languages other than English in jurisdictions where more than 5 percent of the voting-age citizens are members of a particular language minority, if their illiteracy rate is higher than the national illiteracy rate. The reason: "unequal educational opportunities which language minorities have suffered at the hands of State and local officials." Although the *Congressional Record* references "evidence," it cites only statements by three Representatives who supported the amendment. Enacted as "temporary," Section 203 was extended: in 1982 for 10 years, in 1992 for 15 years, and in 2006 for 25 years.

Even if Section 203's "evidence" were true in 1975, which is doubtful, Congress may not interfere constitutionally with the right of state and local officials to conduct elections by imposing a prophylactic remedy—non-English ballots—unless it has evidence of discrimination and enacts a remedy that is "congruent and proportional," in the words of the Supreme Court, to the offense. Because "disparity" does not mean "discrimination," let alone the intentional discrimination by state and local officials that allows extra-constitutional action by Congress, Section 203 is unconstitutional, if not in 1975, then certainly in 2011, given Congress's rote reauthorization of the provision over the decades.

Experts such as Center for Equal Opportunity Chairman Linda Chavez argue that, even in 1975, lack of English language fluency was likely not the result of discrimination but factors such as growing up in a home where English is not spoken enough. Furthermore, how likely is it that the English language deficiencies Congress "found" in 1975 exist four decades later? If not likely, why are hundreds of jurisdictions still covered? Because the Census Bureau labels those who say they speak English "Well" (as opposed to "Very Well") with any who say "Not Well" or "Not at All" as having "Limited English Proficiency" (LEP) and covered by Section 203.

That citizens do not need non-English ballots was demonstrated by a 1986 General Accounting Office (GAO) study, which found that over half of the reporting jurisdictions said no one used the bilingual materials. In 1996, a Yuba County (California) official reported that, in 16 years, only one person requested bilingual materials, yet the county spent $30,000 a year preparing them. In May of 2011, Cuyahoga County (Ohio) spent $100,000 for bilingual ballots in a "light" primary season. Bilingual ballots create another concern for election officials: their ability to prevent fraud. As Ms. Chavez puts it, the only people who need bilingual ballots are non-citizens who want to vote.

Sadly, this costly, useless federal mandate, which undermines national unity, facilitates voting fraud, and violates the Constitution, is likely with us forever. That is, unless a courageous election official asks the Supreme Court to strike it down.

NOVEMBER 2011

CHAPTER TWENTY-THREE

Equal Access to Justice

On March 5, 2012, the Colorado Supreme Court issued its ruling in MSLF's lawsuit on behalf of a national group and three University of Colorado (CU) students who wish to exercise their right to carry concealed weapons on campus. One of our clients was a woman who sought the right to protect herself. Despite an array of friend of the court briefs filed by anti-gun groups, the decision was unanimous! I drafted a press release and spent the day responding to inquiries from reporters. I was particularly delighted by a comment from David B. Kopel, Esq., of the Independence Institute, who filed an *amici curiae* brief on behalf of the Institute and the County Sheriffs of Colorado, "It is an especially impressive accomplishment for . . . a small public-interest law firm to win a unanimous state Supreme Court victory against an institution whose largest campus (Boulder) has an annual budget of over a billion dollars."

Soon, however, efforts were underway across the street from the Supreme Court at the State Capitol in the Colorado General Assembly to eviscerate our victory. One leader said women are too emotional to have guns to defend themselves from rape and should use whistles instead. Another said women should use "ballpoint pens" to defend themselves. Yet another said to use the "buddy system" or "judo." In news coverage of the debate, a liberal commentator told Fox News there is no "rape on a college campus." Finally, CU advised coeds to fight rapists, not with guns, but with "passive resistance," including the use of bodily fluids.

Then, on April 17, 2012, I read a *Los Angeles Times* editorial ("Obama anti-gun? Says who?"), which declared "Obama hasn't proposed any anti-gun legislation in his first term, and has rarely mentioned the topic." Obama, opined the *Times*, rather than being "a wolf in sheep's clothing is really just a sheep." Second Amendment defenders should stop "crying wolf," lectured the editorial writer, because "the battle against gun control has been largely won." I did not believe it. Regarding the attack on the Second Amendment, I knew the worst was yet to come.

ENDANGERED SPECIES ACT:
LIKE THE *HOTEL CALIFORNIA*

The Eagles' memorable hit, *Hotel California*, ends hauntingly, "You can check-out any time you like; but you can never leave." Don Henley, who with Don Felder and Glenn Frey, share the writing credits, says "it's basically a song about the dark underbelly of the American dream and about excess in America . . . ," but, in light of a new, draft Obama administration regulation, it could be about plants and animals listed pursuant to the Endangered Species Act (ESA). Once they get on, they never leave.

The 1973 ESA defines "species" as "any subspecies of fish or wildlife or plants, and any distinct population segment of any species of vertebrate fish or wildlife which (sic) interbreeds when mature." Under the Act, an "endangered species" is one "in danger of extinction throughout all or a significant portion of its range," and a "threatened species" is one "likely to become an endangered species within the foreseeable future throughout all or a significant portion of its range." Amazingly, "a significant portion of its range" remained undefined for almost 35 years.

In 2007, the U.S. Department of the Interior Solicitor issued a legal memorandum that defined the term as "a substantive standard for determining whether a species [is covered by the ESA]," which permits the Secretary to list a species as subject to the Act's protections only "in that portion of its range where it [meets the Act's requirements.]" Based on the Solicitor's Opinion, the U.S. Fish and Wildlife Service (FWS) concluded that several species met the Act's requirements only in a significant portion of their range but not in all of their range; thus, the FWS delisted them where they were neither threatened nor endangered.

Not surprisingly, environmental groups quickly challenged those delisting decisions in Montana (wolves), Colorado (mice), and Arizona (prairie dogs). The Obama administration provided a half-hearted defense of the former Solicitor's Opinion in the Montana and Arizona cases, but, in the Colorado case, federal lawyers informed the district court that the FWS would revoke the 2007 Opinion and embark upon new rulemaking. Late last year, the FWS published its draft rules in the *Federal Register*; the agency will receive comments on the rules until next week and then issue final rules later this year.

The FWS concludes that, if a species is threatened or endangered any-where in its range, it must be listed as threatened or endangered through-out the entirety of its range. The agency reaches this self-serving conclusion because it conflates two terms in the ESA: "a significant portion of its range" [SPR], and a "distinct population segment" [DPS]. Because the ESA pro-vides authority for the FWS to delist a species that qualifies as a DPS, the FWS concludes that the DPS language would become redundant, which is impermissible when interpreting a statute, if a species could be delisted, effectively, by use of the SPR language.

Instead, it is the SPR language that the FWS renders of no effect con-trary to the intent of Congress and the holdings of federal appellate courts. When Congress amended the 1969 Endangered Species Conservation Act in 1973, it specifically included the SPR phrase to require that the FWS first, identify a species covered by the Act, and second, determine where in its range it is threatened or endangered. The FWS calls this congressional mandate a mere "bookkeeping provision" it may ignore, which is rebutted further by the requirement that the FWS ascertain if a species meets the ESA's requirements in "all or a [] portion" of its range.

This is no lawyer's quibble. A FWS decision to list a species and impose its Draconian mandates over an entire region or the refusal of the agency to lift such rules where a species is thriving has devastating consequences. Just ask the farmers in California's San Joaquin Valley (delta smelt), the ranch-ers and roughnecks in Wyoming's Sublette County (sage grouse), or the communities in the Texas Panhandle (sand dunes lizard).

MARCH 2012

MASSIVE LAND-LOCK UP THREATENS
NUCLEAR FUTURE

President Obama's commitment to "all of the above" energy development apparently does not include nuclear power in light of a January of 2012 order issued by his Secretary of the Interior, Ken Salazar, locking-up a million acres of federal land in northwestern Arizona that hold the nation's highest-grade uranium ore. That is according to lawsuits filed in Arizona federal district court by two mining groups—the Northwest Mining Association of Spokane, Washington, and the National Mining Association of Washington, D.C. allied with the Nuclear Energy Institute—challenging the legality and the constitutionality of the order.

"The Arizona Strip," which lies north of the Colorado River in northern Arizona, is bordered to the south by the northern rim of Grand Canyon National Park. In the 1984 Arizona Wilderness Act, Congress designated 250,000 acres of federal land on or near the Arizona Strip as wilderness and released 600,000 acres of land in the same area for multiple use, including uranium mining, as a result of a historic compromise among environmental groups, uranium mining interests, the livestock industry, and others. It was that compromise that permitted exploration for domestic sources of uranium. In fact, according to the U.S. Geological Survey, lands withdrawn by Salazar's order contain uranium that, if mined to capacity, would generate sufficient electricity to power the City of Los Angeles for 154 years.

Experts believe the United States must develop domestic sources of uranium in the face of higher prices and increased global demand. America is over 90 percent dependent on foreign sources of uranium to fuel the 104 nuclear reactors that provide power for 1 in 5 American homes and businesses. A major source of U.S. imports is uranium from dismantled Russian warheads; however, the agreement under which the U.S. purchases that uranium expires in 2013. There is currently a global supply shortfall of about 40 million pounds of uranium per year, which comes from existing stockpiles. With nuclear power generation around the world projected to increase substantially—even after Fukushima—these shortfalls will increase and stockpiles will dwindle. There are 435 nuclear reactors operating worldwide, but, according to the Nuclear Energy Institute, there are 65 reactors under construction and 491 reactors planned or proposed around the world. The World Nuclear Association estimates that there will be between 602 and 1,350 reactors in the world by 2030, a 38 percent to 210 percent increase. Therefore, worldwide competition for uranium will increase dramatically.

Nonetheless, environmental groups consistently attack efforts to develop domestic sources of uranium. For example, at the national level, leasing of uranium lands by the U.S. Department of Energy was halted by a lawsuit by environmental groups demanding more study. At the state level, a permit issued by Colorado for a uranium mill in economically hard-pressed Montrose County is under attack by environmental groups. Meanwhile, in 2009, Salazar joined in the assault by proposing to withdraw the million acres in Arizona allegedly to "protect the Grand Canyon watershed." Even though studies found no significant risk of environmental harm, Salazar issued his "emergency" withdrawal order in June of 2011.

According to the lawsuit, Salazar's order violates the Federal Land Policy and Management Act (FLPMA), the National Forest Management Act (NFMA), and the National Environmental Policy Act (NEPA). The lawsuit also complains that the FLPMA's provision permitting the Secretary to make withdrawals of 5,000 acres or more is illegal because it is linked to FLPMA's legislative veto provision, which unconstitutionally permits Congress to veto excessive Secretarial withdrawal orders. That is, Congress, which with the passage of FLPMA reasserted its constitutional authority over federal lands, would not have authorized the Secretary to withdraw more than 5,000 acres if Congress did not retain the right to reject any such order.

If America is to have a nuclear energy future, a federal court, perhaps the Supreme Court of the United States, will have to issue the order opening the door to that future.

APRIL 2012

JUNK SCIENCE, WEIRD SCIENCE, AND JUST PLAIN NONSENSE

At a recent three-day hearing before an Idaho federal district court on whether the court should restrict oil and gas and ranching activities over a vast area of federal land in western Wyoming, an expert summoned by the environmental group that filed the lawsuit testified, "The greater sage grouse is one stochastic, catastrophic event away from extirpation in Sublette County." That the moment passed without the judge, lawyers, and spectators convulsing into laughter indicates just how absurd what passes for scientific debate about the Endangered Species Act (ESA) has become. After all, everything on the planet is "one. . . . catastrophic event" away from annihilation.

Sadly, the outcome of that hearing, following briefings last month, is deadly serious. At risk are the future of energy development in Sublette County, which has two of America's largest, producing natural gas deposits, and the fate of family-owned ranching operations. It is just the beginning; the Sublette County case involves but one of 16 federal planning areas, covering 25 million acres in six western states, in the Idaho court. Worse yet, environmental groups demand the sage grouse's accommodation, regardless of the cost to humans and other species, all across its former range: 156 million acres in 11 western states. In response to one such plan, an expert called the sage grouse, "the northern spotted owl on steroids!"

The Wyoming case, says Dr. Rob Roy Ramey, illustrates the plan by the U.S. Fish & Wildlife Service (FWS) and environmental groups—one of whose leaders said, "[Why] sit in trees when there's [the ESA to] make people do whatever we want"—to narrow infinitely the ESA's focus and to widen exponentially its application. Dr. Ramey, the wildlife biologist who blew the whistle on the junk science used to list "the so-called Preble's meadow jumping mouse (PMJM)," says problems with the ESA go far beyond a lack of effective peer review.

The problems begin for the ESA when the FWS defines a "species," "sub-species," or "distinct population segment" because the FWS has no consistent thresholds and its listing decisions are highly subjective. For example, the "so-called PMJM" did not qualify for listing, argues Dr. Ramey, because the degree of measured difference between it and other purported subspecies of meadow jumping mice is less than that among mouse populations of the same subspecies. Dr. Ramey argues, only half-jokingly, that applying the FWS's approach to *Homo sapiens* would yield numerous subspecies and distinct population segments of mankind.

Moreover, as the Sublette County lawsuit shows, the FWS and environmental groups label a species "imperiled" in one location despite its vitality elsewhere—the sage grouse, for example, is a game bird in Wyoming and Montana. They make the same argument for species "peripheral populations" that are naturally at risk because the species have colonized, perhaps during unique climatic conditions, historically inhospitable areas. Finally, species advocates use national boundaries to create pockets of "imperiled" species that thrive across the border.

"Scientific findings" historically meant "reproducible" findings, but not for the FWS, which now uses models to predict conditions 30 to 100 years hence! Furthermore, the agency increasingly relies on published studies that are incestuous or self-serving (posted online by environmental groups, *e.g.*) and for which the underlying data are never made public. The FWS's greatest deficiency, however, is conflict of interest: its work is the product of "species cartels" afflicted with group think, confirmation bias, and a common desire to preserve the prestige, power, and appropriations of the agency that pays or employs them. For example, in a recent sage grouse monograph, 41 percent of the authors were federal workers and the editor, a federal bureaucrat, authored one-third of the papers!

There is good news. Congress, at least one federal judge, and conservation experts worldwide question the FWS's approach and call for reforms. Meaningful change, however, will not come in time for the areas targeted by environmental groups and like-minded federal bureaucrats.

JUNE 2012

COLORADO FIRES FAN FLAMES OF FEDERAL FOREST CONTROVERSY

It's hot in Colorado! It is not just that summer began officially a little over a week ago. Nor is it that last week Denver, with an average high temperature of 103.5°, hit the record of 105°, twice! Nor is it that a drought, which began in the winter of 2011-2012 and lasted through the spring, continues unabated. What makes Colorado so hot is that it appears to be burning up.

Colorado's 2012 "wildfire season" got a frighteningly early start with a March blaze in the forested foothills southwest of Denver. Caused by a controlled ("prescribed") burn—in warm weather and high winds—by the Colorado Forest Service, which got out of control, the Lower North Fork Fire forced the evacuation of 900 homes, destroyed or damaged two dozen homes, and killed three residents. Despite valiant efforts by firefighters, the weeklong blaze ended only with the arrival of an early April snow and cold temperatures. Although state officials ended prescribed burns, Coloradoans were fearful.

Then, on June 9, lightning struck in the Arapaho-Roosevelt National Forest west of Fort Collins; the High Park Fire was underway. A month later, with only 85 percent containment, the fire has blackened over 87,000 acres, destroyed 257 homes, and killed one resident. Suddenly it appeared that all of Colorado was ablaze: the Woodland Heights Fire near Rocky Mountain National Park, the Treasure Fire near Leadville, the Stateline Fire at the New Mexico border, the Little Sand Fire near Durango, and the Weber Fire near Mesa Verde National Park. The worst was yet to come.

On June 23, the Waldo Canyon Fire erupted in the Pike National Forest west of the state's second largest city, Colorado Springs, forced the evacuation of portions of that city and Manitou Springs, and closed The Garden of the Gods, Pike's Peak Highway, and the Air Force Academy to visitors. At 55 percent containment, the fire has destroyed nearly 18,000 acres and 346 homes—the most in Colorado history—and killed two residents. Colorado's fires may have put the state in the news, but it is not alone. The Little Bear Fire (near the home of Smokey the Bear) in New Mexico's Lincoln National Forest swept across 38,000 acres and destroyed 224 homes. Forest fires also burned in Arizona, Washington, and Wyoming.

The courage, dedication, and tenacity of the firefighters, on the ground and airborne, cannot be overstated; however, the ability of the U.S. Forest Service to fight these fires has been questioned. For example, FOX News contributor Michelle Malkin, who was evacuated from her Colorado home, derides the Forest Service's 2011 decision to cancel a contract for firefighting planes; later, the company shut down. Congressman Dan Lungren (R-3rd CA) condemned the action, "Our aerial firefighting fleet is already seriously undercapitalized."

Congressman Steve Pearce (R-2nd NM) argues, "We just can't keep managing our forests this way. It's not a question of if our forests in the West are going to burn; it's a matter of when." It is little wonder that the national forests in the West are tinderboxes. Environmental groups and activist judges use the Endangered Species Act, the National Environmental Policy Act (NEPA), and other federal laws to prevent forest management; in fact, days before the High Park Fire started, an Idaho federal judge killed a forest thinning project in response to the demands of environmental groups worried about the Canadian lynx.

Recently the U.S. Court of Appeals for the Ninth Circuit was asked to uphold the ruling of a Montana federal judge who rejected demands by environmental groups to stop a federal-state-local/public-private forest health project undertaken to prevent loss of human life during catastrophic fires. At oral argument, one judge inquired, "How many will die?" Apparently not enough; the three-judge panel reversed the decision because the plan did not provide enough elk cover. Today, in Colorado and the West, forests burn, homes are lost, and human beings die.

JULY 2012

'GUN-FREE ZONES' ARE NEVER GUN FREE

In the very early morning hours on July 20, I was in Aurora preparing to fly out of Denver International Airport when, standing at the gate, I pulled up the terrible news on my mobile telephone. As a Colorado resident since 1989, I was reminded of the day in 1999 when I rushed to pick up my sons from their Jefferson County public schools after gunmen invaded Columbine High School.

I thought as well of a snowy December day in 2007 when a gunman murdered missionaries and church-goers in Arvada and Colorado Springs. As in the hours following those tragic days, much remains unknown about the murders and the man who committed them; soon we will know more than we ever would have wanted.

Likewise, as occurred following those tragedies, yesterday, even before my flight landed on the East Coast, there were declarations by some, including New York City's Mayor Michael Bloomberg, that guns, gun-ownership, and Second Amendment rights are the reasons for these tragedies.

I write this in the darkness of Saturday's early morning hours knowing that, because the organization I lead defends the rights of law-abiding citizens to exercise their federal and state constitutional rights to keep and bear arms and, if they qualify, to carry concealed weapons, we will be described as part of this alleged "national problem." Such accusations ignore, not only that gun rights are supported overwhelmingly by the American people, but also that the Supreme Court of the United States affirmed those rights in two landmark rulings in 2008 and 2010. (In the latter case, Justice Alito cited to our brief.)

Furthermore, earlier this year, in a case we brought on behalf of Students for Concealed Carry on Campus and three Colorado students, a unanimous Colorado Supreme Court upheld the Colorado Concealed Carry Act, which allows those who qualify to carry firearms throughout Colorado—with four specific exceptions: locations prohibited by federal law, K-12 schools, public buildings with metal detectors, and private property. The court overruled attempts by the University of Colorado to set its own policies and bar concealed carry weapons and the exercise of Second Amendment rights on its campuses.

It appears that Cinemark Holdings Inc., owner of the theater where these murders took place exercises its rights as an owner of private property in Colorado to bar those who hold concealed carry permits from exercising their rights in its theaters. As a result, law-abiding citizens, including owners of concealed carry permits, who were in the theater that dreadful night were unarmed and thus unable to defend themselves and their fellow movie goers from the murderous attack visited upon them.

Opponents of the Second Amendment and concealed carry laws call the areas created by Cinemark's decision "gun-free zones." They are not. As we discovered to our great horror in the early morning hours of July 20 and as we have discovered in the past, they are free only of the guns owned by law-abiding citizens.

JULY 2012

EQUAL ACCESS TO JUSTICE ACT—
NEITHER EQUAL NOR JUST

Last month, Karen Budd-Falen, a Cheyenne, Wyoming attorney, presented her findings on the Equal Access to Justice Act (EAJA) to the 100th Anniversary Conference of the Rocky Mountain Coal Mining Institute in Vail, Colorado. After years researching court documents—the federal government keeps no records of EAJA disbursements—Ms. Budd-Falen found that environmental groups have amassed tens of millions of dollars in EAJA awards.

The EAJA was written for nobler purposes, however, which was to allow Americans forced to litigate against the federal government to be paid their attorneys' fees and expenses if they prevail and if the government's legal position is not "substantially justified." There is a cap on the hourly fees for which recovery is permitted, which according to Ms. Budd-Falen, has not limited fees paid to environmental groups, and an eligibility restriction based on net worth ($2 million for individuals and $7 million for entities), which specifically excepts tax-exempt (environmental) groups. The use of the EAJA by environmental groups is unique in two other ways, one not intended by Congress, the other not anticipated. Environmental groups recover fees for suing over non-injurious, technical violations of federal law, whereas most other EAJA applicants sue to vindicate constitutional or statutory rights. Finally, while environmental groups are paid quickly, private litigants are paid only after years, if ever.

Take John Shuler of Dupuyer, Montana, who killed a grizzly bear in self-defense—as allowed under the Endangered Species Act—but was prosecuted by the federal government for nearly a decade. Shuler prevailed only after his attorneys expended $225,000; however, federal courts denied his EAJA application, holding that the federal government's position in his case was "substantially justified." The courts did so despite the risible factual and legal arguments of federal lawyers: 1) Shuler did not act in self-defense despite that the bear charged and fell mortally wounded 20 feet from him; 2) Shuler, by leaving his house, unlawfully placed himself in the "zone of imminent danger," 3) Shuler's dog "Boone," by going on point, provoked the bear and "escalated" the conflict; and 4) bears are entitled to a higher standard of self-defense because they are not capable of sapient thought.

Or take Donald Eno, a disabled veteran on fixed income, seeking to eke out a living as a miner on his gold and travertine claim in the Plumas National Forest in northern California. In 1996, the U.S. Forest Service took legal action to drive Mr. Eno off his valuable claim. The government asserted, for example, that any mining would interfere with cultural myths allegedly important to some Maidu Indians; in fact, one Forest Service attorney met, unsuccessfully, with the Maidu urging them to so assert. In December of 2003, after years of pre-hearing preparation, testimony, and post-hearing briefs, an administrative law judge ruled in favor of Mr. Eno. The federal government appealed, but in February of 2007, Mr. Eno again prevailed. Although federal lawyers did not appeal, they challenged Mr. Eno's EAJA claim for nearly $200,000, a battle that, after more than five years, remains in federal court!

Or take Stanley K. Mann, a professor, lawyer, and alternative-energy entrepreneur, whose extremely valuable geothermal wells were seized illegally by federal officials. Beginning in April of 1998, Mr. Mann fought to recover payment for what had been taken from him; in April of 2009, Mr. Mann was awarded nearly $1 million. Despite his clear victory, the years invested in it, and the absence of any justification for the government's illegal actions, federal lawyers contested his nearly $300,000 EAJA claim. Almost three years later, Mr. Mann awaits a ruling.

Representative Cynthia Lummis (R-WY) has introduced legislation to restore the EAJA to its original intent, but passage of her bill is unlikely in the days that remain in the 112th Congress. Meanwhile, environmental groups are on the way to the bank with their huge awards while private citizens sit empty handed on the courthouse steps.

AUGUST 2012

UNIVERSITY OF COLORADO'S DUBIOUS COMMITMENT TO SAFETY

Late last month the University of Colorado (CU) made national news with its decision to segregate students who hold concealed carry permits in their own dormitory. CU's latest announcement on the subject—CU floated a different idea in April—comes in response to CU's stunning defeat at the Colorado Supreme Court in March of 2012. That is when a unanimous court held, "[T]he [Colorado Concealed Carry Act's] comprehensive statewide purpose, broad language, and narrow exclusions show that the General Assembly intended to divest the [CU] Board of Regents of its authority to regulate concealed handgun possession on campus."

The lawsuit that yielded the ruling was filed in 2008 by a national group with 43,000 members, Students for Concealed Carry on Campus, and three members—one a female—from CU's Boulder, Denver, and Colorado Springs campuses. In April of 2009, a state district court dismissed the case, but in April of 2010, a unanimous Colorado Court of Appeals reversed, holding, "Had the legislature intended to exempt [CU], it knew how to do so." Days earlier, a television station reported that "several people were attacked and robbed on [CU's Denver] campus or inside their dorm rooms," and "2 students were stabbed with a hatchet." The day after the ruling, the FBI, Secret Service, and the U.S. Department of Education reported targeted violence on college campuses was up sharply over the last two decades.

Despite "friend of the court" assistance from several anti-gun groups that filed a brief at the Colorado Supreme Court in support of CU and notwithstanding the court's reported liberal bent, CU lost resoundingly. Nonetheless, the litigation is not yet complete; it returns to the El Paso County district court for entry of judgment against CU and, if necessary, for a ruling on CU's ability to implement its evolving regulations to snatch victory from the jaws of defeat.

CU clearly does not like guns, even in the possession of those who pass the rigorous requirements imposed by the Colorado Concealed Carry Act as implemented by county sheriffs across the state. Firearms on campus, CU concluded and then argued in its briefs, "'seriously undermines' its academic mission, 'threatens the tranquility of the educational environment,' and 'contributes in an offensive manner to an unacceptable climate of violence.'" Averred CU, it alone possesses the "constitutional and statutory power[] to govern the University and pass regulations designed to promote the safety of students, employees, and campus visitors."

Ironically, CU's words ring hollow today, given criminal court proceedings regarding a former CU student who posed a real danger to himself and others. As the world now knows, on July 20, a former CU student slipped unseen into a midnight showing in a crowded Aurora theater; when he emerged, twelve people lay dead or dying and 70 people were wounded. In days, the media reported that he had been under the care of a CU mental health professional. What is not known is when did CU employees learn of the danger the student posed, to whom did they convey the information, and what action, if any, did they take to protect human life?

All the facts about CU and its former student are under a gag order; but, days ago a Colorado prosecutor asserted that CU knew, not in June, when the student dropped out of school and, as a non-student, had his key card deactivated, but in March. Thus, CU's apparent treatment of a threat posed by a potentially psychotic killer differed markedly from its attitude, at least prior to the March ruling, toward the non-existent threat from students with concealed carry permits. Alas, CU has posted a notice that it will bar permit-holders exercising their rights under Colorado law from any CU "concert, athletic event, or performance," the very type of venue in Aurora, Colorado, that declares itself "gun-free" and did so to the deadly detriment of innocent movie goers one terrible night in July.

SEPTEMBER 2012

CHAPTER TWENTY-FOUR

President Obama's Department of the Interior

———

In *Sagebrush Rebel, Reagan's Battle with Environmental Extremists and Why It Matters Today* (Regnery, 2013), I noted that "Reagan foresaw that the Soviet Union would collapse of its own weight, and he no doubt thought that the radical environmental movement—'environmental extremists,' as he called them—would share that fate. Unfortunately, the latter has not happened—yet. That is not to say that Reagan failed in his toe-to-toe battles with environmental groups, their allies in Congress, and the media. In the 1980s, Reagan deprived these extremists of the aura of inevitability, invincibility, and infallibility with which they had been cloaked for almost two decades. . . . When they said they spoke for the planet and the needs of all living things not human, he responded that he spoke for the dream of the American people and for unborn generations to be free and prosperous. Reagan countered the religious mysticism that drives the radical environmental movement with his own deep religious faith, which insists on the preeminence of human life. . . . [H]e exposed the childishness of radical environmentalists, who are incapable of being satisfied, always demand their own way, and, like the tyrants they are, never bring anything to the negotiating table—not even their good will or a sense of fair play. As Reagan succinctly put it in 1983, 'I do not think they will be happy until the White House looks like a bird's nest.'"

Oddly, "what allowed environmental extremists to continue to get their way was the economic recovery for which Reagan was responsible. . . . The demands by environmental groups for restrictions, limits, or land closures, which in tougher times would have resulted in a harsh economic burden, could be absorbed by [Reagan's] constantly growing economy. . . . No more. For twenty-five years, Gallup has asked people whether the economy or the environment is more important, and the environment has consistently out-polled the economy. In 2009, however, the lines crossed for the first time; those polled said the economy is more important. Given the state of the economy, the outlook for the future, and the intractable demands of the environmental movement, the lines may never cross again. . . . Ronald Reagan, I am confident, will turn out to have been right about the future of radical environmentalism."

IT'S STILL OBAMA'S DEPARTMENT OF THE INTERIOR

In the 1970 western, *Monte Walsh*, Lee Marvin plays the title character, a tough cowhand who ekes out a living in the last days of the old west hiring out for anything he can do from a horse. Barbed wire and railroads, however, close up the wide open prairie Walsh loves and condemn cowboys like him to obsolescence. After his partner (Jack Palance) and paramour (Jeanne Moreau) die tragically, Walsh goes on a drinking binge and rides an unbroken steed, destroying Main Street in the process. The owner of a wild west show watches in amazement and offers Walsh fame and, if not fortune, at least steady pay to wear fancy buckskins and perform for city folks. Walsh refuses with a snarl. "I ain't gonna spit on my whole life."

Monte Walsh comes to mind with President Obama's nomination of Sally Jewell, president and chief executive officer of Recreational Equipment, Inc. (REI), to replace Ken Salazar as Secretary of the Interior. The media mentions often that the British-born and Seattle-raised Jewell is a mechanical engineer whose first post-graduate job was with Mobil Oil in Oklahoma. After three years, Jewell hired on with a bank interested in the oil boom that needed engineers "to understand the value of the collateral in the ground." That bank was acquired by another; Jewell ran its business-banking activities. In her last role in a 20-year banking career, she led Washington Mutual's commercial-banking business. In 1996, she joined REI's board, in 2000 became its chief operating officer and, in 2005, its CEO. Neither Jewell's engineering degree nor her long ago and limited years in the oil patch define her as Monte Walsh's cowboying defined him.

That Jewell contributes almost exclusively to Democratic candidates is irrelevant; a president's nominee should support his party's views. Of concern, however, is REI's funding of the Conservation Alliance whose grantees brag of killing energy development in Arizona, Colorado, and Utah, for example. Also worrisome is Jewell's receipt of the Audubon Society's Rachel Carson Award for Environmental Conservation, unlikely had she, as an engineer, noted Carson's sloppy science, obvious overstatements, and dubious documentation, not to mention the human impact of *Silent Spring's* inspired DDT ban. Finally, despite the December of 2009 collapse of the house of cards that was the purported scientific basis for climate change doomsayers, REI pushes a "climate change" regulatory agenda and Obama, who called her a "climate expert," would not have nominated her if she were a climate change skeptic, let alone a "denier."

The bottom line is Secretary Jewell serves Obama whose views on oil and gas are well-known, especially since a *Wall Street Journal* report on his meeting with oilman Harold Hamm. Obama cut short Hamm's briefing on the revolution in the oil and gas industry, which would enable America to replace OPEC, "[W]e need to go on to green and alternative energy." Even had Jewell the inclination, let alone knowledge not three decades old, what luck will she have persuading Obama?

Obama brags about the revolution Hamm sought to discuss; however, the majority of hydraulic fracturing occurs on state and private lands (96 percent of the growth in oil production from 2007 to 2010 was on such lands), not federal lands, notwithstanding that the federal government owns a third of the nation's onshore acreage. Worse yet, Obama's Interior wants to require federal approval of fracturing—the activity has been regulated by states for nearly 60 years—at a cost of $1.6 billion annually. Meanwhile, Obama's Fish and Wildlife Service fines oil and gas operators for the occasional and accidental bird death while ignoring wind energy's regular avian slaughter. Finally, most of the billion acres the federal government owns on the Outer Continental Shelf (OCS) is closed to energy development.

The frequency with which Jewell's oil patch days are mentioned demonstrates an eternal hope that is uniquely American, but at Obama's Interior, there will be no change.

MARCH 2013

RONALD REAGAN'S GREATEST LEGACY:
DEFENDERS OF FREEDOM

In 1958, President Dwight D. Eisenhower proclaimed May 1 as "Law Day" and called upon Americans to "remember with pride and vigilantly guard the great heritage of liberty, justice, and equality under the law [that] our forefathers bequeathed to us." On the first Law Day, President Eisenhower urged Americans to "honor not only the principle of the rule of law," but also all "who actively work to preserve our liberties under law."

In 1982, President Ronald Reagan, marking the twenty-fifth anniversary of Law Day, paid tribute to "those courageous, far-sighted individuals who two centuries ago had the faith to believe that men and women could live in freedom under law." "In other parts of the world," Reagan noted, "May 1st is used for a different kind of celebration—a forced, unnatural observance of a system that promises a freedom it systematically denies, proclaims justice while practicing tyranny, and uses what it calls law as little more than a thin veneer for the edicts of a totalitarian elite." "We can and should be grateful to God that such is not true in America," he stressed; here "law remains the cornerstone of the freedom that we've been given. [But] we bear a solemn obligation to preserve it."

Long before he was president or even governor of California, Reagan spoke of that obligation. In March of 1961, he declared, "[F]reedom is never more than one generation away from extinction. We didn't pass it on to our children in the bloodstream. The only way they can inherit the freedom we have known is if we fight for it, protect it, defend it and then hand it to them with the well-thought lessons of how they in their lifetime must do the same. And if you and I don't do this, then you and I may well spend our sunset years telling our children and our children's children what it once was like in America when men were free."

Reagan knew the fight to protect and defend freedom must occur in the courtroom. In fact, it was his response to attacks on his legislative reform efforts by leftist groups that gave rise to the first freedom-based, public-interest legal foundation focused on a range of free enterprise, economic, and property rights issues. Of course, since 1968, the National Right to Work Legal Defense Foundation had battled *pro bono* in court to protect employees' legal rights against forced unionism abuses. Reagan, however, saw the need for a liberty-based legal defense group with a broader focus; so, in 1973, with his full support, Pacific Legal Foundation (PLF) opened its doors in Sacramento.

By the time Reagan ended his weekly radio addresses, which he had begun on leaving the governor's mansion, legal groups similar to PLF had spread across the country. In 1979, in his final radio address before he began his campaign for president of the United States, one titled "Miscellaneous and Goodbye," Reagan began, "The first item is, in my opinion, very serious for all of us and another indication of how far we are straying from the very basics of our system. The Mountain States Legal Foundation has filed a suit with the federal government claiming that the constitutional rights of several states are being violated. . . ."

Today, the liberty-based law movement, which began with the inspired response of Governor Reagan to the threats to the freedom of individual Americans is alive, well, and thriving. More importantly, from the point of view of Reagan's prime directive of defending freedom, that movement's *pro bono* representation of those who could not appear in the nation's courtrooms otherwise has made history. In fact, many of those clients reached the Supreme Court of the United States and there set legal precedents to benefit all Americans.

On Law Day 2013, America recognizes one of the greatest of Reagan's legacies: public-interest legal foundations dedicated to constitutional liberties and the rule of law.

MAY 2013

LAST [MINER] STANDING IN A COLORADO NATIONAL FOREST

At the Metropolitan Museum of Art (MOMA) in New York City, alabaster—calcite or gypsum, but also, onyx-marble, Egyptian or Oriental alabaster—with its swirls of cream and brown, form works from antiquity. From Egypt come "Fragmentary face of King Khafre" (*ca.* 2520–2494 B.C.), "Cosmetic Jar in the Form of a Cat," with inlaid eyes of rock crystal and copper (*ca.* 1991–1783 B.C.), and "Canopic Jar Lid," with glass and stone inlays (*ca.* 1340–1336 B.C.). Other exhibits, which span the centuries and the continent, include "Christ on the Road to Calvary" (German), "Saint James the Greater" (Spanish), and "Charity" (Franco-Flemish). Because of its ease of being carved, soft, smooth texture, white, delicately shaded color and translucence, alabaster is still sought after for decorative objects. It may be popular with the ancients, artisans over the ages, and admirers of sculpture, but it is not favored when modern man seeks to mine it.

One such man is Coloradoan Robert Congdon who owns ten mining claims within the White Banks Quarry—an alabaster, marble, and gypsum deposit—beneath Mount Sopris in the White River National Forest in north-central Colorado near Carbondale in Pitkin County. He located the claims in 1988 and, in 1992, filed a mining permit with the county and a plan of operations with the U.S. Forest Service. In 1998, the county granted a 20-year permit. Meanwhile, pursuant to the National Environmental Policy Act (NEPA), the Forest Service conducted an Environmental Analysis (EA) and approved his plan but limited operations to May 1 to November 15; however, the plan contemplated year-round operations after an initial trial period of Forest Service monitoring. Over the years, amendments were approved by the Forest Service, but Congdon was not authorized to operate during the winter and early spring.

In 2003, he sought authority to operate year-round, but Forest Service officials procrastinated and Congdon was forced to shut down. Despite the value of his deposit and the desire for his world-class alabaster, Congdon cannot operate economically unless he is able to work year round—frankly no business can afford to close six months each year. When the original plan of operations expired in 2010, he submitted a new plan to operate during the winter months. In April of 2011, after meeting with Forest

Service and Pitkin County officials, he modified his plan to reduce winter operating hours, minimize lighting, end winter camping by employees, and limit outdoor winter surface activity to loading and removing ore. Again the Forest Service procrastinated and approved an interim plan that allowed Congdon to work as before, but that was economically infeasible.

In response to the 2011 proposal, the Forest Service prepared yet another EA in which it considered three options: (1) take no-action; (2) approve Congdon's plan, or (3) restrict mining, once again, to the May through November period. In March of 2012, the District Ranger published a "Decision Notice and Finding of No Significant Impact (FONSI)" that barred all winter operations due to "issues raised about potential impacts to bighorn sheep during critical winter periods." Congdon appealed the decision and, in August of 2012, the Forest Supervisor reversed the District Ranger's decision after finding there was not enough evidence in the EA linking Congdon's proposed winter operations to the declining bighorn sheep population. The Forest Supervisor vacated the earlier decision and remanded the case to the District Ranger who, relying on the fatally flawed study, barred Congdon's full use of his mine.

Unfortunately, there are scores of NEPA-abuse cases by federal agencies across the country and over the decades but Congdon decided he would not be victimized by bureaucrats too cowardly to admit that, under the law, he must be granted reasonable use of his property. He sued the Forest Service and its officials. If his case makes it to the Supreme Court of the United States, perhaps he will go to MOMA and see its alabaster displays.

JUNE 2013

FEDERAL COURT: A RIGHT TO CARRY
OPENLY OUTSIDE THE HOME

Last month, a Colorado federal district court struck down a U.S. Postal Service regulation barring a rural man from possessing a firearm in his car when he parks in the Post Office parking lot to retrieve and send his mail. The news made headlines across the country as one of the first favorable federal court rulings after President Obama declared war on the Second Amendment in the wake of the Connecticut tragedy.

Tab Bonidy drives miles from his home to Avon to collect his mail, but because he regularly carries a concealed handgun pursuant to Colorado law, he is barred by a Postal Service regulation, adopted in 1972, from parking in the Post Office parking lot and entering the Post Office itself. In 2010, after landmark rulings by the Supreme Court of the United States in *District of Columbia v. Heller* and *McDonald v. City of Chicago*, Bonidy asked the Postal Service if he would be prosecuted if he carried his firearm into the Post Office or locked it in his vehicle in the Post Office parking lot. The Postal Service's top lawyer wrote back, "carrying firearms, openly or concealed, onto any real property under the charge and control of the Postal Service" is still barred by Postal Service regulation.

On two separate occasions the district court denied attempts by the U.S. Department of Justice to dismiss Bonidy's lawsuit and during oral arguments sharply challenged the federal lawyer's assertion that the Avon Post Office parking lot is a "sensitive" place that allows the Postal Service to curtail Second Amendment rights. Then, last month during oral arguments on cross motions for summary judgment, the judge upbraided the federal lawyer thusly, "there's a difference between all of this broad, general restriction and an individual situation.... You know, this is more of what we are seeing[;] regulatory authority prevails, period. It isn't going to happen [here]."

Days later the district court issued its ruling. Because it was bound by recent precedent from the U.S. Court of Appeals for the Tenth Circuit regarding the right to carry a concealed weapon outside the home, the district court addressed whether the Second Amendment protects the right to carry openly outside the home. The district court concluded that the Supreme Court in *Heller* upheld a constitutional right to carry firearms openly outside the home for self-defense subject only to reasonable public safety related restrictions. Just what are those restrictions?

As to the interior of the Avon Post Office, the district court found it a "sensitive" place and thus the Postal Service's regulation presumptively valid there. The matter of the public parking lot, however, is another story. Government ownership alone is not sufficient, held the district court, to restrict constitutional liberties. The lot is not a government building, nor is it a place where government business is conducted, nor is there meaningful limitation on those who enter it; in fact, the Postal Service lot is little different from other nearby public lots.

Therefore, the Postal Service justifies its regulation with "a history of firearm violence on postal property based on a study of workplace violence [on the basis of which it] makes broad, conclusory statements..." That rationale, which involves "administrative convenience and saving expenses," might be sufficient, held the district court, except that the case involves Bonidy's right to protect himself, "the core concern of the Second Amendment."

"In sum," ended the district court, "openly carrying a firearm outside the home is a liberty protected by the Second Amendment.... The parking lot adjacent to the building is not a sensitive place and the [Postal Service] failed to show that an absolute ban on firearms is substantially related to [its] important public safety objective." Thus, it is "unconstitutional."

The expected appeal by federal lawyers is due in early September at the Tenth Circuit, the next stop in a case likely to reach the Supreme Court of the United States.

AUGUST 2013

OILMAN WITH REAGAN-ERA LEASE STILL
WAITING TO DRILL, SUES

In September of 1981, President Reagan determined whether to grant permission to drill on a federal oil and gas lease in Wyoming. In the summer of 1981, two federal agencies completed months of study of an application for permit to drill (APD) by an oil company that owned a lease in the Bridger-Teton National Forest southeast of Jackson in Teton County. They concluded the APD should be granted. When the recommendation reached Washington, Wyoming's congressional delegation was briefed that Secretary Jim Watt would approve the APD. Meanwhile, environmental groups were gearing up for a major battle on the issue.

Future Wyoming Governor Mike Sullivan, a Democrat, learned the opposition had gone beyond angry words. Death threats had been issued against Watt, threats that Sullivan thought serious enough to convey directly to his fraternity brother Watt. Then Watt heard from a unanimous and Republican Wyoming delegation: deny the APD! In time, Watt had a meeting in the Oval Office; he feared he was about to let Reagan down. Reagan stiffened Watt's backbone. "No," Reagan declared and then uttered a paraphrase of remarks that would become famous in his Second Inaugural Address: "If not us, who? If not now, when?"

President Reagan consistently demonstrated rare courage in his efforts to permit Americans to discover energy on the nation's "federal lands," which he reminded, "the very term means it belongs, to us—to the people of America." Reagan would be shocked to learn that a man issued a federal oil and gas lease less than a year after that White House meeting has been unable to drill for over 30 years.

In June of 1982, the Bureau of Land Management (BLM) issued Sidney M. Longwell of Baton Rouge, Louisiana, a 6,247 acre oil and gas lease in the Badger-Two Medicine Area of Lewis and Clark National Forest in Glacier County in northwestern Montana. In 1983, Mr. Longwell assigned the lease to America Petrofina Company of Texas, which later became Fina Oil and Chemical Company (Fina). In October of 1983, Fina submitted an APD to drill to evaluate the natural gas potential of that part of the Overthrust Belt. After extensive review pursuant to the National Environmental Policy Act (NEPA) and the National Historic Preservation Act

(NHPA), seventy-six (76) separate appeals, and a ruling by the Interior Board of Land Appeals (IBLM), the BLM, in consultation with the U.S. Forest Service, the Montana Department of Fish, Wildlife, and Parks, and the U.S. Fish and Wildlife Service, approved the APD in 1985, in 1987, in 1991, and in January of 1993.

In April of 1993, seven environmental groups filed a lawsuit challenging the approved APD; the lawsuit ended in 1997. Meanwhile, Senator Max Baucus (D-MT) introduced legislation to bar surface disturbances on oil and gas leases in the area and to evaluate the area for wilderness designation; he also demanded Secretary Bruce Babbitt impose a moratorium on oil and gas drilling there. In June of 1993, Secretary Babbitt suspended activity on the lease purportedly to await congressional action. In 1994 and 1995, he extended the suspension for the same reason. In 1996, he continued the suspension, this time asserting it was necessary to comply further with the NHPA. In 1997, he extended the NHPA-related suspension and finally, in 1998, he continued it indefinitely!

In 1999, in the face of the interminable delay, Fina assigned its lease and APD rights back to Mr. Longwell. In July of 2004, he assigned his rights to his company Solenex, LLC, which, in May of 2013, asked that the suspension be lifted; that request was denied. In June of 2013, Mr. Longwell sued Secretary Sally Jewell and others.

Is it any wonder that the miracle of hydraulic fracturing that has produced untold energy riches all across the country has been exclusively on state and private lands, and not on the third of the country owned by the federal government?

SEPTEMBER 2013

SCOTS-IRISH ENCOUNTER THE KING'S MEN IN THE OZARK FOREST

In 1808, a Scots-Irish family named McIlroy heard news of the Louisiana Purchase and farmland that was plentiful there, left their home in Tennessee, and headed west. Across the Mississippi River, two hundred miles west of Memphis, south of the Ozark Plateau's Boston Mountains, and north of the Arkansas River, the family homesteaded three parcels at Fly Gap, Beech Grove, and Cass. Arkansas Territory was established in 1819; Arkansas won statehood in 1836; and the million-acre Ozark National Forest, which surrounded the McIlroy farm, was proclaimed in 1908.

In 1933, Congress created the Civilian Conservation Corps (CCC), units of which were located on federal land managed by, among other entities, the U.S. Forest Service. One CCC camp was placed in the Ozark National Forest and was responsible for constructing over 300 miles of trails. After World War II, the CCC was discontinued, but in 1964 President Johnson signed the Economic Opportunity Act—part of his Great Society campaign and War on Poverty—which created the Job Corps, modeled after the CCC, to provide "vocational and academic training." A Job Corps camp was established in the Ozark National Forest near Cass.

Beginning in the late 1960s, W.C. McIlroy complained that Job Corps students were trespassing on and littering his property, damaging his fences, and destroying his hay; his objections went unanswered. In 1971, he died and his son, W.L. McIlroy, took over the farm only to discover that the Forest Service had drilled a well on his property. He protested, but Forest Service officials said the well, used as a water source for Job Corps facilities, was on federal land. Over the years, a string of Job Corps directors, Forest Service rangers, and Forest Service officials repeated that statement, over the family's protestations.

In 1973, unbeknownst to W.L. McIlroy, the Job Corps used heavy equipment to tear down a 100-year old levee built just upstream of the farm at the confluence of Mulberry River and Fane's Creek to protect the farm and the site of the Job Corps facility. The result was flooding and erosion downstream, alteration of the bed of Mulberry River due to silting and deposits of eroded rock, and destruction of 10 acres of the farm. Subsequent actions by the Forest Service, which included removing fill, laying culverts, and pouring concrete, only exacerbated the problem: water widened the channel across the farm to Mulberry River.

In 1998, Matthew McIlroy, W.L.'s son, who had taken over the farm, discovered part of his fence had been flattened, a sewage effluent line installed over it and across 50-60 yards of the farm, and Job Corps sewage effluent discharged from his property into Mulberry River. Subsequently, he discovered the Forest Service installed a "temporary" water line that ran a quarter mile across his land and blocked entry to his farm; continued to use the water well—even though a later federal survey proved the well was on the farm; trespassed with heavy equipment onto the farm to blade dirt and drag drainage ditches; built a service road across the farm to access the well and the sewage effluent line and poured concrete on the road when it eroded; used parts of the farm for heavy equipment training, digging down to creek rock, causing serious erosion, destroying fences, and resulting in the loss of escaping livestock; and, dumped concrete and construction waste on its property near the farm, effluent from which washed onto the farm.

In January of 2013, a Forest Service official "document[ed] the encroachment on [the McIlroy's] property." Nonetheless, the Forest Service refused to compensate Mr. McIlroy or remove those encroachments. Under the Federal Tort Claims Act, which permits recompense when the government's employees commit torts, Mr. McIlroy filed an administrative claim on which he will sue if it is denied. Meanwhile, he wonders whether his clansmen in the days of William Wallace ever saw greater abuses by "the King's men."

OCTOBER 2013

JEWELL'S ACTIONS DASH HOPE FOR CHANGE AT INTERIOR

Early on Secretary of the Interior Sally Jewell was welcomed with bipartisan enthusiasm. She is a petroleum engineer who spent: a few years working for a major energy company in the Oklahoma oil patch; 19 years as a commercial banker; and, over a decade as an executive with REI, finally as its CEO. To find a secretary with a similar life-long business background, one must go back to Ethan A. Hitchcock (1899 to 1907). In his early sixties Hitchcock left business for his first presidential appointment; Jewell did so in her late fifties. Today, however, Secretary Jewell has lost her luster.

Secretary Jewell's first episode of political thuggery was her ham-handed attempt to silence those who dissent from the received wisdom on climate change. She warned Interior employees, "I hope there are no climate change deniers in the Department of Interior." The former engineer, who should be used to scholarly disagreement, did not say "skeptics," "dissenters," or "doubters," but "deniers," a pejorative linked to the Holocaust.

Her timing is odd. Climate change orthodoxy began collapsing in November of 2009 with the release of data from the Climate Research Unit at the University of East Anglia. Weeks before her comments, the *Economist*, long alarmist on the subject, wrote "Over the past 15 years air temperatures at the Earth's surface have been flat while greenhouse-gas emissions have continued to soar." Days ago, three prominent scientists faulted the promotion of "scary scenarios as if they were forecasts," noting they are "neither forecasts nor the product of a validated forecasting method."

In another political call, Secretary Jewell forged ahead with plans to regulate hydraulic fracturing. Days ago thousands of comments were filed, most of which were in opposition, including those from energy producing states, which have been regulating the activity for decades. In a bit of irony given Secretary Jewell's pledge to respect tribal sovereignty, the strongest opposition came from the Southern Ute Indian Tribe.

States, tribes, and energy groups argue the rules address a remote, speculative, and totally non-existent harm; one association called them, "a solution in search of a problem." They are duplicative, vague, and unduly burdensome, impose financial burdens on the states, ensure delays, including endless litigation by environmentalists after the BLM issues permits, and generate additional costs for the energy industry and hence the American public. The Western Energy Alliance says the cost to 13 states will exceed $345 million annually and cost $100,000 per well.

These two issues—involving matters of scientific integrity and potential energy self-sufficiency—pale by comparison with actions by the National Park Service (NPS). In October, the agency whose employees were once the proud protectors of and friendly facilitators of visitors to America's beautiful and historic places became the service that barred veterans, their survivors, families, and friends from access to national war memorials.

At Mount Vernon, the NPS kept visitors from the privately owned home of George Washington and, elsewhere across the country, the NPS closed or sought to close or bar access to private facilities located on or accessed via federal land. In South Dakota, the NPS blocked scenic overlooks with views of Mount Rushmore. In Arizona, access to the Grand Canyon through the town of Tusayan was shut down with devastating effect on private businesses. Finally, in Wyoming, at Yellowstone National Park, a tour group was locked in a hotel under armed NPS guard.

Reporters fault the NPS or even the NPS's career director; that is not where the blame lies. The NPS has its faults but it zealously protects its reputation for non-partisan professionalism. The speed with which the NPS moved, its attempt to inconvenience the maximum number of people, and its expenditures of additional time, money, and material demonstrate that the order came, not from the NPS Director, but from the Office of the Secretary and likely Secretary Jewell herself. So much for "hope and change" at Obama's Interior Department.

NOVEMBER 2013

MODERN-DAY LUDDITES IN MORA COUNTY, NEW MEXICO

President Reagan would not have been surprised by the 2-1 vote of the Mora County, New Mexico Commission in April of 2013 prohibiting oil and gas activities, not just those using hydraulic fracturing, and waging war on corporate entities. Reagan would call them "modern-day Luddites." "For those who don't know," Reagan explained, "the Luddites were people who wanted to stop the industrial revolution back in the last century. They took to the streets and tried to smash factory machinery then."

"Modern-day Luddites," however, need not take to the streets; instead, they can rush to a courthouse. Declared one, "We're crazy to sit in trees when there's this incredible law[, the Endangered Species Act (ESA),] where we can make people do whatever we want." Therefore, as Stephen Moore wrote in the *Wall Street Journal*, environmental groups, using the ESA, sue federal officials who in turn quickly settle the lawsuits, pay off the groups, and close lands to oil and gas activity.

Meanwhile, encouraged by the lawlessness in Washington, D.C., where federal officials imperially channel Humpty Dumpty ("When I use a word, it means just what I choose it to mean—neither more nor less."), local officials who want to stop energy development adopt a "sue us if you dare" strategy. Using a perfect storm of environmental extremism, leftwing political demagoguery, and runaway NIMBY-ism (not-in-my-back-yard-ism), these officials blatantly ignore constitutional guarantees and federal and state laws.

Thus it was that Mora County, New Mexico, population 4,881, which sits astride I-25, assisted by a radical "environmental" group from Pennsylvania, adopted a "local bill of rights" that bars use of hydraulic fracturing, forbids all oil and gas development, and strips corporate entities of their constitutional and legal rights across the county's 1,993 square miles. The Community Environmental Legal Defense Fund, which drafted the ordinance and 150 others like it around the country, says it is part of a "growing people's movement for community and nature's rights."

Although some ordinance supporters are dismayed that Mora County is being used by an outside advocacy group as a "soapbox," especially given its potential cost—$100,000, even with free lawyers—others are eager to slug it out in court. "We're ready for this fight," said one commissioner in response to a lawsuit filed in November by three landowners and a trade organization—the Independent Petroleum Association of New Mexico—asserting a host of constitutional violations and breaches of federal and state law.

Much is at stake. New Mexico has been a major producer of oil and natural gas since their discovery in the state in the 1920s; they are a lynch-pin of the state's economy and are essential for its continued fiscal health. In 2012, 27 percent of New Mexico's general fund revenues came from taxes and royalties on oil, natural gas, and carbon dioxide production. Over the years, oil and gas activity has contributed over 90 percent of the principal in the Severance Tax and Land Grant Permanent Funds, the earnings on which are used to fund schools, special charities and institutions, and other state governmental operations. Other petroleum tax receipts go directly into the state's general budget. More than 88,000 New Mexican citizens are employed directly by the oil and gas industry.

Since 1978, that industry has been regulated by the New Mexico Oil and Gas Act, which created the Oil Conservation Commission and Oil Conservation Division; they have complete "jurisdiction, authority and control" over the development of oil or gas. The Division regulates these activities to protect fresh water, public health, safety and the environment and issues rules for "safety procedures for drilling and production of oil and gas wells."

The battle in Mora County is not about protecting people, land, or water; that is obvious from the ordinance's narrow, oil patch, focus. Instead it is over the primacy of the Constitution and the rule of law or whether America devolves into Chicken-Little Mob Rule.

DECEMBER 2013

CHAPTER TWENTY-FIVE

Still Fighting After All These Years

★ ★ ★ ★ ★

On January 14, 2014, I sat at counsel table before the justices of the Supreme Court of the United States. It was three days short of 19 years from the day of my first of three appearances at the Court in the *Adarand* case. My son Perry, a Marine Judge Advocate, who had been sworn in as a member of the Bar of the Court by Chief Justice Roberts, sat directly behind me. Today, however, I would not argue for MSLF's client, Marvin Brandt of Fox Park, Wyoming. Steven J. Lechner, MSLF's Vice President and Chief Legal Officer did that.

I reflected that the case began on February 23, 2006, when I received an email from Bob Johnson, president of the Fox Park Home Owners Association, "Since you graduated from the UW Law School, you probably know where our community is located." I did.

"On January 12, 2006," he wrote, "the U S. Forest Service notified the majority landowner in our subdivision, Mr. Marvin Brandt that the Forest Service has requested the Department of Justice to file a legal action in the United States District Court for the District of Wyoming to declare the abandoned railroad bed through Fox Park, Albany, and Mountain Home as property of the United States [to] pave the way for a 'Rails to Trails' project to run through the gut of each of the three communities..." He noted he prepared a package of materials, including federal court rulings, "in favor of the property owners. We have pointed this out to the Forest Service, but they are bringing the big guns after us." Finally, "We have met with the Forest Service in Laramie, and have been told that they intend to take this to the Supreme Court to set a precedent that applies across the Country. This is extremely upsetting because the three communities do not have the resources to fight this." I sent the email to one of MSLF's attorneys; days later he was at Mr. Brandt's home.

In early June of 2006, MSLF approved representation of Mr. Brandt; therefore, when the federal government brought a quiet title action against him on July 14, 2006, MSLF filed an answer and a counterclaim. For nearly eight years, MSLF represented Mr. Brandt before five federal courts culminating in an appearance before the Supreme Court. On March 10, 2014, the Court ruled 8-1 in favor of Mr. Brandt and remanded the case to the lower federal courts.

MELVIN AND LULA BRANDT'S SON
BEFORE THE U.S. SUPREME COURT

In 1936, Melvin and Lula Brandt, in a Chevy they owned outright, drove from Mountain View, Missouri to the Medicine Bow National Forest of southeastern Wyoming. When they reached Fox Park, which grew out of the transcontinental railroad's need for cross ties made from the lodgepole pine that carpets mid-elevations of the forest, they had two dollars. Like thousands of other young men in the midst of the Great Depression, Melvin Brandt was looking for work and found it among the hearty Scandinavians who logged the forest.

He hired on to cut ties for Ole Alexander. With borrowed tools and boots, Melvin Brandt hiked into the woods, cut down a tree of at least an 11-inch diameter with a one-man crosscut saw, scored the sides with a six-pound double-bit axe to create a minimum seven inch by four inch face, removed the scored wood with a broadaxe, and cut the shaped wood into eight foot lengths, each of which he lugged to the nearest road. Melvin Brandt got a nickel a tie. Soon he could produce twenty a day.

John Wicklund who left Sweden at 14, arrived in New York City speaking no English, and worked in Minnesota logging camps, was Ole Alexander's wood's boss. He and Melvin Brandt became friends, bought out Ole Alexander in 1946, formed Brandt & Wicklund Forest Products, and, by 1951 built a permanent sawmill. The U.S. Forest Service, responsible for the 284 million board feet of annually producible timber generated by the forest's million plus acres, had planned for such a mill on the "Fox Park Industrial Site" tract.

John Wicklund ran the men and horses that harvested the timber and hauled it to the mill that Melvin Brandt operated; at its height it was processing six million board feet annually, employing 60 men. Since 1910, the Laramie, Hahn's Peak & Pacific Railway Company had run a railroad from Laramie, Wyoming, through the Fox Park site, and then south to the Wyoming-Colorado border along a 200-foot-wide, 66 miles long right-of-way. The railroad brought in supplies and transported milled timber to Laramie and beyond. In 1976, the Forest Service traded 200 acres Melvin Brandt owned on Sheep Mountain plus 40 acres near Fox Park for

83 acres in Fox Park occupied by the mill, houses and cabins, a church, pool hall, hotel, general store, school and saloon.

Melvin and Lula's son Marvin, raised amidst the woods, the mill, and the hard work, went to college, but soon returned. Unfortunately, after the 1980 recession, times were hard and changing. The Forest Service was no longer interested in letting Marvin Brandt harvest the timber; instead, it left it to the pine beetle. It did not matter that the vast forest, properly managed, could sustain scores of operations like Brandt's mill.

In 1991, a young woman spoke to locals at the Hungry Woodsmen of her vision that, after the Wyoming and Colorado Railroad, as it was then known, pulled up its tracks and ties, a high-altitude bicycle trail could be built in its place all paid for by local businesses; Marvin Brandt proclaimed he was that local business and was nearly finished. That year, he sold the mill and its equipment for pennies on the dollar.

In 2003 Marvin Brandt accidently learned of Forest Service plans to build the trail; the agency "forgot" to tell him and his neighbors. Despite the 9,000 foot elevation, snow cover from November to mid-June, and the lodgepole pine's attempt to reclaim the path, the Forest Service audaciously predicted 120,000 bikers annually! First, however, the Forest Service sued Marvin Brandt and seized the abandoned railroad right-of-way across his land.

On January 14, Marvin Brandt will sit before the justices of the Supreme Court of the United States to hear a government lawyer argue why the laws, documents, and court rulings that apply to everyone else do not apply to the federal government.

JANUARY 2014

IDAHO WOMAN DEFEATS OBAMA'S
TOP LAWYERS ON GUNS

President Obama's Justice Department left nothing to chance last month in a major Second Amendment battle being fought in Idaho that will affect millions of acres of federal land throughout the country. Pushing aside Idaho's United States Attorney, a top Justice lawyer flew to Boise to argue that the U.S. Army Corps of Engineers' prohibition on possession of a functional firearm at its public recreational sites in 43 states is constitutional. Shortly after the lawyer got back to Washington, but likely before he filed his expense report, the Idaho federal district court ruled for the Idaho woman who filed the lawsuit.

Most Americans would be surprised to learn that the Corps is the nation's largest provider of water-based outdoor recreation; in fact, it administers 422 lake and river projects in 43 states spanning 12 million acres, including over 700 dams—that hold back over 100 trillion gallons of water—encompassing 55,000 miles of shoreline, 4,500 miles of trails, 90,000 campsites, and 3,400 boat launch ramps. Waters under its control constitute 33 percent of all U.S. freshwater fishing and attract 300 million visitors a year. Unfortunately for those visitors and contrary to the Supreme Court's 2008 ruling in *District of Columbia v. Heller*, a regulation adopted by the Corps in 1973 bars the carrying of firearms for self-defense and the possession of functional firearms in temporary residences on its lands.

The Corps' regulation is a problem for Elizabeth E. Morris of Lewiston in Nez Perce County who was issued an emergency license in 2012 by the Nez Perce County Sheriff to carry a concealed handgun due to threats and physical attacks against her by a former neighbor. She regularly carries a handgun for self-defense and regularly uses Corps-administered public lands near the Snake River in Lewiston, Idaho, to boat with friends, regularly walks the Corps-administered paths in the area with her dog, and/or her family, and must travel across Corps-administered lands to reach Hells Gate State Park, which accesses Hells Canyon, the deepest river gorge in North America.

After seeking an exemption from the Corps' regulation via its federal attorneys and getting no response, in August of 2013, Ms. Morris and another Idahoan filed a lawsuit in Idaho federal district court and sought an immediate, nationwide preliminary injunction barring the Corps from enforcing its regulation against her and subjecting her to arrest—or worse. The Corps opposed that motion and moved to dismiss her lawsuit. The Idaho federal district court not only rejected the dismissal motion, it also ruled that Ms. Morris was likely to win her lawsuit and was entitled to the injunction.

Noting that the Corps' "regulation bans carrying a loaded firearm for the purpose of self-defense [and] carrying an unloaded firearm along with its ammunition" and that "[a]n unloaded firearm is useless for self-defense purposes without its ammunition," the district court held that the regulation "burden[s] [Morris'] Second Amendment rights." Further, the district court held that the regulation's ban on "firearms and ammunition in a tent on the Corps' sites" "poses a substantial burden on a core Second Amendment right. . . ." Finally, the district court concluded that, because the "regulation contains a flat ban on carrying a firearm for self-defense purposes[,]" which "completely ignor[es] the right of self-defense, [it] cannot be saved. . . ." As a result, the district court found the regulation "simply too broad [because] it violates the Supreme Court's description of Second Amendment rights in [*Heller*]. This regulation needs to be brought up to date."

The Idaho district court did not stop there. After determining that Ms. Morris is likely to prevail following an "evidentiary hearing or trial," the district court prohibited the Corps from enforcing its regulation "as to law-abiding individuals possessing functional firearms on Corps-administered public lands for the purpose of self-defense." That means, in time, on Corps sites from California to Connecticut, from Minnesota to Mississippi, Second Amendment rights prevail. Over to you, Mr. President.

FEBRUARY 2014

NEW YORK LANDOWNERS FIGHT BACK, SUE GOVERNOR CUOMO

In February, a coalition of New York landowners and three property owners sued Governor Andrew Cuomo, two state agencies, and their top officials demanding the right to develop the rich Marcellus Shale beneath their land. After nearly six years of a moratorium barring landowners from developing energy on their land pending an environmental study, rural residents have waited long enough. One of them is Jonathan R. Kark of Fenton.

Jon Kark represents his family's sixth generation on the land; he and his wife Patricia own 353 acres of land in north-central Broome County, northeast of Binghamton, the county seat, where they run 50 head of cattle. Jon Kark and his wife have four children and four grandchildren. Jon Kark prefers to run cattle, operate his trucking company, help with the nonprofit, non-denominational Christian camp his father created in 1970 on part of the farm, and be with his family, but for the last six years he has been everywhere but home.

In July of 2007, he leased his mineral rights to an independent oil and gas company for a five-year term; if the company drilled, made a discovery, and produced natural gas, it would pay a royalty. Bad news accompanied the good news; the potential value of that gas increased his property taxes. More bad news came in July of 2008. Then Governor Paterson imposed a moratorium on permits for wells using horizontal drilling and hydraulic fracturing (HF)—the six decades old technology whose modern day application unlocked vast amounts of energy on state and private land across America—until completion of an environmental study.

In June of 2009, anticipating completion of the study and seeking to make the highest and best use of Jon Kark's mineral estate by producing its oil and gas, his lessee filed six horizontal well applications. By that time, Jon Kark had left town. Fearing loss of the family farm under the pressure of its mortgage and the county's taxes, he hired on as a heavy equipment operator to develop energy resources from coast to coast. In 2012, Jon Kark got lucky: in July, his lessee extended its term for another five years—until 2017—and in December, he was home for two weeks at Christmas. In 2013, he was home one week.

The irony for Jon Kark and those with whom he joined in filing the lawsuit—including the Joint Landowners Coalition of New York with its 38 landowner groups that represent over 70,000 landowners and a million acres across fourteen counties—is that the policy of New York is to promote development of indigenous oil and natural gas resources so as to prevent waste, protect correlative rights, and provide for greater ultimate recovery of these resources. Plus, every agency and its officials are mandated to adhere to the state's energy policy, including processing oil and gas well permit applications "as expeditiously as possible."

Specifically, the Department of Environmental Conservation (DEC), which oversees the regulation of oil and natural gas drilling, is required by the State Environmental Quality Review Act (SEQRA) not only to consider various factors prior to approving activities that may have an adverse effect on the environment but also to expedite proceedings to minimize procedural and administrative delays in obtaining drilling permits. In fact, in 1992, to streamline the well permitting process, the DEC prepared a Generic Environmental Impact Statement (GEIS) that recognized use of horizontal drilling and HF. In 2008, the Environmental Conservation Law was amended as to spacing requirements of drilling units for wells using horizontal drilling and HF, and the DEC began its study.

In nearly six years, the DEC released a "draft supplemental" GEIS, received thousands of public comments, held multiple public meetings, and issued a "revised draft supplemental" GEIS, but the final GEIS remains unpublished! Meanwhile, Jon Kark does whatever it takes to save his farm that is dying from high taxes and regulatory overkill.

MARCH 2014

OBAMA'S EPA HANGS ITSELF;
SECRETARY JEWELL HOLDS THE ROPE

In an administration infamous for ignoring the Constitution and the rule of law, the Environmental Protection Agency (EPA) stands out. President Obama's EPA: administratively implemented "cap and trade" after the Senate refused to enact requisite legislation; killed a multimillion dollar West Virginia coal mine by vetoing the Army Corps of Engineers' approval—action so unprecedented 27 state attorneys general urged Supreme Court review; and, sought to "crucify" energy companies in the nation's most productive oil and gas region, all while a senior, regulation-writing, job-killing employee masqueraded as a CIA agent and defrauded American taxpayers of nearly $900,000.

In December, however, the EPA outdid itself with the extraordinary decision that a million acres of land in west-central Wyoming, including the town of Riverton, lie within the Wind River Indian Reservation. Purportedly, the EPA's action is required by the Clean Air Act's provision allowing tribes to obtain the authority available to states to regulate their air quality programs but, in doing so, the EPA subjected land long known to be outside the Reservation to the tribal jurisdiction of the Northern Arapaho and Eastern Shoshone. In February, Wyoming challenged the EPA's ruling in the U.S. Court of Appeals for the Tenth Circuit in Denver. Days later, the Wyoming Farm Bureau Federation, on behalf of its members who live and/or work in Riverton and in greater Fremont and Hot Springs Counties, joined in the lawsuit.

Westerners, elected officials, and commentators nationwide heaped deserved abuse on the EPA, but there is plenty of blame to go around. The EPA wrote that it received "input from other federal agencies," and that its "determination is consistent with a 2011 Opinion of the Solicitor of the U.S. Department of the Interior." Secretary Sally Jewell's Interior, home of the Indian Bureau since 1824, is the 500-pound gorilla on this issue, as it has been since 1873 when Congress transferred territorial responsibilities for the American West there from the State Department.

The Reservation was established in 1868, but, in 1904, the Tribes entered into an agreement with the United States to cede 1.48 million acres of land in exchange for per capita payments to tribal members and capital improvement projects within the Reservation. In 1905, Congress ratified the agreement, declared the lands were "ceded, granted, relinquished, and conveyed" to the United States, and referenced the new Reservation as "the diminished reserve." In 1906, the ceded lands were opened for settlement by Presidential Proclamation; the land was sold to non-Indians, including land that became Riverton. In 1939, some of the unsold ceded lands were restored to the Reservation, but much of the land, including all land within Riverton city limits, was not.

Over the decades, Congress, the Supreme Court of the United States, and the Wyoming Supreme Court wrote of "lands formerly embraced in the [Reservation]," of the "diminished reservation," and of lands that were "ceded, granted, and relinquished." Challenges by tribal members of their convictions in state court for crimes committed in Riverton—putative "Indian country"—were rejected, on one occasion with *amicus* support for Wyoming from the United States.

Unfortunately, the Solicitor made unmitigated hash of this undisputed history. In fact, her opinion slavishly tracks the Tribes' 2008 EPA application in which they cherry-pick bits of congressional hearings and self-serving tribal documents but ignore court rulings, the 1904 agreement, the 1905 Act, and their precise and binding language. Most egregious is the Solicitor's failure to address a 1998 ruling of the Supreme Court on another tribe's similar assertion. A unanimous Court, in an opinion by Justice O'Connor, held Congress set forth "the most certain statutory language, evincing [its] intent to diminish the [Reservation] by providing for total cession and fixed compensation."

Last month, in another case from Wyoming, the Supreme Court rebuked the federal government for ignoring 139 years of legal precedent. The EPA will suffer the same fate, to paraphrase that ruling, for its "improbable (and self-serving) reading" of history.

APRIL 2014

SAGEBRUSH REBELLION HITS COLORADO'S WESTERN SLOPE

Reed Williams is a most unlikely Sagebrush Rebel. Like his hero Ronald Reagan however, he has had it with those Reagan called "environmental extremists" and the federal bureaucrats who slavishly do their bidding so he is preparing a lawsuit to reclaim his energy leases that a federal agency illegally revoked.

He was born and raised in Beaumont, Texas home of Spindletop, the huge discovery in 1901 that started the Texas oil boom and helped make the USA the world's largest oil producer. His father, a farm boy, served on the War Production Board in World War II (an arrhythmia kept him a civilian), built a successful pipe valve and fitting company to supply the burgeoning Gulf Coast oil patch, and planned for his son to take over the business. Young Williams, however, had other plans.

A turn as a 12-year-old performer in *Bye Bye Birdie* hooked him, so on his arrival at the University of Colorado, he started a rock band, "The Beautiful Morning." As the group's lead vocalist, Reed Williams scheduled gigs throughout the Mountain West; his favorite was Cheyenne's Hitching Post Inn, especially during Frontier Days. In 1970, he got his B.S. degree in business at Boulder, but show business beckoned. He inked a deal with Capitol Records and then, eager to see the world and serve his country, signed with the Department of Defense to entertain the troops Bob Hope's USO tour did not reach.

From Tin City Air Force Station at the westernmost tip of Alaska's Seward Peninsula, where a C-130 taxied his band into a cave dug into a mountain, to the Naval Support Facility on Diego Garcia south of the Equator in the midst of the Indian Ocean, where 3,000 Seabees who had not seen a woman in a year enthusiastically welcomed the band's two dancers, to a military installation in Turkey after an all-night flight from Colorado, where an Air Force pilot greeted him after the show with, "You were better two nights ago in Boulder," Mr. Williams toured the world. He developed a great love of his country, profound respect for the men and women who wear its uniform, and an appreciation for America's unique, fortunate, and hard-won place in the world.

At 32, he tired of the road and returned full-time to Colorado. He teamed up with experts who knew the Denver-Julesburg (DJ) Basin petroleum province, which lies northeast of Denver and has been producing since the year Spindletop hit, and they leased acreage and miraculously drilled 70 successive successful wells. Of course, today the DJ Basin is even hotter thanks to the energy, economic, and environmental miracle that is hydraulic fracturing, the six-decades-old technology that has unlocked shale oil and gas. Unfortunately, in towns along the Front Range it has drawn the virulent opposition of environmental radicals.

Meanwhile, Mr. Williams acquired seven federal oil and gas leases in the White River National Forest in the vast rural counties in Colorado's northwest corner where Bureau of Land Management (BLM) and Forest Service lands predominate. Because he cares about the lands, he worked with federal agencies to decrease impacts, but it was not enough for the groups that oppose all oil and gas activity; they demand that the BLM cancel 65 area leases. That demand recently drew a standing-room-only crowd in De Beque (pop. 504) in Mesa County where families from Parachute, Silt, Grand Junction, and the semi-rural stretches around affluent towns like Aspen that oppose all drilling, protested to the BLM.

"There is enormous pressure on us to pack up, take huge federal tax credits, and abandon these people," says Mr. Williams. "It's a battle between those who have already made it or had it handed to them and those trying to provide for their families and achieve the American dream." Reminiscent of Reagan's Second Inaugural Address, he concludes, "If I don't fight back, who will?"

JUNE 2014

MICHIGAN LANDOWNERS REBEL
AGAINST FEDERAL RULES

In Gogebic County at the western end of Michigan's Upper Peninsula is the last place one expects to find landowners who feel a kinship with Sagebrush Rebels in the news across the West. David and Pamela Herr do; not because the federal government is their landlord—controlling grazing and watering of their cattle, use of their ATVs, or the right to develop their energy leaseholds—but because it is their neighbor, a bad one at that. Little wonder the Herrs sued the U.S. Forest Service.

Every summer, since the 1990s, the Herrs traveled from their home in Wisconsin to Watersmeet—from whence the Ontonagon River flows north into Lake Superior, the Wisconsin River flows south into the Mississippi River, and the Paint River flows east into Lake Michigan—to a privately owned cabin at the edge of Crooked Lake in the midst of the million-acre Ottawa National Forest, with its spruce, balsam, maple, birch, and aspen. In 2010, they bought the cabin. There are other privately owned cabins on lots along the water's edge, but the largest landowning, waterfront-sharing neighbor is the Forest Service and its Sylvania Wilderness. In fact, the wilderness area, created by the Michigan Wilderness Act of 1987, surrounds 95 percent of Crooked Lake.

As owners of lakefront property, the Herrs hold riparian water rights, that is, they own the right to use the entire surface of the lake for recreational purposes so long as their use does not interfere with the reasonable use of their neighbors. The Forest Service may be the biggest landowner, but it holds no greater rights to the surface of Crooked Lake than do the Herrs and each of their neighbors. In fact, the federal law that created the wilderness area went out of its way to protect just those rights by preserving all "valid existing rights." The Forest Service does not see it that way; instead, it argues not only that it is a neighbor with riparian rights, but also the government that makes the rules as to what is reasonable.

That might be an arguable point in need of resolution by a federal judge, except for one thing. The Michigan federal district court where the Herrs filed their lawsuit ruled already on what riparian rights were preserved and on whether those rights may be trumped by the Forest Service. In fact, the ruling came in 1997 in a lawsuit involving three of the

Herrs' neighbors, Kathy Stupak-Thrall and Bodil and Michael Gajewski. The court ruled that, because the "valid existing rights" were preserved and because such rights include riparian recreational rights, the Forest Service has no authority to restrict landowners' access.

Needless to say, in 2006, when the Forest Service issued an edict restricting the size of electric motors that may be used on Crooked Lake and further limiting "[a]ll watercraft" to "a slow no-wake speed," the Herrs believed the district court's ruling protected their rights. In June of 2013, the Forest Service wrote that the district court's ruling applied only to the parties in the lawsuit and did not bind the agency when it restricts the rights of other landowners. The assertion is patently ridiculous. The district court did not just rule as to the riparian rights of the landowners; it also ruled the Forest Service had zero authority to restrict those rights.

The Forest Service is doing more than spurning the district court's on-point ruling; it is thumbing its nose at the rebuke of the Supreme Court of the United States: "[A]n agency literally has no power to act . . . unless and until Congress confers power upon it. . . . To permit an agency to expand its power in the face of a congressional limitation on its jurisdiction would be to grant to the agency power to override Congress." This nation was meant to be ruled by law and not by mankind's caprice; in Michigan's Upper Peninsula, it is not.

JULY 2014

SUING THE FEDS:
LIKE WAITING FOR *GODOT*!

There is a reason so many citizens who reach the Supreme Court of the United States in their battles with the federal government and emerge to face reporters and their cameras are elderly, white-haired widows. Fighting the world's largest law firm is like *Waiting for Godot*, but worse; Samuel Beckett's absurdist play was fiction but the ludicrous lengths to which federal lawyers go to avoid judgment day is all too real. Stanley K. Mann of Colorado, now 82, spent 20 years awaiting that day.

On November 1, 1981, Mr. Mann and the Bureau of Land Management (BLM) entered into a 10-year lease for geothermal resources—a clean, efficient, renewable energy source—on federal lands near Las Cruces, New Mexico. Wells capable of production in paying quantities were drilled and Mr. Mann spent many years and over a million dollars to commercialize his discovery. Meanwhile, he paid annual royalties to BLM's sister agency in the Department of the Interior, the Minerals Management Service (MMS).

In September of 1989, Mr. Mann moved to California where he received mail, including mail forwarded from Colorado. Regarding his geothermal lease, he was in frequent telephonic and written communication with the BLM and the MMS and repeatedly advised both agencies of his address to ensure he received all correspondence. Nonetheless, on or about November 23, 1993, the BLM sent him an undated document at a wrong address as a result of what was later discovered to be a data-keeping error by an unnamed BLM employee. Not surprisingly, it was returned unclaimed; in 1994, the BLM cancelled his lease. In 1996, Mr. Mann visited the BLM's Las Cruces office and learned of the cancellation; his administrative appeal was denied.

In April of 1998, Mr. Mann filed a breach of contract lawsuit against the United States for failing to provide him the notice required by federal law; however, in September of 2002, the Court of Federal Claims held the BLM's general rules as to "constructive notice" trumped its specific geothermal regulations compelling "actual receipt of notice." Mr. Mann appealed. On June 3, 2003, the U.S. Court of Appeals for the Federal Circuit held oral arguments. Just 24 days later, the three-judge panel reversed:

the United States breached Mr. Mann's lease by failing to send notice of a potential cancellation to his "last address of record."

Mr. Mann was vindicated; however, documents that proved his case were in the federal government's hands the entire time. Those documents showed: employees from one agency did not speak to their colleagues in a sister agency; federal employees either did not or could not read the plain English of official documents; and federal employees either did not know what the law and regulations provided or refused to do what they required. Worse yet, federal lawyers defending the BLM failed to provide a sworn affidavit from a single federal employee as to why the BLM sent the notice to the wrong address.

The Court of Federal Claims conducted a trial in November of 2005 and completed post-trial briefing in March of 2006. Mr. Mann argued he was owed "lost profits," or "reliance damages," or "restitution," while federal lawyers asserted he was owed nothing; however, in April of 2009, the court awarded him $869,501.52 in damages. In August of 2009, he timely filed his bill of costs and an Equal Access to Justice Act (EAJA) application for attorneys' fees and non-taxable expenses. Although the court awarded him in excess of five thousand dollars in costs in June of 2010, slightly less than what was billed, no EAJA order was issued. Finally, earlier this summer, after numerous pleas to the court that it act on his application, including a recent notice citing his advancing years and nearly two decades seeking justice, the court awarded him nearly a third of a million dollars.

Godot has come for Mr. Mann, but thousands of other unhappy citizens still wait.

OCTOBER 2014

OBAMA STILL LOSING HIS WAR ON THE SECOND AMENDMENT

Last month, two Pennsylvania state legislators walking to their apartment after an evening meal in Harrisburg were accosted by an armed assailant demanding their wallets. When the gunman put a 9mm handgun to the head of Representative Ryan Bizzarro (D-Erie), Representative Marty Flynn (D–Scranton), a former county corrections officer with a concealed carry permit, drew his .380 Smith & Wesson and fired. The gunman, his accomplice, and two others—teenagers all—were arrested nearby; they later admitted committing a Capitol Hill robbery a day earlier that netted cash, cell phones, and computers.

Last summer, at a hospital in Darby, a Philadelphia suburb, caseworker Theresa Hunt brought a patient to psychiatrist Dr. Lee Silverman for his appointment. The patient extracted a hidden pistol, killed Hunt, and turned the gun on Silverman. Silverman, who has a concealed carry permit, ducked behind his desk, grabbed his weapon, and, though grazed in the temple and hand, returned fire. The wounded patient fled but was subdued and his pistol seized. Although hospital policy bars weapons by other than active-duty police, the local chief said, "[T]he doctor saved lives."

Meanwhile last fall, in Moore, a suburb of Oklahoma City, at the offices of Vaughan Foods, Mark Vaughan, the chief operating officer and a reserve county deputy, heard cries alerting him to the murder of Colleen Hufford by beheading and the stabbing of another female employee. Vaughan rushed to his car, retrieved his weapon secured there under Oklahoma's Bring Your Gun to Work law, and returned. While an employee spoke with 911, Vaughan cornered and shot the perpetrator in the midst of his one-man Islamic jihad. Said a police sergeant, "This [killing] was not going to stop if [Vaughan] didn't stop it."

Elizabeth Moore, a nurse in Lewiston, Idaho, two hundred miles north of Boise, seeks to exercise the Second Amendment rights employed so effectively by Flynn, Silverman, and Vaughan, not to protect herself on a city's mean streets, in a psyche ward, or even at work, but when recreating in the middle of nowhere on federal lands in the Pacific Northwest, specifically lands managed by the U.S. Army Corps of Engineers. Morris has an emergency concealed carry license from the Nez Perce County Sheriff due to 2012 threats and physical attacks by a former neighbor and regularly carries a handgun for self-defense, but she may not do so when she uses Corps-administered public lands near the Snake River in Lewiston, Idaho, to boat with friends, to hike with her dog, or to reach nearby Hells Gate State Park.

Late last month, ruling in a lawsuit brought by Morris, an Idaho federal district court struck down a 1973 Corps regulation, unchanged since the landmark 2008 decision of the Supreme Court of the United States in *District of Columbia v. Heller*. The case is headed for the Ninth Circuit Court of Appeals but the Idaho judge argues that Ninth Circuit precedent requires his holding ("banning the use of handguns on Corps' property by law-abiding citizens for self-defense purposes violates the Second Amendment") be upheld.

Meanwhile, a Tenth Circuit Court in Denver heard an appeal by the U.S. Postal Service from a Colorado federal district court's invalidation of its unconstitutional 1972 regulation that bars firearms in locked cars in its parking lots. The Colorado man who brought the case, Tab Bonidy of Avon, cross appealed for the right to enter, armed, his closed post office to retrieve or drop mail late at night. During oral argument in early October, one judge asked about the Obama administration's concern that criminals could be using the building to transport drugs. All the more reason, answered Bonidy's lawyer, for him to have his concealed weapon at hand.

The Ninth and Tenth Circuit preside over more than a third of the country. Favorable rulings there limiting the federal government's powers over the Second Amendment will have a huge impact; moreover, in any case, the Supreme Court awaits.

DECEMBER 2014

EPILOGUE

As discouraging as it is to realize, much does not change with the election of new leaders sent to Washington or our State Capitols. Not that the election of the right people is unimportant; it is vitally so. Unfortunately, however, notwithstanding their election, mischief continues apace. Therefore, the fight for liberty is never-ending. We can never declare victory and retire from the battlefield. We must not just be "eternal[ly] vigilant" as great men have told us since 1790, but also vigorously engaged in the defense of freedom.

Governments, and especially the federal government, are just too vast for any one leader and his—one hopes—loyal, principled, and energetic team to seize control and reverse course. Like the enchanted broom in Walt Disney's *The Sorcerer's Apprentice* (based on Goethe's 1797 poem) in the 1940 film *Fantasia*, once set in motion it continues indefatigably performing as instructed. It is not just that, as Reagan put it so well, "a government bureau is the nearest thing to eternal life we'll ever see on this earth!" It is that an agency's day-to-day activities continue uninterrupted and largely without adult supervision regardless of who is in the large office down the hall, in the suite on the building's top floor, or in the Oval Office far across town. As I write this, I have just finished reviewing filings in a lawsuit on behalf of a man who obtained a federal oil and gas lease in 1982; an application for permit (APD) to drill on the lease was filed expeditiously the very next year. Today, some thirty-two years later, he remains barred from drilling on the lease. Thus, over the course of three plus decades, during the administrations of both political parties, federal bureaucrats through sloth, ineptitude, or bad faith in the performance of their duties denied the man his rights. Unfortunately, the Department of Justice, "which above all should be the defender of constitutional rights" as Reagan put it in a radio address about an MSLF case, in this case and in all others of which I am aware defends the indefensible, seeking not justice but victory.

Meanwhile, Congress appears helpless to protect the rule of law and constitutional liberties when it comes to the manner in which agencies execute their duties, implement federal statutes, and impose their regulatory regimes. Set aside that Congress stampedes into passing unnecessary laws that supplant the role of states, that are overly broad and vague, and that leave entirely too much to agency discretion. Later, when the not unexpected unintended consequences occur, Congress is unable to break its own bewitching spell; instead, it holds no one accountable, continues extravagantly funding future mischief, and looks the other way even as to conduct that truly shocks the conscience because "the matter is in litigation."

Unfortunately as well, too many jurists envision themselves, not as judges, but as administrators believing that it is their judgment that should be substituted for that of the agency. Some call these robed souls "judicial activists" but Chief Justice of the Michigan Supreme Court, Robert P. Young, Jr., calls them "empathetic judges" who substitute their emotional response for the "harshness" of the Constitution, the rule of law, or the express terms of contract. At the appellate level too many judges know that, should they decide as they desire rather than as the fact and law mandate, it is unlikely (but a one percent chance) the Supreme Court of the United States will review and reverse their decision. It is the hope of people like me that the Supreme Court will grant *certiorari*, reverse a ruling, and set a legal precedent to benefit all Americans and thereby help preserve a little piece of freedom for another generation.

After all of these years in this battle, I still awaken each morning thankful for the days before, the day that lies ahead, and the new opportunity, on learning of an injustice, to be able to respond. I am thankful too that I was born, raised, and allowed to live in the greatest country in the history of the world, an exceptional country with unlimited opportunity and a commitment to excellence, not just individually, but as a nation. As to the need perpetually to persevere and perfect, I share the perspective of English professor Katharine Lee Bates who in 1893 standing atop Pike's Peak—just 56 miles southeast and some 6,000 feet above the mountain top on which I live—was inspired to write in her poem, *America the Beautiful*: "May God thy gold refine/Till all success be nobleness/And every gain divine."

May it always be so.

ACKNOWLEDGMENTS

I am indebted to many for their assistance in the completion of this project; first as always, I acknowledge the support of my wife, lawyer, and friend, Lis. The others include: Ron Arnold, Amber Colleran, Kelli Escalante, Pam Janz, Val Orr, Diane Patrick, and Ryan Scheife.